TEACH YOURSELF BOOKS

GERMAN

Acknowledgements

The author and publishers would like to thank the following for their permission to reproduce material:
Lufthansa; AMK Berlin; Café 7 Heidelberg; Zentralkellerei Rheinischer Winzergenossenschaften EG Gau-Bickelheim; Ford Werke Germany; Deutsche Bank Bonn; Sparkasse; Deutsche Bundesbahn; DPA; Eurocard Brussels; Visacard (Banco de Santander FA) Frankfurt; Südwestfunk Baden-Baden; AOK; Bunte; Zweites Deutsches Fernsehen; Süddeutsche Zeitung Munich; Badische Zeitung Freiburg; Sozialistiche Einheitspartei Deutschlands Berlin.

Every effort has been made to trace copyright holders of material reproduced in this book. The publishers will be glad to make suitable arrangements with any copyright holder not acknowledged within this printing.

GERMAN

Paul Coggle

Board of Applied Languages and Linguistics
University of Kent at Canterbury

TEACH YOURSELF BOOKS

My thanks are due to Etta Ites-Pätzold, DAAD Lektorin, for reading and commenting on the manuscript and for making numerous suggestions for improvements in the German text.

Long-renowned as the authoritative source for self-guided learning – with more than 30 million copies sold worldwide – the *Teach Yourself* series includes over 200 titles in the fields of languages, crafts, hobbies, sports, and other leisure activities.

British Library Cataloguing in Publication Data
Coggle, Paul
German. – (Teach yourself books)
1. Spoken German language
I. Title
438.3′421
ISBN 0 340 55332 4

Library of Congress Catalog Card Number: 92-80896

First published in UK 1989 by Hodder Headline Plc, 338 Euston Road, London NW1 3BH

First published in US 1992 by NTC Publishing Group, 4255 West Touhy Avenue, Lincolnwood (Chicago), Illinois 60646 – 1975 U.S.A.

Typeset by Cotswold Typesetting Ltd, Gloucester
Printed in Great Britain by Cox & Wyman Ltd, Reading, Berkshire.

Second edition 1991
Reissued 1992

Impression number	22 21 20 19 18 17 16 15
Year	1999 1998 1997 1996

Contents

List of Language Functions

Lektion 1
Introductions and saying where people come from.

Lektion 2
Greetings, enquiries about health, personal information (nationality, marital status, languages spoken etc.).

Lektion 3
Asking and answering questions concerning accommodation (type and situation) and about the surrounding area.

Lektion 4
Stating requirements—specifically, in relation to booking a room in an hotel.

Lektion 5
Making proposals for leisure activities. Accepting and rejecting proposals.

Lektion 6
More ways of making suggestions. How to ask for and give directions.

Lektion 7
Ordering food in a restaurant. Stating likes and dislikes concerning food and drink.

Lektion 8
More ways of asking and giving directions. Prepositions needed for expressing location and direction.

Lektion 9
Talking about past events.

Introduction

This is a course for beginners and requires no previous knowledge of the language. It has been designed for self-study, but may also be used for group study in a conventional classroom situation.

The course introduces German typical of both the spoken and written forms, in informal as well as some formal contexts. The emphasis is firmly on learning to ***use*** German in a variety of situations. Each of the 18 course units (**Lektionen**) presents German being used for a specific purpose, e.g. for making polite requests (**Lektion 4**) or for proposing and accepting/rejecting arrangements (**Lektion 5**). The structures of German have been carefully graded and are presented and practised in meaningful contexts. In addition, grammatical explanations are offered of all the main structures of German. No knowledge of grammar terminology is presupposed; each term is defined as it is introduced.

The majority of the approximately 2,600 words introduced in the course are those most frequently used in everyday communication. A few less useful items, such as *action painter* and *uncut diamond*, have been included because they appear in comprehension materials taken from real-life sources. All the vocabulary items are listed in the **German-English Vocabulary** at the end of the book.

How to use this course

Dialog

The English introduction sets the scene for the **Dialog** (*Dialogue*). First, try to get the gist of the dialogue, consulting the **Vokabeln** (*Vocabulary*) for key words. Then make a more detailed study of the dialogue noting ***all*** the new vocabulary and language forms. Work through the dialogue in a number of different ways—sometimes concentrating on the meaning, sometimes on the language forms. The **Fragen zum Dialog** (*Questions on the dialogue*) are designed to assist you in becoming more familiar with the language presented in the dialogue. The answers to these questions can be found in the **Key to the Exercises**.

Try also reading the dialogue aloud or even reciting it from memory. If you have a study partner, you can check each other's performance. Writing out the dialogue from memory is a good test as to whether you are ready to go on to the next section of the course unit.

Bear in mind that understanding—whilst this is an important part of language learning—does not on its own enable you to ***produce*** German fluently and accurately. A considerable amount of practice is necessary before the gap between recognition and production is bridged.

Try to learn new vocabulary by remembering the context in which the item appears. In the case of nouns, learn not only the word itself but also the gender and plural. In the case of verbs, you should—from **Lektion 9** onwards—learn the 'principal parts' as listed in the German-English vocabulary.

Was Sie wissen sollten

This section (*What you ought to know*) contains information on various aspects of German life and culture, from brief descriptions of German institutions to advice on social interaction.

Wichtige Redewendungen

In this section (*Important phrases*) the language functions introduced in the dialogue are isolated and listed in a systematic way. The aim is to assist you in progressing from recognising the phrases in a specific context to both recognising and using them in many different contexts. Make sure that you are thoroughly familiar with all the phrases and sentence patterns in this section.

From **Lektion 3** onwards this section also contains additional vocabulary grouped around certain themes.

Grammatik

Knowing ***about*** a language does not necessarily mean that you can ***use*** that language fluently and accurately. It is, however, generally recognised that most adult language learners wish to acquire a conscious understanding of the way in which the foreign language works, and that—for most learners—such an understanding provides the foundation on which to base a good command of the language.

Coming to grips with German grammar is renownedly difficult, but the **Grammatik** (*Grammar*) section attempts to simplify the task as far as possible by providing easy-to-follow explanations illustrated with numerous examples.

It is recommended that you study the **Grammatik** (*Grammar*) with reference to the main dialogue and to the exercises that follow.

Übungen

As this is a self-instruction course, all the **Übungen** (*Exercises*) are self-correcting. The correct answers are given in the **Key to the Exercises**. The nature of the course also means that the exercises have to be completed in writing. You should, however, say the answers out loud wherever appropriate to help you develop oral expertise. Watch out particularly for the language forms that have been introduced in the latest course unit. Make sure you understand what is going on.

Verstehen Sie?

The **Verstehen Sie?** (*Do you understand?*) section contains a **Konversation** (*Conversation*) and a **Lesetext** (*Reading text*). Some of the later units contain a second **Lesetext** and **Lektion 17** contains a radio news item instead of a **Konversation**.

The idea is to present you with material that reinforces the language items that have already been introduced, but that also goes slightly beyond the level that you have so far achieved. You are ***not*** expected to understand everything, merely to follow the gist. If you go on to make a thorough study of these materials, so much the better, but first see what you can manage without reference to the vocabulary. The English questions relating to the **Lesetexte** sometimes offer you important clues to the meaning. It is therefore often a good idea to read through the questions before tackling the **Lesetext**. Even in the early units the **Lesetexte** are often taken from or based on real-life sources in order to confront you from the outset with ***real*** German as opposed to German which has been specially written for English-speaking learners.

Using the course with the cassette

Although this course-book has been designed to be self-contained, you will find it of great benefit to work with the cassette that has been produced to accompany the course. The native-speaker recordings provided on the cassette will assist you considerably in (i) recognising and understanding spoken German and (ii) achieving pronunciation and patterns of intonation and stress that will make you intelligible to German speakers. The cassette contains recorded versions of the **Dialoge**, the **Konversationen**, a road traffic report and two items from a newscast.

It is suggested that in the initial stages you start each **Lektion** by listening a number of times to the recording of the **Dialog** at the same time as you read it, sometimes concentrating on the meaning of what is being said and sometimes paying special attention to the pronunciation and intonation. Later on in the course you may find that you can manage to get the gist of the new **Dialog** without looking at the printed text, before you refer to the book in order to learn the new vocabulary and study the new language forms. In either case, you should go on working with the recording until you are able to follow everything said in the **Dialog** without referring to the text. Re-playing the cassette whilst you are involved in other activities (such as exercising or gardening) will help to ensure that the newly learned items become more firmly fixed in your long-term memory.

Transcribing the **Dialog** is also a useful activity once you feel you are familiar with it. Play the cassette one sentence at a time, pausing to write down each sentence as you hear it. Check your written version with that printed in the book.

At the end of each **Lektion**, the **Konversation** can be used as a listening comprehension exercise. If you have problems understanding, have a look at the vocabulary and check the meanings of key words, then listen again. Remember, you are not meant to understand every single word in this section. The idea is to try and follow the gist—just as you might have to do in a real-life situation. Again, it is well worth playing the recording a number of times.

Beyond the course book

Radio and TV broadcasts

An important source of native-speaker German is, of course, radio and television. Whilst it is admittedly very demanding for the English speaker to try and follow programmes intended for German native speakers, there is no doubt that great benefit can be derived from this source. It is, however, important not to be over-ambitious in what you attempt. Initially you will do well if you are able to recognise short announcements, such as station identification, the time, programme titles and times of transmission, but you will be accustoming your ear to authentic German pronunciation and intonation. After completing this course you should be able to follow at least the gist of what is being said. Television is usually easier to follow than radio, as the visual element aids comprehension.

It is preferable to record the radio or television extract that you want to work on, if you are able to do so. This will enable you to play the extract through as many times as you wish and to make a thorough study of it, looking up those words which you do not understand and noting idiomatic expressions and turns of phrase.

From Britain reception of the following stations is possible:

Radio

Deutsche Welle	Short Wave	6075 kHz
Radio Luxemburg	Short Wave	6090 kHz
BBC World Service*	Medium Wave	648 kHz

After dark on Medium Wave numerous stations can be received, including ***Bayerischer Rundfunk*** (801 kHz), ***Deutschlandfunk*** (756 kHz and 1269 kHz), ***Radio Bremen*** (936 kHz), ***Stimme der DDR*** (783 kHz), ***Südwestfunk*** (1017 kHz), ***Westdeutscher Rundfunk*** (1593 kHz).

Television

Satellite channels, including ***SAT 1, RTL Plus*** and ***3 SAT***, transmit a number of news and documentary programmes.

Newspapers and magazines

West German newspapers and magazines are readily available in many British supermarkets and newsagents. The formal, complex German frequently used in the 'quality press' (such as ***die Zeit, Süddeutsche Zeitung, der Spiegel***) can be quite daunting. You will need to spend time on sorting out the sentence structure and looking up vocabulary in a good general dictionary. It is a good idea to start by tackling shorter news items. Popular illustrated magazines (such as ***Stern*** and ***Bunte***) should provide more accessible reading material, though here again judicious use of the dictionary will be required.

*Broadcasts in German are at certain times only

Pronunciation

The aim of this brief pronunciation guide is to assist you in recognising and producing the sounds of spoken Standard German (known as **Hochdeutsch**). It *is* only a guide and cannot by itself teach you to master the pronunciation, stress and intonation patterns of German. Listening to and imitating native speakers will provide the best results. Opportunities for listening to native-speaker German are suggested in the **Introduction**.

The following descriptions of German vowels and consonants are only approximate. All comparisons are made with ***Standard*** British English unless otherwise stated. There are also a few hints for helping you to overcome the natural tendency to produce English sound patterns when you speak German.

Vowels

Vowels in German may be short or long. You will often be able to determine whether a vowel is short or long from the spelling of the word in which it occurs. Vowels followed by two or more consonants are usually short, e.g. **Land, Mann, Sicht** (though there are exceptions, such as **Buch, Kuchen**), whereas vowels followed by one consonant or by **h** plus a consonant are often long, e.g. **rot, Ruf, nehmen** (though there ***are*** exceptions, such as **von, um** and **das**—all of which contain short vowels).

The main difficulty for English speakers (whether British, North American or Antipodean) is to produce 'pure' vowels in German and not the double vowels or diphthongs so common in English. For instance, German **Mann** and **rot** are ***not*** pronounced like Standard British English *man* and *wrote*.

Long vowels

a	like the *a* in *father*, *last*	Vater	Name
	long **a** is also spelt **ah** or **aa**	**Bahn**	**Haar**
e	like the *ay* in Scots English *day*	wen	Leder
	long **e** is also spelt **eh** or **ee**	nehmen	**Tee**

ä	rather like long **e** above, but slightly more open	Mädchen	Käse
i	like the *ea* in *pea*, *dean*	Kilo	aktiv
	long **i** is also spelt **ie** or **ih**	wie	ihm
o	like the *oa* in Welsh English *loan*	rot	Dom
	long **o** is also spelt **oh**	Sohn	Bohne
ö	a little like the *er* in *her*, *refer*	hören	schön
u	like the *oo* in *moon*, *food*	du	Ruf
	long **u** is also spelt **uh**	Schuh	ruhig
ü	try to say a long **i** through tightly rounded lips; also spelt **üh**	müde	fühlen

Short vowels

a	like the *u* in *but*, *gutter*	Mann	halb
e	like the *e* in *bend*, *test*	essen	Ende
ä	as for long **e** above	fällt	Länder
i	like the *i* in *bin*, *grin*	billig	links
o	like the *o* in *god*, *rotten*	kommen	noch
ö	shorter and more closed than long **ö** above	können	Wörter
u	like the *u* in *butcher*, *put*	Bus	dunkel
u	between *ew* in *few* and *i* in *bin*	fünf	Glück
Unstressed **e**: has the quality often given to the unstressed vowel(s) in such words as *never*, *conductor*		haben	Leben

Diphthongs

au	a combination of long **a** and **u**	Haus	grau
eu/äu	like the *oi* in *soil*, *toil*	deutsch	Häuser
ei/ai	like the *i* in *bite*, *right*	ein	Mai

Consonants

The pronunciation of German consonants is generally similar to that of English consonants. The following are the main exceptions:

At the end of a word or syllable:

b	is pronounced as **p**	halb	abholen
d	is pronounced as **t**	Deutschland	freundlich
g	is pronounced as **k**	Tag	weggehen
ch	let the air rush through the back of the throat after pronouncing short **o**. Then try this again with short **i**. Two distinct pronunciations of **ch** should emerge.		

	The first **ch** is used after **a, o, u, au**	**Lachen**	**kochen**
		Buch	**auch**
	The second **ch** is used after **ä, e, i, ö, ü, äu, eu, ei**	**Fächer**	**Recht**
		mich	**Köche**
		Bücher	**reich**
chs	is pronounced as *x* in *six*, *mix*	**sechs**	**Wachs**
j	is pronounced as *y* in *yes*, *young*	**ja**	**Junge**
l	In Standard British English the word *little* contains two distinct pronunciations of **l**. The first is called 'clear' and the second 'dark'. In American English only the dark **l** is used. In Standard German it is the clear **l** that is used. Practise pronouncing the clear **l** at the end of words like **voll, Kohl** and in the middle of words like **Balkon, helfen**.		
ng	as in *bring* (***not*** as in *linger*)	**bringen**	**Klingel**
qu	is pronounced as **kv** (***not*** **kw**)	**Qualität**	**Quadrat-meter**
r	is quite different from English **r**. It is formed in that position of the throat where gargling takes place. A trilled **r** (as in Scots English) is used by some speakers. Towards the end of a word **r** is very weakly articulated and sometimes not pronounced at all e.g. **Vater, Wert, Geburt, hier**.		
s	at the beginning of a word or syllable and before a vowel **s** is pronounced as *z* in *zoo*, *ozone*	**Sohn**	**lesen**
	sp and **st** are pronounced **shp** and **sht** when they occur at the beginning of a word or syllable	**sprechen**	**verstehen**
ß	is used instead of **ss** at the end of a word, before a **t** or after a long vowel. It is pronounced as **ss**	**muß**	**mußten**
		grüßen	**heißen**
v	is pronounced as *f* in *full*, *fat*	**voll**	**bevor**
w	is pronounced as *v* in *vat*, *love*	**Wasser**	**Ausweis**
z	is pronounced as *ts* is *hats*, *coats*	**zehn**	**Herz**

Glottal stop

In British English there is an increasing tendency in ordinary speech not to pronounce the *t* in such phrases as *What a day!*, *a bottle of beer*. Instead a so-called ***glottal stop*** is used to separate the two vowels: *Whaʔ a day!*, *boʔle of beer*. The glottal stop is used in German before every word that begins with a vowel (e.g. **ʔist, ʔAbend, ʔEnde**) and at the junction of compounds of which the second element begins with a vowel (e.g. **Fernsehʔapparat, Hausʔarzt**).

Word Stress

In all German words of two or more syllables, one syllable is given more prominence than all the others. It is said to bear the main stress. In most German words of two or more syllables it is the first syllable that bears the main stress: **lángsam, Mántel, Mútter**. This also applies to most compound words: **Áutobahn, Fáhrstreifen, Áutobahnfahrstreifen**.

The main exceptions to this general rule are:

(*a*) words beginning with the prefixes **be-**, **ge-**, **ent-**, **emp-**, **er-**, **ver-**, **zer-**.

(*b*) some verbs beginning with the prefixes **über-**, **unter-**: **überréden, unterríchten**.

(*c*) a number of foreign loan words, such as **Grammátik, Maschíne, Partéi, Studént.**

(*d*) Some German place names, such as **Berlín, Hannóver**.

1 Wie heißen Sie, bitte?

In this unit you will learn how to ask people's names and where they come from, as well as how to give your own name and say where you come from.

Dialog

Frank Thoma and Michael Stein meet up at a gathering of senior personnel at their company's headquarters. They exchange information about various colleagues.

Frank Thoma	Entschuldigen Sie, bitte. Sind Sie Bernd Schröder?
Michael Stein	Nein, mein Name ist Stein, Michael Stein. Bernd Schröder steht da drüben. Und wie heißen Sie?
Frank Thoma	Ich heiße Frank Thoma und bin aus Dresden.
Michael Stein	Ach, Sie kommen aus Dresden? Ich komme aus Hamburg. Elke Richter kommt aus Dresden, nicht wahr?
Frank Thoma	Ja, und Heike Graf auch. Wer ist das neben Elke Richter?
Michael Stein	Das ist Ursula Lieb.
Frank Thoma	Und woher kommt sie?
Michael Stein	Sie kommt aus Innsbruck.
Frank Thoma	Ach so. Ist Rainer König nicht auch aus Innsbruck?
Michael Stein	Nein, er kommt aus Salzburg, nicht aus Innsbruck.
Frank Thoma	Ach ja, natürlich. Aber sie sind beide aus Österreich und nicht aus Deutschland.
Michael Stein	Ja, das stimmt.

Entschuldigen Sie, bitte *Excuse me, please*
Sind Sie . . . ? *Are you . . . ?*
nein *no*
Ich heiße . . . Mein Name ist . . . *My name is . . .*
steht *is standing*
da drüben *over there*
und *and*
Wie heißen Sie? *What's your name?* (lit. *How are you called?*)
Ich heiße . . . *I am called . . .*
Ich bin aus . . . *I am from . . .*
Sie kommen aus . . . *You come from . . .*
Ich komme aus . . . *I come from . . .*
Elke kommt aus . . . *Elke comes from . . .*
auch *also, too, as well*
nicht wahr? lit. *not true?*
ja *yes*
Wer ist das? *Who is that?*
neben *next to*
Das ist . . . *That is . . .*
Woher kommt sie? *Where does she come from?*
ach so *oh, I see*
nicht *not*
er he
natürlich *of course*
Sie sind aus . . . *They are from . . .*
beide *both*
Österreich *Austria*
Deutschland *Germany*
Das stimmt *That's right*

Fragen zum Dialog

1 Richtig (R) oder Falsch (F)? (*True or false?*) Re-write those statements which are false.

1 Frank Thoma ist aus Dresden.
2 Michael Stein kommt aus Dresden.
3 Ursula Lieb kommt aus Innsbruck.
4 Rainer König ist auch aus Innsbruck.
5 Ursula Lieb und Rainer König kommen beide aus Österreich.

2 Welche Antwort paßt? (*Which answer is the most appropriate?*)

1 Sind Sie Bernd Schröder?
(*a*) Ich heiße Frank Thoma.
(*b*) Nein, ich heiße Michael Stein.
(*c*) Ja, und Heike Graf auch.

2 Heike Graf kommt auch aus Dresden, nicht wahr?
(*a*) Ja, und Elke Richter auch.
(*b*) Nein, Heike Graf steht da drüben.
(*c*) Nein, er kommt aus Salzburg.

3 Kommt Rainer König nicht auch aus Innsbruck?
   (*a*) Nein, ich bin aus Dresden.
   (*b*) Nein, er ist aus Salzburg.
   (*c*) Ja, sie kommt aus Innsbruck.

4 Aber sie kommen beide aus Österreich, nicht wahr?
   (*a*) Nein, Rainer König ist aus Salzburg.
   (*b*) Ja, ich bin aus Österreich.
   (*c*) Ja, Rainer ist aus Salzburg und Ursula ist aus Innsbruck.

Was Sie wissen sollten

Although the names of German and Austrian cities in the dialogue are written the same in both German and English, you must not assume that all cities can be treated in this way. Look at the following examples of cities where the difference is considerable:

Köln	*Cologne*	Braunschweig	*Brunswick*
München	*Munich*	Wien	*Vienna*

You will need to make a special effort to give the correct German pronunciation to those names which have been borrowed directly into English (such as Hamburg, Dresden and Berlin).

As you will have noticed from the dialogue, names of countries, too, are often different in German from their English counterparts. Here are a few examples.

Frankreich	*France*	Spanien	*Spain*
Italien	*Italy*	Belgien	*Belgium*
Dänemark	*Denmark*	Norwegen	*Norway*

The main English-speaking countries can easily be recognised:

England, Schottland, Wales, Irland, Kanada, Australien, Neuseeland

Only the *United States of America* presents a bit more of a challenge:

die Vereinigten Staaten von Amerika

Since this is rather long, people often use **die USA** instead.

Wichtige Redewendungen

How to:

1 Ask someone's name and give your name.

4 *German*

Wie heißen Sie?	}	Ich heiße Kurt Meyer
Wie ist Ihr Name?		Mein Name ist Anita Schmidt.

2 *Ask people where they are from and say where you are from.*

Woher kommen Sie?	*or*	Wo kommen Sie her?*	*or*	Woher sind Sie?
Ich komme aus Köln.		Ich komme aus Dresden.		Ich bin aus München

Note that* **Woher? can be split: **Wo . . . her?**

3 *Excuse yourself—for instance, when asking a stranger for information.*
Entschuldigen Sie, bitte.

Grammatik

1 ***Sie*** (*you, she, they*)
You will have noticed from the dialogue that the word for *you* is **Sie** with a capital S. The word for both *she* and *they* is also **sie**, but with a small **s**—unless, of course, it is the first word in a sentence:

Kommen Sie aus Berlin?	*Are you from Berlin?*
Woher kommt sie?	*Where is she from?*
Kommen sie nicht aus Salzburg?	*Aren't they from Salzburg?*

You might think that German speakers would have difficulties in distinguishing **sie** (*they*) from **Sie** (*you*), expecially in the spoken language when no difference can be ***heard*** between

Kommen **sie** aus Dresden? *and* Kommen **Sie** aus Dresden?

In fact, the context will almost always provide the solution and misunderstandings rarely arise.

2 **Statements and questions**
The statements that you have so far learned to make in German have a very similar pattern to their English counterparts:

Ich bin aus Dresden.	*I'm from Dresden.*
Das ist Ursula Lieb.	*That's Ursula Lieb.*
Sie kommt aus Innsbruck.	*She comes from Innsbruck.*

The pattern for asking questions in German is like the English pattern in sentences such as:

Are you Bernd Schröder? and	*Is that Elke Richter over there?*
Sind Sie Bernd Schröder?	Ist Das Elke Richter da drüben?

but unlike English in such sentences as:

Do you come from Dresden? and	*Does he come from Salzburg?*
Kommen Sie aus Dresden?	Kommt er aus Salzburg?

This principle of simply reversing the subject and verb (the first two words in the English examples above) also applies to questions beginning with a 'question word' such as *Who? Where? How?*:

Wer ist das?	*Who is that?*
Wo ist Rainer?	*Where is Rainer?*
Woher kommt Ursula?	*Where does Ursula come from?*
Wie heißen Sie?	*What* (lit. *how*) *are you called?*

There was in the dialogue an example of yet another type of question:

Elke Richer kommt aus Dresden, nicht wahr?

The speaker is making a statement and then seeks confirmation by adding a question element at the end. 'Tag questions', as they are called, are easy to construct in German, since the 'tag' element is normally **nicht wahr?**, unlike English which requires many different kinds of 'tag':

Sie sind Bernd Schröder, nicht wahr?	*You're Bernd Schröder, **aren't you**?*
Ursula kommt aus Innsbruck, nicht wahr?	*Ursula comes from Innsbruck, **doesn't she**?* etc.

In colloquial German the 'tag' **oder?** (lit. *or?* meaning *or am I wrong?*) is often used:

Klaus kommt aus München, oder?	*Klaus comes from Munich, **doesn't he**?*

A further very common way of checking on information is by the use of the word **doch** together with a questioning intonation pattern:

Klaus kommt doch aus München?

3 Possessive Adjectives

Words indicating possession, such as *my*, *your*, *her*, *his* are called **possessive adjectives**. You have already met two of these words in German, in the sentences:

Wie ist **Ihr** Name?	*What is your name?*
Mein Name ist Stein.	*My name is Stein.*

Note that **Ihr** (*your*), like **Sie** (*you*), is written with an initial capital letter.

Two more possessive adjectives are: **sein** (*his*) and **ihr** (*her*)

Sein Name ist Klaus.	*His name is Klaus.*
Ist **ihr** Name nicht Magda?	*Isn't her name Magda?*

4 Negation

Both statements and questions can be negated by using the word **nicht** in the appropriate position in the sentence:

Ich komme **nicht** aus Berlin. Ich komme aus München.
Kommen Sie **nicht** aus Frankfurt?
Kommt Klaus **nicht** auch aus Frankfurt?

5 *Kommen* (*to come*) and *heißen* (*to be called*)

Note the various forms of the two verbs **kommen** and **heißen**. Many other verbs form their present tense in the same way:

ich komm**e**	aus Deutschland.	*I come . . .*
Sie komm**en**	aus Österreich.	*you come . . .*
er komm**t**	aus Dresden.	*he comes . . .*
sie komm**t**	aus Innsbruck.	*she comes . . .*
wir komm**en**	aus Berlin.	*we come . . .*
Sie komm**en**	beide aus Bern, nicht wahr?	*you come . . .*
sie komm**en**	beide aus Italien.	*they come . . .*
ich heiß**e**	Fritz.	*I am called . . .*
Sie heiß**en**	Klaus, nicht wahr?	*you are called . . .*
er heiß**t**	Bernd.	*he is called . . .*
sie heiß**t**	Ursula.	*she is called . . .*
wir heiß**en**	Paul und Anna.	*we are called . . .*
Sie heiß**en**	Max und Moritz.	*you are called . . .*
sie heiß**en**	Heike und Rainer.	*they are called . . .*

6 *Sein* (*to be*)

As you have seen in Section 3 above, **sein** can mean *his* as well as *to be*. The meaning will always be clear from the context. Like the English verb *to be*, **sein** in German is irregular. Note and learn its various forms:

ich bin	aus Dresden.	*I am . . .*
Sie sind	Bernd Schröder, nicht wahr?	*you (singular) are . . .*
er ist	da drüben.	*he is . . .*
sie ist	aus Salzburg.	*she is . . .*
wir sind	nicht aus Deutschland.	*we are . . .*
Sie sind	beide aus Bern, nicht wahr?	*you (plural) are . . .*
sie sind	beide aus Österreich.	*they are . . .*

Übungen

ÜBUNG 1.1

(A) **Lesen Sie den folgenden Dialog.** (*Read the following dialogue*)

Karin	Entschuldigen Sie, bitte. Wie ist Ihr Name?
Klaus	Ich heiße Görner, Klaus Görner.
Karin	Und woher kommen Sie?
Klaus	Ich komme aus Deutschland, aus Dresden.

Look at the Lufthansa baggage label above and answer as if you were the owner of the baggage:

1 Wie ist Ihr Name, bitte?
2 Und woher kommen Sie?

(B) Now answer the same questions using the following information:

	NAME	LAND (*country*)	STADT (*town, city*)
1	Kurt Ziegler	Deutschland	Köln
2	Tracy Lowe	Australien	Sydney
3	Juan Sanchez	Spanien	Madrid
4	Heide Rebel	Österreich	Wien

ÜBUNG 1.2 **Sagen Sie es anders.** (*Say it another way*)
Example: Wie *heißen Sie*, bitte? You provide the near-alternative version for the words in italics: ***Wie ist Ihr Name, bitte?***

1 *Ich heiße* Fritz Bauer.
2 *Heißen Sie* Claudia Henkel?
3 *Heißt er* Franz oder Frank?
4 *Sie heißen* Dagmar Werner, nicht wahr?
5 *Heißt sie* Hedi oder Heidi?

ÜBUNG 1.3 **Sagen Sie es anders.**
Example: Kommen Sie aus Deutschland? You provide the near-alternative version for the words in italics:
Sind Sie aus Deutschland?

1 Ich *komme* nicht aus Deutschland, ich *komme* aus Österreich.
2 *Kommt* Bruce aus England oder aus Australien?
3 Nicole *kommt* aus Frankreich, nicht wahr?
4 *Kommen* Helga und Dieter aus Stuttgart?
5 Wir *kommen* aus Bergen in Norwegen.

ÜBUNG 1.4 **Welche Antwort paßt zu der Frage?** (*Which answer fits the question?*)

1 Heißen Sie Frank Brown?	(*a*) Sie ist aus Braunschweig.
2 Kommen Sie aus Irland?	(*b*) Das ist Paula Zech.
3 Und wer ist das?	(*c*) Ja, ich bin aus Dublin.
4 Ach so. Und woher kommt sie?	(*d*) Nein. Mein Name ist Sean Kelly.

ÜBUNG 1.5 **Ergänzen Sie den Dialog.** (*Complete the dialogue*)

A Wer sind Sie, bitte?
B (1)
A Ich heiße Peter Meyer. Woher kommen Sie?
B (2)
A Ach so. Das ist in Australien, nicht wahr?
B (3)
A Nein, Ich bin aus Österreich. Und wer ist das da drüben?
B (4)

(*a*) Ja. Sind Sie aus Deutschland?
(*b*) Ich bin aus Brisbane.
(*c*) Das ist Bettina Fleischmann. Sie ist auch aus Brisbane.
(*d*) Ich heiße Bergmann, David Bergmann. Und wie ist Ihr Name?

Verstehen Sie?

Bear in mind that in this section you are not expected to understand every single word. You should try and follow the gist of what is meant.

1 Konversation

Dieter Klein and Mary Watts are both on holiday in West Germany. They meet up at the bar of their camp site.

Dieter Klein	Entschuldigen Sie, bitte, aber Sie sind nicht aus Deutschland, oder?
Mary Watts	Nein, ich bin aus England.
Dieter Klein	Ach so. Kommen Sie aus London?
Mary Watts	Nein. Ich bin aus Manchester. Und Sie, woher kommen sie?
Dieter Klein	Ich bin aus Bozen in Südtirol.
Mary Watts	Ach, Sie kommen aus Österreich.
Dieter Klein	Nein! Südtirol ist in Italien, nicht in Österreich.

Richtig (R) oder Falsch (F)? Re-write those statements which are false:

1 Mary Watts kommt nicht aus Deutschland.
2 Sie ist aus London.
3 Dieter Klein kommt aus Bozen (oder Bolzano) in Südtirol.
4 Südtirol ist in Österreich, nicht in Italien.

2 Lesetext

Berlin als Zentrum für Tourismus und Kongresse.

Berlin ist ein Zentrum für Tourismus und Kongresse. Touristen kommen nicht nur aus Deutschland, sondern auch aus den anderen europäischen Ländern, aus Nordamerika, aus Japan, ja aus der ganzen Welt nach Berlin. Nach Berlin kommen auch viele Kongreßdelegierte. Berlin ist heutzutage eine Kongreßmetropole. Es begann mit dem »Berliner Kongreß« am 13. Juni 1878. Seit dem 2. April 1979 gibt es in Berlin das ICC (das Internationale Congress Centrum).

Answer the following questions in English:

1 How is Berlin described here?
2 Where do tourists in Berlin come from?
3 What do other people come to Berlin for, according to the text?
4 Why is the date 13 June 1878 mentioned?

2 Was sind Sie von Beruf?

In this unit you will learn how to greet people, enquire about their health and ask for certain personal information (concerning nationality, languages spoken, employment, marital status, etc.).

Dialog

Doris Zehnder and her cousin, Marga Koch, meet a neighbour, Hans Krämer, in the lift of their apartment block.

Hans Krämer	Guten Tag, Frau Zehnder. Wie geht es Ihnen?
Doris Zehnder	Danke, gut, Herr Krämer. Das ist übrigens meine Kusine aus Chicago, Frau Dr. Marga Koch.
Hans Krämer	Guten Tag, Frau Dr. Koch. Sprechen Sie Deutsch?
Marga Koch	Oh ja! Ich wohne zwar in Amerika, aber ich bin Deutsche. Ich bin jetzt im Urlaub hier in Deutschland.
Hans Krämer	So. Und was sind Sie von Beruf, wenn ich fragen darf?
Marga Koch	Ich bin Ärztin. Sind Sie vielleicht Arzt?
Hans Krämer	Nein, leider nicht. Ich bin Englischlehrer. Meine Frau ist aber Kinderärztin. Sind Sie auch verheiratet?
Marga Koch	Ja. Mein Mann ist Amerikaner. Er ist Journalist.
Hans Krämer	Spricht er auch Deutsch?
Marga Koch	Er versteht es ziemlich gut, aber er spricht nicht sehr fließend. Dafür spricht er aber sehr gut Spanisch und Französisch.
Hans Krämer	Und Sie sprechen wohl perfekt Englisch?
Marga Koch	Perfekt nicht. Aber mein Mann versteht mich meistens!

Guten Tag *see* ***Greetings*** *below* (lit. *good day*)
Frau Zehnder *Mrs Zehnder*
Wie geht es Ihnen? *How are you?* (lit. *How goes it to you?*)
danke, gut *fine, thank you*
Herr Krämer *Mr Krämer*
übrigens *by the way*
meine Kusine *my cousin*
Dr. = Doktor (*normally abbreviated*)
Sprechen Sie Deutsch? *Do you speak German?*
Ich wohne in . . . *I live in . . .*
zwar *admittedly*
Ich bin Deutsche *I'm a German* (*woman*)
jetzt *now*
im Urlaub *on holiday*
hier *here*
Was sind Sie von Beruf? *What do you do for a living?* (lit. *What are you by profession?*)
. . . wenn ich fragen darf *Might I ask . . .?*(lit. *if I ask may*)
Ärztin (*female*) *doctor*
vielleicht *perhaps*
Arzt *doctor*
leider nicht *I'm afraid not* (lit. *unfortunately not*)
Englischlehrer English teacher
meine Frau *my wife*
aber *however*
Kinderärztin (*female*) *paediatrician* (lit. *child doctor*)
verheiratet *married*
mein Mann *my husband*
Amerikaner *American*
Journalist *journalist*
Spricht er . . .? *Does he speak . . .?*
verstehen *to understand*
es *it*
ziemlich *fairly*
sehr *very*
fließend *fluent*(*ly*)
dafür *but* (*to compensate*)
wohl *no doubt*
perfekt *perfect*(*ly*)
mich *me*
meistens *mostly; most of the time*

Fragen zum Dialog

1 Richtig (R) oder Falsch (F)? Re-write those statements which are false.

1 Frau Dr. Koch ist aus Boston.
2 Sie spricht gut Deutsch.
3 Sie ist Amerikanerin.
4 Sie ist jetzt im Urlaub in Deutschland.
5 Sie ist Journalistin.
6 Sie ist verheiratet.
7 Herr Koch versteht ziemlich gut Deutsch.
8 Er spricht es auch fließend.

2 Beantworten Sie die Fragen (*answer the questions*)
1 Wo wohnt Frau Dr. Koch in Amerika?
2 Was ist sie von Beruf?

3 Ist Herr Krämer Arzt?
4 Spricht Herr Koch Spanisch?
5 Was spricht er auch sehr gut?

Was Sie wissen sollten

Greetings

Although the greeting *Good day* does exist in English, and is in widespread use in Australian English, it tends in British English to sound rather formal. In German, however, **Guten Tag** is the standard greeting and is used even in quite informal situations (though it is often shortened to **Tag**) from early morning till late in the afternoon.

Guten Morgen (*good morning*), **Guten Abend** (*good evening*) and **Gute Nacht** (*good night*) may be used at the appropriate times; there is in German no equivalent of *good afternoon.*

In Southern Germany and Austria **Grüß Gott** is the normal greeting, though this is nowadays giving way to **Guten Tag** in more formal situations.

Hand-shaking as part of the greeting and leave-taking processes is much more common in continental Europe than in the English-speaking countries. The English way of greeting is often considered somewhat casual and cool.

Titles

Considerable store is set by titles in German-speaking countries. The titles of professor and doctor are held in particularly high regard. The holders of these titles are addressed as **Herr/Frau Professor, Herr/Frau Dr.**

The wives of professors and doctors used to enjoy their husband's titles, even if they had no qualifications of their own, i.e. **Frau Professor, Frau Dr.** This custom still persists in some conservative areas.

The titles of **Herr . . ., Frau . . .,** and **Fraülein . . .** are more or less equivalent to *Mr . . ., Mrs . . .* and *Miss . . .,* although unmarried women are nowadays almost always given the **Frau** title, as are widows.

Wichtige Redewendungen

How to exchange information about:

1 Health	Wie geht es Ihnen? *To which the standard reply is:* Danke, gut (und Ihnen?)

2 *Nationality*	Sind Sie Amerikanerin? Nein, ich bin Deutsche. Sind Sie Amerikaner? Nein ich bin Engländer.
3 *Occupation*	Was sind Sie von Beruf? Ich bin Journalist.
4 *Languages spoken*	Sprechen Sie Englisch (Spanisch, Französisch)? Ja, ich spreche Englisch (Spanisch, Französisch). Nein, ich spreche nur (*only*) Deutsch.
5 *Marital status*	Sind Sie verheiratet? Ja, meine Frau heißt Christiane. Nein, ich bin ledig (geschieden, verwitwet) (*single*, *divorced*, *widowed*).

Grammatik

1 Gender

In English, nouns referring to people's nationality or occupation are often the same for both men and women:
e.g. *American*, *Spaniard*, *Canadian*, *sales assistant*, *cleaner*, *teacher*.

On other occasions the sex of the person referred to is clear from the noun: e.g. *English*(*wo*)*man*, *French*(*wo*)*man*, *milkman*, *postman*, *landlady*, *barmaid;* or: *Actor/actress*, *author/authoress*, *poet/poetess* etc. (though increasingly the *-ess* versions are disappearing from common usage).

In German, too there are many nouns referring to nationality or occupation that have both a masculine and a feminine form. Nouns of this kind that refer to males are said to be of the ***masculine gender***, whereas those referring to females are of the ***feminine gender***.

(*a*) ***Staatsangehörigkeit*** (*Nationality*)

Masculine	*Feminine*	
Amerikaner	Amerikanerin	*American*
Engländer	Engländerin	*English*(*wo*)*man*
Kanadier	Kanadierin	*Canadian*
Australier	Australierin	*Australian*
Spanier	Spanierin	*Spaniard*

	Schweizer	Schweizerin	*Swiss*
	Österreicher	Österreicherin	*Austrian*
	Neuseeländer	Neuseeländerin	*New Zealander*
	Franzose	Französin	*French(wo)man*
	Türke	Türkin	*Turk*
	Schwede	Schwedin	*Swede*
But	Deutscher	Deutsche	*German*

(*b*) ***Beruf*** (*Profession*)

Lehrer	Lehrerin	*teacher*
Journalist	Journalistin	*journalist*
Arzt	Ärztin	*doctor (medical)*
Mechaniker	Mechanikerin	*mechanic*
Ingenieur	Ingenieurin	*engineer*
Graphiker	Graphikerin	*graphic artist*
Tennisspieler	Tennisspielerin	*tennis player*
Verkäufer	Verkäuferin	*sales(wo)man*
Student	Studentin	*student*

Note that the indefinite article (*a*/*an* in English) is ***not*** required in German when stating nationality or occupation:

Ich bin Engländer.	*I'm an Englishman.*
Sie ist Journalistin.	*She's a journalist.*
Franz ist Ingenieur.	*Franz is an engineer.*

Ich bin Engländer(in)/Amerikaner(in) etc. is the standard way of giving one's nationality. The English way of using an adjective instead of a noun (*I'm English*, *American* etc.) is not normally acceptable, although it ***is*** possible to say **Ich bin deutsch**.

2 Capital letters

Like English, German requires names of places and people (***proper nouns***) to be written with an initial capital letter:

Dresden, Deutschland, Herr Krämer, Frau Dr. Koch

Unlike English, German also requires an initial capital letter for ***all*** other nouns:

Mein **N**ame ist Doris Zehnder.
Das ist meine **K**usine aus Chicago.
Was sind Sie von **B**eruf?
Ich bin **A**rzt.

3 Verbs

Verbs are normally quoted in their ***infinitive*** i.e. the form which is given in dictionaries:

sein	*to be*
kommen	*to come*
heißen	*to be called*

These are the verbs which you encountered in **Lektion 1**. In **Lektion 2** the following new verbs have occurred:

> **gehen** (*to go*), **sprechen** (*to speak*), **wohnen** (*to live*), **fragen** (*to ask*), **verstehen** (*to understand*).

The present tense of these verbs is formed in the same way as that of **kommen** and **heißen** (**Lektion 1**, **Grammatik**, Section 5):

ich versteh**e**	Englisch.	ich wohn**e**	in London.
Sie versteh**en**	Deutsch, nicht wahr?	Sie wohn**en**	in Paris, oder?
er versteh**t**	gut Französisch.	er wohn**t**	in Sydney.
sie versteh**t**	nur Spanisch.	sie wohn**t**	auch in Sydney.
wir versteh**en**	nur Deutsch.	wir wohn**en**	in Dresden.
Sie versteh**en**	beide nur Deutsch?	Sie wohn**en**	beide in Berlin?
sie versteh**en**	Englisch und Deutsch.	sie wohn**en**	in New York.

Sprechen, whilst following this same pattern, also modifies the **e** to an **i** in the **er/sie** forms (or ***third person singular***, as it is called):

> Marga spricht sehr gut Englisch. Sie spricht auch Spanisch.
> Hans spricht Deutsch. Spricht er auch Englisch?

Übungen

ÜBUNG 2.1 Lesen Sie.

> Ich heiße Dieter Schulz. Ich bin Deutscher und wohne in Stuttgart. Ich bin verheiratet und bin Graphiker von Beruf.

Use the following information to compose self-introductions on the same pattern as the one given above:

Name	Staatsangehörigkeit	Wohnort (*residence*)	Familienstand (*marital status*)	Beruf
1 Rainer Naumann	Deutschland	Frankfurt	ledig	Graphiker
2 Helga Aue	Schweiz	Zürich	verheiratet	Verkäuferin
3 Karl Miller	Kanada	Toronto	geschieden	Arzt
4 Barbara Martin	Australien	Sidney	verwitwet	Lehrerin
5 Christel Kuhn	Österreich	Salzburg	verheiratet	Ärztin

ÜBUNG 2.2 Fragen Sie.

Write questions to which the following sentences form the answers:

Wie heißen Sie?	Mein Name ist Horst Schneider.
1	Ich bin Deutschlehrer.
2	Nein, ich bin ledig.
3	Nein, ich bin Schweizer.
4	Ich wohne in Zürich.
5	Nein, ich spreche nur Deutsch und Englisch.

ÜBUNG 2.3 Welche Antwort paßt?

1 Wer ist das da drüben?
(*a*) Das ist in England.
(*b*) Er ist Ingenieur.
(*c*) Das ist Peter Heine.

2 Was ist Peter Heine von Beruf?
(*a*) Er ist Kinderarzt.
(*b*) Sie ist Verkäuferin.
(*c*) Ich bin Journalist.

3 Ist er Deutscher oder Schweizer?
(*a*) Sie ist Deutsche.
(*b*) Er ist nicht Amerikaner.
(*c*) Er ist Deutscher.

4 Wo wohnt er?
(*a*) Er wohnt in Mainz.
(*b*) Sie wohnen in Dresden.
(*c*) Er wohnt nicht in Köln.

5 Spricht er nur Deutsch?
(*a*) Ja, er spricht Englisch.

(*b*) Nein, er spricht es nicht sehr gut.
(*c*) Nein, er spricht auch Spanisch.

6 Ist er verheiratet?
(*a*) Nein, sie ist verheiratet.
(*b*) Ja, seine Frau heißt Elke.
(*c*) Nein, sie sind geschieden.

ÜBUNG 2.4 **Schreiben Sie einen Dialog** (*Write a dialogue*)
Arrange the following sentences in sequence, so as to create a dialogue.

1 Guten Tag, Frau Koch. Sprechen Sie Deutsch?
2 Leider nicht. Ich spreche nur Deutsch.
3 Danke, gut. Und Ihnen?
4 Meine Kusine spricht leider nur Englisch. Sprechen Sie vielleicht Englisch, Herr Meyer?
5 Guten Tag, Herr Meyer. Wie geht es Ihnen?
6 Auch gut, danke. Das ist übrigens meine Kusine, Frau Susi Koch aus Amerika.

ÜBUNG 2.5
(A) **Ergänzen Sie.** (*Complete*)
Complete the following sentences, using the words given below:

1 Peter Schmidt ist . . .
2 Er ist Lehrer und . . . aus Dortmund.
3 Er ist jetzt . . . in Kanada.
4 Er . . . sehr gut Englisch.
5 Französisch . . . er auch.
6 Seine Kusine . . . in Montreal.
7 Sie ist . . .
8 Sie spricht Deutsch, Französisch und . . . auch Englisch.

(*a*) spricht (*b*) im Urlaub (*c*) versteht (*d*) Deutscher
(*e*) natürlich (*f*) Journalistin (*g*) kommt (*h*) wohnt

(**B**) Imagine you are Peter Schmidt. Write a few sentences about yourself, using the information given in 1–6 above. Start with:

Ich heiße Peter Schmidt und . . .

Verstehen Sie?

1 Konversation

In a London restaurant Werner Krause recognises a face from back home.

Werner Krause Entschuldigen Sie bitte, aber sind Sie nicht Olaf Dahme aus Köln?

Olaf Dahme Ja. Und wer sind Sie, wenn ich fragen darf?

Werner Krause Ich heiße Werner Krause und komme auch aus Köln.

Olaf Dahme Ach so, ja natürlich! Sie sind Journalist, nicht wahr?

Werner Krause Ja, das stimmt. Sind Sie im Urlaub hier in London?

Olaf Dahme Ja, zusammen mit meiner Frau. Und Sie? Sind Sie auch im Urlaub hier?

Werner Krause Nein, ich wohne jetzt hier in London. Meine Frau ist Engländerin.

Olaf Dahme Ach. Dann sprechen Sie wohl sehr gut Englisch?

Werner Krause Ja. Haben Sie denn Probleme mit der englischen Sprache?

Olaf Dahme Ich verstehe fast alles, aber ich spreche es nicht sehr gut.

Werner Krause Das lernt man sehr schnell, wenn man hier wohnt.

Richtig (R) oder Falsch (F)? Re-write those statements which are false.

1 Olaf kommt aus Koblenz.
2 Werner ist Journalist.
3 Olaf ist ledig.
4 Er ist im Urlaub in London.
5 Werner ist auch im Urlaub in London.
6 Seine Frau ist Engländerin.
7 Werner spricht sehr gut Englisch.
8 Olaf versteht ziemlich gut Englisch, aber er kann nicht sehr gut sprechen.

2 Lesetexte

(A) ***Advertisement in a London newspaper:***

> Ich bin Österreicher und 28 Jahre alt. Ich spreche nur Deutsch. Von Beruf bin ich Verkäufer. Vom 3. bis zum 17. Juli komme ich im Urlaub nach London. Wenn Sie Deutsch verstehen und mir London zeigen können, schreiben Sie bitte an:
> Otto Wiegel,
> Gymnasiumstraße 6,
> A-1180 Wien,
> Österreich.

Answer the following questions in English:

1 What are the nationality, age and occupation of the person advertising?
2 What is he planning to do for the two weeks 3–17 July?
3 What kind of person is he looking for to show him London?

(B) ***Advertisement in a Frankfurt newspaper***

> Ich bin 60 Jahre alt und verwitwet. Von Beruf bin ich Sekretärin. Als Hobby lerne ich Englisch und suche deshalb Kontakte mit Engländern. Wenn Sie im Stadtzentrum wohnen und mit mir Englisch sprechen wollen, dann schreiben Sie mir.
> Helene Falke,
> Bismarkstraße 23a
> 60326 Frankfurt am Main.

Answer the following questions in English:

1 What are the marital status and occupation of the person advertising?
2 Why is she seeking contact with English people?
3 What should people do, if they wish to speak English with her?
4 What geographical restrictions does Frau Falke, however, impose?

3 Wo wohnen Sie?

In this unit you will learn how to ask and answer questions concerning accommodation (type and situation) and about the surrounding area.

Dialog

Renate Schwarz is planning to rent a house in Southern Bavaria for the summer months. Her agent, Herr Harz, has found a house which interests her in the town of Füssen, but she wants to ask a few questions before booking.

Renate Schwarz	Wo liegt das Haus, und was für ein Haus ist es?
Herr Harz	Das Haus liegt in der Nähe von Füssen in Südbayern. Es ist ein Einfamilienhaus, modern und bequem.
Renate Schwarz	Und wie groß ist es? Wieviel Zimmer hat es?
Herr Harz	Es ist ziemlich groß—110 (hundertzehn) Quadratmeter. Es hat ein Wohnzimmer, zwei (2) Schlafzimmer und natürlich auch eine Küche und ein Badezimmer. Der Garten ist etwas klein aber sehr schön.
Renate Schwarz	Kann man dort schwimmen gehen? Meine Kinder schwimmen nämlich sehr gern.
Herr Harz	Ja, sicher. Das Haus liegt direkt am Forggensee und in Füssen selbst ist ein Freibad und auch ein Hallenbad. Wieviel Kinder haben Sie eigentlich?
Renate Schwarz	Drei (3)—zwei (2) Jungen und ein (1) Mädchen. Die Jungen sind zwölf (12) und zehn (10) Jahre alt und das Mädchen wird bald acht (8). Was für Sehenswürdigkeiten gibt es in der Umgebung von Füssen?

Herr Harz Nicht weit von Füssen findet man das Schloß Neuschwanstein. Das Schloß ist ja sehr berühmt.

Renate Schwarz Ja, ich kenne das Schloß schon, aber meine Kinder noch nicht. Sie finden es bestimmt sehr interessant. Aber was kostet denn das Haus? Hoffentlich ist es nicht zu teuer!

Herr Harz Eintausend Mark im Monat. Das ist ja sehr preiswert, finde ich.

Wo liegt das Haus? *Where is* (lit. *lies*) *the house?*
Was für ein Haus ist es? *What kind of house is it?*
in der Nähe von Füssen *near Füssen*
das Einfamilienhaus *detached house* (lit. *one-family house*)
bequem *comfortable*
Wie groß ist es? *How big is it?*
Wieviel Zimmer hat es? *How many rooms does it have?*
das Wohnzimmer *living room*
das Schlafzimmer *bedroom*
die Küche *kitchen*
das Badezimmer *bathroom*
Der Garten ist sehr klein aber sehr schön *The garden is very small but very beautiful*
Kann man dort schwimmen gehen? *can you* (lit. *one*) *go swimming there?*
Meine Kinder schwimmen sehr gern *My children like swimming very much*
sicher *certain*(*ly*), *sure*(*ly*)
das Freibad *open-air swimming pool*
das Hallenbad *indoor swimming pool*
direkt am Forggensee *right on Lake Forggen*
Wieviel Kinder haben Sie? *How many children do you have?*
Zwei Jungen und ein Mädchen *Two boys and a girl*
Das Mädchen wird bald acht Jahre alt *The girl will soon be* (lit. *is becoming*) *eight years old*
die Sehenswürdigkeiten *Sights* (lit. *worth seeing*)
in der Umgebung *in the surrounding area*
nicht weit von . . . *not far from . . .*
Das Schloß Neuschwanstein ist sehr berühmt *Neuschwanstein Castle is very famous*
Ich kenne das Schloß schon *I know the Castle already*
noch nicht *not yet*
Was kostet das Haus? *What does the house cost?*
Hoffentlich ist es nicht zu teuer! *I hope it isn't too expensive!*
Eintausend Mark im Monat *One thousand marks per month*
Das ist preiswert, finde ich *That's reasonable* (*in price*), *I think* (lit. *I find*)

Fragen zum Dialog

1 Richtig (R) oder Falsch (F)?

1. Das Haus liegt in der Nähe von Oberammergau.
2. Es ist modern und bequem.
3. Das Haus hat fünf (5) Zimmer.
4. Der Garten ist sehr groß und auch sehr schön.
5. Renate hat zwei Jungen und zwei Mädchen.
6. Nicht weit von Füssen findet man das Schloß Neuschwanstein.
7. Die Kinder kennen schon das Schloß.
8. Das Haus kostet zweitausend Mark im Monat.

2 Beantworten Sie die Fragen

1. Was für ein Haus ist es?
2. Ist es ziemlich groß?
3. Kann man dort schwimmen gehen? (Ja oder nein?)
4. Kennt Renate das Schloß?
5. Findet Herr Harz das Haus zu teuer?

Was Sie wissen sollten

Floor space and rent

Whilst English-speakers tend to describe the size of their living accommodation in rather vague terms (such as 'I've got a fairly big house' or 'My apartment is tiny'), German-speakers normally know the area of the homes much more precisely:

> Meine Wohnung ist 82m² (zweiundachtzig Quadratmeter) groß. *My apartment is* 82 *square metres* (*large*).

People usually also know the going rate for buying or renting accommodation in their area:

> Wohnungen kosten in München zirka 14 DM (vierzehn Mark) pro Quadratmeter. *In Munich apartments cost about* 14 *marks per square metre.*

This would refer to the price of rented accommodation **per month**. Rents, salaries and wages are paid monthly. The price of holiday accommodation and hotels can, of course, be quoted for shorter periods:

> Das Zimmer kostet 100 DM (hundert Mark) pro Tag (pro Woche). *The room costs* 100 *marks a day* (*a week*).

When giving the number of rooms in a house or flat the kitchen is normally regarded as half a room and the bathroom/shower/toilet/lobby do not count as rooms at all. So a flat with a living room, dining room, two bedrooms, kitchen, bathroom and lobby would be described as **eine $4\frac{1}{2}$** (viereinhalb) –**Zimmer-Wohnung**.

Wichtige Redewendungen

How to exchange information on:

1	*Situations of towns or buildings.*	
	Wo liegt Füssen?	In Südbayern.
	Wo liegt das Haus?	Direkt am Forggensee.
2	*Type of accommodation.*	
	Haben Sie ein Haus oder eine Wohnung?	Wir haben ein Haus.
	Was für ein Haus ist es?	Es ist ein Einfamilienhaus.
3	*Size of accommodation.*	
	Wie groß ist das Haus?	Es ist ziemlich groß—110m^2.
	Wieviel Zimmer hat die Wohnung?	Sie hat drei Zimmer—ein Wohnzimmer und zwei Schlafzimmer.
4	*Price of accommodation.*	
	Was kostet das Zimmer?	100,–Mark pro Tag.
	Wieviel kostet die Wohnung?	1000,–Mark im Monat.
5	*Number and age of children.*	
	Haben Sie Kinder?	Ja, wir haben zwei Jungen und ein Mädchen.
	Wie alt sind Ihre Kinder?	Die Jungen sind zwölf und zehn Jahre alt, und das Mädchen wird bald acht.

Die Zahlen 0–29

0	null	5	fünf	10	zehn
1	eins	6	sechs	11	elf
2	zwei	7	sieben	12	zwölf
3	drei	8	acht	13	dreizehn
4	vier	9	neun	14	vierzehn

15	fünfzehn	20	zwanzig	25	fünfundzwanzig
16	sechzehn	21	einundzwanzig	26	sechsundzwanzig
17	siebzehn	22	zweiundzwanzig	27	siebenundzwanzig
18	achtzehn	23	dreiundzwanzig	28	achtundzwanzig
19	neunzehn	24	vierundzwanzig	29	neunundzwanzig

Note that **eins** can only stand on its own. As soon as you want to say, for example, *one Englishman* or *one Frenchwoman*, then **ein** or **eine** must be used: **ein** Engländer, **eine** Französin (see **Grammatik** below for further details).

Note also that the numbers 21–29 are said 'back to front'—a system which was used in English too in former times (cf. the four-and-twenty blackbirds of nursery rhyme fame).

Grammatik

1 Gender

To the concept of masculine and feminine gender which was introduced in the grammar section of **Lektion 2** we now need to add a third category—that of ***neuter***. An example of a neuter noun taken from the **Dialog** is **Haus**. This might seem logical, since *house* falls into the category of 'things' rather than into the category of 'masculine' or 'feminine'.

Unfortunately, the gender of nouns in German is not determined on such a straightforward basis. Many 'things' are not neuter, but masculine (e.g. **Garten** *garden*) or feminine (e.g. **Wohnung** *flat, apartment*) and the word for *girl*—**Mädchen**—is neuter. This means that whenever you learn a new noun in German, you must also learn its gender before you can use it correctly.

2 *Der/die/das*

The word for *the* (or ***definite article***) is

der for masculine nouns:	**der** Garten, **der** Junge, **der** Monat
die for feminine nouns:	**die** Küche, **die** Wohnung, **die** Spanierin
das for neuter nouns:	**das** Haus, **das** Schloß, *das* Zimmer

3 *Ein/eine*

The word for *a/an* (or ***indefinite article***) is:

ein for masculine and neuter nouns:	**ein** Garten, **ein** Junge, **ein** Monat **ein** Haus, **ein** Schloß, **ein** Zimmer
eine for feminine nouns:	**eine** Küche, **eine** Wohnung, **eine** Spanierin

4 Plural of nouns

You may have already noticed that the plural of nouns in German is ***not*** formed as in English simply by adding an 's' to the singular noun (*one room, two rooms; one house, two houses*). There are, of course, certain 'irregular' plurals in English (such as *fish, oxen, brethren, children*, etc.) which have to be learned individually and this is basically what has to be done with the plurals of German nouns. Examples from the nouns you have met so far are:

ein Junge, zwei Junge**n**	ein Garten, zwei G**ä**rten
eine Küche, zwei Küche**n**	eine Wohnung, zwei Wohnunge**n**
ein Haus, zwei H**ä**us**er**	ein Zimmer, zwei Zimmer

Note that the two dots (or ***Umlaut***) over **a**, **o** and **u** do make a difference to the pronunciation (see the **Guide to Pronunciation** p. xiv). The ***Umlaut*** is often the sole indication of the plural, as in **Garten/Gärten**, or it can appear in conjunction with an **-er** or **-e** ending, as in **Haus/Häuser**, or **Nacht/Nächte**.

Because it is so important to know both the gender and plural of German nouns, all nouns in the vocabulary section at the end of this book are listed with both the definite article and an indication of how to form the plural:

e.g. der Garten (¨)	der Mann (¨er)
die Küche (-n)	die Wohnung (-en)
das Haus (¨er)	das Zimmer (-)

The definite article is **die** for all genders in the plural:

Der Garten ist klein.	Die Küche ist modern.	Das Haus ist teuer.
Die Gärten sind klein.	**Die** Küche**n** sind modern.	**Die** H**ä**us**er** sind teuer.

5 *Haben* (*to have*)

The verb **haben** follows the pattern outlined in section 3 of the **Grammatik** of **Lektion 2** except that the **b** is dropped in the **er/sie/es** form:

	Ich habe	zwei Jungen und ein Mächen.
Frau Schwarz,	**Sie haben**	ein Haus in Süd-bayern, nicht wahr?
Und die Wohnung,	**sie hat**	fünf Zimmer?
	Wir haben	ein Einfamilien-haus.
Herr und Frau Zehnder,	**Sie haben**	eine Kusine in Chi-cago, oder?
Sie kennen Marga und Hans;	**sie haben**	ja eine Wohnung in München.

6 *Finden* and *antworten*

You may have spotted in the **Fragen zum Dialog 2/5** that the **er/sie/es** form of **finden** is **findet**, i.e., an extra **e** has been inserted between the stem **find-** and the ending **-t**. All verbs with stems ending in **-d** or **-t** behave in this way:

Herr Harz find**e**t das Haus sehr preiswert.
Er antwort**e**t nicht.

7 *Er/sie/es*

You have already met these so-called ***personal pronouns*** in contexts where **er, sie, es** meant *he*, *she*, *it* respectively. In fact **er** is used to refer to masculine nouns, **sie** to feminine nouns and **es** to neuter nouns. **Er** and **sie** can therefore both mean *it* and **es** can even mean *she*:

Ist der Garten klein?	Ja, **er** ist sehr klein.
Ist die Küche modern?	Ja, **sie** ist sehr modern.
Ist das Mädchen berühmt?	Ja, **es** ist sehr berühmt.

In the plural **sie** (*they*) is used for all genders:

Sind die Gärten (Küche**n**, Zimmer) groß?
Ja, **sie** sind groß.

In very colloquial speech, as opposed to written or more carefully spoken German, **der, die, das** are used instead of **er, sie, es**:

Ist der Arzt schon da?	Ja, **der** ist schon da.
Ist die Wohung groß?	Ja, **die** ist groß.
Ist das Schloß modern?	Nein, **das** ist alt!
Sind die Kinder noch nicht da?	Nein, **die** sind noch nicht da.

8 Word Order

You will note from the following examples that in German statements the verb is the second ***idea*** (not necessarily the second ***word***) in the sentence:

1	2	3	4
Das Haus	liegt	in Südbayern	
Nicht weit von Füssen	findet	man	das Schloß
Das Schloß	kenne	ich	

In the first example, the word order happens to be the same as in English, but in the other two examples it is not. Only practice will give you a 'feel' for this rule.

Übungen

ÜBUNG 3.1 **Schauen Sie sich den Wohnungsplan an.** (*Have a look at this plan of a flat.*)

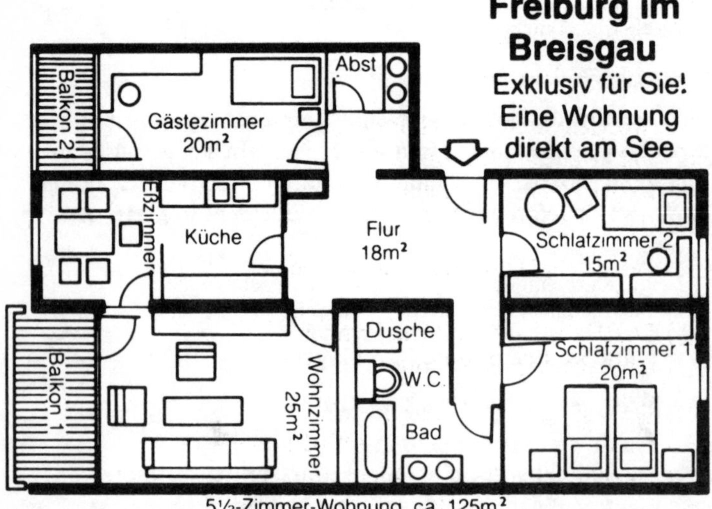

das Bad (¨er) *bath*
der Balkon (-s) *balcony*
das Bett (-en) *bed*
die Dusche (-n) *shower*
das Eßzimmer (-) *dining room*
der Flur (-e) *hall, lobby*
das Gästezimmer (-) *guest room*
das WC (-s) *WC*
Abst. = der Abstellraum (¨e) *storeroom*
ca. = cirka *approximately*

Antworten Sie.

Beispiel: Wieviel Zimmer hat die Wohnung? ***Sie hat 5½ (Fünfeinhalb) Zimmer***

1 Wieviel Gästezimmer hat die Wohnung?
2 Sie hat nur ein Schlafzimmer, nicht wahr?
3 Hat die Wohnung ein Bad oder eine Dusche?
4 Wieviel Balkons hat die Wohnung?
5 Wie groß ist das Wohnzimmer?
6 Wie groß ist Schlafzimmer Nummer 1?
7 Ist der Flur 20 (zwanzig) Quadratmeter groß?
8 Die Wohnung ist 200 (zweihundert) Quadratmeter groß, nicht wahr?
9 Wo liegt sie?

ÜBUNG 3.2 **Welche Antwort paßt?**

1 Wo wohnen Sie, wenn ich fragen darf?
(*a*) Ich heiße Frank Henkel.
(*b*) In der Nähe von Freiburg.
(*c*) Ich bin Arzt.

2 Haben Sie ein Haus oder eine Wohnung?
(*a*) Es hat ein Wohnzimmer.
(*b*) Das Haus hat zwei Schlafzimmer.
(*c*) Ich habe eine Wohnung.

3 Ist die Wohnung groß oder klein?
(*a*) Sie ist ziemlich groß—125 Quadratmeter.
(*b*) Es ist sehr groß—200 Quadratmeter
(*c*) Er ist nicht sehr groß—nur 35 Quadratmeter.

4 Wieviel Zimmer hat die Wohnung?
   (*a*) Sie hat natürlich eine Küche.
   (*b*) Die Zimmer sind sehr groß.
   (*c*) Sie hat $4\frac{1}{2}$ (viereinhalb) Zimmer.

5 Hat sie ein Bad oder eine Dusche?
   (*a*) Sie hat ein Bad.
   (*b*) In Freiburg ist ein Hallenbad.
   (*c*) Es hat eine Dusche.

6 Wie alt ist die Wohnung?
   (*a*) Hoffentlich ist sie nicht zu alt!
   (*b*) Sie ist 5 (fünf) Jahre alt.
   (*c*) Sie hat 200 Quadratmeter.

ÜBUNG 3.3 **Sagen Sie es anders.**

Provide the near-alternative versions for the words in italics.:

1 Wo *ist* das Haus?
2 Es liegt *nicht weit von* Freiburg.
3 Das Haus ist *nicht alt*.
4 *Wie teuer ist* das Haus?
5 900,—Mark im Monat—das ist *nicht teuer*, finde ich.
6 Das Wohnzimmer *hat* $25m^2$.

ÜBUNG 3.4 **Welche Antwort paßt zu der Frage?**

1 Wohnen Sie direkt in Füssen?	(*a*) Nein, sie kennen es noch nicht.
2 Haben Sie ein Haus dort?	(*b*) Ja, es ist sehr berühmt.
3 Kann man dort schwimmen gehen?	(*c*) Nein, aber wir wohnen in der Nähe von Füssen.
4 Kennen Sie das Schloß Neuschwanstein?	(*d*) Nein, wir haben eine Wohnung.
5 Wo liegt es?	(*e*) Ja, die Wohnung liegt direkt am See.
6 Kennen die Kinder das Schloß?	(*f*) Es liegt nicht weit von Füssen.

ÜBUNG 3.5 **Lesen Sie.**

Ich wohne in Düsseldorf. Ich habe ein Zimmer in der Altstadt.

Das Zimmer ist 25 Quadratmeter groß und kostet 220,—Mark im Monat.

Using the information given below, write sentences on the same pattern as those provided:

Wohnort	Haus Wohnung Zimmer	Lage (*situation*)	m^2	Miete (*rent*)
1 Berlin	W	in Charlottenburg	120	450 DM
2 Köln	H	in der Severinstr.	350	1200 DM
3 Bremen	Z	in der Violenstr.	28	180 DM
4 München	H	im Englischen Garten	420	1550 DM
5 Rothenburg	Z	am Marktplatz	18	120 DM

Verstehen Sie?

1 Konversation

Joachim Deicke tells fellow-student, Doris Beck, about the flat he has just found.

Joachim Deicke Du, ich habe eine Wohnung gefunden!

Doris Beck So. Und was für eine Wohnung ist das?

Joachim Deicke Sie ist nur klein—etwa 28 Quadratmeter. Aber sie ist sehr schön.

Doris Beck Wunderbar! Und was kostet sie?

Joachim Deicke Nur 250,—Mark im Monat.

Doris Beck Das ist ja preiswert. Und wo liegt die Wohnung?

Joachim Deicke In der Kaiserstraße.

Doris Beck Ach. Das ist gar nicht weit von der Universität.

Joachim Deicke Und meine Wohnung hat eine kleine Küche und auch eine Dusche.

Doris Beck Das finde ich sehr praktisch.

Richtig (R) oder Falsch (F)?

1 Joachim hat eine Wohnung.
2 Die Wohnung ist sehr groß.
3 Sie kostet nur 250,—Mark im Monat.
4 Das ist ja sehr teuer.
5 Die Wohnung liegt nicht weit von der Universität.
6 Sie ist in der Königstraße.
7 Die Wohnung hat ein Bad.
8 Doris findet das sehr praktisch.

2 Lexetext

Antworten Sie auf Deutsch:

Travemünde, 24. Juli

Lieber Herr Schulz,
Wie geht es Ihnen? Wir haben eine Ferienwohnung hier in Travemünde. Das ist nicht weit von Lübeck. Die Wohnung ist phantastisch. Sie hat drei Zimmer und ist 95 Quadratmeter groß. Doris und ich gehen oft schwimmen. Aber die Ostsee ist sehr kalt!

Herzliche Grüße
Peter Gruber

Herrn
Karl Schulz
Bayerstraße 5
80333 München

1 Haben Peter und seine Familie eine Wohnung oder ein Zimmer in Travemünde?
2 Wo liegt Travemünde?
3 Wie findet Peter die Wohnung?
4 Wieviel Zimmer hat sie?
5 Doris und Peter schwimmen gern, nicht wahr?
6 Finden sie die Ostsee warm oder kalt?
7 Wo wohnt Herr Schulz?

4 Haben Sie ein Zimmer frei?

In this unit you will learn how to ascertain and state requirements—specifically, in relation to booking a room in an hotel.

Dialog

Kurt Braun arrives at an hotel and enquires about a single room with a bath. The receptionist (**Empfangsdame**) is only able to offer him a room with a shower.

Kurt Braun	Guten Abend! Haben Sie ein Zimmer frei?
Empfangsdame	Ja. Möchten Sie ein Einzelzimmer oder ein Doppelzimmer?
Kurt Braun	Ich möchte ein Einzelzimmer mit Bad, bitte.
Empfangsdame	Wir haben leider nur noch ein Einzelzimmer mit Dusche. Geht das?
Kurt Braun	Ja, das geht. Was kostet das Zimmer, bitte?
Empfangsdame	Das Zimmer kostet mit Frühstück 75 DM (fünfundsiebzig Mark).
Kurt Braun	Gut, ich nehme es.
Empfangsdame	Würden Sie sich bitte eintragen?
Kurt Braun	Gerne. Wo kann ich hier parken?
Empfangsdame	Wir haben eine Tiefgarage. Da können Sie parken. Parken kostet 10 DM (zehn Mark) pro Nacht.
Kurt Braun	Gut, danke. Darf ich bitte meinen Schlüssel haben?
Empfangsdame	Bitte schön. Sie haben Zimmer 38 (achtunddreißig) im 3. (dritten) Stock.
Kurt Braun	Danke. Haben Sie keinen Aufzug? Ich habe nämlich ziemlich viel Gepäck.
Empfangsdame	Doch, natürlich. Der Aufzug ist gleich um die Ecke. Da finden Sie auch den Fernsehraum.

Möchten Sie . . .? *Would you like . . .?*
das Doppelzimmer (-) *double room*
Ich möchte . . . *I'd like . . .*
Wir haben nur noch ein Einzelzimmer *We've only a single room left* (lit. *we have only still a single room*)
Geht das? *Is that all right?*
das Frühstück (-e) *breakfast*
Gut, ich nehme es *All right, I'll take it*
Würden Sie sich bitte eintragen? *Would you register, please?*
Wo kann ich hier parken? *Where can I park here?*
die Tiefgarage (-n) *underground car park*
dürfen (ich darf) *to be allowed to (I am allowed to, I may)*
der Schlüssel (-) *key*
bitte schön *there you are*
Zimmer 38 im dritten Stock *Room 38 on the third floor (US fourth floor)*
kein *no, not a*
der Aufzug (¨e) *lift*
viel *a lot, much*
das Gepäck *luggage*
doch *yes (in reply to a negative question)*
gleich um die Ecke *just around the corner*
der Fernsehraum (¨e) *TV room*

Fragen zum Dialog

1 Ja (J) oder nein (N)? Answer the questions with either *yes* (J) or *no* (N):

1 Ist im Hotel ein Zimmer frei?
2 Möchte Kurt Braun ein Doppelzimmer?
3 Kostet das Zimmer achtundfünfzig Mark?
4 Hat das Hotel eine Tiefgarage?
5 Ist Kurts Zimmer im dritten Stock?
6 Hat das Hotel einen Aufzug?

2 Welche Antwort paßt?

1 Haben Sie ein Zimmer frei?
(*a*) Ja, das geht.
(*b*) Ja. Möchten Sie ein Einzelzimmer oder ein Doppelzimmer?
(*c*) Ja, sicher. Das Haus liegt direkt am See.

2 Ich möchte ein Einzelzimmer mit Bad.
(*a*) Gut, ich nehme es.
(*b*) In Füssen selbst ist ein Freibad.
(*c*) Wir haben leider nur noch ein Einzelzimmer mit Dusche.

3 Wo kann ich hier parken?
(*a*) Wir haben eine Tiefgarage. Da dürfen sie parken.
(*b*) Der Aufzug ist gleich un die Ecke.
(*c*) Parken kostet 10,—Mark pro Nacht.

4 Haben Sie keinen Aufzug?
(*a*) Nein, leider nicht. Ich bin Englischlehrer.
(*b*) Doch, natürlich. Der ist gleich um die Ecke.
(*c*) Ja, das geht.

5 Was kostet das Zimmer?
(*a*) Zweitausend Mark im Monat. Das ist ja sehr preiswert.
(*b*) Es kostet mit Frühstück fünfundsiebzig Mark.
(*c*) Hoffentlich ist es nicht zu teuer!

Was Sie wissen sollten

Hotel accommodation

If you have not booked accommodation in advance, you should on arrival in a German town make your way to the **Verkehrsamt** (*tourist office*) which you will find by looking out for the internationally recognised symbol.

The **Verkehrsamt** is open only during normal working hours, so it is advisable to phone ahead if you plan to arrive in the evening. In some towns a list of hotels is displayed at the **Verkehrsamt**, and in large cities help with accommodation may be available at the train station or airport.

Whilst 'luxury' hotels of the international kind are on the increase, a more typical German atmosphere is to be found in the smaller, often family-run hotels which are usually very clean, comfortable and reasonably priced. Many such hotels are found in the **Hotel garni** (*bed and breakfast hotel*) category.

Bitte schön

The expression **bitte schön** is widely used and has a number of different meanings. In the **Dialog** it is used to mean *There you are* or *There you go* and requires the response **Danke** or **Danke schön**.

Used by a sales assistant, **Bitte schön?**—with a questioning intonation—means *Can I help you?* or *Yes, please?*

Bitte or **Bitte schön** is almost always the automatic response to **Danke** or **Danke schön**. German speakers are often at a loss as to what to say in English in response to *Thank you.* Whilst *You're welcome* sometimes fits the bill, it is by no means as common as **Bitte schön**.

Wichtige Redewendungen

How to

1 *State requirements.*
Ich möchte ein Einzelzimmer mit Bad, bitte.
Wir möchten ein Doppelzimmer mit Dusche.
Wir möchten in der Tiefgarage parken.

2 *Ask people politely to do something.*
Würden Sie sich bitte eintragen?
Würden Sie bitte in der Tiefgarage parken?

3 *Grant or refuse permission.*
Da dürfen Sie parken.
Hier dürfen Sie nicht parken.

4 *Ask politely for something.*
Darf ich bitte meinen Schlüssel haben?
Dürfen wir bitten das Doppelzimmer haben?

Die Zahlen 30–1 000 000

30	dreißig	70	siebzig	101	hundert(und)eins
40	vierzig	80	achtzig	121	hunderteinundzwanzig
50	fünfzig	90	neunzig	1000	(ein)tausend
60	sechzig	100	(ein)hundert	1 000 000	eine Million

999 999 neunhundertneunundneunzigtausendneunhundertneunund-neunzig

Grammatik

1 Indirect forms (*möchten* and *würden*)

When we state requests or ask people to do things, we tend to avoid the bluntest forms, such as *I want a room with a bath* or *Park in the underground car park*, as these could be regarded as abrupt and impolite. Instead, we prefer to use indirect forms such as ***I should like*** *a room with a bath* and ***Would you please*** *park in the underground car park*.

For these purposes **möchte/möchten** (from the verb **mögen** *to like*) and **würde/würden** (from the verb **werden** *to become* may be used:

> Ich möchte ein Einzelzimmer mit Bad
> Würden Sie bitte in der Tiefgarage parken?

Note that with both these forms, any infinitive verb that is introduced automatically goes to the end of the clause or sentence:

> Wir möchten bitte in der Tiefgarage **parken**.
> Würden Sie sich bitte **eintragen**?

2 *Dürfen* and *können*

Also with **dürfen** (*to be allowed to*) and **können** (*to be able to*) (which belong to a group called ***modal verbs***) the infinitive goes to the end of the clause or sentence:

Dürfen wir jetzt **gehen**?	*May we go now?*
Darf Hans schwimmen **gehen**?	*May Hans go swimming?*
Können wir dort **parken**?	*Can we park there?*
Kann man dort **schwimmen**?	*Is it possible to swim there?* (lit. *Can one swim there?*)

Dürfen and **können** are irregular in that their **ich** form is the same as their **er/sie/es** form (**darf** and **kann**). The plural forms (**wir, Sie, sie**) are the same as the infinitives (**dürfen** and **können**).

3 Accusative cases

In the sentence *The girl understands the American*, ***the girl*** is said to be the ***subject*** of the verb *to understand* and ***the American*** is said to be the ***object***. In German the object of a sentence has to be in what is called the ***accusative case***. Fortunately, for feminine and neuter nouns and all nouns in the plural, the accusative forms of the definite and indefinite articles are the same as the ***nominative*** forms (that is, those used for the subject of the sentence):

Subject	*Verb*	*Object*
Nominative case		*Accusative case*
Die Wohnung	hat	eine Küche (*fem. sing.*)
Der Junge	kennt	die Stadt (*fem. sing.*)
Das Haus	hat	ein Gästezimmer (*neuter sing.*)
Die Kinder	kennen	das Schloß (*neuter sing.*)
Die Engländer	verstehen	die Amerikaner (*masc. plur.*)
Die Kinder	verstehen	die Lehrerinnen (*fem. plur.*)
Die Australier	kennen	die Schlösser (*neut. plur.*)

Only the articles of ***masculine singular*** nouns have a special form in the accusative:

Das Mädchen	versteht	**den** Amerikaner (*masculine sing.*)
Der Junge	versteht	**den** Lehrer (*masculine sing.*)
Das Hotel	hat	**einen** Aufzug (*masculine sing.*)
Das Haus	hat	**einen** Garten (*masculine sing.*)

The same **-en** ending is found on **mein, sein, ihr, Ihr** (the so-called ***possessive adjectives***) in the masculine singular accusative:

Franz	kennt	**meinen** Lehrer
Dieter	versteht	**seinen** Lehrer
Dagmar	versteht	**ihren** Arzt

This may seem a little complicated, but you will in time get a feel for what is correct. The German system has the advantage that it is possible to produce such sentences as:

Den Engländer versteht der Lehrer aber den Amerikaner nicht.

which, perhaps rather confusingly for an English-speaking person, means:

The teacher does understand the Englishman but not the American.

rather than what the word order might at first glance suggest, namely:

The Englishman understands the teacher but not the American.

Perhaps you can now see some justification for the accusative case!

Certain verbs—such as **sein** (*to be*) and **werden** (*to become*)—are ***not*** followed by the accusative:

Das ist **der** Garten

Das Gästezimmer wird jetzt **der** Fernsehraum

The accusative forms of the ***personal pronouns*** (words like *me*, *you*, *us*, *him*) are as follows:

Mein Mann versteht **mich** meistens.	*My husband understands me most times.*
Ich kenne **Sie** schon, nicht wahr?	*I know you already, don't I?*
Kurt kennt **ihn (sie)** gut.	*Kurt knows him (her) well.*
Das Zimmer ist klein, aber ich nehme **es**.	*The room is small but I'll take it.*
Die Empfangsdame kennt **uns** nicht.	*The receptionist doesn't know us.*
Wer sind Hans und Maria? Ich kenne **sie** nicht.	*Who are Hans and Maria? I don't know them.*

4 *Kein*

Kein is normally used to mean *no*, *not a*, *not any*:

Kein**e** Wohnung (*nom. fem. sing.*) hat einen Aufzug.	*No apartment has a lift.*
Das Hotel hat kein**en** Aufzug. (*acc. masc. sing.*)	*The hotel has no lift* or *The hotel doesn't have a lift.*
Kurt ist kein Journalist. (*nom. masc. sing.*)	*Kurt is not a journalist.*
Ich kenne kein**e** Lehrerinnen. (*acc. fem. plur.*)	*I don't know any (female) teachers.*

Kein can also be used to mean *not one*:

Das Hotel hat kein**en** (einzigen) Aufzug.	*The hotel doesn't have one (single) lift.*
Kein**e** (einzige) Wohnung hat einen Aufzug.	*Not one (single) apartment has a lift.*

Note that **kein** behaves like **ein** (and like the possessive adjectives **sein, ihr** etc.) in that it takes an **-e** in the feminine singular and in the plural (all genders) and an **-en** in the masculine accusative (see examples above).

5 *Nehmen*

Nehmen (*to take*), like **sprechen** (*to speak*) which you met in **Lektion 2**, undergoes a vowel change in the third person singular form:

Ich nehme ein Einzelzimmer mit Bad, aber Andreas **nimmt** eins mit Dusche.

The third person singular form of verbs that undergo a vowel change of this kind is given after the infinitive in the **Vokabeln** at the end of the book:

nehmen, (nimmt, . . .) *to take*; **sprechen, (spricht, . . .)** *to speak.*

Übungen

ÜBUNG 4.1 Write three sentences about each of the following hotels, using as a model the example provided:

> Das Hotel Oper in Hamburg hat 220 (zweihundertzwanzig) Betten.
> Einzelzimmer kosten von 135,— (hundertfünfunddreißig) bis (*up to*) 158,— (hundertachtundfünfzig) Mark.
> Doppelzimmer kosten von 180,— (hundertachtzig) bis 218,— (zweihundertachtzehn) Mark.

Name	*Stadt*	*Bettenzahl*	*Einzel-zimmer*	*Doppel-zimmer*
Hotel Oper	Hamburg	220	135–158	180–218
1 Schloßhotel	Karlsruhe	180	143–160	215–253
2 Hotel Körner	Hannover	140	109–129	139–163
3 Hotel Bristol	Köln	60	113–165	175–240
4 Hotel Domus	Kassel	66	99–119	155–177

ÜBUNG 4.2 State the accommodation requirements of the following people, using as models the two examples provided:

> Norbert Jens möchte ein Einzelzimmer mit Bad. Er möchte auch einen Parkplatz (**der Parkplatz,** *parking place*) in der Tiefgarage.
>
> Klaus und Beate Weber möchten ein Doppelzimmer mit Dusche. Sie möchten aber keinen Parkplatz in der Tiefgarage.

	Einzel zimmer	*Doppel zimmer*	*Bad*	*Dusche*	*Parkplatz*
Norbert Jens	√		√		√
Klaus u.Beate Weber		√		√	X

1 Peter Trost	√				√	X
2 Bernd u.Claudia Hummel		√	√	und	√	√
3 Anna Lohr	√		√			√
4 Paul Krause u. Sylvia Bachmann	2		√	oder	√	√

ÜBUNG 4.3 Answer the following requests or questions in the negative, using as a model the example provided:

> Ich möchte bitte ein Einzelzimmer mit Bad.
> ***Wir haben leider keine Einzelzimmer mehr mit Bad.***

1 Dann möchte ich bitte ein Einzelzimmer mit Dusche.
2 Dann nehme ich ein Doppelzimmer mit Bad.
3 Dann möchte ich bitte ein Doppelzimmer mit Dusche.
4 Was? Haben Sie denn keine Zimmer mehr frei?

ÜBUNG 4.4 Answer the following questions, using as models the two examples provided:

> Kann man in Schottland Englisch sprechen?
> ***Ja, in Schottland kann man Englisch sprechen.***

> Kann man in Spanien Deutsch sprechen?
> ***Nein, in Spanien versteht man meistens kein Deutsch.***

1 Kann man in Österreich Deutsch sprechen?
2 Kann man in Norwegen Spanisch sprechen?
3 Kann man in Dänemark Französisch sprechen?
4 Kann man in Australien Englisch sprechen?
5 Kann man in Belgien Französisch sprechen?
6 Kann man in Neuseeland Deutsch sprechen?

ÜBUNG 4.5 Complete the list of rooms etc. which are to be found in the apartment shown in the plan on the next page:

Die Wohnung hat (*a*) einen Flur
(*b*) ein Wohnzimmer
1 ....
2 ....
3 ....

4 ....

5 ....

6 ....

7 ....

8 ....

Note that the rooms on the list will need to be in the accusative case, which means you should check on the gender (and in two instances on the plural forms) of the nouns concerned. All the nouns used can be found in the German-English vocabulary at the end of the book.

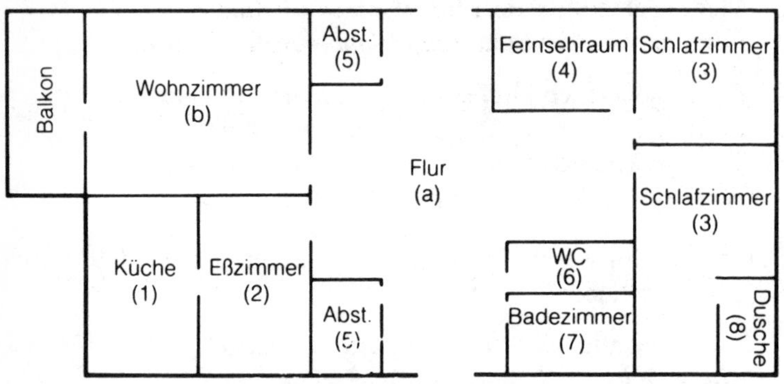

Verstehen Sie?

1 Konversation

Heike Klein enquires about a room at the reception desk.

Empfangsherr	Guten Tag. Was möchten Sie, bitte?
Heike Klein	Guten Tag. Haben Sie ein Zimmer frei?
Empfangsherr	Was für ein Zimmer möchten Sie denn?
Heike Klein	Ein Einzelzimmer mit Dusche, bitte.
Empfangsherr	Und für eine Nacht?
Heike Klein	Nein, für drei Nächte (bitte).
Empfangsherr	Kleinen Moment. Mit Dusche habe ich leider keine Einzelzimmer mehr frei. Mit Bad hätte ich noch ein Einzelzimmer. Möchten Sie das nehmen?
Heike Klein	Und was kostet es?

Empfangsherr	Es kostet inklusive Frühstück hundertfünfundzwanzig Mark.
Heike Klein	Dann nehme ich es.
Empfangsherr	Gut. Sie bekommen Zimmer vierundzwanzig im zweiten Stock. Hier ist Ihr Schlüssel.
Heike Klein	Danke schön.
Empfangsherr	Bitte schön.

Richtig (R) oder Falsch (F)?

1 Heike Klein möchte ein Einzelzimmer mit Bad.
2 Sie möchte das Zimmer für eine Nacht haben.
3 Der Empfangsherr hat keine Einzelzimmer mit Dusche mehr.
4 Er hat aber eins mit Bad
5 Das Zimmer kostet mit Frühstück hundertfünfunddreißig Mark.
6 Heike nimmt das Zimmer.
7 Sie hat Zimmer vierundzwanzig im zweiten Stock.

2 Lesetext

Read the descriptions of hotels taken from a publicity brochure shown on the next page:

Answer the following questions in English:

1 For what two purposes does the first class Hotel Bellaria claim to be suited?
2 Where it is situated? (*Two parts to the answer*)
3 Which mountain does the hotel have a view of?
4 What is informal about the medium-priced Hotel Kronprinz?
5 Where is it situated? (*Two parts to the answer*)
6 What two features are drawn to the traveller's attention?
7 What is said here about the condition, the location and the style of the Hotel Schloß, which is opposite the spa rooms?
8 Which two qualities are claimed for this hotel, along with that of friendliness?
9 What is the hotel's geographic situation?
10 What conference facilities do the three hotels have?

« ASTA » HOTELS DEUTSCHLAND

Hotel Bellaria Berchtesgaden

Erstklassiges Ferien- und Konferenzhotel in bester Lage von Berchtesgaden mit Ausblick auf den Watzmann. 5 Minuten vom Stadtzentrum entfernt.

Konferenzmöglichkeit: Ein Konferenzraum bis zu 20 Personen.

Hotel Kronprinz Aachen

Mittelklasse-Hotel mit familiärer Atmosphäre, nur 10 Minuten außerhalb vom Stadtzentrum. In der Nähe der Autobahnen nach Köln und Belgien. Ein Minigolfplatz sowie eine Kaffeeterrasse gehören ebenfalls zum Hotel.

Konferenzmöglichkeit: Konferenzräume von 20 biz 120 Personen.

Hotel Schloß Bad Tolz

Komplett renoviertes Traditionshotel in idyllischer Lage gegenüber dem Kurhaus. Stileinrichtung in klassischem Barock.
Bequemlichkeit – Atmosphäre – Freundlichkeit. 40 km südlich von München gelegen. Hotel Garni.

Konferenzmöglichkeit: Konferenzraum bis zu 20 Personen.

5 Kommst du heute abend mit?

In this unit you will learn how to propose arrangements for leisure activities and how to accept or reject such arrangements.

Dialog

Udo Glunk suggests a visit to the cinema. Ruth Bock reviews her commitments before agreeing to accept. Udo is unable to go out for a meal first, but agrees to pick Ruth up at about 8.15 pm.

Udo Glunk	Ich möchte heute nachmittag ins Kino gehen. Kommst du vielleicht mit?
Ruth Bock	Tut mir leid. Heute nachmittag kann ich nicht. Da muß ich einkaufen.
Udo Glunk	Hast du dann heute abend Zeit?
Ruth Bock	Ja, vielleicht. Wann fängt der Film an, und wie heißt er?
Udo Glunk	Um halb neun. Es läuft der alte amerikanische Film »Manche mögen's heiß«.
Ruth Bock	Ach, den Film möchte ich ja sehen! Aber wie lange dauert er? Ich muß nämlich morgen arbeiten. Da muß ich schon um sechs Uhr aufstehen.
Udo Glunk	Der Film dauert ungefähr zwei Stunden. Bis elf Uhr bist du sicher wieder zu Hause.
Ruth Bock	Gut, das geht noch. Möchtest du vorher noch essen gehen?
Udo Glunk	Das kann ich nicht. Gegen Viertel vor sieben gehe ich meine Mutter besuchen. Sie erwartet mich zum Abendbrot. Ich kann dich erst um Viertel nach acht treffen.
Ruth Bock	Gut, holst du mich dann bitte ab? Ich habe zur Zeit keinen Wagen mehr.
Udo Glunk	Gerne. Wohnst du noch in der Adelbertstraße?
Ruth Bock	Ja. Also, bis nachher, Tschüs!

heute nachmittag *this afternoon* (lit. *today afternoon*)
ins Kino gehen *to go to the cinema (movies)*
du *you (informally, see below)*
mitkommen (*sep.*) *to come along*
(es) tut mir leid *I'm sorry* (lit. *it does to me sorrow*)
Hast du heute abend Zeit? *Do you have time this evening?*
anfangen (ä) (*sep.*) *to begin*
um halb neun *at half past eight* (lit. *at half way on the way to nine*)
es läuft . . . (*from* **laufen (äu)**) *. . . is on* (lit. *is running*)
»Manche mögen's heiß« *"Some like it hot"*
sehen (ie) *to see*
Wie lange dauert der Film? *How long does the film last?*
aufstehen (*sep.*) *to get up*
ungefähr zwei Stunden *about two hours*
bis elf Uhr *by eleven o'clock*
zu Hause *at home*
Möchtest du vorher essen gehen? *Would you like to go for a meal first?*
gegen Viertel vor sieben *around a quarter to seven*
Ich gehe meine Mutter besuchen *I'm going to visit my mother*
Sie erwartet mich zum Abendbrot *She's expecting me for supper*
erst um Viertel nach acht *not until a quarter past eight*
treffen (i) *to meet*
Holst du mich ab? *Will you pick me up? Are you picking me up?*
zur Zeit *at present*
Bis nachher. Tschüs! *Till later* (lit. *afterwards*). *Bye!*

Fragen zum Dialog

1 Richtig (R) oder Falsch (F)?

1 Udo möchte heute nachmittag schwimmen gehen.
2 Ruth muß heute nachmittag einkaufen.
3 Sie hat aber heute abend Zeit.
4 Ruth muß morgen erst um neun Uhr aufstehen.
5 Der Film dauert ungefähr drei Stunden.
6 Udo kann vorher nicht essen gehen.
7 Er muß seine Mutter besuchen.
8 Er kann Ruth aber schon um halb acht treffen.
9 Udo holt Ruth um Viertel nach acht ab.
10 Ruth wohnt noch in der Adelbertstraße.

2 Welche Antwort paßt?

1 Ich gehe heute nachmittag ins Kino. Möchtest du mitkommen?

(*a*) Gut, das geht noch.
(*b*) Ja, vielleicht. Wann fängt der Film an?
(*c*) Gut, danke. Darf ich bitte meinen Schlüssel haben?

2 Wann fängt der Film an?
(*a*) Um halb neun.
(*b*) Ungefähr zwei Stunden.
(*c*) Bis elf Uhr.

3 Wie lange dauert der Film?
(*a*) Um sechs Uhr.
(*b*) Ungefähr zwei Stunden.
(*c*) Es läuft »Manche mögen's heiß«.

4 Möchtest du vorher essen gehen?
(*a*) Ja. Also, bis nachher. Tschüs!
(*b*) Ja. Ich habe nämlich ziemlich viel Gepäck.
(*c*) Das kann ich leider nicht.

5 Holst du mich bitte ab?
(*a*) Gut, das geht noch.
(*b*) Gerne.
(*c*) Gut. Ich nehme es.

Was Sie wissen sollten

Du

As a general rule, you should address every one with **Sie**, unless they are close friends, members of the family or children, in which case **du** is the appropriate form of address.

Du can be used to establish solidarity—students, for instance, normally use **du** to each other, even when they are complete strangers.

Early rising

Despite some decline in recent years in the traditional German 'work ethic', work in factories, schools and offices still starts about an hour earlier than in Britain. This means, of course, that people generally need to get up earlier in Germany. Even people working flexi-time often prefer to make an early start, so that they 'still have something of the day' (**noch etwas vom Tag haben**) after work.

Meals

Das Abendbrot mentioned in the **Dialog** is in fact a cold meal normally consisting of assorted sliced meats and cheeses (**der Aufschnitt**) on bread of various kinds, such as **das Schwarzbrot** (*brown* – lit. *black* – *rye bread*), **der Pumpernickel, das Bauernbrot** (*coarse rye bread*). A selection of salads is also often offered (such as **der Kartoffelsalat** (*potato salad*), **der Fleischsalat** (*meat salad*), **der Gurkensalat** (*cucumber salad*).

The main meal of the day is usually **das Mittagessen** (*lunch*). This may be taken at home, if circumstances permit, but is very often taken at the place of work.

Breakfast usually consists of **der Kaffee** (*coffee*) and **die Brötchen** (neut. plur.) (*rolls*) with **die Marmelade** (*jam*) or **Aufschnitt. Ein gekochtes Ei** (*boiled egg*) is also relatively common, especially in hotels, where **das Frühstücksbüffet** (*self-service breakfast buffet*) may offer an extensive range of foods.

Das zweite Frühstück (*second breakfast*) consisting of rolls with meat or cheese filling is often taken at about 9.30 or 10.00 am. **Kaffee und Kuchen** (*coffee and cake*) may be taken in the afternoon, particularly at weekends.

Wichtige Redewendungen

How to:

1 *Propose arrangements.*
Ich gehe ins Kino. Kommst du mit?
Möchtest du mit mir ins Kino gehen?

2 *Suggest a time*
(*a*) *general*
Kannst du heute abend?
Hast du heute abend Zeit?
(*b*) *specific*
Geht es um acht Uhr?
Kannst du um acht Uhr?

3 *Show some interest in a proposed arrangement.*
Ja, vielleicht. Wann denn?

4 *Turn down a proposal.*
Tut mir leid, das geht nicht.
Tut mir leid, das kann ich nicht.

5 *Give a reason for refusal.*

Da muß ich	meine Mutter besuchen.
	morgen schon um 6 Uhr aufstehen.
Da möchte ich	meine Kusine abholen.
	einkaufen.
	arbeiten . . .

Die Uhrzeit

The twelve-hour clock is used in everyday speech. The twenty-four hour clock is used in timetables, programme schedules, etc. as well as in time checks on radio and television.

Wie spät ist es? *What's the time* (lit. *how late is it?*)*?*
Wieviel Uhr ist es? *What time is it?*

03.00	Es ist	3 Uhr	3 Uhr (drei Uhr)
03.05		5 nach 3	3 Uhr 5 (drei Uhr fünf)
03.06		6 Minuten nach 3	3 Uhr 6 (drei Uhr und sechs Minuten)
03.15		Viertel nach 3	3 Uhr 15 (drei Uhr fünfzehn)
03.20		20 nach 3	3 Uhr 20 (drei Uhr zwanzig)
03.25		5 vor halb 4	3 Uhr 25 (drei Uhr fünfund-zwanzig)
03.30		halb 4	3 Uhr 30 (drei Uhr dreißig)

22.35	Es ist	5 nach halb 11	22 Uhr 35 (zweiundzwanzig Uhr fünfunddreißig)
22.40		20 vor 11	22 Uhr 40 (zweiundzwanzig Uhr vierzig)
22.45		Viertel vor 11	22 Uhr 45 (zweiundzwanzig Uhr fünfundvierzig)
22.54		6 Minuten vor 11	22 Uhr 54 (zweiundzwanzig Uhr vierundfünfzig)
22.55		5 vor 11	22 Uhr 55 (zweiundzwanzig Uhr fünfundfünfzig)
23.00		11 Uhr	23 Uhr (dreiundzwanzig Uhr)

Wann kommst du?	Um (*at*) Viertel nach acht.
Um wieviel Uhr (*at what time*) kommst du?	Gegen (*around*) halb neun.

When using the 12-hour clock there is sometimes a need to add the time of day:

02.00	2 Uhr **nachts** (*in the night*)
05.00	5 Uhr **morgens** (*in the morning*)
12.00	12 Uhr **mittags** (*noontime*)
14.00	14 Uhr *oder* 2 Uhr **nachmittags** (*in the afternoon*)
19.00	19 Uhr *oder* 7 Uhr **abends** (*in the evening*)

Grammatik

1 The *du* form

The ending on the verb in the **du** form is normally **-st**:

Komm**st** du aus Berlin? Versteh**st** du Deutsch?
Lern**st** du Französisch? Kenn**st** du das Schloß?

If, however, the verb stem ends in **-d** or **-t**, for example **find**en or **antworten**, then the **du** form ending is **-est**:

Wie find**est** du meine Wohnung? Antwort**est** du oder nicht?

Verbs like **heißen** whose stems end in **-ß** merely add a **-t** in the **du** form:

Wie heiß**t** du?

Verbs like **sprechen, nehmen** and **werden** which modify their middle vowel in the **er/sie/es** form, do so in the **du** form as well:

Spr**i**chst du Englisch? N**i**mmst du die Wohnung?
Du w**i**rst jetzt 24, nicht wahr? Wann f**ä**ngst du an?

These same rules apply to modal verbs (such as **dürfen, können** and **müssen**) and other verb-forms which you have met in Units 1–4:

Du darf**st** jetzt gehen. Kann**st** du bitte um 8 Uhr kommen?
Du mußt ein Zimmer suchen.

Möcht**est** du schwimmen gehen? Würd**est** du Deutsch sprechen.

The verbs **haben** and **sein** are irregular:

Hast du heute abend Zeit?
Wann **bist** du wieder zu Hause?

2 Position of expressions of time

When two phrases—one of them indicating time—come together after the main verb, the time phrase comes first:

	time		
Ich möchte	**heute abend**	ins Kino	gehen.
Du kannst	**morgen abend**	in meiner Garage	parken.
Ich gehe	**gegen sieben Uhr**	meine Mutter	besuchen.
Ich habe	**zur Zeit**	keinen Wagen mehr.	
Kommst du	**heute nachmittag**	vielleicht	mit?

When two time expressions occur together, the more general one comes first:

	general	*specific*	
Ich muß	**morgen**	***um sechs Uhr***	aufstehen.
Kannst du mich	**heute nachmittag**	***gegen drei Uhr***	abholen.

Since the order of these items tends to be the reverse in English:

I should like to go to the cinema this evening.
Can you pick me up around 3 o'clock this afternoon?

you will need some time to get used to the German order. Practice will help!
In statements, as opposed to questions, it is possible to 'front' the time phrase. Remember that the verb has to be the second idea in the sentence:

Morgen abend kannst du in meiner Garage parken.
Zur Zeit habe ich keinen Wagen mehr.
Gegen 7 Uhr gehe ich meine Mutter besuchen.

3 Separable verbs

Verbs such as **abholen, aufstehen, einkaufen, mitkommen** and **anfangen** are referred to as ***separable verbs*** because, in straightforward statements and questions, the particle (**auf, ein, mit, an,** etc.) 'floats away' from the main stem of the verb:

Ich hole dich morgen abend **ab.**
Ich stehe jeden Tag (*every day*) um 7 Uhr **auf**.
Kaufst du morgen nachmittag **ein**?
Kommst du vielleicht **mit**?
Wann fängt der Film **an**?

When the separable verb is used in the infinitive form however, the main stem of the separable verb joins up with its particle at the end of the clause or sentence:

Mußt du morgen schon um 6 Uhr **auf**stehen?
Kannst du heute nachmittag **ein**kaufen?
Würdest du bitte **mit**kommen?
Der Film kann ja nicht schon um 4 **an**fangen!

Note that when you pronounce a particle verb, the stress always falls on the particle.

Another group of verbs, though not actually separable verbs, behaves in a very similar fashion. You have had only two examples from this group so far, namely **essen gehen** and **schwimmen gehen**:

Gehst du heute abend **essen**?	Ich kann heute abend leider nicht **essen** gehen.
Ich gehe gern **schwimmen**.	Möchtest du morgen nachmittag **schwimmen** gehen?

Other examples of this category are: **tanzen gehen** (*to go dancing*), **spazierengehen** (*to go for a walk*) and **kennenlernen** (*to get to know*) the last two of which have, through frequent use, become regarded as single units and are therefore written as one word in the infinitive, just like a separable verb:

Ich gehe heute abend **tanzen**.	Möchtest du auch **tanzen** gehen?
Wir gehen jetzt **spazieren**.	Möchtest du auch **spazieren**gehen?
Morgen lerne ich den Mann **kennen**.	Möchtest du den Mann auch **kennen**lernen?

In the **Vokabeln** the abbreviation (*sep.*) indicates that a verb is separable.

4 Use of *da*

Da is frequently used at the beginning of a sentence in colloquial speech. Two such uses occurred in the **Dialog**:

Heute nachmittag kann ich nicht. **Da** muß ich einkaufen.
Ich muß morgen arbeiten. **Da** muß ich schon um 6 Uhr aufstehen.

In the first example, **da** has the meaning of *then*, *at that time*, whereas in the second example, **da** means *so*, *for that reason*.

5 English meanings of the German Present Tense

Note that for such sentences as

Ich wohne in Köln.

there are two possible English versions:

(*a*) *I live in Cologne.* (Present Simple)
(*b*) *I am living in Cologne.* (Present Continuous)

The two English tenses are covered by the one tense in German.

The Present Continuous is often used in English to refer to the future:

I am going to the cinema this afternoon.

The German Present Tense is similarly used with future meaning:

Ich gehe heute nachmittag ins Kino.

In fact the German Present Tense is also often used where English would require a Future Tense:

Bis 11 bist du wieder zu Hause.	*You **will** be home again by* 11.
Holst du mich um 8 ab?	***Will** you pick me up at* 8?

Übungen

ÜBUNG 5.1 Provide the 12-hour clock versions for the following times. Use the chart to assist you establish the time of day:

00.00–02.59	03.00–11.59	12.00–13.59	14.00–17.50	18.00–23.59
12.00		1.59	2.00 5.59	6.59 11.59
nachts	*morgens*	*mittags*	*nachmittags*	*abends*

Beispiele: 04.00. *Es ist vier Uhr morgens.*
16.00. *Es ist vier Uhr nachmittags.*

1 05.00	2 17.00	3 13.00	4 20.00
5 01.00	6 23.00	7 12.00	8 21.00

ÜBUNG 5.2 The following list shows times in cities around the world when the time in London is 12 o'clock midnight:

(*a*) New York: 19.00	(*b*) Wien: 01.00
1 Mexiko City: 18.00	5 Wellington: 12.00
2 San Franzisko: 16.00	6 Karatschi: 05.00
3 Hamburg: 01.00	7 Hong Kong: 08.00
4 Sydney: 10.00	8 Moskau: 03.00

Write out the time (on the 12-hour clock) in each of the cities mentioned, using the words **schon** (*already*) and **erst** (*only*) to establish a comparison with London time.

In London ist es 12 Uhr nachts.
(*a*) ***In New York ist es dann erst 7 Uhr abends.***
(*b*) ***In Wien ist es dann schon 1 Uhr nachts.***

ÜBUNG 5.3

(A) Imagine the following are activities which you are planning for today as you lie in bed. Those activities marked with a tick are those which you are looking forward to; those marked with a cross are those which you have to do, like it or not:

(*a*) 07.30 aufstehen ×
(*b*) 08.15 mit Dieter spazierengehen √

1 09.45 für Frau Körner einkaufen ×
2 10.30 mit Dieter schwimmen gehen √
3 12.00 in der »Forelle« essen gehen √
4 13.15 für Frau Körner arbeiten ×
5 16.15 Beate abholen ×
6 16.45 mit Beate Tennis spielen (*to play*) √
7 18.30 ins Kino gehen √
8 22.00 mit Dieter und Beate tanzen gehen √

Write out what you would like to do and what you have to do in the course of the day.

(*a*) Um halb 8 muß ich aufstehen.
(*b*) Um Viertel nach 8 möchte ich mit Dieter spazierengehen.

(B) Now imagine that the list refers to Heinz Bäcker. Write out what he is doing in the course of the day:

(*a*) Um halb 8 steht Heinz auf.
(*b*) Um Viertel nach 8 geht er mit Dieter spazieren.

ÜBUNG 5.4 **Können oder müssen?**

Provide the appropriate form of either **können** or **müssen**:

Wilfried ***muß*** morgen um 7 Uhr arbeiten. Da ***muß*** er schon um halb 6 austehen. Er ***kann*** erst um 4 Uhr ins Kino gehen.

Morgen . . (1) . . Helga nicht arbeiten. Da . . (2) . . sie bis 9 Uhr schlafen (*to sleep*). Sie . . (3) . . erst um halb 10 einkaufen.

Claudia . . (4) . . wir heute nachmittag leider nicht besuchen. Heute abend . . (5) . . wir meine Mutter besuchen. Morgen um 10 . . (6) . . ich Tennis spielen. Morgen nachmittag . . (7) . . du arbeiten. Da . . (8) . . wir erst morgen abend Claudia besuchen.

ÜBUNG 5.5 **Was paßt zusammen?** (*What goes together with what?*)

Ergänzen Sie den Dialog.

1	Ich möchte essen gehen. Kommst du mit?	(*a*)	Holst du mich bitte vorher ab?

2	So gegen 8.	(*b*)	Gut. Dann bist du bis 10 Uhr wieder zu Hause.
3	Der »Ratskeller« ist sehr gut.	(*c*)	Nein. Möchtest du nachher noch vielleicht tanzen gehen?
4	Gut. Dann gehen wir in das »Orgelchen«.	(*d*)	Ja gern. Wann denn?
5	Ja gerne. Hast du zur Zeit keinen Wagen?	(*e*)	Gut. Wo gehen wir dann hin?
6	Das kann ich leider nicht. Ich muß morgen schon um 5 aufstehen.	(*f*)	Der ist aber zu teuer. Dafür ist das »Orgelchen« viel preiswerter.

Verstehen Sie?

1 Konversation

Listen to the following radio announcement giving details of the programmes. Note the key phrase **nach den Nachrichten** (*fem. plur.*) *after the news.*

Programmhinweis

Bayern 3. Dreizehn Uhr achtundfünfzig.
Und jetzt vor den Nachrichten ein kurzer Blick in das Programm der kommenden Stunde:

—Bayern 1 bringt um vierzehn Uhr ein Programm für Kinder.
—Um vierzehn Uhr dreißig kommt eine Volksmusik-Wunschsendung. Am Mikrophon Fritz Meyer.
—Im Programm Bayern 1 läuft seit elf Uhr dreißig die Oper »Carmen«.
—Im Programm Bayern 3 läuft nach den Nachrichten bis fünfzehn Uhr das Pop-Musik-Karussell. Ihr Chef am Mikrophon ist Günter Dehmel.

Richtig (R) oder Falsch (F)?

1 Die Zeit ist jetzt drei Minuten vor zwei Uhr nachmittags.
2 Um vierzehn Uhr bringt man im Programm Bayern 3 Nachrichten.
3 Das Programm für Kinder kommt um vierzehn Uhr im Programm Bayern 1.

4 Das Volksmusikprogramm kommt um halb drei.
5 Die Oper »Carmen« dauert dreieinhalb Stunden.
6 Das Pop-Musik-Karussell fängt erst nach den Nachrichten an.
7 Das Pop-Musik-Karussell endet um vier Uhr nachmittags.
8 Für das Volksmusikprogramm ist Günter Dehmel am Mikrophon.

2 Lesetext

Die Teilung und Vereinigung Deutschlands

Ein paar historische Daten:

1945 Die vier Alliierten (Großbritannien, Frankreich, die Sowjetunion und die Vereinigten Staaten von Amerika) besiegen das Hitler-Deutschland. Die vier Siegesmächte teilen das Deutsche Reich (westlich der Oder-Neiße-Linie) in vier Zonen auf. Die Hauptstadt Berlin wird in vier Sektoren geteilt.
1948 Am 20. Juni führen die Westallierten eine neue Währung, die Deutsche Mark (DM), ein. Die Sowjetunion reagiert mit der Blockade von den drei Westsektoren Berlins. Nur die Berliner Luftbrücke rettet West-Berlin vor dem Stalinismus. Am 23. Juni führt die Sowjetunion ihre neue Währung in Ost-Berlin und in der Sowjetzone ein. Das bedeutet zwei Währungen für Deutschland.
1949 Am 15. September wird aus den drei Westzonen die Bundesrepublik Deutschland. Gleich danach, am 7. Oktober, wird aus der Sowjetzone die Deutsche Demokratische Republik (DDR). Die DDR ist ein sozialistisches Land, und ihre Ökonomie ist deshalb nach den Prinzipien der Planwirtschaft organisiert, während die Ökonomie der Bundesrepublik nach den Prinzipien der sozialen Marktwirtschaft organisiert ist.
1961 Am 13. August – Bau der Berliner Mauer. DDR-Bürger dürfen nicht nach West-Berlin und in die Bundesrepublik reisen.
1989 Nach Demonstrationen in der ganzen DDR öffnen sich am 9. November die innerdeutsche Grenze und die Berliner Mauer.
1990 Am 3. Oktober tritt die DDR der Bundesrepublik Deutschland bei und hört zu existieren auf. Der 3. Oktober wird zu einem nationalen Feiertag. Seitdem gibt es wieder nur einen deutschen Staat mit cirka 78,2 Millionen Einwohnern.

Answer the following questions in English:

1945 1 What do the four victorious powers do after they have defeated Hitler's Germany?

1948 2 How does the Soviet Union react to the introduction by the Western Allies of a new currency?

3 How is West Berlin rescued from Stalinism?

4 What measure does the Soviet Union take in the Soviet Zone of Germany?

1949 5 What happens on 15 September and 7 October?

6 Why is the economy of the German Democratic Republic organised according to the principles of planned economy?

7 What kind of economy does the Federal Republic have?

1961 8 What are GDR citizens no longer allowed to do as a result of the building of the Berlin Wall?

1989 9 What happens when the border between the two German states and the Berlin Wall are opened up?

1990 10 Why is 3 October a national holiday?

6 Wo gehen wir hin?

In this unit you will learn more ways of making suggestions and also how to ask for and give directions.

Dialog

Having agreed to have a meal together, Sylvia Rave and Robert Kühn decide where to go and how best to get there.

Sylvia Rave	Es ist schon Viertel nach 7. Hast du Zeit, mit mir essen zu gehen oder mußt du jetzt schon nach Hause?
Robert Kühn	Nein, ich muß erst gegen 10 wieder zu Hause sein. Ich gehe gern mit dir essen. Aber wo gehen wir dann hin?
Sylvia Rave	Ich schlage vor, wir gehen entweder ins Restaurant »Zur Sonne« oder in den Ratskeller. Beide sind ja gleich hier in der Nähe.
Robert Kühn	Welches ist billiger? Ich kann nämlich heute nicht viel Geld ausgeben. Übermorgen gehe ich in die Oper und Donnerstag ins Theater.
Sylvia Rave	Na gut. Gehen wir also in die »Sonne«. Mir gefällt es dort sehr gut. Dort gibt es immer ein interessantes Tagesmenü.
Robert Kühn	Wie kommt man von hier aus am besten in die Krumme Gasse? Wir wollen durch die Fußgängerzone, nicht wahr? Gehen wir hier geradeaus die Hauptstraße entlang und dann rechts in die Lange Straße?
Sylvia Rave	Nein. Am besten gehen wir hier rechts, diese Straße entlang, links in den Bohlweg und erst dann rechts in die Lange Straße.
Robert Kühn	Ach ja. Ich glaube, du hast recht. Im Bohlweg

sind die Geschäfte viel interessanter als die in der Hauptstraße.

Sylvia Rave Ja. Und man kommt auch viel schneller vorwärts. In der Hauptstraße sind immer so viele Touristen.

Robert Kühn Das stimmt. Die meisten besichtigen das Schloß und den Dom und gehen dann einkaufen. Also gut, los geht's!

mit mir *with me*
nach Hause *home* (lit. *to home*)
mit dir *with you*
wo . . . hin? (*or* **wohin?**) *where . . . to?*
vorschlagen (ä) (*sep.*) *to suggest*
entweder . . . oder . . . *either . . . or . . .*
der Ratskeller *cellar of the* **Rathaus** *or Town Hall; nowadays usually a restaurant*
Welches ist billiger? *Which one is cheaper?*
Geld ausgeben (i) (*sep.*) *to spend money*
übermorgen the day after tomorrow
Gehen wir . . . *let's go*
Mir gefällt es *I like it* (lit. *to me it is pleasing*)
das Tagesmenü (-s) *set meal of the day*
Wie kommt man am besten . . .? *What's the best way . . .?* (lit. *How does one come best . . .?*)
die Gasse (-n) *lane, alley*
wollen (will) *to want*
die Fußgängerzone (-n) *pedestrian precinct*
geradeaus *straight on*
die Hauptstraße entlang *along the High Street* (*Main Street*)
rechts *to/on the right*
links *to/on the left*
glauben *to believe, think*
recht haben *to be right*
das Geschäft (-e) *shop, business*
schnell *quick, fast*
besichtigen *to view, to have a look at*
der Dom (-e) *cathedral*
los geht's *off we* (lit. *it*) *go*

Fragen zum Dialog

1 Richtig (R) oder Falsch (F)?

1 Es ist schon neunzehn Uhr fünfzehn.
2 Sylvia möchte mit Robert essen gehen.
3 Robert muß aber schon um 8 Uhr 30 wieder zu Hause sein.
4 Der Ratskeller und die »Sonne« sind beide in der Nähe.

5 Robert geht übermorgen ins Kino.
6 Sylvia schlägt vor, in die »Sonne« zu gehen.
7 Sie wollen durch die Fußgängerzone gehen.
8 In der Hauptstraße sind die Geschäfte viel interessanter als im Bohlweg.
9 Es gibt viele Touristen in der Hauptstraße.
10 Die meisten Touristen gehen nur einkaufen.

2 Welche Antwort paßt?

1 Mußt du jetzt schon nach Hause?
(*a*) Ja. Bis elf Uhr bist du sicher wieder zu Hause.
(*b*) Nein, leider nicht.
(*c*) Nein, ich muß erst gegen 10 wieder zu Hause sein.

2 Hast du Zeit, mit mir essen zu gehen?
(*a*) Nein, ich muß erst gegen 10 wieder zu Hause sein.
(*b*) Ja, gerne. Ich muß erst gegen 10 wieder zu Hause sein.
(*c*) Ja, natürlich. Der Aufzug ist gleich um die Ecke.

3 Gehen wir in den Ratskeller?
(*a*) Gut. Mir gefällt es dort.
(*b*) Nein. Am besten gehen wir hier rechts.
(*c*) Ach ja. Ich glaube, du hast recht.

4 Welches Restaurant ist billiger?
(*a*) Die »Sonne« ist gleich hier in der Nähe.
(*b*) Das Tagesmenü ist im Ratskeller immer interessant.
(*c*) Die »Sonne« ist bestimmt billiger.

5 Wie kommt man am besten in die Krumme Gasse?
(*a*) Am besten gehen wir in den Ratskeller.
(*b*) Am besten gehen wir hier rechts und dann links in den Bohlweg.
(*c*) Am besten geht man in die Krumme Gasse.

Was Sie wissen sollten

Street names

The most common word in German for *street* or *road* is **die Straße**. Other words of similar meaning are: **die Gasse** (*lane*, *alley*), **der Weg** (*road*, *way*) and **die Allee** (*avenue*). Street names are usually written as one word:

die Hauptstraße, die Holzgasse, der Bohlweg, die Königsallee

If, however, an adjective—such as **lang** (*long*) or **krumm** (*crooked*) appears as part of the name, then this name is written as two words:

die Lange Straße, die Krumme Gasse

These same rules apply to the naming of *squares* and *bridges*:

der Marktplatz but **die Alte Brücke**.

Restaurants
The range of restaurants in Germany is enormous. It is still possible in most towns and cities to find good, traditional dishes typical of the area. Immigrants from a number of countries, but particularly from Turkey, Greece, Yugoslavia, Spain, Italy and Vietnam, have opened restaurants specialising in dishes from their particular country. Needless to say, fast food outlets are also well represented. Prices are clearly marked on the menu (which is usually displayed in the window) and include both **Mehrwertsteuer** (*VAT*) and **Bedienung** (*service*), though it is normal to round up the bill.

As a general rule, the best food is found in small restaurants offering a small number of freshly prepared dishes.

Wichtige Redewendungen

How to

1 *Make a suggestion.*

(*a*) Ich schlage vor, | wir gehen ins Restaurant.
wir spielen Tennis.

(*b*) Gehen wir ins Restaurant.
Spielen wir Tennis.

2 *Say you like something.*

Mir gefällt | es hier.
die Wohnung.

Mir gefallen | die Gärten.
die Häuser.

3 *Ask the way*

Wie kommt man (am besten)	dorthin?
	ins Hotel?
	in die Lange Straße?

4 *Give directions.*

Sie gehen hier	geradeaus/rechts/links.
	diese Straße entlang.

5 *Make comparisons.*

Hier sind die Geschäfte (viel)	interessanter als dort.
	billiger.
	schöner.

Die Wochentage (*The days of the week*)

Sonntag *Sunday* **Montag** *Monday* **Dienstag** *Tuesday*
Mittwoch *Wednesday* **Donnerstag** *Thursday* **Freitag** *Friday*
Samstag (im Süden) **Sonnabend** (im Norden) *Saturday*

Grammatik

1 Omission of *gehen* and *fahren*:

The verb **gehen** is often omitted in sentences such as:

Ich muß jetzt nach Hause (gehen).
Möchtest du mit mir ins Kino (gehen)?

You will note that both the examples contain a finite verb (**muß** and **möchtest**) as well as an expression of destination (**nach Hause** and **ins Kino**). The same applies to the verb **fahren** *to go* (*in a vehicle*):

Ich kann leider jetzt nicht nach Paris (fahren).
Wir wollen Donnerstag nach Frankfurt (fahren).

2 Adjectives and adverbs

There is in German normally no difference in form between

adjectives: Das Essen ist dort **billig**. *Food is cheap there.*

and

adverbs: Dort kann man **billig** essen. *One can eat cheaply there.*

3 Comparative

When we wish to make comparisons we use what is known as the ***comparative*** form. In English we either add **-er** to the adjective (*cheaper*, *faster*) or we add ***more*** in front of the adjective (***more*** *interesting*, ***more*** *practical*). In German only the **-er** form exists:

billi**ger**	*cheaper*	schnel**ler**	*faster*
interessan**ter**	*more interesting*	praktisch**er**	*more practical*

Some adjectives add an ***Umlaut*** in the comparative:

groß→**größer**	*bigger, larger*	alt→**älter**	*older*
dumm→**dümmer**	*more stupid*	klug→**klüger**	*cleverer/more clever*

Adjectives which end in **-er** and contain a diphthong (such as **eu** or **au**) in the syllable before the **-er** (for instance **teuer** (*dear*, *expensive*), **sauer** (*sour*, *tart*) drop an **e** before adding the comparative **-er**:

teuer→**teurer**	*dearer*	sauer→**saurer**	*tarter*

The equivalent of the English *than* in comparisons is **als**:

Die Wohnung in Köln ist teurer **als** die in Bremen.	*The flat in Cologne is more expensive than the one in Bremen.*

The comparative form of **gut** is **besser**:

Ihr Wagen ist **besser** als der da drüben.	*Your car is better than the one over there.*

Comparisons may also be made by using **(genau) so . . . wie . . .** (*just*) *as . . . as . . .*

Der Ford ist (genau) so gut wie der Honda.	*The Ford is (just) as good as the Honda.*

The comparative forms of adjectives may normally be used as adverbs:

Dort kommt man viel schneller vorwärts.	*One gets ahead much more quickly there.*
Den Mann kenne ich besser als die Frau.	*I know the man better than the woman.*

4 *Der/die/das* meaning *the one(s), that one, those*

Der/die/das can mean not only *the* or *he*, *she*, *it*, *they*, as described in **Lektion 3**, but also *the one*(*s*), *that one*, *those*:

Dieser Wagen fährt schneller als **der** da. *This car goes faster than that one there.*
Die Universität in Konstanz ist moderner als **die** in Hamburg. *The university in Constance is more modern than the one in Hamburg.*
Das Hotel in der Hauptstraße ist besser als **das** um die Ecke. *The hotel in the High Street is better than the one around the corner.*
Diese Geschäfte hier sind interessanter als **die** in der Hauptstraße. *These shops here are more interesting than those in the High Street.*

5 *Welch-?* and *dies-*

The question-word **welch-?** (*which* (*one*)*?*) and the 'demonstrative' word **dies** (*this* (*one*)) take the following endings:

Singular	*Masculine*	*Feminine*	*Neuter*
Nominative	**-er**	**-e**	**-es**
Accusative	**-en**	**-e**	**-es**

Plural (*masculine*, *feminine* and *neuter*) *nominative* and *accusative:* **-e**

Welch**er** Film, glaubst du, ist besser?	Welch**er** ist besser?
Dies**er** Film ist besser.	Dies**er** ist besser.
Welch**e** Küche ist moderner?	Welch**e** ist moderner?
Dies**e** Küche ist moderner.	Dies**e** ist moderner.
Welch**es** Restaurant ist billiger?	Welch**es** ist billiger?
Dies**es** Restaurant ist billiger.	Dies**es** ist billiger.
Welch**e** Geschäfte sind interessanter?	Welch**e** sind interessanter?
Dies**e** Geschäfte sind interessanter.	Dies**e** sind interessanter.
Welch**en** Film möchtest du sehen?	Welch**en** möchtest du sehen?
Dies**en** Film möchte ich sehen.	Dies**en** möchte ich sehen.
Welch**e** Wohnung nimmst du?	Welch**e** nimmst du?
Dies**e** Wohnung nehme ich.	Dies**e** nehme ich.
Welch**es** Zimmer möchtest du haben?	Welch**es** möchtest du haben?
Dies**es** Zimmer möchte ich haben.	Dies**es** möchte ich haben.
Welch**e** Zimmer möchtest du haben?	Welch**e** möchtest du haben?
Dies**e** Zimmer möchte ich haben.	Dies**e** möchte ich haben.

The fact that it is only the ending on **dies-** or **welch-** in the last four lines of the above examples which indicates whether the singular (*room*) or the plural (*rooms*) is intended, serves to underline the importance of trying to get the endings right.

Welch- can also mean *some*, *any*:

Ich habe keine Eier. Hast du **welche?** *I haven't any eggs. Have you got any?*

6 *In* + accusative

The accusative case is not only used to denote the object in a sentence or clause (see **Lektion 4**), but it is also used with certain ***prepositions*** (words like **für, gegen, um**). After **in** the accusative is used when **in** may be translated as *(in)to:*

Ich gehe	in **den** Garten. in **den** dritten Stock. in **die** Oper. in **die** Stadt. **ins** (in **das**) Bett. **ins** Kino. in **die** Häuser. in **die** Schlafzimmer.

You may be puzzled that the **Dialog** contains examples in which **in** is ***not*** followed by the accusative (such as **Die Geschäfte in *der* Hauptstraße . . .**). Here **in** cannot be translated as *(in)to* and therefore belongs to a different category which will be dealt with later.

7 *Entlang* *(along)*

Note that **entlang** usually follows the noun and that it requires the accusative case:

Gehen wir diese Straße entlang. *Let's go along this street.*

Übungen

ÜBUNG 6.1 Was paßt zusammen?

Ich möchte . . .	Dann gehen Sie . . .
1 französisch essen.	(*a*) in den Ratskeller.

2	einen Kaffee trinken	(*b*)	ins Freibad.
3	tanzen gehen.	(*c*)	in die Hauptstraße.
4	schwimmen gehen.	(*d*)	ins Restaurant »Barcelona«.
5	einen Film sehen.	(*e*)	ins Theater.
6	einkaufen.	(*f*)	in die Discothek »Heaven«.
7	spanisch essen.	(*g*)	ins Bett.
8	Goethe's »Faust« sehen.	(*h*)	ins Café »Sieben«.
9	typisch (*typically*) deutsch essen.	(*i*)	ins Restaurant »L'escargot«.
10	schlafen.	(*j*)	ins Kino.

ÜBUNG 6.2 Renate has a busy week ahead. Look at this extract from her diary and write out what she is doing on each day of the week, following the pattern provided in the examples:

JULI 29. Woche

(a)	Mon 14	18.00	Kino (mit Michael)
(b)	Di 15	19.30	Oper
1	Mi 16	20.00	Theater
2	Do 17	19.15	Ratskeller (mit Klaus)
3	Fr 18	22.30	Discothek (mit Doris und Claudia)
4	Sa 19	21.15	Kabarett
5	So 20	14.00	Konzert (mit Käthe)

Two of the items of vocabulary you have not met before. Although their meanings will present no difficulty, you will nevertheless need to know their genders: **das Kabarett, das Konzert**.

(*a*) Montag um sechs Uhr geht Renate mit Michael ins Kino.
(*b*) Dienstag um halb acht geht sie in die Oper.

ÜBUNG 6.3

(A) Going one better. Reply to the following statements as indicated in these examples:

(*a*) Das Haus um die Ecke ist sehr alt.
Ja, aber dieses hier ist noch älter als das um die Ecke.
(*b*) Der Wagen da drüben ist sehr preiswert.
Ja, aber dieser hier ist noch preiswerter als der da drüben.

1 Das Hotel da drüben ist sehr teuer.
2 Der Garten um die Ecke ist sehr schön.
3 Das Geschäft da drüben ist sehr interessant.
4 Das Zimmer im zweiten Stock ist sehr klein.
5 Die Fußgängerzone in Düsseldorf ist sehr groß.
6 Die Wohnung in der Hauptstraße ist sehr modern.

(B) Now ask questions displaying incredulity at the information given in the answers to **(A)**. Use these examples as models:

(*a*) ***Welches Haus ist älter? Dieses hier?***
(*b*) ***Welcher Wagen ist preiswerter? Dieser hier?***

ÜBUNG 6.4 You are asked whether you like the following items. You answer (guided by the ticks and crosses) either that you like them or that you are afraid you don't like them:

Wie finden Sie (*a*) diesen Film? ***Mir gefällt er.***
(*b*) diese Häuser? ***Mir gefallen sie leider nicht.***

Wie finden Sie

1 diese Oper? √	5 diese Musik? ×
2 diese Gärten? ×	6 diese Namen? ×
3 diesen Wagen? √	7 dieses Wohnzimmer? √
4 dieses Hallenbad? √	8 diesen Plan? ×

ÜBUNG 6.5 Ergänzen Sie den Dialog.

Tourist Guten Abend! Haben Sie ein Zimmer frei?

Empfangsdame	(1)
Tourist	Ein Doppelzimmer mit Bad, bitte, für meine Frau und mich.
Empfangsdame	(2)
Tourist	Das Zimmer nehmen wir.
Empfangsdame	(3)
Tourist	Danke. Wie kommen wir am besten in die Altstadt?
Empfangsdame	(4)
Tourist	Danke. Und wo können wir hier gut essen?
Empfangsdame	(5)
Tourist	Ist es dort aber nicht zu teuer?
Empfangsdame	(6)

(*a*) Würden Sie sich bitte eintragen? Sie haben Zimmer 24 im zweiten Stock. Hier ist Ihr Schlüssel.
(*b*) Gut. Das Zimmer kostet 210,—Mark inklusive Frühstück, Mehrwertsteuer und Bedienung.
(*c*) Ja. Möchten Sie ein Einzelzimmer oder ein Doppelzimmer?
(*d*) Nein. Billig ist es dort nicht, aber auch nicht zu teuer.
(*e*) Das Restaurant »Zum Schiffchen« ist sehr gut. Dort kann man sehr gut essen.
(*f*) Sie gehen hier die Breite Straße entlang, links in die Grabenstraße, dann immer geradeaus.

Verstehen Sie?

1 Konversation

Otto Lamm, who has just arrived in Berlin, asks a taxi driver to take him to his hotel. The taxi driver gives Otto some information on what to see in Berlin.

Taxifahrerin	Wohin möchten Sie?
Otto Lamm	Zum Hotel »Domus«, bitte. Kennen Sie es?
Taxifahrerin	Ja. Das ist doch in der Uhlandstraße.
Otto Lamm	Ja. Uhlandstraße 49 (neunundvierzig). Liegt das Hotel ziemlich zentral?
Taxifahrerin	Ja, sicher. Die Uhlandstraße liegt gleich in der Nähe vom Kurfürstendamm.

Otto Lamm Was ist denn der Kurfürstendamm?

Taxifahrerin Was?! Sie kennen den Kurfürstendamm nicht? Das ist doch wohl eine der berühmtesten Straßen hier in Berlin, wo die ganzen Geschäfte, Kinos, Cafés, Restaurants und Nachtklubs sind. Kennen Sie Berlin also noch gar nicht?

Otto Lamm Nein. Ich bin zum erstenmal hier.

Taxifahrerin Sind Sie auf Urlaub?

Otto Lamm Ja, ich habe acht Tage frei.

Taxifahrerin Sehr schön. In einer Woche kann man sehr viel sehen. Sie müssen unbedingt das Schloß Charlottenburg besichtigen.

Otto Lamm Welches Schloß, bitte?

Taxifahrerin Das Schloß Charlottenburg. Woher kommen Sie denn eigentlich?!

Otto Lamm Aus Buxtehude.*

Richtig (R) oder Falsch (F)?

1 Otto Lamm möchte zum Hotel »Domus«.
2 Die Taxifahrerin kennt das Hotel nicht.
3 Das Hotel liegt gleich in der Nähe vom Kurfürstendamm.
4 Der Kurfürstendamm ist eine sehr berühmte Straße in Berlin.
5 Am Kurfürstendamm findet man nur Nachtklubs.
6 Otto Lamm kennt Berlin ziemlich gut.
7 Otto Lamm hat eine Woche Urlaub.
8 Otto Lamm kommt aus München.

2 Lesetext

das Land (¨er) *(federal) state*	**die Hauptstadt (¨e)** *capital city*
eigen *own*	**die Bevölkerungszahl** *population*
die Regierung (-en) *government*	**das Gebiet (-e)** *area*

Die Länder der Bundesrepublik Deutschland

Die Bundesrepublik Deutschland hat eine föderative Struktur. Die sechzehn »Länder« der Bundesrepublik haben jeweils ein eigenes

*See **Buxtehude** in German–English Vocabulary.

Landesparlament oder »Landtag« und eine eigene Landesregierung. Drei Länder, Hamburg, Bremen und Berlin sind Stadtstaaten. Die anderen dreizehn Länder haben je eine Landeshauptstadt.

Der Freistaat Bayern ist mit 70 551 Quadratkilometern das größte Bundesland. Dieses Land ist ungefähr so groß wie die Niederlande und Belgien zusammen und liegt im Südosten der Bundesrepublik. Bayern hat 11 Millionen Einwohner, von denen 1 297 000 in der Landeshauptstadt München wohnen.

Das Land Nordrhein-Westfalen hat mit 16,9 Millionen Einwohnern die größte Bevölkerungszahl von allen Bundesländern. In Nordrhein-Westfalen liegen nicht nur die Großstädte Düsseldorf, Köln und der Regierungssitz Bonn, sondern auch die Städte des Ruhrgebiets Bochum, Dortmund, Duisburg, Essen usw.

Die Länder der Bundesrepublik Deutschland

Bundesland	**Landeshauptstadt**	**Bundesland**	**Landeshauptstadt**
Baden-Württemberg	Stuttgart	Nordrhein-Westfalen	Düsseldorf
Bayern	München	Rheinland-Pfalz	Mainz
Brandenburg	Potsdam	Saarland	Saarbrücken
Hessen	Wiesbaden	Sachsen	Dresden
Mecklenburg-Vorpommern	Schwerin	Sachsen-Anhalt	Magdeburg
		Schleswig-Holstein	Kiel
Niedersachsen	Hannover	Thüringen	Erfurt

Stadtstaaten: Berlin, Bremen, Hamburg

Answer the following questions in English:

1 How many states or **Länder** does the Federal Republic have?
2 What is the function of the **Landtag** that each federal state has?
3 Why are the cities of Bremen, Hamburg and Berlin specially mentioned?
4 What claim to fame does the Free State of Bavaria have?
5 With what land area is Bavaria compared, in order to give us some idea of its size?
6 What do the figures of 11 million and 1,297,000 represent?
7 Why is the state of North Rhine Westphalia mentioned?
8 In which famous area do the cities of Bochum, Dortmund, Duisburg and Essen lie?
9 What city is the seat of government in the Federal Republic?

7 Wir möchten bestellen

In this unit you will learn how to place orders in a restaurant and how to state likes and dislikes concerning food and drink.

Dialog

Sylvia and Robert arrive at the »Sonne«, choose their table, seek advice from the waiter and select food from the menu.

Kellner	Guten Abend. Sie möchten einen Tisch für zwei Personen? Bitte. Setzen Sie sich entweder an diesen Tisch hier oder an den in der Ecke. Ich bringe Ihnen sofort die Speisekarte.
Sylvia Rave	Danke. Wir nehmen hier Platz. (*Der Kellner gibt ihnen die Speisekarte*) Was können Sie uns heute empfehlen?
Kellner	Die Forelle ist heute ausgezeichnet, und der Rehbraten ist auch sehr gut. Kann ich Ihnen etwas zu trinken bringen?
Robert Kühn	Ja, bringen Sie uns zwei Glas Weißwein—den Mosel, bitte, und eine große Flasche Mineralwasser—mit Kohlensäure. (*Der Kellner geht weg*)
Sylvia Rave	Möchtest du eine Vorspeise? Ich glaube, ich nehme eine Zwiebelsuppe. Französische Zwiebelsuppe esse ich sehr gern.
Robert Kühn	Gut, dann esse ich auch eine Vorspeise. Ich bekomme eine kalte Schinkenplatte. Und als Hauptgericht nehme ich die bayerische Schweinshaxe mit Kartoffelknödel und Salat. Ich möchte heute keinen Fisch essen und Wild mag ich nicht.
Sylvia Rave	Ich auch nicht. Heute esse ich lieber Hähnchen mit Pommes frites. Willst du auch etwas zum Nachtisch?
Robert Kühn	Das weiß ich noch nicht. Das sage ich dir erst später.

Wahrscheinlich bin ich dann satt, aber vielleicht esse ich noch ein Eis oder einen Pudding. Die Puddings schmecken hier phantastisch.

(*Der Kellner bringt ihnen den Wein.*)

Kellner Bitte schön. Zwei Schoppen Mosel.

Sylvia Rave Danke schön. (*Er will weggehen*) Und Herr Ober, wir möchten bitte bestellen.

Kellner Ja. sofort. Die Herrschaften nebenan wollen zahlen. Ich muß zuerst noch bei ihnen kassieren.

Here is the menu from which Sylvia and Robert made their selection:

Speisekarte	***Menu***
Vorspeisen	**Starters**
Französische Zwiebelsuppe	French onion soup
Kalte Schinkenplatte	Cold ham platter
Hauptgerichte	**Main courses**
Forelle Müllerin	Trout á la meunière
Rehbraten	Roast venison
Bayerische Schweinshaxe mit Kartoffelknödel	Bavarian knuckle of pork with potato dumpling
Hähnchen vom Grill mit Pommes frites	Grilled chicken with French fries
Dessert	**Dessert**
Gemischter Eisbecher	Mixed ice-cream sundae
Vanille- oder Himbeereis mit Sahne	Vanilla or raspberry ice-cream with cream
Schokoladenpudding	Chocolate blancmange

der Tisch (-e) *table*
sich setzen *to sit down*
Platz nehmen *to take a seat*
empfehlen (ie) *to recommend*
Das weiß ich nicht *I don't know (that)*
Das sage ich dir später *I'll tell you (that) later*

ausgezeichnet *excellent*
etwas zu trinken *something to drink*
zwei Glas (oder Gläser) Weißwein *two glasses of white wine*
eine Flasche Mineralwasser *a bottle of mineral water*
mit Kohlensäure *fizzy* (lit *with carbonic acid*)
Ich esse gern . . . *I like* (*eating*) . . .
Wild mag ich nicht *I don't like game*
Ich auch nicht *nor do I*
Ich esse lieber . . . *I prefer* (*to eat*) . . .
etwas zum Nachtisch *something for dessert*
wahrscheinlich *probably*
Ich bin satt *I'm full up*
Der Pudding schmeckt phantastisch *The blancmange tastes wonderful*
Herr Ober! *Waiter!*
sofort *straight away*
Wir möchten bestellen *We'd like to order*
die Herrschaften (*fem. plur.*) *the lady and gentleman, the ladies and/or gentlemen*
nebenan *next door;* (*here*) *at the next table*
zahlen *to pay*
kassieren (bei) *to collect money* (*from*)

Fragen zum Dialog

1 Richtig (R) oder Falsch (F)?

1 Der Kellner empfiehlt ihnen das Hähnchen und die Schweinshaxe.
2 Robert bestellt zwei Gläser Moselwein und eine Flasche Mineralwasser.
3 Sylvia bekommt eine französische Zwiebelsuppe.
4 Robert möchte keine Vorspeise.
5 Als Hauptgericht nimmt Robert das Hähnchen mit Pommes frites.
6 Robert möchte heute keinen Fisch essen.
7 Sylvia mag kein Wild essen.
8 Robert ißt vielleicht ein Eis oder einen Pudding zum Nachtisch.
9 Die Puddings im Restaurant »Zur Sonne« schmecken ausgezeichnet.
10 Der Kellner muß noch bei den Herrschaften nebenan kassieren.

2 Welche Antwort paßt?

1 Guten Abend! Wir möchten einen Tisch für zwei Personen.

(*a*) Wie nehmen hier Platz.
(*b*) Sie dürfen sich entweder an diesen Tisch hier oder an den in der Ecke setzen.
(*c*) Gut, ich habe noch acht Tage frei.

2 Was können Sie uns heute empfehlen?
(*a*) Der Rehbraten ist heute ausgezeichnet.
(*b*) Das sage ich Ihnen erst später.
(*c*) Ich schlage vor, Sie gehen in den Ratskeller.

3 Kann ich Ihnen etwas zu trinken bringen?
(*a*) Ja, bringen Sie uns bitte zwei Hähnchen mit Pommes frites.
(*b*) Tut mir leid. Heute nachmittag kann ich nicht.
(*c*) Ja, bringen Sie uns bitte zwei Glas Wein.

4 Nimmst du eine Vorspeise?
(*a*) Ja. Ich nehme eine kalte Schinkenplatte.
(*b*) Ja. Ich nehme die bayerische Schweinshaxe.
(*c*) Nein. Wild mag ich nicht.

5 Willst du auch etwas zum Nachtisch?
(*a*) Ich glaube, ich nehme eine Zwiebelsuppe.
(*b*) Vielleicht esse ich noch ein Eis oder einen Pudding.
(*c*) Heute möchte ich keinen Fisch essen.

Was Sie wissen sollten

Getting served and paying

Whilst **der Kellner** and **die Kellnerin** mean *waiter* and *waitress* respectively, these words are not used when addressing waiters or waitresses or when attracting their attention. **Herr Ober** (short for **Herr Oberkellner** *head waiter*) and **Fräulein** are used for these purposes.

When you wish to pay, you catch the waiter/waitress's eye and say:

Herr Ober,	ich möchte bitte (be)zahlen.
Fräulein,	wir möchten bitte (be)zahlen.

Or simply: **Bitte (be)zahlen.**

German wines

Most of the wine produced in Germany is white wine. Table wine is referred to as **Deutscher Tafelwein** unless it has been blended with wine from another EEC country, in which case it is merely **Tafelwein**.

Quality wine or **Qualitätswein** is subdivided into **Qualitätswein bestimmter Anbaugebiete (QbA)** (*quality wine from specified sites*) and **Qualitätswein mit Prädikat (QmP)** (*quality wine with a specific distinction*).

There are six different distinctions reserved for the latter type of quality wine: **Kabinett, Spätlese, Auslese, Beerenauslese, Trockenbeerenauslese** and **Eiswein**.

In restaurants and pubs wine is usually sold by the glass (20 or 25 cl) and is referred to by the name of one of the thirteen regions from which quality wines come (**Ahr, Hessische Bergstraße, Mittelrhein, Nahe, Rheingau, Rheinhessen, Rheinpfalz, Mosel-Saar-Ruwer, Franken, Württemberg, Baden, Saale-Unstrut, Elbe**). They might be listed as follows on a menu:

Schankweine *draught wines*

110	Rheinpfalz QbA	113	Rheinhessen QbA
111	Mosel QbA	114	Rheingau QmP
112	Franken QmP	115	Württemberg QbA

Wichtige Redewendungen

How to

1 *Order food and drink.*

Bringen Sie	mir		zwei Glas Wein
	uns	bitte	eine Zwiebelsuppe.
Ich möchte			eine Schinkenplatte.
Wir möchten			zwei Hähnchen.

2 *State intentions regarding food and drink (these are also often used for placing orders).*

	die bayerische Schweinshaxe.
Ich bekomme	ein Vanilleneis mit Sahne.
Ich nehme	ein Glas Weißwein.
	ein Mineralwasser.

3 *State likes and dislikes concerning food and drink.*

Ich esse (nicht) gern	Schokoladenpudding.
Ich esse lieber	Eis.
Ich mag kein (e(n))	Zwiebelsuppe.

4 *State preferences concerning food and drink.*

Möchtest du einen Pudding? Danke, ich esse lieber ein Eis.
Möchtest du einen Tafelwein? Danke, ich trinke lieber einen Qualitätswein.

Ißt du gern Pudding? Ja, aber ich esse lieber Eis.
Trinkst du gern Tafelwein? Ja, aber ich trinke lieber Qualitätswein.

5 *Say that something tastes good or bad.*

	(Ihnen)	der Pudding?
Schmeckt	(dir)	das Hähnchen?
		die Suppe?

Ja,	er es sie	schmeckt	gut. sehr gut. phantastisch.

Mir	schmeckt schmecken	diese Suppe diese Pommes frites	(nicht)	. .

Getränke *drinks*
das Mineralwasser *mineral water*
der Apfelsaft *apple juice*
der Kaffee *coffee*
das Bier *beer*
die Milch *milk*
der Weißwein *white wine*
der Rotwein *red wine*
der Tee *tea*
die Cola *coke*

Gemüse *vegetables*
die Kartoffel(-n) *potato*
der Kohl (-e) *cabbage*
der Porree (-s) *leek*
die Erbse (-en) *pea*
die Rübe (-n) *turnip*
die Bohne (-n) *bean*
der Blumenkohl (-e) *cauliflower*
der Spargel(-) *asparagus*
die Möhre (-n) *carrot*

Obst *fruit*
der Apfel (¨) *apple*
die Birne (-n) *pear*
die Kirsche (-n) *cherry*
die Pflaume (-n) *plum*
die Erdbeere (-n) *strawberry*
die Banane (-n) *banana*
die Orange (-n) *orange*
der Pfirsich (-e) *peach*
die Zwetschge (-n) *dark blue plum*

Fleischsorten *meats*
das Rindfleisch *beef*
das Lammfleisch *lamb*
das Schweinefleisch *pork*
das Kalbfleisch *veal*
das Hammelfleisch *mutton*

Grammatik

1 Dative case

In the sentence *The waiter is bringing us the menu*, ***the waiter***—as we saw in **Lektion 4**—is the ***subject*** of the sentence and in German is in the ***nominative*** case. As ***the menu*** is ***what*** the waiter is bringing, we call this the ***direct object***. This in German is in the ***accusative case***. ***Us*** tells us ***to whom*** the waiter is bringing the menu and is referred to as the ***indirect object***. In German indirect objects are in the ***dative case***. So far you have met a few personal pronouns in the dative case:

Ich bringe **Ihnen** die Speisekarte. *I'll bring* (*to*) *you the menu.*
Kann ich **Ihnen** etwas zu trinken bringen? *Can I bring* (*to*) *you something to drink?*
Was können Sie **uns** empfehlen? *What can you recommend* (*to*) *us?*

Bringen Sie	**uns**	zwei Glas Wein.	*Bring*	(*to us*)	*two glasses of wine.*
	mir			(*to*) *me*	

Das sage ich **dir** später. *I'll tell you* (lit. *say to you*) (*that*) *later.*

Other examples are:

Bringen Sie **ihnen** etwas zu trinken. *Bring* (*to*) *them something to drink.*
Können Sie **ihr** ein Hotel empfehlen? *Can you recommend* (*to*) *her an hotel?*
Kannst du **ihm** 10,—Mark geben? *Can you give* (*to*) *him 10 marks?*

Also in this category is another useful verb that you have not yet met—**schenken** (*to give* (*as a present*)):

Schenkst du **ihm** einen Wagen? *Are you giving him a car?*

Certain verbs are followed by the dative case. You have already met **gefallen** and **schmecken** which fall into this category:

Dieser Wagen gefällt **mir** nicht. *I don't like this car* (lit. *This car is not pleasing to me*).
Diese Suppe schmeckt **uns** nicht. *We don't like* (*the taste of*) *this soup.* (lit. *This soup does not taste to us*).

Another useful verb in this category is **helfen (i)** (*to help*):

Kann ich **Ihnen** helfen? *Can I help you?*

In **Lektion 2** you learned the phrase **Wie geht es Ihnen?** (*How are you?* (lit. *How goes it to you?*)) which contains the dative pronoun **Ihnen**. You will now be able to use this construction with other dative pronouns:

Wie geht's **dir**?	*How are you?*
Mir geht's gut, danke.	*I'm well, thanks.*
Wie geht's **Anna**?	*How is Anna?*
Ihr geht's gut.	*She's well.*

Certain prepositions are followed by the dative case. You have already met **mit** and **bei** in this category:

Hast du Zeit, mit **mir** essen zu gehen? *Have you time to go for a meal with me?*
Ich muß zuerst noch bei **ihnen** kassieren. *I still have to collect money from them* (lit. *at them*).

The dative question-word is **wem?**:

Wem gibst du den Kaffee? *To whom are you giving the coffee?* or *Who are you giving the coffee to?*
Wem gefällt es hier nicht? *Who doesn't like it here?*(lit. *To whom is it not pleasing here?*)
Mit **wem** gehst du ins Kino? *With whom are you going to the cinema?* or *Who are you going to the cinema with?*

More information on the dative case will appear in subsequent units.

2 Expressions of quantity

You will already have noticed in the **Dialog** such expressions as

eine Flasche Mineralwasser — *a bottle of mineral water*
ein Glas Weißwein — *a glass of white wine*

English uses *of* to link the measure or container with the substance in question. No such link-word is required in German:

eine Tasse Kaffee — *a cup of coffee*
zwei Tassen Tee — *two cups of tea*
ein Glas Bier — *a glass of beer*
ein Kilo Äpfel — *a kilo of apples*
ein Pfund Tomaten — *a pound of tomatoes*
ein Liter Milch — *a litre of milk*

The plural of **Glas** is **Gläser**, but the **Glas** form is often retained when drinks are being ordered: **Zwei Glas Weißwein, bitte**.

The word **Schoppen** is often used—especially in Southern Germany—instead of **Glas** when wine or beer is involved: **Zwei Schoppen Mosel, bitte**.

3 Word order

In **Lektionen 3** and **4** you learned that German word order is often different from that of English. In this unit there were examples of the ***direct object*** appearing as the first item in the sentence—something that very rarely happens in English:

Direct object	*verb*	*subject*	*Indirect object*		
1	2	3			
Wild	mag	ich		nicht.	*I don't like game.*
Das	weiß	ich		nicht.	*I don't know (that).*
Das	sage	ich	dir	später.	*I'll tell you (that) later.*

In this and the previous unit there were examples of the ***dative pronoun*** appearing as the first item of the sentence:

1	*2*	*3*		
Mir	gefällt	es	dort.	*I like it there.*
Mir	schmeckt	diese Suppe.		*I like (the taste of) this soup.*

Word order differences of this kind can lead to comprehension problems, especially in the earlier stages of learning German. If you are having difficulties understanding, ask yourself whether word order might be the reason. You will soon become used to the various word order possibilities, and after sufficient practice, you will find yourself quite naturally using typically German word order.

4 Imperative

In **Lektion 4** you learned the indirect way of asking someone to do something:

Würden Sie bitte in der Tiefgarage parken? *Would you please park in the underground car park?*

If you wish to give someone a direct command, you use what is called the ***imperative***:

Bringen Sie uns zwei Glas Wein. *Bring us two glasses of wine.*

This blunt command can, of course, be toned down by the simple addition of **'bitte'**.

The **Sie** form of the imperative is very simple. It is only necessary to reverse the order of the present tense form: **Sie bringen** thus becomes **Bringen Sie**. Other examples are:

Setzen Sie sich an diesen Tisch.	*Sit at this table.*
Nehmen Sie hier Platz.	*Take a seat here.*
Kommen Sie mit mir.	*Come with me.*

The **du** form of the imperative is not much more difficult. Merely omit the **-st** and the **du** from the present tense form: **Du bringst** thus becomes **bring**. Other examples are:

Komm mit mir ins Kino.	*Come to the cinema with me.*
Hol mich um 10 ab.	*Pick me up at* 10.
Nimm hier Platz.	*Take a seat.*

Exceptions to this rule are verbs like **anfangen** and **fahren** which do modify the middle vowel in the present tense form (**du fängst an, du fährst**), but which do not modify this vowel in the imperative:

Fang bitte an.	*Please start.*
Fahr doch schneller!	*Do drive faster!*

As you may have already noticed from two of the examples above (those illustrating **abholen** and **anfangen**), the separable particle of separable verbs goes at the end of the sentence in the imperative:

Stehen Sie morgen um 6 Uhr **auf.** **Steh** morgen um 6 Uhr **auf.**	} *Get up at* 6 *o'clock tomorrow.*

Needless to say, the verb **sein** is also irregular in the imperative;

Seien Sie nicht so unfreundlich.	*Don't be so unfriendly.*
Sei lieb!	*Be nice!*

Übungen

ÜBUNG 7.1 Welche Antwort paßt?

1 Möchtest du heute abend mit mir essen gehen?
(*a*) Ja, sicher, mit dir gehe ich immer gerne essen.
(*b*) Ja, sicher, mit ihnen gehe ich immer gerne essen.
(*c*) Nein, mit ihr gehe ich nicht gerne essen.

2 Gehen wir dann in den Ratskeller?
(*a*) Nein, ihm gefällt es dort nicht.
(*b*) Ja, mir gefällt es dort nicht.
(*c*) Ja, mir gefällt es dort.

3 Darf Susi auch mitkommen?
(*a*) Nein, bitte nicht! Mit ihr gehe ich nicht gerne essen.
(*b*) Ja, natürlich, mit dir gehe ich immer gerne essen.
(*c*) Ja, dort hat man immer ein interessantes Tagesmenü.

4 Herr Ober. Was gibt es heute abend zu empfehlen?
  (*a*) Sie empfiehlt uns die Schweinshaxe.
  (*b*) Er empfiehlt uns den Rehbraten.
  (*c*) Ich empfehle Ihnen die Forelle.

5 Und möchten Sie etwas zum Nachtisch?
  (*a*) Ja, bringen Sie uns bitte eine Zwiebelsuppe und eine Erbsensuppe.
  (*b*) Nein, Rotwein trinke ich nicht gern.
  (*c*) Ja, wir bekommen einen Eisbecher und einen Schokoladenpudding, bitte.

6 Bitte schön. Kann ich Ihnen etwas zu trinken bringen?
  (*a*) Bring uns zwei Glas Bier.
  (*b*) Bringen Sie uns bitte zwei Glas Bier
  (*c*) Bringen Sie ihnen bitte zwei Schoppen Mosel.

ÜBUNG 7.2 **Ergänzen Sie den Dialog.**

Klaus Tag, Kurt. Wie geht's dir?
Kurt (1)
Klaus Ach ja. Schenkst du ihr etwas?
Kurt (2)
Klaus Sie gibt eine Party, nicht wahr? Schenk ihr doch einen Kuchen.
Kurt (3)
Klaus Schenk ihr dann eine Flasche Wein.
Kurt (4)
Klaus Dann schenk ihr einen Wagen.
Kurt (5)
Klaus Dann kann ich dir leider nicht helfen!

(*a*) Wein mag sie leider nicht.
(*b*) Das kann ich nicht. Das ist mir viel zu teuer.
(*c*) Danke, gut. Du, Birgit hat morgen Geburtstag (*birthday*).
(*d*) Ich glaube, sie hat schon vier Kuchen.
(*e*) Ja, aber ich weiß noch nicht was.

ÜBUNG 7.3 **Antworten Sie.**

Answer that the following people are well or not so well

Beispiele: Wie geht's Ihnen? ***Mir geht's gut.***
Wie geht's Klaus? ***Ihm geht's nicht so gut.***

1 Wie geht's dir?
2 Wie geht's Maria?
3 Wie geht's Frau Schmidt?
4 Wie geht's Heinz?
5 Wie geht's Klaus und Anna?
6 Wie geht's Ihnen beiden?

ÜBUNG 7.4 **Sagen Sie es anders.**

Transform the following polite requests into commands:

Beispiele: Würden Sie bitte in der Tiefgarage parken?
Parken Sie in der Tiefgarage.

Würdest du mich bitte um 10 Uhr abholen?
Hol mich um 10 Uhr ab.

1 Würden Sie uns bitte eine Flasche Moselwein bringen?
2 Würdest du bitte mit mir ins Kino gehen?
3 Würdest du doch bitte schneller fahren?
4 Würdest du bitte hier Platz nehmen?
5 Würden Sie bitte sofort anfangen?
6 Würden Sie bitte um halb sieben aufstehen?

ÜBUNG 7.5 Move to the front of the sentence the phrase printed in italic and make any further necessary adjustments:

Beispiel: Ich fahre ***morgen*** nach Düsseldorf.
Morgen fahre ich nach Düsseldorf.

1 Ich habe *in Düsseldorf* sehr viel zu tun.
2 Ich muß *deshalb* um 6 Uhr aufstehen.
3 Mein Freund Holger kommt *um halb* 7 und holt mich ab.
4 Man fährt ungefähr 2 Stunden *von Frankfurt nach Düsseldorf.*
5 Wir sind dann *hoffentlich* gegen halb 9 schon in Düsseldorf.
6 Wir wollen *am Abend* noch ins Theater gehen.
7 Wir müssen *nachher* natürlich wieder 2 Stunden auf der Autobahn fahren.
8 Wir sind *wahrscheinlich* erst gegen 1 Uhr morgens wieder zu Hause.

Verstehen Sie?

1 Konversation

Sonja Auer orders a three-course meal, but makes some effort to keep a check on her calorie intake.

Sonja Auer Herr Ober! Ich möchte gerne bestellen.
Kellner Bitte schön. Was wünschen Sie?
Sonja Auer Als Vorspeise nehme ich eine Gemüsesuppe.
Kellner Eine Gemüsesuppe—und als Hauptgericht?
Sonja Auer Das Pfeffersteak mit Grilltomate, bitte. Ich möchte aber keine Pommes frites. Kann ich statt dessen einen gemischten Salat haben?
Kellner Aber selbstverständlich. Und zum Trinken?
Sonja Auer Bringen Sie mir bitte einen Apfelsaft.
(20 *Minuten später*)
Kellner So? Schmeckt es Ihnen?
Sonja Auer Dank. Mir schmeckt's sehr gut.
Kellner Gut! Möchten Sie vielleicht auch etwas zum Nachtisch?
Sonja Auer Ja. Ich bekomme einen gemischten Eisbecher. Aber bitte keine Sahne! Und bringen Sie mir auch eine Tasse Kaffee.
Kellner Einen gemischten Eisbecher ohne Sahne. Möchten Sie den Kaffee sofort oder erst nachher?
Sonja Auer Erst nach dem Eisbecher, bitte.

Richtig (R) oder Falsch (F)?

1 Als Vorspeise bestellt Sonja eine Bohnensuppe.
2 Als Hauptgericht möchte sie das Pfeffersteak, aber ohne Pommes frites.
3 Sie möchte statt dessen einen Kartoffelsalat.
4 Zum Trinken bestellt sie einen Orangensaft.
5 Ihr schmeckt das Steak.
6 Zum Nachtisch bestellt Sonja einen gemischten Eisbecher mit Sahne.
7 Sie nimmt auch eine Tasse Kaffee.
8 Den Kaffee möchte sie sofort mit dem Eisbecher haben.

2 Lesetext

Here is a German recipe (a speciality from Westphalia and the Rhineland), called 'Heaven and Earth'. Some of the vocabulary items will already be known to you. Others, like **Pfeffer, Salz, Zucker** should be instantly recognisable because of their similarity to English. Others again can be guessed from the context. Read through both the ingredients and the method of preparation, then try to answer the questions. Vocabulary assistance is offered opposite, in case you get stuck.

Die Zubereitung:

Kartoffeln schälen und in Würfel schneiden. Äpfel schälen, in Viertel schneiden. Kartoffeln und Äpfel in etwa ½ Liter Wasser mit Salz und Zucker zum Kochen bringen und bei schwacher Hitze so lange kochen lassen, bis sie weich sind. Dann mit Salz, Zucker und Essig abschmecken. Den Speck und die Zwiebeln in Würfel schneiden, braten und beides über die Kartoffeln und Äpfel geben.

Kochzeit: Etwa 45 Minuten.

der Speck *bacon*	**kochen** *to cook, boil*
der Pfeffer *pepper*	**schwach** *weak*
das Salz *salt*	**die Hitze** *heat*
der Zucker *sugar*	**lassen** *to let*
der Essig *vinegar*	**weich** *soft*
schälen *to peel*	**abschmecken** *season*
der Würfel (-) *cube*	**braten** *to fry*
schneiden *to cut*	

Answer the following questions in English:

1 Into what sized pieces do the potatoes and apples have to be cut after they have been peeled?
2 In how much water are they then brought to the boil and what must be added to the water?
3 How long are they to be boiled and at what heat?
4 What is done to the bacon and onions before these are poured over the potatoes and apples?

8 Wie kommen wir dorthin?

In this unit you will learn further ways of asking for and giving directions. Particular attention is paid to the various prepositions used when talking about location and direction.

Dialog

Jörg Arndt and his friend have just arrived in Munich for a week's holiday. They have gone to the Tourist Information Office to pick up a map of the city and some leaflets. Andrea Hahn answers their questions and tells them how to get to **der Englische Garten**.

Jörg Arndt	Entschuldigen Sie, bitte. Mein Freund und ich möchten uns erkundigen, was man hier in München alles unternehmen kann. Hätten Sie vielleicht einen Stadtplan und ein paar Informationsblätter?
Andrea Hahn	Selbstverständlich. Bitte schön. (*Sie gibt ihnen den Stadtplan und die Informationsblätter.*) Wie lange wollen Sie denn in München bleiben?
Jörg Arndt	Wir haben acht Tage Urlaub. Wir wollen nicht nur die Sehenswürdigkeiten besichtigen, sondern uns auch in die Sonne legen, spazierengehen, vielleicht ein bißchen Sport treiben . . .
Andrea Hahn	Und wo wohnen Sie zur Zeit?
Jörg Arndt	Im Hotel Meier in der Schützenstraße.
Andrea Hahn	Ach ja. Das liegt in der Fußgängerzone, nicht weit vom Hauptbahnhof, nicht wahr? Dann rate ich Ihnen, mal in den Englischen Garten zu gehen. Bei diesem Wetter können Sie schöne Spaziergänge durch den Park machen, und sich auf der Liegewiese in die Sonne legen.

Jörg Arndt	Aber wie kommen wir dorthin? Wir kennen uns in dieser Stadt nicht aus.
Andrea Hahn	Ich zeige es Ihnen auf dem Stadtplan. Von hier aus gehen Sie bis zum Marienplatz. Links vom Rathaus ist die Theatinerstraße. Gehen Sie immer geradeaus, die Theatinerstraße entlang, bis zur Ludwigstraße. Auf der rechten Seite sehen Sie den Hofgarten. Gehen Sie durch den Hofgarten bis zur Staatsgalerie. Dort fängt der Englische Garten an.
Jörg Arndt	So, vielen Dank. Wir werden ihn schon finden. Und auf dem Stadtplan sind auch die wichtigsten Sehenswürdigkeiten aufgeführt. Wir müssen unbedingt zum Olympischen Dorf hinausfahren. Und das Schloß Nymphenburg wollen wir auch besichtigen.
Andrea Hahn	Also, ich wünsche Ihnen viel Vergnügen hier in unserer Stadt.

der Freund (-e) *friend*
Wir möchten uns erkundigen, . . . *We should like to enquire . . .*
unternehmen (*insep.*) *to undertake, do*
Hätten Sie vielleicht . . . ? *Would you perhaps have . . . ?*
ein paar Informationsblätter *a few leaflets*
bleiben *to stay*
nicht nur . . . sondern auch . . . *not only . . but also . . .*
sich in die Sonne legen *to lie in the sun*
Sport treiben *to do sport*
der Hauptbahnhof (¨e) *main train station*
raten (+*dat.*) *to advise*
bei diesem Wetter *in this weather*
einen Spaziergang machen *to go for a walk*
die Liegewiese *lawn* (*for sunbathing*) (lit. *meadow for lying on*)
Wir kennen uns hier nicht aus *We don't know our way around here*
auf der rechten Seite *on the right-hand side*
der Hofgarten *Court Garden*
Wir werden ihn schon finden *We shall find it all right*
wichtig *important*
aufgeführt *listed*
das Olympische Dorf *Olympic Village*
Ich wünsche Ihnen viel Vergnügen *I hope you enjoy yourself* (lit. *I wish you much enjoyment*)

Fragen zum Dialog

1 Richtig (R) oder Falsch (F)?

1 Jörg und sein Freund möchten einen Stadtplan und ein paar Informationsblätter haben.
2 Andrea kann ihnen leider keinen Stadtplan und keine Informationsblätter geben.
3 Jörg und sein Freund haben zwei Wochen Urlaub.
4 Sie wohnen zur Zeit im Hotel Meier in der Schützenstraße.
5 Das Hotel liegt nicht weit vom Bahnhof.
6 Andrea rät ihnen, in den Englischen Garten zu gehen.
7 Sie kennen sich in München sehr gut aus.
8 Das Rathaus liegt am Marienplatz.
9 Auf dem Stadtplan finden Jörg und sein Freund auch die wichtigsten Sehenswürdigkeiten aufgeführt.
10 Sie wünschen Andrea viel Vergnügen.

2 Welche Antwort paßt?

1 Hätten Sie vielleicht einen Stadtplan?
(*a*) Bitte schön. Zwei Schoppen Mosel.
(*b*) Selbstverständlich. Bitte schön.
(*c*) Tut mir leid. Heute nachmittag kann ich nicht.

2 Wie lange wollen Sie hier bleiben?
(*a*) Wir wollen uns in die Sonne legen.
(*b*) Wir nehmen hier Platz.
(*c*) Acht Tage.

3 Wo wohnen Sie zur Zeit?
(*a*) Im Hotel Meier in der Schützenstraße.
(*b*) Auf dem Stadtplan.
(*c*) In der Staatsgalerie.

4 Wie kommen wir dorthin?
(*a*) Das liegt in der Fußgängerzone.
(*b*) Dort fängt der Englische Garten an.
(*c*) Ich zeige es Ihnen auf dem Stadtplan.

5 Was kann man im Englischen Garten unternehmen?
(*a*) Auf dem Stadtplan sind auch die wichtigsten Sehenswürdigkeiten aufgeführt.

(*b*) Bei diesem Wetter kann man spazierengehen und sich in die Sonne legen.
(*c*) Am besten geht man hier rechts.

Was Sie wissen sollten

Varieties of German

The German spoken in Munich is, in the main, what is known as **Stadtsprache** (*the language of the city*). This variety is much closer to standard German in syntax and vocabulary than are the true Bavarian dialects, but gains its regional flavour principally from its pronunciation and intonation—which sometimes present the foreigner with difficulties in understanding. Such difficulties are, however, usually overcome fairly quickly, as the ear attunes to the **Münchener Stadtsprache**.

Understanding Bavarian dialects as they are spoken by country-dwellers is quite another matter! Germans themselves—unless they come from the South—have considerable difficulties with these varieties. Young people who speak dialect at home and with friends are encouraged to master **Hochdeutsch** (*High German*) as well.

Whilst the Bavarian dialects are the most extreme examples of non-standard varieties of German, other non-standard varieties exist all over the German-speaking area and most cities have their particular **Stadtsprache**.

German parks

Der Englische Garten in Munich is so-called because of its informal layout which is considered to be particularly English. Whilst it used to be forbidden to walk on, let alone lie on the grass in most German parks, attitudes have in recent years changed and many parks now provide **eine Liegewiese**, specifically for sunbathing. Some—like **der Englische Garten**—set aside an area for nudist sunbathing. Nudism or **Freikörperkultur** has long been much more widely practised in Germany than in the English-speaking countries.

It is nevertheless advisable to look out for notices saying: **Rasen nicht betreten** (*Do not walk on the grass*), especially in parks in small towns, where the older attitudes sometimes still prevail.

Wichtige Redewendungen

How to

1 Ask for information by means of an indirect question

Wir möchten uns erkundigen, Ich möchte mich erkundigen,	was man in München unternehmen kann. wo man hier billig essen kann. wie man zum Rathaus kommt. wie lange man hier parken darf.

2 Offer advice.

Ich rate Ihnen, Ich rate dir,	in den Englischen Garten zu gehen. zum Olympischen Dorf hinauszufahren. das Schloß Nymphenburg zu besichtigen. in der Tiefgarage zu parken.

3 Ask the way (Continued from **Lektion 6***).*

Wie	komme ich kommen wir	(am besten)	zur Fußgängerzone? zum Bahnhof? zum Olympischen Dorf? zur Autobahn?

4 Give directions (Continued from **Lektion 6***).*

Gehen Sie	diese Straße entlang hier geradeaus durch den Hofgarten	bis zur Ludwigstraße. bis zum Marienplatz. bis zur Staatsgalerie.

Links Rechts	vom Dom vom Rathaus von der Galerie vom Bahnhof	sehen Sie finden Sie	das Schloß die Fußgängerzone. den Park die Hauptstraße. den Marktplatz.
Auf der rechten Seite Auf der linken Seite			

5 *Ask very politely and rather tentatively for something.*

Hätten Sie vielleicht	einen Stadtplan? ein paar Informationsblätter? ein Zimmer frei?

Das Wetter (*The weather*)

der Sonnenschein *sunshine*	**der Schnee** *snow*
der Regen *rain*	**der Nebel** *fog*
die Wolke (-n) *cloud*	**das Glatteis** *black ice*
die Hitze *heat*	**die Kälte** *cold*
der Frost *frost*	

Grammatik

1 Dative case (*continued*)

In **Lektion 7** examples of personal pronouns in the dative case were introduced.

Kann ich **Ihnen** etwas bringen? Wie geht es **dir**? Kommst du mit **mir** essen? *etc.*

This description of the dative case now needs to be extended to ***nouns***.

Look at the following sentences:

An einem Tisch sitzen (*sit*) ein Mann, eine Frau und ein Mädchen. Nebenan sitzen drei Amerikaner.

	Indirect object *Dative case*		*Direct object* *Accusative case*
1	De**m** Mann (*to the man*)	bringt der Kellner	ein Glas Bier.
2	De**r** Frau (*to the woman*)	bringt er	eine Tasse Kaffee.
3	De**m** Mädchen (*to the girl*)	bringt er	ein Glas Apfelsaft.
4	De**n** Amerikaner**n** (*to the Americans*)	bringt er	eine Flasche Wein.

Note the endings (in bold print) which are characteristic of the dative case: i.e. **m** for masculine and neuter nouns in the singular (see examples 1 and 3), **r** for feminine nouns in the singular (example 2) and **n** for nouns of all three genders in the plural (example 4). The nouns themselves generally remain unchanged in the singular (although an extra **e** is sometimes added to masculine and neuter nouns of one syllable), but in the plural an **n** is added to the noun if it is possible to do so (as in example 4). Nouns such as **Frau** with the plural **Frauen** clearly cannot add a further **n**.

These endings are characteristic of the dative not only for the definite article as illustrated in the examples above, but also for the indefinite article **ein**, for **kein**, for the possessive adjectives such as **mein** (*my*), **dein** (*your*), **sein** (*his, its*), **unser** (*our*), etc. and for such words as **dies-** (*this, these*); **jen-** (*that, those*) and **jed-** (*each, every*).

Here are some examples to make this point quite clear. Bear in mind that the dative case is required not only for the indirect object, but also after certain verbs (such as **gefallen** and **helfen**) and after certain prepositions (such as **bei** and **mit**):

Masculine nouns **m**
Was sagt Helga **unserem Kellner**?
Da sitzt (*sits*) Birgit **mit einem Amerikaner**!
Feminine nouns **r**
Können Sie **meiner Kusine** ein Hotel empfehlen?
Was schenkst du **deiner Mutter** zum Geburtstag?
Neuter nouns **m**
Können Sie **diesem Fraülein** vielleicht helfen?
Siehst du Klaus da drüben **mit einem Mädchen**?
Plural nouns **n**
Welches Restaurant empfehlen Sie **diesen Engländern**?
Australier? Aber ich wohne doch **bei keinen Australiern**!
Da kommt Frank **mit seinen Freunden**.

2 Prepositions

2.1 Prepositions requiring the dative

The dative case is used after the following prepositions:

aus	*out (of), from*	Andrea kommt gerade (*just*) **aus dem Rathaus**. Bernd kommt **aus der Schweiz**.
bei	*with, at, in*	Du kannst **bei meiner Mutter** wohnen. Darf ich **bei Ihnen** kassieren? **Bei diesem Wetter** gehe ich gern spazieren.
mit	*with*	Kommst du **mit mir** einkaufen? Möchten Sie **mit meinem Freund** den Dom besichtigen?
nach	*after, according to*	**Nach den Nachrichten** bringen wir ein Konzert.

	Die deutsche Ökonomie ist **nach den Prinzipien** der sozialen Marktwirtschaft organisiert.
seit *since*	**Seit dem 2. April 1979** gibt es in Berlin das ICC.
	Heute geht's mir **seit der Konferenz** nicht so gut.
von *from, of, by*	Das sind Pflaumen **von unserem Garten**.
	Von meiner Wohnung bis hierher sind es 3 Km.
zu *to, at, for*	Kommen Sie morgen **zu unserer Wohnung**!
	Ich fahre jetzt **zu meiner Mutter**.

2.2 Contracted forms in the dative

The following contracted forms are commonly found:

bei dem	→	**beim**	**zu dem**	→	**zum**
von dem	→	**vom**	**zu der**	→	**zur**

Dieter ist gerade **beim Arzt**.
Links **vom Rathaus** ist die Theatinerstraße.
Wie kommt man **zum Bahnhof**?
Zum Frühstück trinke ich immer Kaffee.
Gehen Sie geradeaus bis **zur Staatsgalerie**.

2.3 Prepositions requiring the accusative

The accusative case is used after the following prepositions:

durch *through*	Gehen wir **durch die Fußgängerzone**?
	Gehen Sie **durch den Hofgarten**.
für *for*	**Für mich** ein Glas Bier, bitte.
	Und **für meine Freunde** eine Flasche Moselwein.
entlang *along* (*after the noun*)	Gehen wir geradeaus **die Hauptstraße entlang**?
	Nein, wir gehen lieber **den Bohlweg entlang**.
gegen *against, about*	Ich bin eigentlich **gegen die freie Marktwirtschaft**.
	Bist du für oder **gegen meinen Plan**?
ohne *without*	Ursula fährt **ohne ihren Freund** nach London.
	Was? Du gehst **ohne mich** ins Kino?!
um *around*	Der Aufzug ist gleich **um die Ecke**.

2.4 Prepositions requiring either the accusative or the dative

With the following prepositions the accusative case is used when ***direction*** is being indicated, answering the question **wohin**? (*where to?*). The dative case is used when ***position*** or ***location*** is being indicated, answering the question **wo**? (*where, in what location?*):

in	**an**	**auf**	**hinter**	**neben**	**über**	**unter**	**vor**	**zwischen**
in(to)	*at*	*on(to)*	*behind*	*next to*	*over*	*under*	*in front of*	*between*

	Accusative		***Dative***
	(Wohin gehen wir?)		(Wo sitzen wir?)
Wir gehen	**ins** Kino.	Wir sitzen	**im** Kino.
	an den Tisch.		**am** Tisch.
	auf den Marktplatz.		**auf dem** Marktplatz.
	hinter das Hotel.		**hinter dem** Hotel.
	unter die Brücke.		**unter der** Brücke.

Note the commonly found contracted forms:

in das	→	**ins**	**in dem**	→	**im**
an das	→	**ans**	**an dem**	→	**am**

The English versions of the prepositions listed above are only approximate equivalents. You will need to learn which prepositions are most commonly used together with which nouns. For instance **auf** is frequently used with nouns like **Bank** and **Bahnhof**:

Deine Reiseschecks kannst du **auf der Bank** wechseln. *You can change your travellers' cheques at the bank.*

Fahrkarten kann man **auf dem Bahnhof** lösen. *Tickets can be bought* (lit. *one can buy*) *at the station.*

There is a danger that, at this point, you will despair of ever producing the correct form of the accusative or the dative with the appropriate preposition. You should, however, find that you have already learned certain phrases containing the accusative or the dative without really thinking about it. Look through the **Dialoge** from earlier units and spot such phrases. A good example from **Lektion 6** is Sylvia Rave's second utterance:

Ich schlage vor, wir gehen entweder **ins Restaurant** (*acc. neut. sing.*) »**Zur Sonne**« (*dat. fem. sing.*) oder **in den Ratskeller** (*acc. masc. sing.*). Beide sind ja gleich hier **in der Nähe** (*dat. fem. sing.*).

In fact the **Dialoge** of **Lektionen 6** and **8** are full of such examples and you might find it useful to go through them, picking out the prepositional phrases and labelling them as above. With practice and regular exposure to German, you will find you get a 'feel' for what is right.

3 Indirect questions

When a direct question such as **Wo ist der Marktplatz?**
is prefaced by a phrase such as **Können Sie mir bitte sagen,**
or **Ich möchte mich erkundigen,**
an ***indirect question*** is produced and, in German, the verb of the original question is sent to the end:

Können Sie mir bitte sagen, **wo** der Markplatz **ist**?
Ich möchte mich erkundigen, **wann** der Film **anfängt**.

Note that the two clauses are separated by a comma.

Whilst the indirect question, as illustrated above, is merely a more polite way of asking for information than by means of a direct question, it can also be used in other ways, as is shown in the following short dialogue:

Werner:	Was gibt es heute zu essen?
Dagmar:	Ich weiß nicht, **was** es heute zu essen **gibt**. Frag mal den Kellner, **was** er uns heute **empfiehlt**.
Werner:	Sag mir dann, **wo** der Kellner **ist**!

4 Infinitive clauses

When offering advice or making suggestions, it is often appropriate, instead of issuing blunt commands, to make use of introductory phrases as illustrated in the examples below. Such phrases are normally followed by what is known as an ***infinitive clause*** in which the infinitive, preceded by **zu** goes to the end:

Ich rate Ihnen, mal in den Englischen Garten **zu gehen**.
Ich empfehle Ihnen, den Dom **zu besichtigen**.
Ich schlage vor, heute nachmittag ins Kino **zu gehen**.

In the case of separable verbs, the **zu** comes between the separable prefix and the verb and all three elements join together:

Klaus rät uns, morgen gegen 6 Uhr auf**zu**stehen.

5 Reflexive verbs

Verbs that are normally listed together with the pronoun **sich** (*oneself*) are referred to as ***reflexive verbs***. A useful reflexive verb which occurred in the **Dialog** to **Lektion 7** is **sich setzen** (*to sit (oneself) down*).

In this unit you have met **sich erkundigen, sich auskennen** and **sich in die Sonne legen**. Note that the ***reflexive pronoun***—which in the case of the verbs mentioned is the accusative pronoun—changes according to the subject of the verb:

Ich möchte **mich** erkundigen, wann der Film anfängt.
Maria, kennst du **dich** in München aus?
Franz möchte **sich** in die Sonne legen.
Maria möchte **sich** zu dir setzen.
Wir setzen **uns** an diesen Tisch.
Möchten Sie **sich** zu uns setzen?
Franz und Maria wollen **sich** in die Sonne legen.

Other common reflexive verbs include: **sich anziehen** (*to get dressed*), **sich ausruhen** (*to have a rest*), **sich fühlen** (*to feel*):

Zieh **dich** schnell an!	*Get dressed quickly!*
Ich möchte **mich** jetzt ausruhen.	*I should like to have a rest now.*
Wie fühlen Sie **sich**?	*How are you feeling?*

Übungen

ÜBUNG 8.1 Sagen Sie es anders.

Make the following requests and suggestions more tentative as illustrated in the examples:

Examples: Haben Sie einen Stadtplan?
Hätten Sie vielleicht einen Stadtplan?
Kommst du mit?
Möchtest du vielleicht mitkommen?

1 Haben Sie ein Zimmer frei?
2 Spielst du heute nachmittag mit mir Tennis?
3 Fahren Sie morgen mit uns zum Olympischen Dorf hinaus?
4 Hast du Zeit, mit uns spazierenzugehen?
5 Trinkst du mit uns eine Flasche Wein?
6 Haben Sie einen Tisch für vier Personen?

ÜBUNG 8.2 Was paßt zusammen?

(A) Sie möchten . . .	**Wohin gehen Sie dann?**
1 . . . essen gehen.	(*a*) Auf die Liegewiese.

2	... Geld wechseln.	(*b*) In die Fußgängerzone.
3	... sich in die Sonne legen.	(*c*) In die Discothek.
4	... einen Film sehen	(*d*) Auf den Bahnhof.
5	... einkaufen gehen.	(*e*) Ins Kino.
6	... spazierengehen.	(*f*) Auf die Bank. (*oder* Zur Bank.)
7	... Fahrkarten lösen.	(*g*) In den Park.
8	... tanzen gehen.	(*h*) Ins Restaurant.

(B) Modify the answers (*a*)–(*h*) above to provide suitable answers to the following questions:

Wo kann man ...

... einen Film sehen?	***Im Kino.***
... Fahrkarten lösen?	***Auf dem Bahnhof.***

1 ... einkaufen?
2 ... Reiseschecks wechseln?
3 ... essen?
4 ... tanzen?
5 ... in der Sonne liegen?
6 ... einen Spaziergang machen?

ÜBUNG 8.3 Sagen Sie es anders.

Beispiele: Der Kellner empfiehlt uns, »Nehmen Sie die Forelle«.
Der Kellner empfiehlt uns, die Forelle zu nehmen.

Helga schlägt vor, »Gehen wir heute nachmittag ins Kino«.
Helga schlägt vor, heute nachmittag ins Kino zu gehen.

1 Ich empfehle allen Touristen, »Besichtigen Sie den Dom«.
2 Der Arzt rät meiner Frau, »Fahren Sie in Urlaub«.
3 Klaus schlägt vor, »Essen wir heute abend italienisch«.
4 Mein Freund Peter rät mir, »Fahr mal nach Berlin«.
5 Der Empfangsherr empfiehlt der Dame, »Nehmen Sie Zimmer 21«.
6 Hans rät den Engländern, »Gehen Sie in diesem See nicht schwimmen«.

ÜBUNG 8.4 **Ich weiß überhaupt nichts.** ***I know nothing at all.***

Answer each of the following questions by saying that you don't know the required information:

Beispiele: Wo sind Renate und Joachim?
Ich weiß nicht, wo sie sind.
Welchen Film wollen sie sehen?
Ich weiß nicht, welchen Film sie sehen wollen.

1 Wann gehen Renate und Joachim ins Kino?
2 Wie lange dauert der Film?
3 Was machen Renate und Joachim nach dem Film?
4 Wohin gehen sie nachher?
5 Wann fahren sie nach Hause?
6 Wo wohnen sie zur Zeit?

ÜBUNG 8.5 **Ergänzen Sie.**

Am Sonnabend fahre ich . . . (1) . . . Freundin Anna nach Köln. Wir fahren gleich . . . (2) . . . Frühstück los und sind dann gegen 9 Uhr 30 . . . (3) . . . Stadtzentrum. Wir wollen zuerst . . . (4) . . . Wallraf-Richartz-Museum gehen. Das Museum liegt . . . (5) . . . Dom und der Fußgängerzone. Vom Museum . . . (6) . . . Fußgängerzone sind es nur ein paar Meter . . . (7) . . . Schildergasse (nicht weit vom Museum) wohnt eine Freundin von Anna . . . (8) . . . wollen wir dann Kaffee trinken und uns ausruhen. Vielleicht fahren wir auch nachher . . (9) . . . Deutzer Brücke . . . (10) . . . Rheinpark.

(*a*) Bei ihr	(*b*) zwischen dem	(*c*) bis zur
(*d*) mit meiner	(*e*) im	(*f*) über die
(*g*) nach dem	(*h*) bis zum	(*i*) In der
(*j*) ins		

ÜBUNG 8.6 **Antworten Sie.**

Answer the questions making use of **two** of the following cues for each answer:

zwischen . . . , links von . . . , rechts von . . . , hinter . . . , vor . . .

die Bibliothek (-en) *library*	**die Toilette (-n)** *toilet*
die Kirche (-n) *church*	**die Wurstbude (-n)** *sausage stand*
der Brunnen(-) *well, fountain*	
der Parkplatz (¨e) *parking lot*	**der Polizeiwagen (-)** *police car*

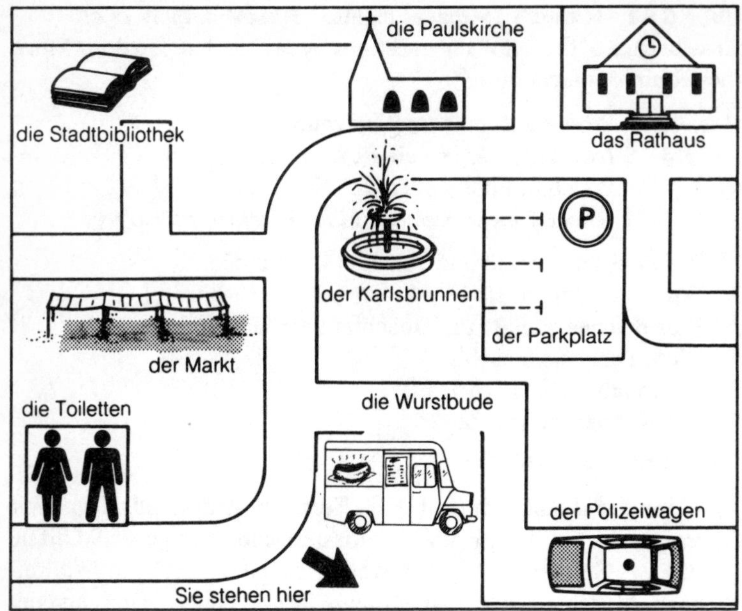

Beispiele: Wo steht die Paulskirche?
Zwischen der Stadtbibliothek und dem Rathaus und hinter dem Karlsbrunnen.

Wo findet man den Parkplatz?
Rechts vom Karlsbrunnen und vor dem Rathaus.

1 Wo steht die Stadtbibliothek?
2 Wo findet man den Markt?
3 Wo steht das Rathaus?
4 Wo findet man den Karlsbrunnen?
5 Wo steht die Wurstbude?
6 Wo findet man die Toiletten?
7 Wo steht der Polizeiwagen?
8 Und wo stehen Sie? (*Using one cue only*)

Verstehen Sie?

1 Konversation

Jörg Arndt and his friend, Bodo Klar, ask a passer-by (**Passant**) their way to the **Alte Pinakothek**, one of Munich's most important museums.

Jörg Arndt	Entschuldigen Sie bitte. Wie kommen wir am besten zur Alten Pinakothek?
Passant	Möchten Sie zu Fuß gehen, oder mit dem Auto fahren?
Jörg Arndt	Zu Fuß gehen. Wir haben keinen Wagen da.
Passant	Gut. Wir sind hier am Odeonsplatz. Drüben links sehen sie eine Straße. Das ist die Brienner Straße. Gehen Sie geradeaus die Brienner Straße entlang bis zum Karolinenplatz.
Jörg Arndt	Und wie weit ist es bis zum Karolinenplatz?
Passant	Vielleicht 500 Meter. Am Karolinenplatz gehen Sie dann rechts in die Barer Straße. Nach ungefähr 300 Metern kommen Sie zur Gabelsbergerstraße. Gehen Sie über die Gabelsbergerstraße rüber, und da auf der linken Seite sehen Sie dann gleich die Alte Pinakothek.
Jörg Arndt	Danke. Wissen Sie zufällig, ob die Alte Pinakothek heute nachmittag aufhat?
Passant	Da kann ich Ihnen leider nicht helfen. Vielleicht sollten Sie telefonieren, bevor Sie hingehen.
Jörg Arndt	Ach nein. Wenn das Museum zuhat, werden wir einfach durch die Gegend weiterspazieren.
Passant	Na gut. Ich wünsche Ihnen viel Spaß.
Jörg Arndt	Danke schön. Auf Wiedersehen!
Passant	Auf Wiedersehen!

Alte Pinakothek, Barerstr. 27,
Tel.: 089/23804-215. tgl. a. Mo. 9–16.30 Uhr.
Di. + Do. 12–16.30 Uhr
Ständige Ausstellung: Europäische
Malerei des 14.–18. Jahrhunderts

Neue Pinakothek, Barerstr. 29,
Tel.: 089/23805-1945. tgl. a. Mo. 9–16.30 Uhr,
Di. + Do. 12–16.30 Uhr
Ständige Ausstellung: Europäische
Malerei und Skulptur des 19. Jahrhunderts
Bis 14.04.1985: Oskar Koller

Richtig (R) oder Falsch (F)?

1 Jörg und Bodo wollen zur Alten Pinakothek.
2 Sie wollen mit dem Wagen dorthin fahren.
3 Sie stehen im Moment am Odeonsplatz.
4 Rechts vom Odeonsplatz ist die Brienner Straße.
5 Vom Odeonsplatz bis zum Karolinenplatz sind es nur 100 Meter.
6 Am Karolinenplatz geht man rechts in die Barer Straße und dann über die Gabelsbergerstraße bis zur Alten Pinakothek.
7 Die Alte Pinakothek steht auf der rechten Seite.
8 Der Passant rät Jörg und Bodo, bei der Alten Pinakothek zu telefonieren, bevor sie hingehen.
9 Wenn das Museum zuhat, gehen Jörg und Bodo einfach wieder ins Hotel.
10 Der Passant wünscht ihnen viel Spaß.

2 Lesetext

Düsseldorf—Altstadt für alle

Zwischen zwei Rheinbrücken und flankiert vom Hofgarten schlägt das Herz der Stadt Düsseldorf. Rund um die Bolker-, Kurze-, Flinger- und Mühlenstraße ist das Stadtbild von Kneipen, Discotheken, alten Brauhäusern und Boutiquen geprägt. In Kontrast dazu findet man im Süden hinter dem Karlsplatz eine Mischung aus alten Wohnhäusern, neuen Kulturinstituten, Antiquitätengeschäften und Galerien. Hier sind auch ein paar Restaurants und »Destillen« oder Bars. Das alles ist die Düsseldorfer Altstadt. Ein Quadratkilometer mit rund 200 Gaststätten aller Art. Man hört Rock und Jazz *live*. Man trinkt das hausgebraute Altbier.

In der Altstadt sind die Bars und die Cafés voll, die Stühle fast immer besetzt. Im Sommer sitzt man gern draußen. Hier kann man Haxe, Sauerbraten, Bratwurst essen, aber man kann auch thailändisch, französisch, italienisch, ägyptisch, japanisch oder wienerisch speisen. Für 10 Mark wird man satt und für 50 Mark kann man schon sehr gut essen.

In den engen Gassen der Altstadt trägt man Jeans oder Seide total—hier ist alles tolerant. Hier und da findet man eine stille Oase—z.B. den Garten auf der einstigen Zitadelle hinter dem Stadtmuseum.

die Kneipe (-n) *pub*	**voll** *full*
das Brauhaus (¨er) *brewery*	**der Stuhl (¨e)** *chair*
die Mischung (-en) *mixture*	**besetzt** *occupied*
die Gaststätte (-n) *eating place*	**draußen** *outside*
die Art (-en) *kind*	**eng** *narrow*

Answer the following questions in English:

1 Where is the heart of the city of Düsseldorf?
2 What dominates the scene in the area around the four streets mentioned here?
3 Where does one find a marked contrast to this part of the old city?
4 What does the contrast consist of?
5 How large is the area covered by the old city?
6 What does the figure of 200 represent?
7 Why is it often difficult to get a seat in the old city bars and cafes?
8 What do people like to do here in summer?
9 What is it possible to do for 10 marks? And for 50 marks?
10 What are the streets like in the old city?
11 Why is it acceptable in the old city to be dressed in jeans or in silk from top to toe?
12 Why is the garden on the former citadel behind the city museum mentioned here?

9 Was hast du gestern gemacht?

In this unit you will start learning how to talk about past events.

Dialog

Else Frick meets Olaf Amm on the Münsterplatz in Freiburg and asks him about the trip he made yesterday to visit his brother Michael's family in Strasbourg. This leads to talk about how Michael came to marry Hélène and live in France.

Else Frick Olaf! Wo warst du gestern? Ich habe mehrmals versucht, bei dir anzurufen, aber es hat sich niemand gemeldet.

Olaf Amm Nein. Ich war nicht zu Hause. Ich habe meinen Bruder Michael und seine Frau Hélène in Straßburg besucht. Michael hat gestern Geburtstag gehabt.

Else Frick Ach so! Erzähl mir doch davon! Was hast du alles gemacht?

Olaf Amm Also, die Fahrt mit dem Auto von Freiburg nach Straßburg hat ungefähr eine Stunde gedauert. In der Stadtmitte habe ich in einem Parkhaus geparkt und habe dann den Dom besichtigt. Anschließend habe ich Geld gewechselt und habe Geschenke für meine Nichte und meinen Neffen gekauft.

Else Frick Und was hast du ihnen geschenkt?

Olaf Amm Ach, nur ein paar Kleinigkeiten. Aber sie haben sich richtig gefreut. Am Nachmittag habe ich dann stundenlang mit ihnen Karten gespielt. Ich habe mit ihnen Französisch geredet und dadurch meine Französischkenntnisse verbessert!

Else Frick Du hast mal in Frankreich gearbeitet, nicht wahr?

Olaf Amm Ja. Vor zwei Jahren habe ich in den Sommerferien bei einer Familie in Paris gewohnt und in einem Büro gearbeitet. Da habe ich auch viel gelernt.

Else Frick Das glaube ich dir. Seit wann wohnt dein Bruder Michael in Frankreich?

Olaf Amm Seit fast zehn Jahren. Hélène hat er hier in Freiburg kennengelernt, als sie bei einer Reisegesellschaft gearbeitet hat. Nach zwei Jahren haben sie geheiratet und sich beide Arbeit in Straßburg gesucht.

Else Frick Und haben sie auch Glück gehabt?

Olaf Amm Ja. Die Firma von meinem Bruder hat alles organisiert. Michael hat man einfach in ihre Straßburger Zweigstelle versetzt, und Hélène hat man dort in der Personalabteilung angestellt.

Wo warst du? *Where were you?*
Ich habe mehrmals versucht, bei dir anzurufen *I tried several times to call you (your home)*
Es hat sich niemand gemeldet *No-one answered*
Erzähl mir davon! *Tell me about it!*
die Stadtmitte *city centre*
anschließend *following that, next*
das Geschenk (-e) *present*
die Nichte (-n) *niece*
der Neffe (-n) (weak noun) *nephew*
Sie haben sich richtig gefreut *They were really pleased*
stundenlang *for hours on end*
reden *to talk, speak*
dadurch *in this way, thus*
Ich habe meine Französischkenntnisse verbessert *I improved my knowledge of French*
vor zwei Jahren *two years ago*
die Sommerferien (plur.) *the summer holidays*
das Büro (-s) *office*
Das glaube ich dir *I can believe that (of you)*
als *when*
heiraten *to marry*
Arbeit suchen *to look for work*
Glück haben *to be lucky*
einfach *simply*
versetzen *to transfer*
die Zweigstelle (-n) *branch*
die Personalabteilung *personnel department*
anstellen to appoint

Fragen zum Dialog

1 Richtig (R) oder Falsch (F)?

1. Else hat gestern mehrmals versucht, bei Olaf anzurufen.
2. Es hat sich aber nur seine Mutter gemeldet.
3. Olaf war gestern nicht zu Hause.
4. Die Fahrt von Freiburg nach Straßburg hat fast zwei Stunden gedauert.

5 Er hat in der Stadtmitte in einem Parkhaus geparkt.
6 Dann hat er das Schloß besichtigt.
7 Seiner Nichte und seinem Neffen hat er ein paar Kleinigkeiten geschenkt.
8 Er hat am Abend stundenlang mit ihnen Karten gespielt.
9 Er hat mit ihnen nur Deutsch geredet.
10 Olaf hat vor zwei Jahren in den Sommerferien in Paris gearbeitet.
11 Sein Bruder Michael hat Hélène in Freiburg kennengelernt.
12 Hélène hat dort in der Personalabteilung gearbeitet.

2 Welche Antwort paßt?

1 Wo warst du gestern?
(*a*) Ich war in der Stadtmitte.
(*b*) Ich habe meinen Bruder und seine Frau in Straßburg besucht.
(*c*) Ich habe mehrmals versucht, bei dir anzurufen.

2 Was hast du deiner Nichte und deinem Neffen geschenkt?
(*a*) Ich habe mit ihnen Französisch geredet.
(*b*) Ich habe stundenlang mit ihnen Karten gespielt.
(*c*) Ach, nur ein paar Kleinigkeiten.

3 Hast du mal in Frankreich gearbeitet?
(*a*) Ja, sie hat in Straßburg in der Personalabteilung gearbeitet.
(*b*) Ja, vor zwei Jahren habe ich in Paris in einem Büro gearbeitet.
(*c*) Ja, in Frankreich habe ich nur Französisch geredet.

4 In Frankreich habe ich meine Französischkenntnisse verbessert.
(*a*) Das glaube ich dir.
(*b*) Ach so! Seit wann wohnt dein Bruder in Frankreich?
(*c*) Ach so! Erzähl mir doch davon!

5 Seit wann wohnt dein Bruder in Straßburg?
(*a*) Vor zwei Jahren.
(*b*) Seit fast zehn Jahren.
(*c*) Nach zwei Jahren.

Was Sie wissen sollten

Visiting in Germany

It is the 'done thing' to take small presents when visiting a German family. For this reason, many shops sell **Mitbringsel** (*things to take with you*) specifically for this purpose.

It is also very common to take flowers (rather than a bottle of wine) when you have been invited to somebody's house for a meal. Flower shops are generally of a high standard and—for people who need to make a last minute purchase—flowers can usually be bought from automatic vending machines. You should remove the wrapping paper before handing the flowers over to your host or hostess. Red roses have romantic connotations.

Celebrations

Germans generally make a considerable effort when it comes to marking occasions—even those occasions, such as adults' birthdays, which tend to pass almost unnoticed in certain countries. Hence the German verb **feiern** is more frequently used than its English counterpart *to celebrate*. Celebrating will almost always involve a special meal, served at a specially decorated table.

Changing money

In Germany banks are normally open from 8.30 am till 12.30 pm and 2.00 till 3.45 pm, Mondays to Fridays. Some have a later closing time, usually one day a week. Banks and **Sparkassen** (*savings banks*) offer the most favourable exchange rates, although **Wechselstuben** (*exchange offices*) at airports and railway stations are open for much longer periods.

Credit cards and Eurocheques can often be used if you are short of local currency.

Wichtige Redewendungen

How to

1 Ask for and give information about past whereabouts of people or things.

Wo warst du gestern?	Ich war in Frankreich.
Wo war dein Auto?	Es war im Parkhaus.

2 *Make statements about past events.*

		meinen Bruder	besucht.
	gestern	Geburtstag	gehabt.
	in einem Parkhaus		geparkt.
Ich habe	dann	den Dom	besichtigt.
	anschließend	Geld	gewechselt.
		Geschenke	gekauft.
	stundenlang	Karten	gespielt.

3 *Ask questions about past events.*

Was hast du	gestern	alles	gemacht?
		deinem Neffen	geschenkt?
Wo hast du	heute nachmittag	dein Auto	geparkt?
	in Paris		gewohnt?
	in Frankreich		gearbeitet?
Hast du	in Paris	Französisch	gelernt?
	heute	Glück	gehabt?

4 *Ask and give information about how long a state of affairs has been going on.*

	wohnt dein Bruder	in Straß-
Seit wann	kennst du Hélène?	burg?
	lernen Sie Deutsch?	

Er wohnt	seit fast 10 Jahren in Frankreich.
Ich kenne sie	seit ungefähr 12 Jahren.
Ich lerne Deutsch	seit drei Monaten.

Freunde und Verwandte (*Friends and relatives*)

der Vater (¨) *father*	**der Onkel(-)** *uncle*
die Eltern (pl.) *parents*	**die Tante (-n)** *aunt*

die Schwester (-n) *sister*	**der Schwager (¨)** *brother-in-law*
der Sohn (¨e) *son*	**die Schwägerin (-nen)** *sister-in-law*
die Tochter (¨) *daughter*	**die Schwiegermutter (¨)** *mother-in-law*
der Vetter (¨) *(male) cousin*	**die Großeltern (pl.)** *grandparents*
die Enkelin (-nen) *grand-daughter*	**der/die Bekannte (-n)** *acquaintance*
der Enkel (-) *grandson, grand-child*	**die Freundin (-nen)** *(female) friend, girlfriend*

Grammatik

1 Perfect Tense (weak verbs)

In the English sentence

I have often played cards with them.

the verb *to play* is being used in what is often called the ***Perfect Tense***. This tense is formed by using the verb *to have* together with what is known as the ***Past Participle*** of the verb in question. In the case of the verb *to play*—as indeed in the case of many other verbs—the ending *-ed* is added to the infinitive to form the past participle.

Similarly, in the German sentence

Ich habe oft mit ihnen Karten gespielt.

the verb **spielen** is being used in the perfect tense. The verb **haben** is being used together with the past participle of the verb in question. As with many verbs, the past participle of **spielen** is formed by taking the stem of the verb (i.e. **spiel-**) and adding the prefix **ge-** and the ending **-t**. The past participle goes to the end of the sentence.

Verbs that form their past participles in this way are referred to as ***Weak Verbs***. They include:

Infinitive	*Past Participle*
dauern	**gedauert**
fragen	**gefragt**
machen	**gemacht**
sagen	**gesagt**
wohnen	**gewohnt**

When the stem of an infinitive ends in a **-d** or a **-t**, an extra **-e** is added in the past participle:

antworten	**geantwortet**
kosten	**gekostet**
reden	**geredet**

Verbs ending in **-ieren** do not add the prefix **ge-** in the past participle:

kassieren	**kassiert**
organisieren	**organisiert**
renovieren	**renoviert**

Verbs containing the inseparable prefixes **be-**, **ent-**, **emp-**, **er-**, **ge-**, **miß-**, **ver-**, **wider-**, **zer-** do not add the prefix **ge-** in the past participle:

besichtigen	**besichtigt**
gehören	**gehört**
erwarten	**erwartet**

Verbs containing a separable prefix or 'double' verbs, such as **kennenlernen**, form their past participles as follows:

abholen	**abgeholt**
ausruhen	**ausgeruht**
einkaufen	**eingekauft**
kennenlernen	**kennengelernt**

The German perfect tense is used not only in all those instances in which the perfect tense would be used in English (except those containing *since* or *for* together with an expression of time—see Section 2 below), but also in many other instances as well:

Ich habe mit ihm geredet.	*I* ***have spoken*** *with him.*
Ich habe gestern mit ihm geredet.	*I* ***spoke*** *with him yesterday.*
Karl hat schon den Dom besichtigt.	*Karl* ***has*** *already* ***viewed*** *the cathedral.*
Karl hat heute den Dom besichtigt.	*Karl* ***viewed*** *the cathedral today.*

Whilst more will be said in subsequent units about the use of the perfect tense, it will suffice at this point for you to know that the perfect tense is the most commonly used past tense in German and that it is particularly useful for the informal narration of past events whether in speech or writing.

2 Present tense used with *seit*, etc.

Whilst in English the perfect tense is used in such sentences as:

I have lived in Australia	*since* 1986. *for many years.*

it is the present tense which is used in German:

Ich wohne	seit 1986 seit vielen Jahren schon viele Jahre	in Australien.

The German is perhaps more logical, as the action or state expressed by the verb is still continuing. These same German sentences would also be used to cover the English:

I have been living in Australia	*since* 1986. *for many years.*

Übungen

ÜBUNG 9.1 Ergänzen Sie.

Gestern nachmittag hat Frank Jens seinen Freund Jan Frey vom Bahnhof . . . (1) . . . Frank hat seinen Wagen in einem Parkhaus im Stadtzentrum . . . (2) . . . , und sie haben dann die Paulskirche am Marktplatz . . . (3) . . . Die Kirche hat man vor ein paar Monaten . . . (4) . . . Im Café Sieben gegenüber von der Kirche haben sie sich eine Tasse Kaffee . . . (5) . . . und sich eine halbe Stunde . . . (6) . . . Der Kaffee war sehr teuer und hat Frank fast 5 Mark . . . (7) . . . Nachher haben sie Franks Freundin Anna . . . (8) . . . Jan hat ihr Blumen . . . (9) . . . , und sie hat sich natürlich . . . (10) . . . Am Abend haben sie im Radio Musik . . . (11) . . . und Karten . . . (12) . . .

(*a*) besichtigt	(*e*) besucht	(*i*) abgeholt
(*b*) ausgeruht	(*f*) gespielt	(*j*) geparkt
(*c*) renoviert	(*g*) bestellt	(*k*) geschenkt
(*d*) gekostet	(*h*) gefreut	(*l*) gehört

ÜBUNG 9.2 Welche Antwort paßt?

1 Wo waren Sie gestern?
(*a*) Sie waren gestern in Düsseldorf.
(*b*) Wir waren den ganzen Tag in München.
(*c*) Wir sind den ganzen Tag hier.

2 Und wie war es dort?
(*a*) Dort haben wir Tennis gespielt.
(*b*) Sehr schön. Es hat nur eine Stunde gedauert.
(*c*) Sehr schön. Wir haben uns gefreut, die Stadt kennenzulernen.

3 Was haben Sie alles gemacht?
(*a*) Wir haben selbstverständlich die wichtigsten Sehenswürdigkeiten besichtigt.
(*b*) Er hat den Dom besichtigt.
(*c*) Wir haben den ganzen Tag Kartoffeln geschält.

4 Haben Sie die Alte Pinakothek besucht?
(*a*) Nein, das Stadtmuseum hat leider zugehabt.
(*b*) Ja, und auch das Stadtmuseum.
(*c*) Ja, dort haben wir gewohnt.

5 Waren Sie auch im Restaurant »Zum goldnen Adler«?
(*a*) Nein, wir haben es gesucht, aber ich glaube, es war nicht mehr da.
(*b*) Nein, das Restaurant hat gestern aufgehabt.
(*c*) Ja, ich habe es meinem Freund auf dem Stadtplan gezeigt.

6 Haben Sie auch viel gekauft?
(*a*) Ja, wir haben im Stadtzentrum geparkt.
(*b*) Nein, es hat sich niemand gemeldet.
(*c*) Nein, gestern haben viele Geschäfte ja zugehabt.

ÜBUNG 9.3 Rearrange the following sentences in the most appropriate order:

Detlef und Waltraud Krempe

1 Damals (*at that time*) war Detlef Automechaniker bei Volkswagen in Wolfsburg . . .
2 . . . und Waltraud hat fünf Jahre lang in der Abendschule Spanisch gelernt.

3 Seit 2 Jahren hat sie jetzt aber einen Sohn und arbeitet nur halbtags.
4 Detlef und Waltraud Krempe haben sich vor acht Jahren kennengelernt.
5 Sie haben sich natürlich über die eigene Wohnung sehr gefreut.
6 Sie hat dort auch ihre Französisch- und Englischkenntnisse verbessert.
7 Detlef hat dann abends fünf Jahre lang studiert . . .
8 Vor 6 Monaten haben sie eine Eigentumswohnung (d.h. die eigene Wohnung) gekauft.
9 . . . und Waltraud war Assistentin in der Personalabteilung.
10 Vor sechs Jahren im April haben sie geheiratet.

ÜBUNG 9.4 Dieses Jahr und letztes Jahr *This year and last year*
Diese Woche und letzte Woche *This week and last week*

Dieter Bachmann lists a number of things he would like to do again (**wieder**) this year (or this week). You ask him whether he actually did these things last year (or last week).

Beispiele: **Dieter Bachmann**: Dieses Jahr im August möchte ich meine Großeltern in Leipzig wieder besuchen.
Sie: ***Haben Sie denn letztes Jahr im August Ihre Großeltern in Leipzig besucht?***

Dieter Bachmann: Diese Woche möchte ich am Mittwoch wieder einen freien Tag haben.
Sie: ***Haben Sie denn letzte Woche am Mittwoch einen freien Tag gehabt?***

1 Dieses Jahr möchte ich meinem Vater wieder eine Flasche Cognac zum Geburtstag schenken.
2 Dieses Jahr möchte ich in den Sommerferien wieder in Frankreich arbeiten.
3 Diese Woche möchte ich am Sonntag wieder den ganzen Tag im Bett bleiben.
4 Diese Woche möchte ich mir am Freitag Abend in der »Eisdiele« wieder einen Eisbecher bestellen.
5 Dieses Jahr möchte ich im Urlaub in Italien wieder versuchen, Italienisch zu lernen.

6 Dieses Jahr möchte ich an meinem Geburtstag wieder mit Heike Fischer tanzen.

ÜBUNG 9.5 Lesen Sie.
Was ich Freitag nachmittag normalerweise (*normally*) mache.

1 Um 2 Uhr besuche ich meine Tochter in Neuß.
2 Ich parke vor ihrer Wohnung.
3 Ich freue mich sehr, meine Tochter zu sehen.
4 Ich setze mich in die Küche, und mache es mir bequem.
5 Meine Tochter arbeitet noch eine Stunde in der Küche.
6 Wir reden über dies und das.
7 Um 3 Uhr setzt sie sich, und ruht sich eine halbe Stunde aus.
8 Um halb 4 holt sie meine Enkelin vom Kindergarten ab.
9 Ich spiele dann mit meiner Enkelin.
10 Um 4 Uhr kocht meine Tochter Kaffee.

Above is a description of Sabine Merck's normal pattern of activities for a Friday afternoon. Last Friday she kept to her usual pattern. Narrate what happened as if you are Sabine Merck:

Was ich Freitag nachmittag gemacht habe.
1 Um 2 Uhr habe ich meine Tochter in Neuß besucht . . .

Verstehen Sie?

1 Konversation

Dagmar Ahrends is calling on the Personnel Manager of a local firm to enquire about the possibility of spending time at the company's headquarters in Spain.

Personalleiter	Seit wann wohnen Sie hier in Ludwigsburg, Fräulein Ahrends?
Dagmar Ahrends	Seit vier Jahren. Die Stadt gefällt mir.
Personalleiter	Und woher kommen Sie eigentlich?
Dagmar Ahrends	Aus Kiel. Meine Eltern wohnen immer noch dort. Aber ich habe in Stuttgart studiert. Und ich habe mir nach dem Studium in der Umgebung von Stuttgart Arbeit gesucht.
Personalleiter	Und wo haben Sie dann gearbeitet?

Dagmar Ahrends	Bei der Firma Pfauter in der Verkaufsabteilung.
Personalleiter	So. Die Firma Pfauter kenne ich. Dort stellt man Werkzeugmaschinen her, nicht wahr?
Dagmar Ahrends	Ja. Die Firma hat auch eine Zweigstelle in Chicago. Dort habe ich vor zwei Jahren 6 Monate lang gearbeitet.
Personalleiter	Sie haben also sicher Ihre Englischkenntnisse in Chicago verbessert.
Dagmar Ahrends	Ja, und jetzt möchte ich gerne auch noch meine Spanischkenntnisse verbessern. Bloß hat die Firma Pfauter in Spanien leider keine Zweigstelle.
Personalleiter	Aber wir haben in Madrid unseren Hauptsitz!
Dagmar Ahrends	Ja! Hätte ich vielleicht eine Chance, in Madrid eine Stelle zu bekommen?
Personalleiter	Allerdings. Sie würden aber zuerst mindestens ein Jahr bei uns hier in Ludwigsburg arbeiten müssen.
Dagmar Ahrends	Aber selbstverständlich!

Answer the following questions in English:

1 How long has Dagmar been living in Ludwigsburg?
2 How does she come to be living there?
3 Where did she find work after finishing her studies?
4 How did Dagmar manage to spend 6 months in Chicago?
5 What does the Personnel Manager assume Dagmar was able to do in Chicago?
6 Why is Dagmar not entirely happy to stay with her present firm?
7 And why has she chosen this particular firm to start her enquiries?
8 What condition does the Personnel Manager stipulate in answer to her request?

2 Lesetext

Read the following *curriculum vitae*.

Lebenslauf

Persönliche Daten:

Paul Rosenbaum
geboren am 30. Oktober 1956 in Neuß
verheiratet, 1 Sohn u. 1 Tochter

Schulbildung

1962-1969	Volksschule in Neuß
1969-1975	Wirtschaftsgymnasium in Düsseldorf, Abitur

Studium

1975-1981	Studium der Betriebwirtschaftslehre an der Ruhr-Universität Bochum

Sprachkenntnisse Englisch und Französisch

Tätigkeiten

1981-1985	Mitarbeiter im Personalbüro der Familienfirma Rosenbaum Werkzeugmaschinen
1985-	Personalleiter der Firma Rosenbaum Werkzeugmaschinen

die Schulbildung *schooling* (lit. *school education*)
die Volksschule *primary school*
das Wirtschaftsgymnasium *grammar school* (*with an economics bias*)
das Abitur *school leaving exam* (*needed for University entrance*)
das Studium *study*
die Betriebswirtschaftslehre *business economics, management studies*
die Tätigkeit (-en) *employment* (lit. *activity*)
der Mitarbeiter (-) *employee*
die Firma (Firmen) *firm*
die Werkzeugmaschine (-n) *machine tool*

Richtig (R) oder Falsch (F)?

1. Paul Rosenbaum hat am 30. Februar Geburtstag.
2. Er ist verheiratet und hat zwei Söhne.
3. Von 1962 bis 1969 hat er eine Volkschule in Neuß besucht.
4. Von 1969 bis 1976 hat er ein Wirtschaftsgymnasium in Düsseldorf besucht.
5. Dort hat er auch das Abitur gemacht.
6. Paul hat sechs Jahre lang studiert.
7. Er hat Betriebswirtschaftslehre an der Philipps-Universität Marburg studiert.
8. Er spricht sowohl Englisch als auch Französisch.
9. Er hat vier Jahre lang als Mitarbeiter im Personalbüro gearbeitet.
10. Seit 1985 ist er Produktionsleiter der Firma Rosenbaum Werkzeugmaschinen.

10 Seid ihr geflogen?

In this unit you will learn more of how to talk about past events and how to address two or more people informally.

Dialog

Martina Linker runs into Christel Petzing whom she has not seen for a while. Christel explains that she and her husband, Thomas, have been away on vacation for three weeks. Martina wants to know all about the trip.

Christel Tag, Martina!

Martina Tag, Christel! Ich habe dich lange nicht gesehen. Wo bist du gewesen?

Christel Thomas und ich haben ganz ungeplant drei Wochen Urlaub genommen und haben eine Englandreise gemacht.

Martina Ach wie schön! Seid ihr geflogen oder mit der Bahn gefahren?

Christel Weder noch. Wir sind mit dem Wagen gefahren. Von Düsseldorf sind es ja nur 5 Stunden Fahrt bis zur französischen Küste. Und von Calais fährt man nur anderthalb Stunden mit dem Schiff bis nach Dover. Die Reise ist also gar nicht anstrengend.

Martina Und wo seid ihr gewesen, und was habt ihr alles gesehen?

Christel Als wir in Dover angekommen sind, war es schon ziemlich spät. Wir haben uns zuerst also ein Hotel gesucht, haben schnell 'was gegessen und sind dann schlafen gegangen. Am nächsten Tag sind wir früh morgens um 7 aufgestanden, haben im Hotel gefrühstückt und sind in Richtung Canterbury losgefahren.

Martina Ach, Canterbury soll ja sehr schön sein. Ihr habt doch sicher den berühmten Dom besichtigt?

Christel Ja, klar! Der Dom ist wirklich sehenswert. Aber es war Sonntag, und die Geschäfte waren alle zu. Dann hat es noch stark geregnet. Wir konnten nicht viel von der Stadt sehen. Wir haben einfach in unserem Hotelzimmer gesessen und haben Bücher und Zeitungen gelesen und ferngesehen.

Martina Ach wie schade! Habt ihr denn die ganze Zeit schlechtes Wetter gehabt?

Christel Nein. Nur an diesem ersten Tag. Wir sind noch zwei Tage in Canterbury geblieben und haben uns alles angesehen. Das Wetter war herrlich. Dann sind wir nach London gefahren und haben zwei Wochen bei Freunden verbracht.

Martina Seid ihr in London ins Theater gegangen?

Christel Oh ja! Dreimal sogar! Wir sind auch fast jeden Tag entweder ins Museum gegangen oder haben eine Galerie besucht. In London gibt es ja so viel zu sehen.

Wo bist du gewesen? *Where have you been?*
ganz ungeplant *quite unplanned*
Wir haben 3 Wochen Urlaub genommen *We took 3 weeks' vacation*
Seid ihr geflogen? *Did you fly?*
Seid ihr mit der Bahn gefahren? *Did you go by rail?*
Weder noch *neither* (lit. *neither . . . nor*)
bis zur französischen Küste *as far as the French coast*
anderthalb Stunden *one and a half hours*
das Schiff (-e) *ship, boat*
astrengend *tiring, strenuous*
ankommen* (sep.) *to arrive*
Wir haben uns zuerst also ein Hotel gesucht . . . *So we first of all looked for a hotel . . .*
Wir haben 'was gegessen *We had something to eat* (lit. *we ate something*)
in Richtung Canterbury (*in the*) *direction* (*of*) *Canterbury*
losfahren* (sep.) *to set off*
Canterbury soll sehr schön sein *Canterbury is supposed to be very beautiful*
Ja, klar *Yes, of course* (lit. *clear*(*ly*))
wirklich sehenswert *really worth seeing*
zu *closed*
stark regnen *to rain heavily* (lit. *strong*(*ly*))
Wir konnten nicht viel sehen *We were not able to see much*
sitzen (sitzt, saß, gesessen) *to sit*
das Buch (¨er) *book*
die Zeitung (-en) *newspaper*
lesen (ie, a, e) *to read*
fernsehen (sep.) *to watch television*
Wie schade! *What a pity!*

Wir sind ins Bett gegangen *we went to bed*
am nächsten Tag *on the next day*
früh morgens *early in the morning*
Wir sind um 7 Uhr aufgestanden *We got up at 7 o'clock*
die ganze Zeit *the whole time*
schlecht *bad*
sich (dat.) **etwas ansehen** (sep.) *to have a look at something*
herrlich *great, wonderful*
verbringen *to spend (of time)*
sogar *even*

Fragen zum Dialog

1 Richtig (R) oder Falsch (F)?

1 Martina hat Christel lange nicht gesehen.
2 Thomas und Christel haben vier Wochen Urlaub genommen.
3 Sie sind mit der Bahn nach England gefahren.
4 Von Düsseldorf kann man in 5 Stunden bis nach Calais fahren.
5 Es war früh morgens, als Christel und Thomas in Dover angekommen sind.
6 Am nächsten Tag sind sie von Dover nach Canterbury gefahren.
7 Sie haben dort den berühmten Dom besichtigt.
8 Sie haben in Canterbury die ganze Zeit schlechtes Wetter gehabt.
9 In London haben Thomas und Christel bei Freunden gewohnt.
10 Sie sind dort zweimal ins Theater gegangen.

2 Welche Antwort paßt?

1 Christel! Wo bist du gewesen?
(*a*) Thomas und ich sind noch zwei Tage in Canterbury geblieben.
(*b*) Thomas und ich sind in Dover angekommen.
(*c*) Thomas und ich haben eine Englandreise gemacht.

2 Seid ihr geflogen?
(*a*) Ja, die Fahrt bis zur französischen Küste hat nur 5 Stunden gedauert.
(*b*) Nein, wir sind mit dem Wagen gefahren.

(*c*) Ja, mit der Bahn ist die Reise nicht so anstrengend.

3 Wo habt ihr gefrühstückt?
(*a*) Im Hotel.
(*b*) Mit dem Schiff.
(*c*) Im Dom.

4 Habt ihr den Dom besichtigt?
(*a*) Nein, nur am ersten Tag.
(*b*) Ja, klar! Der Dom ist ja sehr berühmt.
(*c*) Ja, wir sind fast jeden Tag ins Museum gegangen.

5 Habt ihr die ganze Zeit schlechtes Wetter gehabt?
(*a*) Nein, das Wetter war herrlich.
(*b*) Oh Ja! Dreimal sogar!
(*c*) Nein, in London gibt es so viel zu tun.

Was Sie wissen sollten

Motorway driving

There is no blanket speed limit on the German motorways, although busy sections of the network are increasingly subject to restriction – usually 100 km per hour (62 mph) – strictly enforced by on-the-spot-fines. There is also growing pressure from environmentalists for the introduction of a blanket limit of 100 km per hour, since the death of large numbers of trees in German forests, or **Waldsterben** as it is known, is considered to be attributable – at least in part – to pollution caused by road traffic. Nevertheless, speeds of 200 km per hour (120 mph) are by no means rare. The German automobile industry is, after all, renowned for the manufacture of powerful and fast cars (such as Porsche, Mercedes, BMW).

Wichtige Redewendungen

How to

1 Ask for and give information about past whereabouts of people (*continued from* **Lektion 9**).

Wo bist du gewesen?	Ich bin im Urlaub gewesen.
Wo seid ihr gewesen?	Wir sind nach Canterbury gefahren.

2 *Make statements about past events* (*continued from* **Lektion 9**).

1

	ganz ungeplant	3 Wochen Urlaub	genommen
Wir haben	schnell	etwas	gegessen.
	im Hotelzimmer	Bücher	gelesen.
Wir haben	im Sommer	2 Wochen in London	verbracht.

	mit dem Wagen	gefahren.
Wir sind	ins Bett	gegangen.
	um 7 Uhr	aufgestanden.
	3 Tage	geblieben.

3 *Ask questions about past events* (*continued from* **Lektion 9**).

Was habt ihr	in England	gesehen?
Was haben Sie	zum Frühstück	gegessen?

Sind Sie	nach England geflogen?
Seid ihr	mit der Bahn gefahren?
Bist du	ins Theater gegangen?

Verkehrsmittel (*Means of transport*)

das Flugzeug (-e) *aeroplane*
der Bus (-se) *bus*
die Maschine (-n) *plane* (lit. *machine*)
der Zug (¨e) *train*
der Lastwagen (-) *lorry, truck*
das Auto (-s) *car*
die Untergrundbahn (-en) *underground railway*
das Taxi (-s) *taxi*
der Personenkraftwagen (-) *private car* (*or* **der Pkw (-s)**)
der Flughafen (¨) *airport*
der Taxistand (¨er) *taxi rank*
der Hauptbahnhof (¨e) *main station*
die Busstation (-en) *bus station*

Grammatik

1 Perfect Tense (continued)

1.1 Strong Verbs

In addition to the ***weak verbs*** dealt with in **Lektion 9**, there is in German a further group of verbs, called ***strong verbs***, which form their past participles in a less predictable way:

Infinitive	*Past participle*
sehen	gesehen
fahren	gefahren
finden	gefunden
fliegen	geflogen
gehen	gegangen
sitzen	gesessen
stehen	gestanden
verstehen	verstanden

As can be seen from the above examples, the past participles of strong verbs – like those of weak verbs – take the prefix **ge–** (except for verbs with the inseparable prefixes listed in **Lektion 9**). The ending of strong verb past participles is **-en**.

In some cases the verb stem is retained in the past participle (as with **sehen/gesehen**), in other cases the vowel of the stem is modified (as with **fliegen/geflogen**) and in still other cases, the stem is so drastically changed that it is barely recognisable (as with **gehen/gegangen**).

The only reliable solution is to learn the past participle of every strong verb that you encounter. The vocabulary list at the end of this book assists you by listing the past participle of strong verbs in brackets after the infinitive, in third place after (*i*) the third person singular present tense and (*ii*) the third person singular imperfect tense (to be dealt with later). For instance:

finden (findet, fand, gefunden) *to find*
↑
past participle

The verb **sein** (*to be*), being quite irregular, has the past participle **gewesen**.

1.2 Mixed Verbs

Mixed verbs are so called because they have features of both weak and strong verbs. They are like weak verbs in so far as they usually form their past participles with the prefix **ge-** (except for inseparable verbs) and with the ending **-t**, but they resemble strong verbs in that the verb stem usually undergoes a vowel change and sometimes a consonant change as well:

Infinitive	*Past participle*
kennen	gekannt
nennen (*to name*)	genannt
wissen (*to know*)	gewußt
denken (*to think*)	gedacht
bringen	gebracht
verbringen	verbracht

Mixed verbs are listed in the vocabulary section in the same way as strong verbs:

brennen (brennt, brannte, gebrannt) *to burn*
↑
past participle

1.3 Verbs forming the perfect tense with sein

Whilst weak verbs, strong verbs and mixed verbs normally form the perfect tense by using the verb **haben** together with the past participle:

Wir haben eine Englandreise gemacht.
Wir haben zwei Wochen bei Freunden in London verbracht.
Wir haben in unserem Hotelzimmer gelesen.

certain verbs form their perfect tense not with **haben** but with **sein**:

Klaus **ist** gestern nach Frankfurt geflogen.
Wir **sind** bis zur französischen Küste gefahren.
Ich **bin** schon um 10 Uhr ins Bett gegangen.
Wo **bist** du die ganze Zeit gewesen?
Wir **sind** zwei Tage in Canterbury geblieben.

Such verbs are nearly always both strong verbs and 'verbs of motion' (like **gehen, fahren, fliegen**), although some verbs in this category, such as **sein, bleiben** and **sterben** (*to die*) admittedly cannot be described as 'verbs of motion'.

Verbs forming their perfect tense with **sein** are asterisked in the vocabulary section:

fliegen* **sterben***

A few verbs are treated as **haben** verbs in Northern Germany and **sein** verbs in Southern Germany. **Liegen, stehen** and **sitzen** are three such verbs:

In the North
Ich **habe** ein paar Minuten auf dem Teppich (*carpet*) gelegen.
Ich **habe** lange gestanden.
Wir **haben** in unserem Hotelzimmer gesessen.

In the South
Ich **bin** ein paar Minuten auf dem Teppich gelegen.
Ich **bin** lange gestanden.
Wir **sind** in unserem Hotelzimmer gesessen.

Some of the verbs forming their perfect tense with **sein** may occasionally be used transitively, that is with an object. The perfect tense is, in these cases formed with **haben:**

Ich **habe** den neuen Mercedes gefahren.

1.4 Separable verbs

Strong and mixed verbs, like weak verbs, often take separable prefixes which, in the perfect tense are added to the past participle as well as the **ge-** prefix:

Infinitive	*Past participle*
aufstehen	aufgestanden
losfahren	losgefahren
fernsehen	ferngesehen
einbringen (*to bring in*)	eingebracht

The same principle also applies to 'double verbs':

spazierengehen	spazierengegangen
stehenbleiben (*to stop, come to a halt*)	stehengeblieben

2 *Ihr*

The **ihr**-form, which was introduced in the **Dialog** of this **Lektion**, is usually described as the plural of the **du-** form. In so far as **ihr** is used when addressing more than one person (or animal) each of whom would individually normally be addressed by **du**, this is a correct description.

However, in practice, whilst **ihr** is less formal than **Sie**, it is nevertheless felt, in certain circumstances, to be less intimate than **du**. For instance, a group containing both friends and strangers might well be addressed as **ihr**. Similarly, a couple might be addressed as **ihr** before they are individually addressed as **du**.

The ending characteristic of the **ihr-** form is **-t**. For instance, the present tense is formed by the addition to the verb stem of **-t**, or **-et** if the verb stem ends in **-t** or **-d**:

Ihr kommt heute abend zu uns, nicht wahr?
Was antwortet ihr?
Wie findet ihr meine Wohnung?

Verbs which modify their vowel in the 2nd and 3rd person singular of the present tense (such as **sprechen** – **du sprichst** – **er spricht**) do *not* do so in the **ihr** form:

Ihr **sprecht** ja sehr gut Deutsch.
Was **nehmt** ihr – Weißwein oder Rotwein?
Fahrt ihr mit der Bahn?

The **-t** ending is also used for the imperative:

Kommt heute abend zu uns!
Steht morgen un 6 Uhr auf!
Antwortet auf alle Fragen!

The modal verbs, too, add the **-t** ending:

Ihr **könnt** beide zu uns kommen.
Vor der Wohnung **dürft** ihr nicht parken.
Möchtet ihr morgen abend ins Theater gehen?
Wollt ihr denn zu Hause bleiben?
Müßt ihr jetzt gehen?

Haben behaves regularly in the **ihr** form, although **sein** does not:

Ihr **habt** eine sehr schöne Wohnung.
Ihr **seid** ja gute Freunde.
Habt ihr den Dom besichtigt?
Seid ihr mit dem Wagen gefahren?

Both the accusative and the dative forms of **ihr** are **euch**:

Ich sehe **euch** dann morgen gegen acht.
Ich bringe **euch** ein paar Blumen.
Ich gehe dann nachher mit **euch** ins Kino.

The possessive adjective *your* is **euer**. When an ending is added to **euer** the medial **-e-** is often omitted:

Kommt **euer** Freund Klaus morgen abend mit in die Oper?
Ich möchte **eure** neue Wohnung sehen.

Übungen

ÜBUNG 10.1 Sagen Sie es anders.

The following statements have been made by Lutz and Käthe Breitmann in answer to questions put to them by a friend. Produce the questions that the friend asked. The item to be questioned is always printed in italic:

Beispiele: Wir wollen morgen *nach Wien* fahren.
Wohin wollt ihr morgen fahren?

Wir fahren *mit der Bahn* dorthin.
Wie fahrt ihr dorthin?

1 Wir stehen morgen *um halb sieben* auf.
2 Und wir fahren *um halb acht* los.
3 *Unser Freund Gerd* bringt uns zum Hauptbahnhof.
4 Unsere Fahrkarten haben wir *schon vor einer Woche* gelöst.
5 Die Fahrt Düsseldorf-Wien dauert *ungefähr zwölf Stunden.*
6 Wir kommen *gegen 20 Uhr* in Wien an.
7 *Unsere Freunde Trudi und Rolf* holen uns vom Bahnhof ab.
8 Wir wollen *acht Tage* in Wien bleiben.

ÜBUNG 10.2 Welche Antwort paßt?

1 Wo wart ihr gestern abend? Ich habe mehrmals versucht, bei euch anzurufen.
(*a*) Wir haben im Hotel gefrühstückt.
(*b*) Wir haben zu Hause Karten gespielt.
(*c*) Wir waren nicht zu Hause.

2 Wo seid ihr denn gewesen?
(*a*) Wir haben meine Schwiegermutter besucht.
(*b*) Wir haben ganz ungeplant eine Englandreise gemacht.
(*c*) Wir sind ziemlich früh aufgestanden.

3 Hat es aber gestern abend nicht stark geregnet?
(*a*) Nein, wir haben den ganzen Tag schlechtes Wetter gehabt.
(*b*) Doch, aber wir sind mit dem Wagen dorthin gefahren.
(*c*) Doch, aber wir haben uns in die Sonne gelegt.

4 Habt ihr auch dort gegessen?
(*a*) Nein, wir sind mit meiner Schwiegermutter essen gegangen.
(*b*) Ja, wir haben eine Flasche Wein getrunken.
(*c*) Nein, wir haben im Wohnzimmer gegessen.

5 Ach schön. Hat es aber nicht viel gekostet?
(*a*) Nein, es hat sehr gut geschmeckt.
(*b*) Nein, wir sind nur zwei Stunden geblieben.
(*c*) Nein, im Restaurant »Zur Krone« kann man immer noch sehr billig essen.

6 Was habt ihr nachher gemacht?
(*a*) Wir sind natürlich geflogen.
(*b*) Wir sind nach Hause gegangen und haben ferngesehen.
(*c*) Wir haben anschließend zwei Wochen bei Freunden verbracht.

ÜBUNG 10.3 Rearrange the following sentences in the most appropriate order:

Was wir letztes Jahr im Sommer gemacht haben.

1 Wir sind nach Chicago geflogen. Der Flug Frankfurt-Chicago hat 7 Stunden gedauert.
2 Von San Franzisko sind wir südlich die Küste entlang gefahren bis nach Los Angeles.
3 Letztes Jahr im Sommer haben wir 6 Wochen in den Vereinigten Staaten verbracht.
4 Sie haben uns zu ihrem Haus am Michigansee gebracht.
5 Die Fahrt war sehr interessant und wir haben vieles gesehen.
6 Nach einer Woche haben wir dann einen Wagen gemietet (*rented*) und sind bis nach Kalifornien gefahren.
7 Von Los Angeles sind wir wieder nach Deutschland zurückgeflogen (*flew back*).
8 Bei unseren Freunden haben wir eine Woche gewohnt.
9 Am besten hat uns San Franzisko gefallen.
10 Unsere amerikanischen Freunde haben uns vom Flughafen abgeholt.

ÜBUNG 10.4 Hast du alles gemacht?

Elke and Rudi Hübner are about to set off on a trip to Spain. Elke looks down the check-list which she prepared for Rudi and asks him whether he has completed each job on the list. Some jobs he has already completed (√), but others he has not yet completed (X). You speak for Rudi; (*a*) and (*b*) are provided as examples for you to follow:

(*a*) Geld wechseln (✓)
(*b*) Stadtplan von Madrid kaufen (x)
1 Frau Stein anrufen (✓)
2 Flugscheine (air tickets) beim Büro abholen (x)
3 Hotelzimmer reservieren (✓)
4 Taxi bestellen (x)
5 Sonnenöl (suntan oil) kaufen (✓)
6 Mietze* zu Frau Böhm bringen (x)

*Mietze ist natürlich die Katze (*cat*) von den Hübners!

(a) Geld habe ich schon gewechselt.

(b) Einen Stadtplan von Madrid habe ich noch nicht gekauft.

ÜBUNG 10.5 Berichten Sie *(report)*.

Der Lebenslauf des deutschen Schriftstellers Heinrich Böll

(*a*)	1917	am 21. Dezember in Köln geboren
(*b*)	1924–28	besucht die Volksschule Köln-Raderthal
1	1928–37	besucht das Kaiser-Wilhelm-Gymnasium in Köln
2	1937	macht das Abitur
3	1937	beginnt in Bonn die Buchhandelslehre
4	1939	studiert Germanistik an der Universität Köln
5	1939–45	Soldat im Zweiten Weltkrieg
6	1942	heiratet Annemarie Zech
7	1946–49	veröffentlicht Kurzgeschichten in Zeitungen und Zeitschriften
8	1949	erscheint sein erstes Buch (*Der Zug war pünktlich*)
9	1949–1985	schreibt viele literarische Werke
10	1972	erhält den Nobelpreis für Literatur
11	1985	stirbt am 16. Juli in Hürtgenwald/Eifel

der Schriftsteller (-) *author*	**veröffentlichen** *to publish*
der Buchhandel *book trade*	**die Geschichte (-n)** *story*
die Lehre (-n) *apprenticeship*	**die Zeitschrift (-en)** *journal*
die Germanistik *German language & literature*	**erscheinen (ei, ie, ie)*** *to appear*
der Soldat (-en) *soldier*	**das Werk (-e)** *work*
der Weltkrieg (-e) *World War*	**erhalten (ä, ie, ie)** *to receive*

Give a report on Heinrich Böll's life:

1917 ist Heinrich Böll am 21. Dezember in Köln geboren.
Von 1924 bis 1928 hat er die Volksschule Köln-Raderthal besucht.
usw.

Verstehen Sie?

1 Konversation

Markus Weinreich has been learning in primary school about the post-war period. He asks his father, Horst, a few questions on the subject.

Markus Du, Vati, heute hat uns unser Lehrer erzählt, daß 1945 hier in Köln viele Leute im Keller gewohnt haben. Stimmt das eigentlich?

Horst Ja, das stimmt! Im Krieg sind ja so viele Wohnungen zerstört worden. Ich war damals erst 4 Jahre alt und habe zusammen mit meiner Schwester, deiner Tante Gerda, in den Ruinen gespielt.

Markus Habt ihr auch im Keller gewohnt?

Horst Ja, 6 Monate lang, bis wir eine 2-Zimmer-Wohnung in der Friesenstraße bekommen haben. Dort haben Gerda und ich im Schlafzimmer geschlafen. Oma mußte im Wohnzimmer schlafen.

Markus Und wo hat Opa geschlafen?

Horst Der war noch in Rußland. Er ist erst 1947 zurückgekommen. Ich war schon 6 Jahre alt, als ich ihn kennengelernt habe.

Markus Und habt ihr auch zu wenig zu essen gehabt?

Horst Ja! Wir sind öfters aufs Land gefahren und haben dort nach Kartoffeln, Obst und so weiter gesucht.

Markus	Haben denn Obst und Gemüse so viel gekostet?
Horst	Man mußte entweder viel Geld bezahlen oder gegen wertvolle Sachen tauschen. Oma hat zum Beispiel eines Tages ihren Pelzmantel gegen ein paar Kilo Kartoffeln getauscht.
Markus	Ach, so was! Das kann ich mir kaum vorstellen!

der Krieg (-e) *war*
zerstören *to destroy*
Oma *Grandma*
Opa *Grandpa*
Rußland *Russia*
aufs Land fahren *to go to the country*
wertvoll *valuable*
die Sache (-n) *thing*
tauschen *to exchange*
der Pelzmantel (¨) *fur coat*
sich vorstellen *to imagine*

Richtig (R) oder Falsch (F)?

1 Nach dem Krieg haben viele Leute in Köln im Keller gewohnt.
2 Horst war 1945 vierzehn Jahre alt.
3 Seinen Vater hat er erst 1947 kennengelernt.
4 1947 ist Horsts Vater aus der Sowjetunion zurückgekommen.
5 Horst hat nach dem Krieg zusammen mit seinem Freund in den Ruinen gespielt.
6 In der 2-Zimmer-Wohnung haben Horst und Gerda im Wohnzimmer geschlafen.
7 Damals haben sie zu wenig zu essen bekommen.
8 Für ihren Pelzmantel hat Horsts Mutter nur ein paar Kilo Kartoffeln bekommen.

2 Lesetext

Renate and Paul are spending a few days in Berlin. Renate writes a letter to their friends back home:

Berlin, am 5. Mai

Liebe Sabine, lieber Achim,

Wir sind gestern abend rechtzeitig in Berlin angekommen. Trudi und Hans haben uns mit dem Wagen vom Flughafen abgeholt. Sie haben eine sehr schöne Wohnung in Charlottenburg. Wir wollten keine Zeit verlieren und sind noch um 11 Uhr auf dem Kurfürstendamm spazierengegangen. Da war enorm viel los! Hans hat uns erzählt, daß das Nachtleben in Berlin erst gegen 11 Uhr anfängt.

Heute (Sonntag) haben uns Trudi und Hans etwas von der Stadt gezeigt. Wir haben natürlich das Reichstagsgebäude und das Brandenburger Tor besichtigt. Morgen machen Paul und ich eine Busrundfahrt durch die Stadt.

Als wir vom Brandenburger Tor die Straße des 17. Juni runtergefahren sind, hat Trudi vorgeschlagen, den Flohmarkt zu besuchen. So was gibt's bei uns überhaupt nicht! Ich habe ein paar alte Postkarten von Berlin gekauft. Paul hat nach alten Münzen gesucht – er hat aber keine gefunden. Trudi und Hans haben sich für Porzellan der Zwanziger und Dreißiger Jahre interessiert. Gekauft haben sie aber nichts, weil ihnen die Preise zu hoch waren.

Zu Mittag haben wir in einem kleinen türkischen Restaurant in Charlottenburg gegessen. Ich glaube, wir waren die einzigen Deutschen im Restaurant. Alle haben türkisch gesprochen. Nachher sind wir zur Wohnung zurückgekommen und haben uns ein wenig ausgeruht. Bald geht es wieder los – diesmal nach Spandau.

Viel herzlich gegrüßt von
Renate und Paul

rechtzeitig	*punctual(ly)*	**hoch**	*high*
das Leben	*life*	**schade!**	*a pity!*
die Postkarte (-n)	*postcard*	**wert**	*worth*

Answer the following questions in English:

1. What two items does Renate have to report concerning their arrival in Berlin?
2. What did they do the same evening and why was this not particularly late by Berlin standards?
3. What famous buildings did Renate and Paul go and see?
4. What are their plans for tomorrow?
5. What did Renate buy at the flea market?
6. Did Paul buy any coins?
7. What were Trudi and Hans interested in and why did they not make any purchases?
8. Where did they all eat lunch and to what extent were they typical of the clientele?
9. Why did they go back to the flat after the meal?

11 Ich hab' ein kleines Problem!

In this unit you will increase your ability to describe people and things. This mainly involves learning more adjectives, but also includes names for parts of the body and clothing.

Dialog

Stefan Görler calls his friend, Reinhard Drenkmann, to ask whether he can help out by picking up Stefan's parents from the main station tomorrow afternoon. Reinhard agrees to help, but wants to know what kind of people to look out for. He also tells Stefan what he will be wearing.

Stefan Du, ich hab' ein kleines Problem! Meine Eltern wollen ein langes Wochenende bei mir verbringen. Sie haben gerade angerufen, daß sie morgen um 14 Uhr 23 am Hauptbahnhof eintreffen. Da bin ich noch im Büro und kann sie also nicht abholen. Kannst du mir vielleicht helfen?

Reinhard Ja, gerne. Morgen gehe ich nicht in den Betrieb. Ich habe zufällig einen freien Tag. Am Vormittag gehe ich mit meinem englischen Freund Peter im neuen Sportzentrum schwimmen. Für den Nachmittag bin ich aber noch nicht verabredet.

Stefan Prima! Ich komme also heute abend bei dir vorbei und gebe dir meinen Reserveschlüssel, und du bringst meine Eltern dann morgen nachmittag hierher.

Reinhard Ja, gut. Aber Moment mal! Ich kenne deine Eltern noch gar nicht! Ich weiß überhaupt nicht, wie sie aussehen.

Stefan Das weiß ich! Ich beschreibe sie dir ja gleich. Meine Mutter ist klein und ziemlich dick. Sie hat graue Haare, ein rundes Gesicht und blaue Augen. Mein Vater ist etwas größer, schlank und immer elegant gekleidet. Er hat ein schmales Gesicht und braune Augen und trägt meistens einen Hut, weil er fast keine Haare mehr hat.

Reinhard Ich werde sie schon erkennen.

Stefan Und was trägst du morgen, damit ich meinen Eltern Bescheid sagen kann?

Reinhard Mmm . . . blaue Sportschuhe, meine rote Hose, ein gelbes Hemd und . . . was paßt zu meinem gelben Hemd? . . . ach ja, meine weiße Jacke!

Stefan Dich werden sie bestimmt nicht verpassen!

Meine Eltern wollen ein langes Wochenende bei mir verbringen *My parents intend* (lit. *want to*) *spending a long weekend with me*
gerade *just*
eintreffen* (*sep.*) *to arrive*
zufällig *by chance*
am Vormittag *in the morning*
Ich bin verabredet *I have an appointment, date*
Prima! *Super! Great!*
Ich komme bei dir vorbei *I'll call in on you*
hierher (*to*) *here*
Moment mal! *Just a minute!*
Ich kenne deine Eltern noch gar nicht *I don't know your parents at all yet*
aussehen (*sep.*) *to look*
Ich weiß überhaupt nicht, wie sie aussehen *I don't know what they look like at all*
Das weiß ich! *I know that!*
beschreiben *to describe*
dick *fat*
graue Haare (*pl.*) *grey hair*
ein rundes Gesicht *a round face*
blaue Augen (*pl,*) *blue eyes*
etwas größer *a bit taller*
schlank *slim*
elegant gekleidet *smartly, elegantly dressed*
schmal *narrow, thin*
Er trägt meistens einen Hut *He mostly wears a hat*
. . . weil er fast keine Haare mehr hat *. . . because he's hardly got any hair left*
Ich werde sie schon erkennen *I'll recognize them (don't worry)*
. . . damit ich meinen Eltern Bescheid sagen kann *. . . so that I can let my parents know*
der Sportschuh (-e) *training shoe, plimsoll, sneaker*
meine rote Hose (*sing.*) *my red trousers*
Was paßt zu meinem gelben Hemd? *What goes with my yellow shirt?*
die Jacke (-n) *jacket*
Dich werden sie bestimmt nicht verpassen! *They certainly won't miss* ***you!***

Fragen zum Dialog

1 Richtig (R) oder Falsch (F)?

1. Stefans Eltern haben angerufen, daß sie übermorgen um 14 Uhr 23 am Hauptbahnhof eintreffen.
2. Morgen um 14 Uhr 23 ist Stefan noch im Büro und kann also seine Eltern nicht abholen.

3 Reinhard kann ihm helfen, weil er morgen einen freien Tag hat.
4 Am Vormittag ist er mit seinem englischen Freund Peter verabredet.
5 Er spielt mit Peter im neuen Sportzentrum Fußball (*football*).
6 Am Nachmittag kann er aber Stefans Eltern vom Hauptbahnhof abholen.
7 Heute abend bringt ihm Stefan seinen Reserveschlüssel.
8 Reinhard kennt Stefans Eltern schon sehr gut.
9 Stefans Mutter ist klein und ziemlich schlank.
10 Stefans Vater hat ein rundes Gesicht und braune Augen.
11 Er trägt meistens einen Hut, weil er graue Haare hat.
12 Morgen trägt Reinhard blaue Sportschuhe, seine rote Hose, ein gelbes Hemd und seine weiße Jacke.

2 **Welche Antwort paßt?**

1 Holst du deine Eltern morgen nachmittag vom Hauptbahnhof ab?
(*a*) Nein, ich war nicht zu Hause.
(*b*) Das kann ich leider nicht. Da bin ich noch im Büro.
(*c*) Ja, gut. Aber Moment mal! Ich kenne sie noch gar nicht!

2 Kannst du mir vielleicht helfen?
(*a*) Ach ja. Ich glaube, du hast recht.
(*b*) Ja. Also, bis nachher!
(*c*) Ja, gerne.

3 Gehst du also morgen nicht in den Betrieb?
(*a*) Nein, heute bleibe ich zu Hause.
(*b*) Doch, morgen gehe ich ins Büro.
(*c*) Nein, morgen habe ich zufällig einen freien Tag.

4 Ich weiß überhaupt nicht, wie deine Eltern aussehen.
(*a*) Das weiß ich. Ich beschreibe sie dir ja gleich.
(*b*) Gut, dann esse ich auch eine Vorspeise.
(*c*) Gut, das geht noch.

5 Und was trägst du morgen?
(*a*) Meistens trägt er einen Hut.
(*b*) Meine blaue Hose, ein weißes Hemd und gelbe Sportschuhe.

(*c*) Sie hat ein rundes Gesicht und braune Augen.

Was Sie wissen sollten

Clothing

Whilst the German textile and clothing industry is not famous for its high-fashion creations, it nevertheless enjoys the reputation of German industry in general—that of producing quality goods to guaranteed deadlines. In the English-speaking world a perhaps surprising number of articles of clothing nowadays bears the label 'Made in Germany'. This healthy demand from both home and abroad provides work for over half a million people.

Training schemes

In case you were wondering how Reinhard came to have a day off from his factory, the explanation is that he—in common with many young Germans—has been offered a 4-day-week contract on completion of his apprenticeship or training scheme. Such contracts enable firms to employ 5 young people for every 4 they would previously have employed under the 5-day-week pattern, thus reducing the unemployment figures and offering valuable work experience to a greater number of people. After a fixed period the employee is either offered a full-time contract or has to seek employment with another firm.

Considerable emphasis is placed on vocational training in Germany. The dual system of practical training 'on the job' together with compulsory attendance at a Vocational School **Berufsschule** one or two days per week over the full two- or three-year training period has proved very effective. It means that professional standards are set for occupations such as that of shop assistant for which in countries like Britain (with a few notable exceptions) little or no training is given.

Wichtige Redewendungen

How to

1 Describe people's size.

	sehr	groß.
Mein Vater ist	ziemlich	klein.
Meine Mutter ist	nicht sehr	dick.
	ganz	schlank.

2 Describe facial features.

Er hat Sie hat	ein schmales ein rundes	Gesicht.
	blaue Augen.	
	braune Haare.	

3 Describe what people are wearing.

Er trägt Sie trägt	weiße Sportschuhe. eine rote Hose. eine braune Jacke. ein gelbes Hemd.

Bekleidung *(Clothing)*

der Rock (¨e) *skirt*	**die Bluse (-n)** *blouse*
der Anzug (¨e) *suit*	**das Kostüm (-e)** *costume*
das Kleid (-er) *dress*	**der Strumpf (¨e)** *stocking*
die Socke (-n) *sock*	**der Schuh (-e)** *shoe*
der Gürtel (-) *belt*	**der Mantel (¨)** *coat*
die Krawatte (-n) *(neck)tie*	**der Schlips (-e)** *(neck)tie*
der Stiefel (-) *boot*	**der Pullover (-)** *or* **der Pulli (-s)** *jumper, sweater*

Körperteile *(Parts of the body)*

die Hand (¨e) *hand*	**die Nase (-n)** *nose*
der Mund (¨er) *mouth*	**das Ohr (-en)** *ear*
der Arm (-e) *arm*	**die Schulter (-n)** *shoulder*
das Bein (-e) *leg*	**der Fuß (¨e)** *foot*
der Kopf (¨e) *head*	**der Hals (¨e)** *neck*
der Finger (-) *finger*	**der Magen (-/¨)** *stomach*
der Zeh (-en)/die Zehe (-n) *toe*	**die Brust (¨e)** *chest, breast*

Grammatik

1 Adjectival endings

You have already learned a considerable number of ***adjectives*** in German—words like **kalt, neu, blau, klein**—and may have noticed that such words sometimes add an ending and sometimes do not. For instance, in the **Dialog** of ***Lektion 10*** we find the following exchange:

Martina Ihr habt doch sicher den **berühmten** Dom besichtigt?
Christel Ja, klar! Der Dom ist wirklich **sehenswert.**

Because the adjective **berühmt** (which in this example has added the ending **-en**) stands immediately in front of the noun **Dom** which it qualifies, we call this an ***attributive adjective***. However, the other adjective **sehenswert**, whilst it still refers to the noun **Dom**, stands on its own and not immediately in front of the noun. This use of the adjective we call ***predicative***. In German attributive adjectives require endings whilst predicative adjectives do not.

Examples from earlier dialogues of adjectives used ***predicatively*** are:

Sind Sie auch **verheiratet**? (L2)
Der Garten ist etwas **klein** aber sehr **schön**. (L3)
Haben Sie ein Zimmer **frei**? (L4)
Die Forelle ist heute **ausgezeichnet** (L7)

Examples of ***attributive*** use are:

Es läuft der **alte amerikanische** Film »Manche mögen's heiß«. (L5)
Dort gibt es immer ein **interessantes** Tagesmenü. (L6)
Französische Zwiebelsuppe esse ich sehr gern. (L7)
Auf dem Stadtplan sind die **wichtigsten** Sehenswürdigkeiten aufgeführt. (L8)

For English-speakers the idea of adding endings to adjectives inevitably must seem strange. If, however, you are to speak and write German accurately, the adjectival endings must be mastered. Initially, the system of endings will seem complex and daunting. With exposure to the language and frequent practice, you will gain a 'feel' for what sounds right. There are three sorts of adjectival endings which are normally referred to as ***strong, weak*** and ***mixed***.

1.1 Strong endings

Strong endings are found on those attributive adjectives which appear on their own in front of a noun (i.e. which are ***not*** preceded by such words as **der, dieser, mein,** etc.):

Frisch**er** Fisch schmeckt gut. (*Nom. Masc. Sing.*)
Ich trinke gern kalt**e** Milch. (*Acc. Fem. Sing.*)
Ich habe nur französisch**es** Geld. (*Acc. Neut. Sing.*)
Er hat jetzt grau**e** Haare. (*Acc. Neut. Plur.*)

Here is a summary of the strong endings:

	Masculine singular	*Feminine singular*	*Neuter singular*	*Masc., fem. & neut. plural*
Nominative	-er	-e	-es	-e
Accusative	-en	-e	-es	-e
*Genitive**	-en	-er	-en	-er
Dative	-em	-er	-em	-en

*The Genitive case will be introduced in a later unit. The endings for the Genitive case are included here in order to provide a complete summary for reference purposes.

Here are detailed examples of strong adjectival endings:

Masculine singular
Nom. Frisch**er** Fisch schmeckt gut.
Acc. Frisch**en** Fisch esse ich sehr gern.
Gen. Statt (*instead of*) frisch**en** Fisches esse ich heute Fleisch.
Dat. Zu frisch**em** Fisch esse ich oft Pommes frites.

Feminine singular
Nom. Kalt**e** Milch schmeckt gut.
Acc. Kalt**e** Milch trinke ich sehr gern.
Gen. Statt kalt**er** Milch trinke ich heute Orangensaft.
Dat. Mit kalt**er** Milch schmeckt dieser Tee besser.

Neuter singular
Nom. Frisch**es** Brot schmeckt gut.
Acc. Frisch**es** Brot esse ich sehr gern.
Gen. Statt frisch**en** Brots esse ich heute Toast.
Dat. Zu frisch**em** Brot esse ich oft Marmelade.

Masculine, feminine & neuter plural
Nom. Blau**e** Augen sind sehr schön.
Acc. Braun**e** Augen finde ich aber schöner.
Gen. Statt rot**er** Socken trage ich heute blaue.
Dat. Zu rot**en** Sportschuhen paßt diese Hose nicht.

1.2 Weak endings

Weak endings are found on those attributive adjectives which follow the definite article (**der, die, das**) or such words as **dies-, jed-, jen-** (*that, those*):

Dieser jung**e** (*young*) Herr möchte bei uns wohnen. (*Nom. Masc. Sing.*)
Diesen jung**en** Herrn kenne ich aber gar nicht. (*Acc. Masc. Sing.*)

Das klein**e** Zimmer im 3. Stock nehme ich nicht.	(*Acc. Neut. Sing.*)
Die grün**en** (*green*) Äpfel sind etwas sauer.	(*Nom. Masc. Plur.*)

Here is a summary of the weak endings:

	Masculine singular	*Feminine singular*	*Neuter singular*	*Masc., fem. & neut. plural*
Nominative	-e	-e	-e	-en
Accusative	-en	-e	-e	-en
Genitive	-en	-en	-en	-en
Dative	-en	-en	-en	-en

Here are detailed examples of weak adjectival endings:

Masculine singular

Nom.	Dieser blau**e** Wagen gefällt mir.
Acc.	Diesen grün**en** Wagen mag ich aber lieber.
Gen.	Statt des blau**en** Wagens kaufe ich den grünen.
Dat.	Mit dem grün**en** Wagen kann man sehr schnell fahren.

Feminine singular

Nom.	Diese modern**e** Kirche gefällt mir.
Acc.	Die alt**e** Kirche haben wir gestern besucht.
Gen.	Statt der alt**en** Kirche möchte ich heute die moderne besuchen.
Dat.	In der alt**en** Kirche sind heute viele Touristen.

Neuter singular

Nom.	Jedes neu**e** Haus hat mindestens 2 Schlafzimmer.
Acc.	Dieses neu**e** Haus hat Herr Henning gebaut (*built*).
Gen.	Statt dieses neu**en** Hauses kaufe ich jetzt ein altes.
Dat.	In jedem neu**en** Haus gibt es ja Probleme.

Masculine, feminine & neuter plural

Nom.	Diese grün**en** Äpfel sind alle sauer.
Acc.	Die rot**en** Äpfel esse ich lieber.
Gen.	Statt der billig**en** Kartoffeln nehme ich die teuren.
Dat.	In den best**en** Restaurants bekommt man immer frisches Gemüse.

1.3 Mixed endings

Mixed endings are found on those attributive adjectives which follow the indefinite article (**ein-**), the possessive adjectives (such as **mein-**, **Ihr-**, **sein-**, **unser-** etc.) and after **kein-**:

Mein alt**er** Freund Hans kommt heute aus Köln.
Einen interessant**en** Beruf möchte jeder haben.
Unser neu**es** Haus ist sehr groß.
Wir haben keine rot**en** Äpfel mehr.

Here is a summary of the mixed endings:

	Masculine singular	*Feminine singular*	*Neuter singular*	*Masc., fem. & neut. plural*
Nominative	-er	-e	-es	-en
Accusative	-en	-e	-es	-en
Genitive	-en	-en	-en	-en
Dative	-en	-en	-en	-en

Here are detailed examples of mixed adjectival endings:

Masculine singular
Nom. Ein jung**er** Mann möchte Sie sprechen, Herr Fischer.
Acc. Aber ich erwarte keinen jung**en** Mann.
Gen. Statt eines jung**en** Mannes ist ein Mädchen gekommen.
Dat. Mit meinem alt**en** Freund habe ich schon geredet.

Feminine singular
Nom. Eine jung**e** Frau ist ins Zimmer gekommen.
Acc. Ich habe keine jung**e** Frau gesehen.
Gen. Statt einer jung**en** Frau hat man einen alten Mann angestellt.
Dat. In unserer klein**en** Kirche waren viele Touristen.

Neuter singular
Nom. Ein klein**es** Geschenk liegt auf dem Tisch.
Acc. Vielen Dank für dein schön**es** Geschenk.
Gen. Statt meines lang**en** Kleids trage ich heute meinen Hosenanzug.
Dat. In deinem alt**en** Buch habe ich dieses Photo gefunden.

Masculine, feminine & neuter plural
Nom. Unsere alt**en** Freunde kommen morgen zu Besuch.
Acc. Kennen wir denn euere alt**en** Freunde?
Gen. Statt meiner blau**en** Socken trage ich heute die roten.
Dat. Zu deinen blau**en** Augen paßt dieser Pullover sehr gut.

Note that whilst weak endings are used after **alle** in the plural, strong endings are used after **viele, einige** (*some*) and **wenige** (*few*):

Nicht alle deutsch**en** Dörfer sind schön.
Viele deutsch**e** Dörfer sind aber sehr schön.
Einige deutsch**e** Dörfer sind wunderschön.
Wenige deutsch**e** Dörfer sind nicht schön.

1.4 Omission of the noun

In a sentence such as:

Welchen Pullover nimmst du, den blauen oder den roten?

it is unnecessary to say the word **Pullover** three times. After the first mention, it is clear that **Pullover** is understood in the other two instances. Note that the English would be:

*Which sweater are you taking, the blue **one** or the red **one**?*

Further examples are:

Was für einen Mantel möchtest du?	Einen brauen.
What sort of coat do you want?	*A brown one.*
Welches Kleid gefällt dir?	Das lange.
Which dress do you like?	*The long one.*

2 Adverbs

Just as adjectives supply additional information relating to nouns, so adverbs can be used to supply additional information relating to verbs. For instance, in the sentences:

Mr Peters speaks German fluently
Karin and Paula quickly ate their sandwiches.

the adverbs *fluently* and *quickly* tell us ***how*** Mr Peters speaks German and ***how*** Karin and Paula ate their sandwiches. Whilst in English, this kind of adverb is usually formed by adding *-ly* to the adjective (*fluently*, *quickly* etc.), German rarely distinguishes between adjectives and adverbs, so adjectives such as **fließend** and **schnell** may also be used as adverbs:

Herr Peters spricht **fließend** Deutsch.
Karin und Paula haben **schnell** ihre Butterbrote gegessen.

Note that German also simply uses **gut** in cases where English would distinguish between *good* and *well*:

Das ist ja **gut**!
Ich kenne ihn **gut**.

3 *Werden* and the Future Tense

As you already know, the verb **werden** often has the meaning of *to become, to get*:

Du wirst dick. *You are becoming (getting) fat.*

You may have noticed in **Lektion 8 (Konversation)** and in the **Dialog** of this **Lektion** that **werden** may also be used to form the Future Tense:

Wenn das Museum zuhat, werden wir einfach (. . .) weiterspazieren. *If the museum is closed, we'll simply continue our walk.*
Ich werde sie (deine Eltern) schon erkennen. *I'll recognise them (your parents) all right.*
Dich werden sie bestimmt nicht verpassen! *They certainly won't miss you!*

Note that when **werden** is used to form the Future Tense in this way, the second verb (infinitive) goes to the end of the sentence or clause.

As explained in ***Lektion 5***, the Present Tense is used in German, even more frequently than it is in English, to refer to the future. This means that the Future Tense itself is not used so often in German. There are many cases when both the Present and the Future Tenses may be used to convey more or less the same meaning:

Ich bin morgen abend zu Hause.
Ich werde morgen abend zu Hause sein.

Heute abend gehe ich ins Kino.
Heute abend werde ich ins Kino gehen.

The use of the Future Tense is, if anything, slightly more formal, than that of the Present Tense, but you will often find people shifting between the two tenses for no apparent reason other than that of variety.

You will probably have noted that the **du** and **er/sie/es** forms of **werden** are somewhat irregular:

Du **wirst** bald von mir hören.
Er **wird** bestimmt kommen.

4 Use of *wollen* to express intention

The verb **wollen** may be used not only to express wants or desires:

Ich will jetzt gehen. *I want to go now.*

but also to express intention:

Wir wollen bald ein langes Wochende in Paris verbringen. *We are planning to spend a long weekend in Paris soon.*

Übungen

ÜBUNG 11.1 Sagen sie es anders.

Beispiele: **Herr Amm**
Herr Amm hat ein ovales Gesicht. ***Sein Gesicht ist oval.***
Er hat blaue Augen. ***Seine Augen sind blau.***
Frau Jahn
Frau Jahn hat einen kleinen Mund. ***Ihr Mund ist klein.***
Sie hat lange Haare. ***Ihre Haare sind lang.***

Continue on the same pattern:

A Herr Anders

1 Herr Anders hat ein rotes Gesicht.
2 Er hat braune Augen.
3 Er hat sehr kurze Haare.
4 Er hat große Ohren.
5 Er hat einen kleinen Mund.

B Frau Bendt

1 Frau Bendt hat ein schmales Gesicht.
2 Sie hat grüne Augen.
3 Sie hat lange, braune Haare.
4 Sie hat eine kleine Nase.
5 Sie hat einen ziemlich großen Mund.

ÜBUNG 11.2 Was man (1) am Arbeitsplatz und (2) zu Hause trägt.

The following chart shows what people wear (1) for work and (2) at home. Using the sentences about Udo as a model, write similar sentences about Beate, Frank and Peter:

1 Am Arbeitsplatz trägt Udo einen grauen Anzug, ein weißes Hemd, eine blaue Krawatte und schwarze Lederschuhe (*leather shoes*).
2 Zu Hause trägt er eine rote Hose, ein hellblaues (*light blue*) Hemd, einen dunkelblauen (*dark blue*) Pullover und weiße Sportschuhe.

		Anzug	Jacke	Hose	Rock	Hemd/Bluse	Krawatte	Pullover	Schuhe
Udo	1	grau				weiß	blau		schwarz/Leder-
	2			rot		hellblau		dunkelblau	weiß/Sport-
A Beate	1		dunkelgrün		braun	hellgrün			braun/Leder-
	2			grün		gelb		gelb	grün/Sport-
B Frank	1		grau	schwarz			dunkelblau		grau/Leder-
	2			schwarz		grau		grau	schwarz/Leder-
C Peter	1	blau				hellblau	schwarz		schwarz/Leder-
	2			braun		gelb		grün	keine

ÜBUNG 11.3 **Was paßt zusammen?**

1 Wie gefällt dir diese weiße Bluse?
2 Oder findest du diese blaue schöner?
3 Gut, dann nehme ich die weiße. Ich suche auch eine Hose.
4 Eine schwarze, aber hier sehe ich keine.
5 Die ist schön aber viel zu groß.
6 Ja, die gefällt mir. Ist es auch die richtige Größe (*size*)?
(*Drei Minuten später*)
7 Wie sehe ich denn aus?
8 Dann kaufe ich mir beide.

(*a*) Was für eine möchtest du denn?
(*b*) Ich glaube ja. Zieh sie doch mal an!
(*c*) Hier ist eine. Wie gefällt dir diese?
(*d*) Ich finde sie schön.
(*e*) Sehr elegant! Die weiße Bluse paßt gut zu der schwarzen Hose.
(*f*) Nein, mir gefällt die weiße besser.
(*g*) Gut! Hast du aber Geld bei dir? Ich habe nämlich keins!
(*h*) Ach ja, du hast recht. Diese hier ist vielleicht besser.

ÜBUNG 11.4 **Ergänzen Sie.**

Morgen fahre ich mit meinem . . .(1) . . . Vetter Victor nach Heidelberg. Wir wollen dort das . . .(2) . . . Schloß besichtigen. Für einen . . . (3) Australier wie Victor sind die . . . (4) . . . Schlösser und Kirchen Europas von . . . (5) . . . Interesse. In Australien hat man ja viele ... (6) ... Gebäude, aber sie sind fast alle modern. Natürlich sind nicht alle ... (7) ... Gebäude in Australian schön, aber in Europa sind sie es auch nicht. Victor möchte auch seine ... (8) ... Verwandten in London besuchen, bevor er nach Sydney zurückfliegt. Ich werde auch mitfahren, wenn ich ein paar Tage freibekommen kann. Dann können wir zusammen mit meinem ... (9) ... Wagen fahren. Ich interessiere mich sehr für die moderne ... (10) ... Architektur.

(*a*) britische (*b*) australischen (*c*) modernen (*d*) englischen
(*e*) alte (*f*) jungen (*g*) neuen (*h*) interessante
(*i*) großem (*j*) alten

ÜBUNG 11.5 Sagen Sie es anders.

Am Telefon

Beispiele: **Petra:** Carla, ich bin morgen um 10 Uhr da.
Carla, ich werde morgen um 10 Uhr da sein.
Carla: Gut. Bringst du deinen Freund Gerd mit?
Gut. Wirst du deinen Freund Gerd mitbringen?

1 **Petra:** Nein, morgen arbeitet er den ganzen Tag.
2 **Carla:** Kommst du mit der Bahn?
3 **Petra:** Nein, morgen bekomme ich doch meinen neuen Wagen!
4 **Carla:** Ach ja! Du fährst also mit dem Wagen.
5 **Petra:** Natürlich! Hoffentlich gibt es nicht zu viel Verkehr (*traffic*) auf den Straßen.
6 **Carla:** Glaubst du, du findest meine Wohnung?
7 **Petra:** Oh ja! Wenn nicht, dann rufe ich dich an.
8 **Carla:** Gut. Ich erwarte dich dann gegen 10.

Verstehen Sie?

1 Konversation

Anne Brauer, in Cologne, receives a call from Theo Herzog, who makes arrangements to visit her company. Fräulein Brauer offers to pick Herr Herzog up at the airport.

Anne Brauer Brauer.

Theo Herzog Guten Tag, Fraülein Brauer. Hier Herzog. Ich habe heute früh Ihren Brief bekommen. Es tut mir furchtbar leid, daß Sie Probleme mit unserem

Produkt haben. Ich werde aber morgen, nach Köln fliegen und versuchen, alles wieder in Ordnung zu bringen. Geht das?

Anne Brauer Ja, sicher. Das ist aber nett von Ihnen. Kann ich Sie vielleicht vom Flughafen abholen?

Theo Herzog Da würde ich mich aber freuen! Es kann mit dem Flughafenbus oft sehr lange dauern, bis man in die Stadtmitte kommt. Und manchmal findet man am Flughafen auch kein Taxi. Ich komme um 8 Uhr 35 mit dem Flug Nummer LH 432 in Köln-Bonn an.

Anne Brauer Ich werde auf jeden Fall da sein. Da müßte ich aber wissen, wie ich Sie erkennen kann.

Theo Herzog Ich bin ziemlich groß, etwas rundlich—obwohl nicht dick! Ich habe kurze, blonde Haare. Morgen werde ich einen dunkelblauen Anzug tragen. Und ich lese immer »Die Frankfurter Rundschau«. Die werde ich bestimmt in der Hand haben. Und Sie?

Anne Brauer Ich bin auch ziemlich groß. Ich habe lange, schwarze Haare und morgen werde ich ein graues Kostüm tragen. Oh, und ich trage auch eine graue Brille.

Theo Herzog Also, dann ist ja alles klar. Ich glaube, wir werden uns schon erkennen. Ich erwarte Sie also in der Ankunftshalle.

Anne Brauer Ja gut. Bis morgen dann. Auf Wiederhören!

Theo Herzog Auf Wiederhören!

der Brief (-e) *letter*
in Ordnung bringen *to sort out*
der Flug (¨e) *flight*
auf jeden Fall *definitely* (lit. *in every case*)
rundlich *plump*
die Brille (-n) *pair of glasses*
klar *clear*
die Ankunftshalle *arrivals* (*hall*)

Richtig (R) oder Falsch (F)?

1 Herr Herzog hat heute einen Brief von Fräulein Brauer erhalten.
2 Ihm tut es leid, daß ihre Firma Probleme mit seinem Produkt hat.
3 Herr Herzog möchte Fräulein Brauer nächste Woche besuchen.

4 Herr Herzog freut sich, daß Fräulein Brauer ihn vom Flughafen abholt.
5 Mit dem Flughafenbus ist man schnell in der Stadtmitte.
6 Weil Fräulein Brauer Herrn Herzog noch nicht kennt, möchte sie wissen, wie er aussieht.
7 Er ist ziemlich groß, nicht zu dick und hat kurze blonde Haare.
8 Er liest »Die Frankfurter Allgemeine Zeitung«.
9 Seine Zeitung wird er in der Hand tragen.
10 Fräulein Brauer wird morgen ein dunkelblaues Kostüm und eine schwarze Brille tragen.

2 Lesetext

Read through the following questions and then try to find the answers in the text on page 149:

1 What honour has been accorded the Ford Scorpio?
2 What was the composition of the jury that made the award?
3 How is the honour humorously referred to in the advertisement?
4 What did the jury do before making their choice?
5 What are the first and last of various reasons listed for this particular car having won?
6 Who, it is claimed, is at the centre of all considerations at Ford?
7 What could the Scorpio be for you, the reader of the advertisement?
8 Who, according to the advertisement, will be happy if you drive a Scorpio?

die Aufgabe *task*	**die Sicherheit** *safety*
leicht *easy*	**bauen** *to build*
wählen *to choose, elect*	**sicher** *safe*
verschieden *various, different*	**zuverlässig** *reliable*
der Grund (¨e) *reason*	**glücklich** *happy*

When you have answered the questions, re-read the advertisement, trying to glean more information. Use the vocabulary list at the back of the book to look up those words whose meaning you cannot work out.

Soviel Auto braucht der Mensch

■ Insgesamt 56 Journalisten aus 17 europäischen Ländern haben sich zusammengesetzt. Sie wollten herausfinden, wer in Europa den »Auto-Oscar« verdient hat.

■ Die kritischen Journalisten haben sich alle Kandidaten sehr ganau angesehen. Sie haben sich ihre Aufgabe nicht leichtgemacht. Und dann haben sie den ***Ford Scorpio*** zum Auto des Jahres gewählt

■ Warum hat sich der ***Scorpio*** bei der strengen Jury durchsetzen können? Dafür gibt es verschiedene Gründe. Ein Grund: die moderne Technik. Ein anderer: die Sicherheit. Weitere Gründe: die reichhaltige Ausstattung, das großzügige Platzangebot. Und noch ein Grund: das moderne, aerodynamische Styling. Es gibt noch mehr . . . Aber ehrlich gesagt, wir haben den ***Scorpio*** nicht für die Jury gebaut. Für uns bei Ford steht der Mensch im Mittelpunkt aller Überlegungen. Und so bauen wir unsere Autos. Wie den ***Scorpio***. So sicher, komfortabel und zuverlässig, daß Sie ihn zu Ihrem persönlichen Auto des Jahres machen. Daß Sie und alle, die mit Ihnen fahren, glücklich werden.

12 Ich wollte, aber ich konnte nicht

In this unit you will learn further ways of talking about past events as well as how to link a number of ideas together in one sentence.

Dialog

Herr Jahn and Dr Walz, who have only recently met, exchange information about their jobs and about their job satisfaction.

Herr Jahn Was sind Sie denn von Beruf, wenn ich fragen darf, Herr Doktor Walz?

Dr Walz Ich bin Gymnasiallehrer. Ich unterrichte Englisch und Geschichte. Und Sie?

Herr Jahn Ich habe seit 2 Jahren ein kleines Fotogeschäft in Weissach. Ich war früher mal Schriftsetzer in einer Zeitungsdruckerei. Weil ich aber immer nachts arbeiten mußte, war ich oft krank und mußte mir einen anderen Beruf suchen. Wir haben deshalb mehrere Jahre lang gespart, bis wir uns das eigene Geschäft und die eigene Wohnung leisten konnten.

Dr Walz Und sind Sie mit Ihrem neuen Beruf zufrieden?

Herr Jahn Oh ja! Ich habe mich schon als Junge fürs Fotografieren interessiert, obwohl ich am Anfang nur einen ganz primitiven Fotoapparat hatte. Fotografieren war auch jahrelang mein Hobby, als ich in der Druckerei gearbeitet habe.

Dr Walz Das eigene Geschäft bringt aber sicher eine große Verantwortung mit sich. Was machen Sie zum Beispiel, wenn Sie krank sind? Sie müssen wohl trotzdem ins Geschäft, sonst gehen ihre Kunden woanders hin, nicht wahr?

Herr Jahn Nein, das ist gar kein Problem, wissen Sie, weil meine Frau und zwei von meinen drei Söhnen im Geschäft mitarbeiten. Jeder von uns kann also auch ein paar Stunden für sich allein haben, obwohl der Laden 8 Stunden am Tag aufhat, und wir abends noch Kundenbesuche machen müssen. Ich gehe zum Beispiel einkaufen, wenn es wenig Betrieb gibt . . . Aber wie steht's mit Ihrem Beruf? Sind Sie auch zufrieden?

Dr Walz Im großen und ganzen, ja. Ich interessiere mich sehr für die englische Sprache und ich unterrichte auch sehr gern, aber ich wollte eigentlich Hochschullehrer werden. Obwohl ich meine Doktorarbeit geschrieben habe, konnte ich bisher an keiner Universität eine Stellung finden. Ich sollte aber trotzdem zufrieden sein, denn es gibt heutzutage so viele arbeitslose Lehrer.

Herr Jahn Da haben Sie eigentlich recht!

der Gymnasiallehrer *teacher at a* ***Gymnasium***
unterrichten *to teach, instruct*
das Fotogeschäft *photographic shop*
Ich war früher mal . . . *I used to be . . .*
der Schriftsetzer *compositor, type-setter*
die Druckerei *print shop, printing works*
Weil ich nachts arbeiten mußte . . . *Because I had to work nights . . .*
sich (*dat.*) **etwas suchen** (*sep.*) *to look for something for oneself*
mehrere Jahre lang *for several years*
sparen *to save*
bis (*subord. conj.*) *until*
sich (*dat.*) **leisten** *to afford*
Sind Sie mit Ihrem Beruf zufrieden? *Are you satisfied with your job?*
die Verantwortung *responsibility*
. . . wenn Sie krank sind *. . . when you are ill*
trotzdem *nevertheless, despite that*
Sonst gehen Ihre Kunden woanders hin *Otherwise your customers will go elsewhere*
für sich allein *to oneself* (lit. *for oneself alone*)
der Laden (¨) *shop*
Kundenbesuche machen *to make visits to customers*
. . . wenn es wenig Betrieb gibt *. . . when things are quiet* (lit. *when there is little going on*)
im großen und ganzen *on the whole, by and large*
Ich wollte Hochschullehrer werden *I wanted to be a university teacher*
die Doktorarbeit *doctoral thesis, Ph.D. thesis*

fürs = für das	**Ich konnte . . .** *I was able to, could . . .*
das Fotografieren *photography*	**die Stellung (-en)** *post, position*
obwohl (*subord. conj.*) *although*	**Ich sollte zufrieden sein** *I ought to be satisfied*
am Anfang *in the beginning, to start with*	**denn** (*co-ord. conj.*) *for*
der Fotoapparat (-e) *camera*	**arbeitslos** *jobless, unemployed*
jahrelang *for many years*	
mit sich bringen *to bring with it, to involve*	

Fragen zum Dialog

1 Richtig (R) oder Falsch (F)?

1 Dr Walz ist Universitätslehrer von Beruf.
2 Weil er nachts arbeiten mußte, als er früher mal in der Zeitungsdruckerei gearbeitet hat, war Herr Jahn oft krank.
3 Herr Jahn hat seit 2 Jahren sein eigenes Fotogeschäft.
4 Seine Frau und er haben nur wenige Monate gespart, bis sie sich das eigene Geschäft und die eigene Wohnung leisten konnten.
5 Als Junge hatte Herr Jahn schon einen sehr guten Fotoapparat.
6 Weil seine Frau und zwei Söhne im Geschäft mitarbeiten, hat Herr Jahn wenige Probleme, auch wenn er krank ist.
7 Obwohl der Laden 8 Stunden am Tag aufhat, kann jeder ein paar Stunden für sich allein haben.
8 Dr Walz ist im großen und ganzen mit seinem Beruf zufrieden.
9 Obwohl er seine Doktorarbeit geschrieben hat, konnte er noch keine Stellung als Universitätslehrer finden.
10 Heutzutage kann jeder Lehrer eine gute Stellung finden.

2 Welche Antwort paßt?

1 Was sind Sie denn von Beruf?
(*a*) Mein Beruf ist sehr interessant.
(*b*) Er ist Universitätslehrer.
(*c*) Ich bin Gymnasiallehrer.

2 Warum mußten Sie sich einen anderen Beruf suchen?
(*a*) Weil wir lange gespart haben.

(*b*) Weil ich oft krank war, als ich nachts gearbeitet habe.
(*c*) Weil ich einen ganz primitiven Fotoapparat hatte.

3 Interessieren Sie sich fürs Fotografieren?
(*a*) Ja, sehr. Fotografieren ist mein Hobby.
(*b*) Ja, mein Fotogeschäft ist ein Weissach.
(*c*) Nein, ich war oft krank, als ich in der Druckerei gearbeitet habe.

4 Wann gehen Sie einkaufen?
(*a*) Als ich krank war.
(*b*) Wenn es wenig Betrieb gibt.
(*c*) Weil meine Frau im Geschäft mitarbeitet.

5 Warum haben Sie Ihre Doktorarbeit geschrieben?
(*a*) Weil ich Universitätslehrer werden wollte.
(*b*) Weil ich mich fürs Fotografieren interessiere.
(*c*) Weil es heutzutage wenig Betrieb gibt.

Was Sie wissen sollten

Housing in Germany

A very high proportion of the present German housing stock has been built since the Republic was founded in 1949. In more recent years, greater attention and care than was previously the case has been devoted to the renovation and modernisation of those older dwellings (**Altbauwohnungen**) which survived the bombing raids of the Second World War and the town planners' demolition programmes of the Fifties and Sixties. Lovingly restored **Jugendstil** (*Art Nouveau*) and **Art Deco** apartment blocks are nowadays to be seen in such cities as Düsseldorf and West Berlin.

Millions of **Sozialwohnungen** (in some respects comparable to *council housing* in Britain) have been provided for people on low incomes, for large families, and for handicapped or elderly people.

Whilst many Germans would like to own their own home, the proportion of the population that has actually achieved this ideal is still smaller than in Britain . High unit costs, largely attributable to the high standard of building generally demanded in Germany, together with a widespread preference for living in **Neubauwohnungen** or new dwellings, are perhaps the main reasons for this difference.

The renewal and upgrading of the housing stock in the five new **Länder** is proving to be a challenging and expensive task. Many of the **Altbauwohnungen** were at the time of reunification near the point of collapse through persistent neglect. The much-needed injection of capital has saved for posterity many of the more attractive examples of 19th and early 20th century building.

Schooling in Germany

As education in Germany is a matter for the individual states or **Länder,** there are almost as many education systems as there are **Länder**. This high degree of flexibility has proved an important factor in the incorporation into the Federal Republic of the five Eastern **Länder**. However, throughout Germany, compulsory schooling commences at the age of 6 with attendance at the **Grundschule** (*primary* or *elementary school*). After 4 years (6 years in Berlin) at the

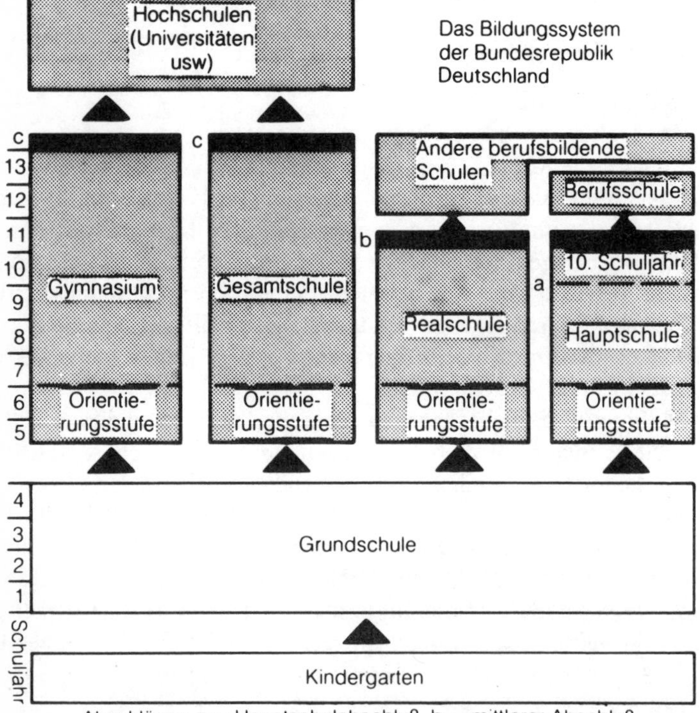

Abschlüsse: a = Hauptschulabschluß, b = mittlerer Abschluß,
c = Hochschulreife.

Grundschule, pupils usually have to choose between three kinds of secondary school (**die Hauptschule, die Realschule** and **das Gymnasium**), although this decision may sometimes be kept open for a further two years by attending a so-called **Orientierungsstufe** (lit. *orientation stage*).

Die Hauptschule is in certain respects comparable to the British *Secondary Modern School*, whilst **das Gymnasium**—although it provides a much broader education—may be compared to the British *Grammar School*. **Die Realschule** fits in between the other two schools and offers courses which tend to lead to careers in business and administration. In some **Länder**, the kinds of courses offered by these three schools are provided under one roof in the **Gesamtschule** or *Comprehensive School*.

Three types of school-leaving certificate are available corresponding to the three kinds of school. **Das Abitur**—the certificate normally obtained at the end of an 8-year academic course—is required for admission to university study.

Wichtige Redewendungen

How to

1 State what used to be the case.

Ich war	früher (mal)	Schriftsetzer.
Hans war		Lehrer.
Rita war		oft krank.
Wir waren		verheiratet.

Ich hatte	früher (mal)	einen ganz primitiven Fotoapparat.
Hans hatte		eine Wohnung in Heidelberg.
Rita hatte		auch samtags auf.
Wir hatten		Freunde in Australien.

2 Talk about past events with particular reference to (a) desires and wishes:

Ich wollte	eigentlich	Universitätslehrer werden
Hans wollte	immer	das eigene Geschäft.
Rita wollte	trotzdem	studieren.
Wir wollten	früher mal	in Berlin wohnen.

(*b*) *obligation, necessity:*

Ich mußte	damals noch	Kundenbesuche machen.
Hans mußte	lange	nachts arbeiten.
Rita mußte	früher mal	im Geschäft mitarbeiten.
Wir mußten	jahrelang	bei den Eltern wohnen.

(*c*) *ability, permission:*

Ich konnte	bisher	keine Stellung finden.
Hans konnte	damals noch	nur Deutsch (sprechen).
Rita konnte	jahrelang	vor dem Haus parken.
Wir konnten		am Wochende Freunde besuchen.

3 Offer advice or make a suggestion (to others or to oneself).
Ich sollte nicht unzufrieden sein.
Hans sollte nicht nachts arbeiten.
Rita sollte sich einen anderen Beruf aussuchen.
Wir sollten einkaufen gehen.

Fachgeschäfte *(specialist shops)*

die Bäckerei (-en) *baker's*
die Konditorei (-en) *cake shop*
der Gemüseladen (¨) *green-grocer's*
die Metzgerei (-en) *butcher's*
die Schlachterei (-en) *butcher's*
die Fleischerei (-en) *butcher's*
die Drogerie (-n) *drug-store*
die Apotheke (-n) *chemist's*
die Buchhandlung (-en) *bookshop*
das Zeitungsgeschäft *newsagent's*
der Waschsalon (-s) *launderette*
die chemische Reinigung *dry cleaner's*

Grammatik

1 Imperfect tense

In previous units, it has normally been the perfect tense that has been used in order to talk about past events. In this unit, a start has been made at introducing the so-called ***imperfect tense***. At this stage, only verbs which are very frequently found in the imperfect tense are dealt with, namely **haben** and **sein** and the modal verbs (**wollen, müssen, können, dürfen** and **sollen**). The imperfect tense will be dealt with in greater detail in a subsequent unit.

1.1 Haben, sein

Whilst it is perfectly correct to say:

> Ich habe früher mal einen Volkswagen gehabt. *I used to have a Volkswagen once.*

or

> Ich bin 10 Jahre lang Lehrer gewesen. *I was a teacher for 10 years.*

it is also very common to find:

> Ich hatte früher mal einen Volkswagen.
> Ich war 10 Jahre lang Lehrer.

In fact, the imperfect tense of **haben** and **sein** is frequently preferred even when the perfect tense is chosen for other verbs:

> Wir haben gespart, bis wir DM 10 000 hatten. *We saved until we had 10,000 marks.*
> Es war sehr spät, als ich gestern abend nach Hause gekommen bin. *It was very late when I got home (came home) yesterday evening.*

Note that for certain persons additional endings are required:

Ich hatte/war ...	Wir hatten/waren ...
Du hattest/warst ...	Ihr hattet/wart ...
Sie hatten/waren ...	Sie hatten/waren ...
Er (sie, es) hatte/war ...	Sie hatten/waren ...

1.2 Modal verbs

The modal verbs, like **haben** and **sein**, tend to be used more often in the imperfect tense than in the perfect tense.

The imperfect tense of the modal verbs is formed as follows:

	wollen	**müssen**	**können**	**dürfen**	**sollen**
Ich	wollte	mußte	konnte	durfte	sollte
Du	wolltest	mußtest	konntest	durftest	solltest
Sie	wollten	mußten	konnten	durften	sollten
Er / Sie / Es	wollte	mußte	konnte	durfte	sollte
Wir	wollten	mußten	konnten	durften	sollten
Ihr	wolltet	mußtet	konntet	durftet	solltet
Sie	wollten	mußten	konnten	durften	sollten
Sie	wollten	mußten	konnten	durften	sollten

Note that the ***Umlaut*** found in the infinitive forms of **müssen, können** and **dürfen** is not found in the imperfect tense forms.

The following examples, together with those from the **Wichtige Redewendungen** should serve to make clear the meaning of the various modal verbs when they are used in the imperfect tense.

Wir wollten gestern schwimmen gehen, aber das Wasser war zu kalt. *We wanted to/intended to go swimming yesterday, but the water was too cold.*
Mußtet Ihr lange auf einen Bus warten? *Did you have to wait long for a bus?*
Warum konntest du gestern abend nicht kommen? *Why couldn't you/weren't you able to come yesterday evening?*
Gerd durfte eine Woche lang nur Wasser trinken. *Gerd was allowed /permitted to drink only water for a week.*
Du solltest deine Mutter besuchen. *You ought to/should visit your mother.*

In the last example **sollen** is—strictly speaking—used in what is known as the ***subjunctive mood*** of the imperfect tense, whilst all the other examples are in the ***indicative mood***. (Whilst the indicative mood expresses matter of fact, the subjunctive mood expresses condition, hypothesis or contingency.) However, the imperfect tense forms of **sollen** are the same in both moods and it is in the subjunctive mood of the imperfect that **sollen** is most frequently used. Further examples using **sollen** are:

Sollte ich vielleicht nach Hause gehen? *Should I perhaps go home?*
Du solltest nicht so schnell essen. *You ought not to eat so quickly.*
Der Lehrer sollte langsamer sprechen. *The teacher ought to speak more slowly.*

2 Conjunctions

The term ***conjunction*** is given to words like *and*, *but* and *or* that are used to link together words, clauses or sentences. The most common conjunction, *and*, may be used for all three purposes:

*I like blackberry pie **and** ice-cream.*
*She drove home **and** went straight to bed.*
*Frank opened the door, **and** the dog bounded in.*

In German, certain conjunctions have an effect on the word order of the clause that they introduce. These are referred to as ***subordinating conjunctions***. Those conjunctions that have no such effect on the word order are called ***co-ordinating conjunctions***.

2.1 Co-ordinating conjunctions

The most common co-ordinating conjunctions in German are
und (*and*), **oder** (*or*), **aber** (*but*), **denn** (*for*).

Here are some examples of these conjunctions in use:

Bernd **und** Christel kommen zum Abendbrot.
Peter spricht gut Englisch **und** versteht auch Spanisch.
Peter spielt heute Tennis, **und** Maria besucht ihre Mutter.

Gehst du mit Gerd **oder** mit Rainer ins Kino?
Spielst du Tennis, **oder** gehst du ins Kino?

Meine Wohnung ist klein **aber** bequem.
Klaus wollte mitkommen, **aber** er hatte kein Geld.

Klaus konnte nicht mitkommen, **denn** er hatte kein Geld.

Note that a comma is used to separate ***sentences*** in the above examples.

Another co-ordinating conjunction that occurs quite frequently is **sondern** which is used to mean *but* in a special sense:

Er ist nicht Engländer **sondern** Deutscher.
Heute geht Nina nicht schwimmen, **sondern** sie spielt Tennis.

Note that in both these examples **sondern** is used to achieve a contrast between a negative and a positive notion.

2.2 Subordinating conjunctions

Subordinating conjunctions are so called, because they introduce a subordinate or dependent clause—that is, a clause which could not normally stand on its own, but depends upon the main clause. For example: *When you are ill* does not mean very much unless it occurs together with a main clause, such as *What do you do, when you are ill?* The German subordinating conjunctions illustrated in the **Dialog** of this **Lektion** are:

als (*when*), **bis** (*until*), **obwohl** (*although*), **weil** (*because*), **wenn** (*whenever, if*)

Look back to the **Dialog** and find the examples of these conjunctions. You will note that in all instances the verb has been sent to the end of the subordinate clause by the subordinating conjunction. Other conjunctions of this kind are:

bevor (*before*), **da** (*as, since*), **damit** (*so that*), **daß** (*that*), **nachdem** (*after*)

Here are examples of these conjunctions in use:

Bevor du nach Hause **gehst**, möchte ich mit dir sprechen.
Da es kalt **war**, wollte Bettina nicht schwimmen gehen.
Gibst du mir Geld, **damit** ich ins Kino mitkommen **kann**?
Ich weiß, **daß** du kein Geld **hast**.
Gehst du heute abend aus, **nachdem** du gegessen **hast**?

Note that, when the subordinate clause comes first, the subject and verb of the main clause are inverted. In German a subordinate clause and a main clause are always separated by a comma.

2.3 Adverbial conjunctions

Certain adverbs may be used to link clauses together and are referred to as ***adverbial conjunctions***. A few such conjunctions are:

dann (*then*), **deshalb** (*for that reason, that is why*), **sonst** (*otherwise*), **trotzdem** (*nevertheless*).

Since these conjunctions are essentially adverbs, their position is not restricted to the beginning of the clause:

Birgit kommt mit uns nach Hause, **dann** kann sie bei uns essen.
Birgit kommt mit uns nach Hause; sie kann **dann** bei uns essen.

Dieter hat kein Geld, **deshalb** kann er nicht mitkommen.
Dieter hat kein Geld; er kann **deshalb** nicht mitkommen.

Du mußt jetzt gehen, **sonst** kommst du zu spät.
Du mußt jetzt gehen; du kommst **sonst** zu spät.

Herr Braun ist sehr alt, **trotzdem** arbeitet er immer noch.
Herr Braun ist sehr alt; er arbeitet **trotzdem** immer noch.

Note that there is inversion of subject and verb after adverbial conjunctions when these occur at the beginning of the sentence or clause.

3 **Reflexive Verbs** (continued)

Some explanation of reflexive verbs was offered in section 5 of the **Grammatik** of **Lektion 8**. In each case, the reflexive pronoun was in the accusative case. There are also reflexive verbs in which the reflexive pronoun is in the ***dative*** case. One such verb occurred in **Dialog 12**: **sich etwas leisten** *to afford something*. Since the **sich** form of the reflexive pronoun is the same in both accusative and dative, the difference between the two verbs doesn't become apparent until some other form of the reflexive pronoun is needed:

Ich interessiere **mich** (*Accusative*) fürs Fotografieren.
BUT Das kann ich **mir** (*Dative*) nicht leisten.

Here are examples illustrating the use of the verb **sich leisten**, so that you are able to see the various forms that the dative reflexive pronoun takes:

Das kann ich **mir** nicht leisten.
Kannst du **dir** dieses Zimmer leisten?
Können Sie **sich** ein neues Auto leisten?
Maria kann **sich** jetzt teuere Kleidung leisten.

Wir können **uns** eine Neubauwohnung leider nicht leisten.
Könnt ihr **euch** ein paar Tage in Paris leisten?
Können Sie **sich** ein Zimmer im Hotel »Astoria« leisten?
Werner und Dagmar können **sich** die Busfahrt nicht leisten.

Other verbs which have a dative reflexive pronoun include:

Sich etwas aussuchen *to choose something for oneself*
Such dir etwas aus. *Choose something for yourself.*
Sich vorstellen *to imagine, visualize*
Stell dir vor! *Just imagine!*

Übungen

ÜBUNG 12.1 Sagen Sie es anders.

Beispiele: Wo bist du die ganze Zeit gewesen?
Wo warst du die ganze Zeit?
Ich habe ein paar Tage Urlaub gehabt.
Ich hatte ein paar Tage Urlaub.

1 Und wo bist denn du gewesen?
2 Ich bin mit meiner Freundin in Österreich gewesen.
3 Habt ihr schönes Wetter gehabt?
4 Ja, wir haben Glück gehabt.
5 Seid ihr in Wien gewesen?
6 Nein, wir sind in Salzburg und Innsbruck gewesen.
7 Seid ihr in Salzburg im Mozarthaus gewesen?
8 Nein, wir haben leider keine Zeit dazu gehabt.

ÜBUNG 12.2 Welches Modalverb paßt?

durfte, konnte, mußte, sollte(n) oder **wollte**?

Sabine Krause: Heute . . . (1) . . . ich in der Tiefgarage parken, weil ich sonst keinen Parkplatz finden . . . (2) . . . Ich . . . (3) . . . eigentlich direkt hinter dem »Kaufhof« parken, aber da . . . (4) . . . ich nicht, weil Parken dort jetzt verboten ist. Es . . . (5) . . . eigentlich im Stadtzentrum mehr Parkplätze auf der Straße geben.

Henny Naumann: Ach was! Im Stadtzentrum . . . (6) . . . Autos verboten sein. Ich . . . (7) . . . heute schnell ein paar Sachen einkaufen, . . . (8) . . . aber nur langsam vorwärts kommen, weil so viele Autofahrer auf dem Fußweg geparkt hatten. Das . . . (9) . . . man früher nicht machen. Ich . . . (10) . . . manchmal sogar auf die Straße gehen, was natürlich sehr gefährlich (*dangerous*) ist.

ÜBUNG 12.3

(A) Join the pairs of sentences together with **weil**.

Beispiele: Ich mußte nachts arbeiten. Ich war deshalb oft krank.
Weil ich nachts arbeiten mußte, war ich oft krank.
Ich war so oft krank. Ich mußte mir deshalb einen anderen Beruf suchen.
Weil ich so oft krank war, mußte ich mir einen anderen Beruf suchen.

1 Wir wollten uns ein eigenes Geschäft kaufen. Wir mußten deshalb mehrere Jahre lang sparen.
2 Ich habe mich immer fürs Fotografieren interessiert. Ich habe mir deshalb ein Fotogeschäft gekauft.
3 Ich bin mit meinem neuen Beruf zufrieden. Ich bin deshalb jetzt nur selten (*seldom*) krank.
4 Meine Frau und zwei Söhne arbeiten im Geschäft mit. Ich kann deshalb ein paar Stunden für mich allein haben.
5 Wir müssen abends noch Kundenbesuche machen. Wir können deshalb nur selten zusammen ausgehen.
6 Mein dritter Sohn interessiert sich nicht für unser Geschäft. Er hat sich deshalb einen anderen Beruf ausgesucht.
7 Wir sind fünf Personen in der Familie. Wir brauchen deshalb einen ziemlich großen Wagen.
8 Hier haben wir sehr viele Freunde und Bekannte. Wir wohnen deshalb so gerne in Weissach.

(B) Now join the clauses together using **denn**. You will need to reorganise the information in each pair of clauses:

Beispiele: Ich mußte nachts arbeiten. Ich war deshalb oft krank.

Ich war oft krank, denn ich mußte nachts arbeiten.
Ich war so oft krank. Ich mußte mir deshalb einen anderen Beruf suchen.
Ich mußte mir einen anderen Beruf suchen, denn ich war so oft krank.

ÜBUNG 12.4 Join the pairs of sentences together with **obwohl**.

Beispiele: Ich war gestern nach der Arbeit sehr müde (*tired*). Ich habe trotzdem noch zwei Stunden Tennis gespielt.
Obwohl ich gestern nach der Arbeit sehr müde war, habe ich noch zwei Stunden Tennis gespielt.
Es war dann ziemlich spät. Ich bin trotzdem noch trinken gegangen.
Obwohl es dann ziemlich spät war, bin ich noch trinken gegangen.

1 Ich verdiene nur wenig Geld. Ich habe trotzdem viel Geld für Bier ausgegeben.
2 Es war dann sehr spät. Ich bin trotzdem noch auf eine Party gegangen.
3 Ich mußte am nächsten Tag arbeiten. Ich bin trotzdem erst um 4 Uhr nach Hause gefahren.
4 Ich hatte gar kein Geld mehr. Ich bin trotzdem mit einem Taxi nach Hause gefahren.
5 Meine Eltern haben natürlich schon geschlafen. Ich mußte sie leider wecken (*waken*).
6 Sie waren sehr böse (*angry*) auf mich. Sie haben trotzdem das Taxi bezahlt.
7 Ich stehe normalerweise um 7 Uhr auf. Heute hat mich mein Vater trotzdem schon um halb 7 geweckt.
8 Ich hatte nur zwei Stunden geschlafen. Ich mußte trotzdem aufstehen und zur Arbeit gehen.

ÜBUNG 12.5 **Was paßt wo?**

Use each of the following conjunctions once to fill the gaps in the text:

damit, daß, als, oder, wenn, aber, obwohl, bis

Jochen: Kommst du heute nachmittag mit mir ins Kino, . . . (1) . . . mußt du noch arbeiten?
Anke: Du weißt ja, . . . (2) . . . ich kein Geld habe!

Jochen: . . . (3) . . . du willst, leihe (*lend*) ich dir 10 Mark, . . . (4) . . . du mitkommen kannst.
Anke: Das ist sehr nett von dir, . . . (5) . . . das mache ich lieber nicht, . . . (6) . . . ich normalerweise sehr gerne ins Kino gehe. . . . (7) . . . ich aber am Freitag wieder Geld bekomme, bleibe ich lieber zu Hause.
Jochen: Gut, das verstehe ich. . . . (8) . . . ich letzte Woche kein Geld hatte, bin ich auch zu Hause geblieben. Freitag bist du aber verabredet—du kommst mit mir ins Kino!

Verstehen Sie?

1 Konversation

Deutsche Bank 

Sind Sie mit Ihrem Beruf zufrieden?

Frau Becker is conducting a survey on job satisfaction. She stops Lothar Pick and asks him a few questions.

Frau Becker Entschuldigen Sie, bitte. Ich mache eine Umfrage und möchte Ihnen ein paar Fragen stellen, wenn Sie nichts dagegen haben.

Lothar Pick Also, gut. Was möchten Sie wissen?

Frau Becker Sind Sie 1. berufstätig, 2. arbeitslos, 3. arbeitsunfähig oder 4. pensioniert?

Lothar Pick Ich bin berufstätig. Ich bin Bankangestellter bei der Deutschen Bank.

Frau Becker Und sind Sie mit Ihrem Beruf 1. sehr zufrieden, 2. zufrieden, 3. relativ zufrieden, 4. relativ unzufrieden oder 5. unzufrieden?

Lothar Pick Na, relativ zufrieden würde ich sagen. Eigentlich wollte ich Anglistik studieren, nachdem ich mein Abitur gemacht hatte. Aber heutzutage ist es ja für Akademiker—und vor allem für Anglisten—sehr schwer, eine Stellung zu finden. Deshalb habe ich mich für eine Banklehre entschlossen.

Frau Becker Und warum sind Sie mit Ihrem Beruf »relativ zufrieden«? Weil Sie gut verdienen?

Lothar Pick Ach nein! So viel Geld verdiene ich noch nicht. Erstens finde ich die Arbeit interessant. Zweitens habe ich gute Chancen, in meinem Beruf voranzukommen, wenn ich fleißig arbeite und die verschiedenen Prüfungen bestehe. Und drittens habe ich die Möglichkeit, später im Ausland zu arbeiten und von meinen Sprachkenntnissen Gebrauch zu machen.

Frau Becker Gut, das wäre's. Vielen Dank.

Lothar Pick Bitte schön.

die Umfrage (-n) *survey*
berufstätig *working, employed*
arbeitslos *unemployed*
arbeitsunfähig *unable to work*
pensioniert *pensioned off, retired*
zufrieden *satisfied*
die Anglistik *study of English language & literature*
der Akademiker (-) *graduate*
sich entschließen für *to decide on*
vorankommen *to get on, make progress*
fleißig *industrious(ly)*
die Prüfung (-en) *examination*
bestehen *to pass (exams)*
der Gebrauch *use*
Das wäre's *That's all*

Richtig (R) oder Falsch (F)?

1 Frau Becker möchte Lothar Pick ein paar Fragen stellen.
2 Lothar arbeitet bei der Dresdner Bank.
3 Er ist mit seinem Beruf relativ zufrieden.
4 Lothar wollte nach dem Abitur Germanistik studieren.
5 Er hat sich aber trotzdem für eine Banklehre entschlossen.
6 Für Akademiker ist es meistens leicht, eine Stellung zu finden.
7 Lothar muß die verschiedenen Prüfungen bestehen, wenn er vorankommen will.
8 Lothar kann vielleicht später im Ausland arbeiten.

2 Lesetext

Read through the following questions and then try to find the answers in the text opposite:

1 Which years are considered by many to number amongst the best?
2 What are the three reasons given for this being so?

3 Whom, according to the advertisement, is it a good time to consult?
4 Why is it claimed here that the new form of saving, 'insurance saving', offers double security?
5 What do both aspects together provide?

Die Zukunft planen. Mit der Sparkasse vorsorgen.

Für viele zählen die ersten Jahre im Berufsleben zu den schönsten. Jetzt machen sich Studium oder Ausbildung bezahlt, jetzt kann man Pläne schmieden und die Zukunft planen. Ein guter Zeitpunkt, um mit dem Geldberater der Sparkasse zu sprechen. Über eine neue Sparform, die genau paßt:

Versicherungssparen.

Die Grundidee: Beim Versicherungssparen geht man doppelt auf Nummer Sicher. Erstens wird aus den Sparbeträgen eine ansehnliche Summe, die man für später einplanen kann. Und zweitens sorgt eine Risikoversicherung dafür, daß die Familie abgesichert ist. Mit beidem zusammen hat Ihre Zukunft eine ganz solide Basis.

Sprechen Sie mit unserem Geldberater über das Versicherungssparen.

Wenn's um Geld geht-Sparkasse

die Zukunft *future*
vorsorgen *to make provisions*
zählen *to count*
die Ausbildung *training*
der Betrag (¨e) *amount*
ansehnlich *considerable, impressive*
dafür sorgen, daß *to see to it that*
absichern *to safeguard*
die Versicherung *insurance*

13 Und was machte dein Vater?

In this unit you will learn more about the uses and forms of the imperfect tense. The **Dialog** illustrates how, in conversation, the imperfect tense sometimes occurs in amongst the more predominant perfect tense.

Dialog

Theo Rauch has had his interest in the immediate post-war period aroused by his teacher. He asks his grandmother, Maria Falk, about her experiences of that period.

Theo Rauch Oma, heute hat uns unser Lehrer von der »Stunde Null« erzählt. Hast du nicht damals in Ostpreußen auf dem Lande gewohnt?

Maria Falk Bis zum Kriegsende wohnten wir dort, aber im August 1945 brachte mich meine Mutter hierher nach Berlin.

Theo Rauch Habt ihr sofort eine Unterkunft gefunden? Waren nicht viele Wohnungen zerstört?

Maria Falk Doch, Berlin lag größtenteils in Ruinen. Tante Gerda hat uns aber aufgenommen. Sie hatte damals eine Villa im Grunewald.

Theo Rauch Wie alt warst du damals, Oma?

Maria Falk Da war ich 13 Jahre alt und ging noch zur Schule. Als wir bei Tante Gerda wohnten, besuchte ich ein Wirtschaftsgymnasium in Wilmersdorf.

Theo Rauch Bist du mit der S-bahn dorthin gefahren?

Maria Falk Zuerst mußte ich zu Fuß in die Schule gehen. Jeden Tag 10 Kilometer hin und zurück. Erst später konnte ich mit der S-bahn fahren.

Theo Rauch Und was machte dein Vater, wohnte er auch bei Tante Gerda?

Maria Falk Leider nicht. Er war 5 Jahre lang in russischer Kriegsgefangenschaft. Ich hab' ihn nicht mehr erkannt, als er endlich zurückkehrte.

Theo Rauch Hattet ihr damals genug zu essen?

Maria Falk Wir aßen, was es gerade gab. Und es gab natürlich sehr wenig. Durch Beziehungen bekamen wir manchmal zusätzliche Lebensmittel.

Theo Rauch Das waren aber harte Zeiten!

die Stunde Null *the period immediately after the Second World War* (lit. *Zero hour*)
auf dem Lande *in the country*
Ostpreußen *East Prussia*
das Kriegsende *end of the war*
bringen (bringt, brachte, gebracht) *to bring*
die Unterkunft (¨e) *accommodation, somewhere to live*
zerstören *to destroy*
größtenteils *for the greater part*
aber *however*
aufnehmen (*sep.*) **(nimmt auf, nahm auf, aufgenommen)** *to take in*
die Villa (Villen) *villa*
der Grunewald *an area of Berlin, partly forest and partly suburb*
Wilmersdorf *a suburb of Berlin*
die S-Bahn (=Stadtbahn) *railway network within a city, mostly above ground*
russisch *Russian*
die Gefangenschaft *captivity*
in russischer Kriegsgefangenschaft sein *to be a Russian prisoner-of-war*
zurückkehren*(*sep.*) *to return*
genug *enough*
was es gerade gab *whatever there happened to be*
sehr wenig *very little*
die Beziehungen (*fem. pl.*) *connections, contacts*
bekommen (bekommt, bekam, bekommen) *to get*
manchmal *sometimes*
zusätzlich *additional, supplementary*
die Lebensmittel (*neut. pl.*) *food(stuffs), groceries*
hart *hard*

Fragen zum Dialog

1 Richtig (R) oder Falsch (F)?

1 Theo hat heute in der Schule etwas über die »Stunde Null« gelernt.
2 Bis August 1945 wohnte Maria in Ostpreußen.
3 Nur wenige Wohnungen waren in Berlin zerstört.
4 Maria und ihre Mutter durften bei Tante Gerda wohnen.
5 1945 war Maria 13 Jahre alt.

6 Maria konnte von Anfang an mit der S-Bahn zur Schule fahren.
7 Marias Vater war 5 Jahre lang in britischer Kriegsgefangenschaft.
8 Als er aus der Gefangenschaft zurückkehrte, erkannte Maria ihren Vater sofort.
9 Damals gab es sehr wenig zu essen.
10 Manchmal bekam man durch Beziehungen etwas mehr zu essen.

2 Welche Antwort paßt?

1 Habt ihr sofort eine Unterkunft gefunden?
(*a*) Nein, bis zum Kriegsende haben wir dort gewohnt.
(*b*) Ja, Tante Gerda hat uns aufgenommen.
(*c*) Ja, damals hatte sie eine Villa im Grunewald.

2 Waren viele Wohnungen in Berlin zerstört?
(*a*) Ja, Berlin lag größtenteils in Ruinen.
(*b*) Doch, Berlin lag größtenteils in Ruinen.
(*c*) Nein, wir wohnten damals auf dem Lande.

3 Gingst du damals noch zur Schule, Oma?
(*a*) Nein, zuerst mußte ich zu Fuß in die Schule gehen.
(*b*) Nein, erst später konnte ich mit der S-Bahn fahren.
(*c*) Ja, ich besuchte ein Wirtschaftsgymnasium in Wilmersdorf.

4 Wohnte dein Vater auch bei Tante Gerda?
(*a*) Tante Gerda hatte damals eine Villa im Grunewald.
(*b*) Leider nicht. Er war 5 Jahre lang in russischer Gefangenschaft.
(*c*) Ich hab' ihn nicht erkannt, als er endlich zurückkehrte.

5 Hattet ihr damals genug zu essen?
(*a*) Leider nicht. Erst später konnte ich mit der S-Bahn fahren.
(*b*) Es gab natürlich sehr wenig zu essen, aber durch Beziehungen bekamen wir zusätzliche Lebensmittel.
(*c*) Ja, jeden Tag 10 Kilometer hin und zurück.

Was Sie wissen sollten

Changes in the political status of Berlin

As the capital of the Third Reich, Berlin was at the end of the Second World War divided into four sectors (**Sektoren**), administered jointly by the four Allied Powers occupying Germany (France, Great Britain, the Soviet Union and the United States), just as the territory of the Third Reich to the West of the Oder-Neiße-Line was divided into four zones of occupation (**Besatzungszonen**). A deterioration in the relationship between the Western Allies and the Soviet Union led to the setting up of two separate German states (the Federal Republic of Germany and the German Democratic Republic) in 1949.

Berlin, however, remained under Four-Power Status for 45 years, even though East Berlin had been declared **Hauptstadt der DDR** and West Berlin was regarded as a **Land** of the Federal Republic. The ideological conflict between East and West often revealed itself in crises in Berlin—the Berlin Blockade and Air Lift of 1948/9, the Workers' Revolt of 1953 and the building of the Berlin Wall in 1961 are the most striking examples. After the Four-Power Agreement on Berlin in 1971 which sought to diminish the risk of conflict over the divided city, the flow of traffic between West Berlin and the Federal Republic through the GDR improved, as did access for West Berliners to East Berlin and the rest of the GDR, though GDR citizens were with few exceptions still prevented from travelling to the West.

It was not until the collapse of the 'socialist' system in the GDR in the autumn of 1989 that the inhabitants of Berlin were able once again to move freely between the Eastern and Western sectors of the city. With the absorption of the GDR into the Federal Republic in July 1990, Berlin finally relinquished its Four-Power-Status and became a re-united self-governing city.

Wichtige Redewendungen

How to

Report events and describe situations in the past, particularly when writing.

Ich wohnte	damals	auf dem Lande.
Hans wohnte	bis zum Kriegsende	in Berlin.
Wir wohnten	Jahre lang	in München.

Im August 1945	brachte mich meine Mutter	nach Berlin.
Später	brachten uns unsere Eltern	hierher.

Berlin	lag	im Jahre 1945	in Ruinen.
Viele Städte	lagen	nach dem Kriege	

Ich aß	soviel wie möglich.
Wir aßen	,was es gerade gab.

Als wir bei Tante Gerda wohnten,	ging ich	noch zur Schule.
Damals	gingen wir	oft in die Kirche.

Die Monate (*months of the year*)

der Januar	**der April**	**der Juli**	**der Oktober**
der Februar	**der Mai**	**der August**	**der November**
der März	**der Juni**	**der September**	**der Dezember**

Zeitausdrücke (*expressions of time*)

im Monat August *in the month of August*
im August *in August*
in diesem August *this August*
Anfang (Ende/Mitte) August *At the beginning (end/in the middle) of August*
Der wievielte ist heute? *What's the date today?*
Welches Datum haben wir heute? *What's the date today?*
Heute ist der 3. (dritte) August. *It's the 3rd of August today.*
Heute haben wir den 3. (dritten) August. *It's the 3rd of August today.*
Am 4. (vierten) August hat Christine Geburtstag. *It's Christine's birthday on 4th August.*
Im Jahre 1982 starb der Prinz. *or*
1982 starb der Prinz. *In 1982 the Prince died.*

Grammatik

1 **Imperfect tense** (continued)

In **Dialog 13** further examples of the imperfect tense have been introduced. As with the perfect tense, it is important to distinguish between weak, strong and mixed verbs.

1.1 Weak verbs

The imperfect tense of weak verbs is formed by taking the stem of the infinitive of the verb in question (e.g. **wohn-**) and adding endings as shown below:

Ich wohnt**e** Du wohnt**est** Sie wohnt**en** Er / Sie / Es } wohnt**e**	Wir wohnt**en** Ihr wohnt**et** Sie wohnt**en** Sie wohnt**en**

When the stem of an infinitive ends in a **-d** or a **-t**, an extra **-e-** is needed:

antworten ich antwortete
reden du redetest

1.2 Strong verbs

As indicated in **Lektion 10,** the vocabulary list at the end of this book assists you with strong and mixed verbs by listing after each verb the three most important forms—(*a*) the third person singular of the present tense, (*b*) the third person singular of the imperfect tense and (*c*) the past participle:

e.g. gehen* (geht, ging, gegangen)

To this third person singular form endings are added for all the other persons except the **ich-** form:

Ich ging Du ging**st** Sie ging**en** Er / Sie / Es } ging	Wir ging**en** Ihr ging**t** Sie ging**en** Sie ging**en**

An extra **-e-** is needed to 'oil the works' in the **du** and **ihr** forms when the third person singular form ends in a **-t** or **-d**:

halten (hält, **hielt**, gehalten) *to stop, hold*
Du hieltest Ihr hieltet
finden (findet, **fand**, gefunden)
Du fandest Ihr fandet

1.3 Mixed verbs

As with strong verbs, the imperfect tense forms of mixed verbs have to be learned and these are therefore listed in the vocabulary at the end of the book. Mixed verbs, however, take the same endings as weak verbs in the imperfect tense:

bringen (bringt, **brachte,** gebracht)	
Ich brach**te** Du brach**test** Sie brach**ten** Er / Sie / Es } brach**te**	Wir brach**ten** Ihr brach**tet** Sie brach**ten** Sie brach**ten**

There are two verbs that each have both a weak and a mixed version of the imperfect tense and of the past participle:

senden (sendet, sandte/sendete, gesandt/gesendet) *to send*
wenden (wendet, wandte/wendete, gewandt/gewendet) *to turn*

Note that when these verbs behave as weak verbs, the imperfect tense and past participle take the extra **-e-** between the **-d** and the **-t**, but that—rather unexpectedly—no extra **-e-** is taken when the mixed pattern is followed.

1.4 Separable verbs in the imperfect tense

Verbs containing a separable prefix (e.g. **abholen** or **aufstehen**) or 'double' verbs (such as **kennenlernen**) behave as follows in the imperfect tense:

(*a*) Separation of prefix occurs in straightforward questions or statements:

Franz **holte** seine Freundin vom Bahnhof **ab**.
Maria **stand** am Tag ihrer Prüfung um 5 Uhr **auf**.
Lerntet Ihr Herrn Plötz durch einen Freund **kennen**?

(*b*) Prefix and verb join together in a subordinate clause:

Es war 14 Uhr 30, als Franz seine Freundin vom Bahnhof **abholte**.
Da Maria um 5 Uhr **aufstand**, was sie schon zu Mittag sehr müde.

Als wir Herrn Plötz **kennenlernten**, arbeitete er bei Siemens.

1.5 Uses of the imperfect tense

It is not easy to give hard and fast rules for the use of the imperfect tense, since German-speakers often use the imperfect and the perfect tenses in the same sentence in an apparently indiscriminate manner, as in the **Dialog**.

Generally speaking, however, the imperfect tense is predominantly used in the written language, especially in narrative fiction and non-fiction and in newspaper reporting. You will also find this tense being used in formal talks and lectures.

The following brief extract from a children's story illustrates the use of the imperfect tense in narrative fiction:

. . . Sie **konnten** aber die Stadt Bremen an einem Tag nicht erreichen und **kamen** abends in einen Wald, wo sie übernachten **wollten**. Der Esel und der Hund **legten** sich unter einen großen Baum, die Katze und der Hahn **machten** sich in die Äste, der Hahn aber **flog** bis in die Spitze, wo es am sichersten für ihn war . . .

»*Die Bremer Stadtmusikanten*«, Gebrüder Grimm

. . . They were, however, unable to reach the city of Bremen in one day and in the evening went into a forest where they planned to spend the night. The ass and the dog lay down under a big tree; the cat and the cockerel made their way up into the boughs; but the cockerel flew up to the (tree-)top where it was safest for him . . .

"*The Bremen Street Musicians*", Brothers Grimm

Although in the everyday conversational narration of events and in informal writing (e.g. personal letters) it is the perfect tense that predominates, examples of the imperfect tense do sometimes occur in these contexts (as illustrated in the **Dialog**). It is sometimes claimed that this use of the imperfect tense is more frequently encountered in North Germany.

Conversely, you will sometimes find the perfect tense being used in contexts in which the imperfect tense predominates. It is common, for example, for a newspaper report to contain one instance of the perfect tense in the first sentence, whilst the rest of the article is written in the imperfect tense:

Tausende verbringen erste Sommertage in Blechlawinen

Sonnenschein und Temperaturen bis zu 25 Grad und darüber **haben** am Gründonnerstag und Karfreitag in Baden-Württemberg Tausende ins Freie

gelockt. Auf den Autobahnen und »Hauptverkehrsadern« des Landes **quälte** sich eine Blechlawine in Richtung Süden.
. . . In Freiburg **gab** es mit 26,3 Grad den ersten Sommertag dieses Jahres. Bisher **galt** für Freiburg als frühester erster Sommertag der 6. April 1961.

Thousands spend first days of summer in mammoth columns of traffic (lit. *avalanches of metal*)

Sunshine and temperatures up to 25°C and above tempted thousands into the open air in Baden-Württemberg on Maundy Thursday and Good Friday. On the State's motorways and main arteries a vast column of traffic struggled its way towards the South.
. . . In Freiburg (a temperature of) 26.3°C brought (lit. *there was*) *the first day of summer this year. Previously (the record for) the earliest first day of summer in Freiburg had been* (lit. *was regarded as*) *6th April* 1961.

2 Word order (pronominal object)

You may have noticed that the first sentence of the **Dialog** seems a little strange in that the subject **unser Lehrer** is not where it might be expected in a sentence of this kind, i.e. next to the verb, but in fourth position after the indirect object **uns**:

1	2	3	4	5	6
Heute	hat	uns	unser Lehrer	von der »Stunde Null«	erzählt.

This only happens when the object (direct or indirect) is a pronoun and the subject is a noun. Otherwise the expected word order is adhered to:

Heute hat unser Lehrer der Klasse von der »Stunde Null« erzählt.
or Heute hat er uns von der »Stunde Null« erzählt.

Further examples of the pronominal object preceding the subject were given in the **Wichtige Redewendungen**:

1	2	3	4	5
Im August 1945	brachte	mich	meine Mutter	nach Berlin.
Später	brachten	uns	unsere Eltern	hierher.

Übungen

ÜBUNG 13.1 Welche Antwort paßt?

1 Der wievielte ist heute?
(*a*) Am 5. Mai.
(*b*) Anfang Juni.
(*c*) Heute haben wir den 3. Juli.

2 Und wann fahrt ihr in Urlaub?
(*a*) Ende Juli.
(*b*) Im Jahre 1986.
(*c*) Heute ist der 7. März.

3 Und wohin fahrt ihr?
(*a*) Im Monat August.
(*b*) Nach Amerika.
(*c*) In Paris.

4 Wie lange bleibt ihr dort?
(*a*) Mitte August.
(*b*) Drei Wochen.
(*c*) Am 16. August.

5 Wann seid ihr wieder zu Hause?
(*a*) Am Freitag, dem 22. August.
(*b*) Im September.
(*c*) Zu Mittag.

6 Gut! Möchtet ihr dann zu meiner Party kommen?
(*a*) Wann hast du Geburtstag?
(*b*) Wann sind wir wieder zu Hause?
(*c*) Wann denn? Schon am Freitag, dem 22. August?

7 Nein! Erst am Samstag, dem 23. August.
(*a*) Am Donnerstag sind wir noch in New York.
(*b*) Gut. Dann kommen wir.
(*c*) Am Samstag sind wir wieder zu Hause.

8 Am 23. August hab' ich nämlich Geburtstag.
(*a*) Und wie alt wirst du?
(*b*) Und wann hast du Geburtstag?
(*c*) Und der wievielte ist heute?

ÜBUNG 13.2 Lesen Sie.

Trudi stand um 7 Uhr auf. Ein paar Sekunden lang sah sie ihren Mann Peter an. Er schlief noch. Sie zog ihren Bademantel an, ging in die Küche und kochte Kaffee. Sie schaute zum Fenster hinaus. Im Park spielten schon Kinder. Trudi setzte sich ins Wohnzimmer, machte das Radio an und trank eine Tasse Kaffee. »Wird er mir glauben?«, dachte sie und lief ins Schlafzimmer, wo sie Peter aus einem tiefen (*deep*) Schlaf weckte.

You have just read an extract from a novel which is written in the imperfect tense. Imagine you are Trudi re-telling her story to a friend, using the perfect tense:

> ***Ich bin um 7 Uhr aufgestanden. Ein paar Sekunden lang habe ich meinen Mann Peter angesehen . . .***

ÜBUNG 13.3 **Was paßt wo?**

Complete the story below by using each of the following verbs once:

(*a*) arbeitete	(*b*) dachte	(*c*) trank	(*d*) sah	(*e*) sagte
(*f*) wartete	(*g*) stand	(*h*) fuhr	(*i*) ging	(*j*) schlug

An diesem vielleicht wichtigsten Dienstag in seinem Leben . . . (1) . . . Karl wie immer um 5 Uhr 30 auf, . . . (2) . . . schnell eine Tasse Kaffee, . . . (3) . . . seiner Mutter, »Tschüs, Mutti« und . . . (4) . . . mit der Straßenbahn bis zum Bahnhof Zoo. Er . . . (5) . . . nämlich in einem kleinen Zeitungsgeschäft in der Fasanenstraße. Heute . . . (6) . . . er aber nicht ins Geschäft, sondern in die Kantstraße, wo er vor dem »Theater des Westens« auf Renate . . . (7) . . . Er . . . (8) . . . an seine Mutter und an seinen Chef, Herrn Krämer. Er würde sie wahrscheinlich nie wiedersehen! Dann . . . (9) . . . er Renate um die Ecke kommen. Ihm . . . (10) . . . das Herz bis zum Hals. Sie wollte also doch mit!

ÜBUNG 13.4 Rearrange the following sentences in the most appropriate order:

Ein Deutscher versucht sein Glück in Amerika

1 Er hat aber trotzdem Schreiben und Lesen gelernt.
2 In wenigen Monaten lernte er Englisch und bekam eine gutbezahlte Stellung in New York.
3 Mit 12 Jahren mußte er arbeiten gehen, um Geld für die Familie zu verdienen.
4 Damals mußte er ohne Schuhe in die Schule gehen.
5 Nach 30 Jahren in Amerika kehrte er als reicher (*rich*) Mann nach Deutschland zurück.
6 Als Kind wohnte Franz Bauer mit seinen drei Brüdern und zwei Schwestern in Berlin.
7 Da er keine Arbeit in Berlin fand, versuchte er sein Glück in Amerika.

8 Als es in den Zwanziger Jahren viel Arbeitslosigkeit in Deutschland gab, verlor auch Franz seine Stellung.

ÜBUNG 13.5 Berichten Sie.

Look back to **Lektion 10, Übung 10.5:** ***Der Lebenslauf des deutschen Schriftstellers Heinrich Böll.*** Use the information to write a formal report (in the Imperfect Tense) on the life of the author. Note that the first sentence stays the same in both versions:

(*a*) ***1917 ist Heinrich Böll am 21. Dezember in Köln geboren.***
(*b*) ***Von 1924 bis 1928 besuchte er die Volksschule Köln-Raderthal.***

You will need to look up in the vocabulary list the Imperfect Tense forms of some of the Strong Verbs.

Verstehen Sie?

1 Konversation

Lutz Bönzli is conducting research into post-war living conditions in Berlin. He approaches an elderly woman, Edith Meyer, who is sitting on a park bench and asks her about her experiences of that period.

Lutz Bönzli Guten Tag! Darf ich Sie bitte einen Augenblick stören? Ich heiße Lutz Bönzli und bin Forschungsassistent an der Freien Universität. Ich interessiere mich für die Lebensbedingungen hier in Berlin gleich nach dem Zweiten Weltkrieg. Waren Sie zufällig zu der Zeit in Berlin wohnhaft?

Edith Meyer Ja, sicher. Ich bin im Frühjahr 1945 mit meinen Kindern vor den Russen aus Ostpreußen geflüchtet. Da ich Verwandte in Berlin hatte, sind wir dann hier geblieben, auch nach der Eroberung der Stadt durch die Russen.

Lutz Bönzli In welchem Stadtteil wohnten Sie damals?

Edith Meyer In Charlottenburg. Wir waren zwar 6 Leute in einem Zimmer, aber das war damals üblich. Die Wohnungsnot war sehr groß, erstens weil die Bombenangriffe so viele Wohnungen zerstört hatten und zweitens, weil es so viele Flüchtlinge in Berlin gab.

Lutz Bönzli Waren Sie zu der Zeit berufstätig?

Edith Meyer Berufstätig würde ich das lieber nicht nennen! Ich war direkt nach dem Krieg eine der sogenannten »Trümmerfrauen«. Ich habe beim Sortieren der Backsteine von zerstörten Gebäuden mitgeholfen. Das war harte Arbeit, aber es hat auch Spaß gemacht.

Lutz Bönzli Da Sie Ihren Mann nicht erwähnt haben, nehme ich an, daß er in den Krieg mußte.

Edith Meyer Ja, leider ist er dann bei Stalingrad gefallen. Wir waren 8 Jahre verheiratet, aber in den letzten 4 Jahren hatte ich ihn nur zweimal kurz gesehen, als er Urlaub hatte. Meine Kinder haben ihren Vater eigentlich nie gekannt.

Lutz Bönzli Ja, so ist es vielen anderen Familien leider auch ergangen.

der Augenblick(-e) *moment*
stören *to disturb*
die Forschung (-en) *research*
die Bedingung (-en) *condition*
wohnhaft *resident*
das Frühjahr *spring*
flüchten (vor +*dat.*) *to flee (from)*
die Eroberung *taking*
der Stadtteil (-e) *part of the city*
üblich *usual*
die Wohnungsnot *housing shortage*
der Angriff (-e) *attack*
der Flüchtling (-e) *refugee*
die Trümmer (*pl.*) *rubble, ruins*
der Backstein (-e) *brick*
erwähnen *to mention*
annehmen *to assume*
fallen *to fall, die in battle*
es ist ihm schlecht ergangen *he fared badly*

Richtig (R) oder Falsch (F)?

1 Lutz Bönzli ist Forschungsassistent an der Technischen Universität Berlin.
2 Er fragt Edith Meyer, ob sie gleich nach dem Krieg in Berlin wohnte.
3 Edith Meyer kam 1945 vor dem Ende des Krieges nach Berlin.
4 Verwandte in Charlottenburg nahmen sie und ihre Kinder auf.
5 Sie hatte damals ihr eigenes Zimmer.
6 Direkt nach dem Krieg arbeitete sie als »Trümmerfrau«.
7 Ihr Mann kehrte 1946 aus sowjetischer Gefangenschaft zurück.
8 Ihre Kinder waren 4 Jahre alt, als sie ihren Vater kennenlernten.

2 Lesetext

Read through the following questions and then try to find the answers in the text below:

1 How is the sculptor, artist and action painter Joseph Beuys described in the first sentence?
2 Why is he a very controversial artist?
3 Why were his sculptures regarded as innovative in the 1970s?
4 Why are some sceptics not convinced by Beuys's international reputation?
5 Why did Beuys feel that the definition of art itself needed to be expanded?
6 What honour was accorded Beuys in 1979 by the Guggenheim Museum?

Soll das denn Kunst sein?

Zu den bekanntesten deutschen Künstlern des 20. Jahrhunderts gehört der Plastiker, Zeichner und Aktionskünstler Joseph Beuys. Beuys ist nicht nur bekannt, sondern auch sehr kontrovers, weil er sich von den traditionellen Vorstellungen von Plastiken abwandte. Seine Werke aus Fett, Fell, Filz, Honig und Wachs zählen zu den Innovationen der Avantgardekunst der 70er Jahre. Obwohl er international hohes Ansehen genießt, stellen viele Skeptiker immer noch die Frage, »Soll das denn Kunst sein?«. Aber gerade die Definition von der Kunst selbst wollte Beuys erweitern. Er war der Meinung, daß jeder Mensch in einem gewissen Sinn ein Künstler ist.

Beuys war 1961–1973 Professor an der Kunstakademie Düsseldorf. Im Jahre 1979 veranstaltete das Guggenheim Museum in New York eine große Ausstellung von seinen Werken. In den 80er Jahren war er für die Grünen politisch aktiv.

Joseph Beuys ist am 12. Mai 1921 in Kleve, einer kleinen Stadt nicht weit von der deutsch-holländischen Grenze, geboren. Er starb am 26. Januar 1986 in Düsseldorf.

die Kunst (¨e) *art*
bekannt *well-known*
der Künstler(-) *artist*
die Vorstellung (-en) *idea, concept*
sich abwenden von *to turn away from*
das Fett *fat*
das Fell (-e) *skin, hide*
der Filz *felt*
der Honig *honey*
das Ansehen *esteem*
die Meinung *opinion*
der Sinn (-e) *sense*
die Ausstellung (-en) *exhibition*
die Grünen (*pl.*) *the 'Greens', Green Party*

14 Ich würde es versuchen

In this unit you will learn how to say what you would do under certain conditions, how to talk about hypothetical situations, and how to offer advice.

Dialog

Marta Friedl, on vacation from the USA, meets unemployed teacher, Stefan Krain, on the Frankfurt-Stuttgart train. She advises him to try his luck in the States.

Marta Friedl Entschuldigen Sie, bitte. Ist hier frei?

Stefan Krain Bitte schön. Nehmen Sie ruhig Platz. (*Sie nimmt Platz.*) Fahren Sie bis nach Stuttgart durch?

Marta Friedl Nein. Nur bis Heilbronn. Ich fahre zum ersten Mal seit 18 Jahren wieder dorthin. Ich wohne nämlich in den Vereinigten Staaten und besuche jetzt Verwandte in der Bundesrepublik.

Stefan Krain Ach so. Ich würde gern mal nach Amerika fahren, wenn ich mir ein Flugticket leisten könnte.

Marta Friedl Sind Sie denn Student?

Stefan Krain Nein, ich bin fertig mit dem Studium. Ich bin voll ausgebildeter Mathematiklehrer. Wegen der hohen Arbeitslosigkeit bei Akademikern habe ich aber trotz vieler Bewerbungen noch keine Stellung gefunden.

Marta Friedl Ach, wie schrecklich! Da sollten Sie lieber nach Amerika auswandern. Dann hätten Sie bestimmt bessere Zukunftsaussichten.

Stefan Krain Das wäre ja keine schlechte Idee! Müßte ich aber nicht ein Visum, eine Aufenthaltserlaubnis und eine Arbeitsgenehmigung beantragen?

Marta Friedl Doch. Da würden Sie mit Ihren Qualifikationen sicher auf keine großen Schwierigkeiten stoßen. Sie müßten natürlich sehr gute Englischkenntnisse vorweisen können.

Stefan Krain Das wäre kein Problem. In der Schule habe ich neun Jahre Englisch gehabt, und außerdem habe ich immer jede Gelegenheit wahrgenommen, Englisch zu sprechen. Für mein Fach mußte ich auch englischsprachige Artikel und Zeitschriften lesen.

Marta Friedl An Ihrer Stelle würde ich es dann versuchen. Sie würden ja nichts dabei verlieren.

Stefan Krain Da haben Sie recht! Da würde ich wenigstens Erfahrungen als Lehrer und als Ausländer in einem fremden Land sammeln.

Ist hier frei? *Is this seat free/vacant?*
Bitte schön (*here*) *go ahead*
Nehmen Sie ruhig Platz *Feel free to sit down* (lit. *Calmly sit down*)
Fahren Sie bis nach Stuttgart durch? *Are you going through to Stuttgart?*
wenn ich mir ein Flugticket leisten könnte *if I could afford the air fare* (lit. *an air ticket*)
Ich bin fertig mit dem Studium *I've finished my studies* (lit. *I am ready/finished . . .*)
voll ausgebildet *fully trained, fully qualified*
wegen (+*gen.*) *on account of, because of*
trotz (+*gen.*) *in spite of, despite*
die Bewerbung (-en) *application*
Wie schrecklich! *How terrible!*
auswandern (*sep.*) *to emigrate*
Sie hätten bessere Zukunftsaussichten *You would have better prospects (for the future)*
ein Visum beantragen *to apply for a visa*
die Aufenthaltserlaubnis (-se) *residence permit*
die Arbeitsgenehmigung (-en) *work permit*
auf Schwierigkeiten stoßen *to encounter* (lit. *run into*) *difficulties*
Englischkenntnisse vorweisen können *to have a knowledge of English* (lit. *to be able to demonstrate . . .*)
außerdem *besides, in addition*
eine Gelegenheit wahrnehmen *to take* (lit. *perceive*) *an opportunity*
englischsprachig *English language, English-speaking*
der Artikel (-) *article*
an Ihrer Stelle *in your place, if I were you*
Sie würden dabei nichts verlieren *You would have nothing to lose*
wenigstens *at least*
Erfahrungen sammeln *to gain* (lit. *collect*) *experience*

Das wäre keine schlechte Idee! *That wouldn't be a bad idea!*
Müßte ich nicht . . .? *Wouldn't I have to . . .?*
der Ausländer (-) *foreigner*
fremd *foreign, strange*

Fragen zum Dialog

1 Richtig (R) oder Falsch (F)?

1 Marta Friedl fährt bis nach Stuttgart durch.
2 Sie war seit 18 Jahren nicht in Heilbronn.
3 Marta Friedl wohnt in den USA.
4 Sie hat keine Verwandten mehr in Deutschland.
5 Stefan Krain möchte gern nach Amerika fahren, aber er kann sich ein Flugticket nicht leisten.
6 Stefan studiert Mathematik.
7 In Deutschland gibt es viele arbeitslose Lehrer.
8 Wenn man in den USA arbeiten will, braucht man eine Arbeitsgenehmigung.
9 Stefan hat nur selten Englisch gesprochen.
10 Stefan hat nichts dagegen, in einem fremden Land zu arbeiten.

2 Welche Antwort paßt?

1 Entschuldigen Sie, bitte. Ist hier frei?
(*a*) Bitte schön.
(*b*) Danke schön.
(*c*) Ja, sehr schön.

2 Fahren Sie bis nach Stuttgart durch?
(*a*) Nein. Nur bis Stuttgart.
(*b*) Ja. Nur bis Heilbronn.
(*c*) Nein. Nur bis Heilbronn.

3 Sind Sie Student?
(*a*) Ja. Ich bin voll ausgebildeter Mathematiklehrer.
(*b*) Nein. Ich habe fertigstudiert.
(*c*) Ja. Ich bin jetzt fertig mit dem Studium.

4 Trotz vieler Bewerbungen habe ich noch keine Stellung gefunden.
(*a*) Das wäre keine schlechte Idee!

(*b*) Ach, wie schrecklich!
(*c*) Das wäre kein Problem.

5 An Ihrer Stelle würde ich versuchen, nach Amerika auszuwandern.
(*a*) Da haben Sie recht!
(*b*) Da würde ich lieber nach Amerika auswandern.
(*c*) Das wäre vielleicht keine schlechte Idee.

Was Sie wissen sollten

Die Deutsche Bundesbahn

Despite the rapid growth in road traffic, the German railway network still plays a vitally important role, particularly in the transportation of people and heavy goods over long distances. The state-owned and heavily subsidised railway company, **Deutsche Bundesbahn (DB)**, has made strenuous efforts to compete with road and air traffic by a concerted programme of modernisation and automation. Inter-City trains (**Intercity-Züge**) reach speeds of 100–120 mph and offer numerous office facilities to business travellers. Punctuality and cleanliness—for which the Germans have long enjoyed a reputation—have, on the whole, been maintained.

In densely populated areas, such as those surrounding the cities of Hamburg, Frankfurt, Stuttgart and Munich and in the Ruhr, the railways fulfil an important function in the rapid and efficient transport of commuters.

Following German unification in 1990, large-scale investment was necessary to incorporate the former East German **Reichsbahn** into the Western system and to bring this part of the German railway network up to modern standards.

DER FAMILIEN-PASS:

EIN GANZES JAHR LANG MIT DER BAHN ZUM HALBEN FAHRPREIS

Die Bahn.

Wichtige Redewendungen

How to

1 *Say what you would do under certain (perhaps rather improbable) conditions.*

Ich würde nach Amerika fahren,	wenn ich reich wäre. wenn ich genug (*enough*) Geld hätte. wenn ich mir ein Flugticket leisten könnte. wenn ich auswandern müßte.

2 *Say what someone would have to do (in a given set of circumstances).*

Sie müßten	eine Arbeitsgenehmigung beantragen. gute Englischkenntnisse vorweisen können. als Ausländer in einem fremden Land arbeiten.

3 *Say what possibilities would be open to someone (in a given set of circumstances).*

Sie könnten	bei mir wohnen. in Amerika mehr Geld verdienen. Ihre Verwandten in Kalifornien kennenlernen.

Auf dem Bahnhof *(At the station)*

der Fahrplan (¨e) *timetable, schedule*
die Abfahrt (-en) *departure*
die Ankunft (¨e) *arrival*
der Personenzug (¨e) *slow train*
der Eilzug (¨e) *fast stopping train*
zuschlagpflichtig *subject to an additional charge*
der Fahrkartenschalter (-) *ticket office*
die Gepäckaufbewahrung *left-luggage office*
der Bahnsteig (-e) *platform*
das Gleis (-e) *track*
der Expreßzug (¨e) *express train*
der D-Zug (¨e) *fast train*
der Schnellzug (¨e) *fast train*
der Schlafwagenplatz (¨-) *sleeper*
der Liegewagenplatz (¨e) *couchette*
das Zug-Sekretariat *office services on board a train*

Grammatik

1 Imperfect Subjunctive (*werden, sein, haben* and the modal verbs)

Three forms of polite request which were introduced earlier in the book as set expressions do in fact contain examples of what is termed the ***Imperfect Subjunctive:***

> **Würden** Sie sich bitte eintragen: *Would you please register.* **(Lektion 4)**
> Ich **möchte** ein Einzelzimmer mit Bad. *I should like a single room with a bath.* **(Lektion 4)**
> **Hätten** Sie vielleicht einen Stadtplan? *Would you perhaps have a map of the city?* **(Lektion 8)**

The **Dialog** of this unit illustrates a further use for the Imperfect Subjunctive—that of expressing conditions. The verbs most frequently used in the expressing of conditions are: **sein, haben,** and **werden** and the modal verbs.

1.1 Forms of the Imperfect Subjunctive

(*a*) **sein**	(*b*) **haben**	(*c*) **werden**
ich wäre	ich hätte	ich würde
du wärest	du hättest	du würdest
Sie wären	Sie hätten	Sie würden
er } sie } wäre es }	er } sie } hätte es }	er } sie } würde es }
wir wären	wir hätten	wir würden
ihr wär(e)t	ihr hättet	ihr würdet
Sie wären	Sie hätten	Sie würden
sie wären	sie hätten	sie würden

(*d*) *the modal verbs*

können	**müssen**	**wollen**	**dürfen**	**mögen**	**sollen**
ich könnte	ich müßte	ich wollte	ich dürfte	ich möchte	ich sollte
du könntest	du müßtest	du wolltest	du dürftest	du möchtest	du solltest
Sie könnten	Sie müßten	Sie wollten	Sie dürften	Sie möchten	Sie sollten
er } sie } könnte es }	er } sie } müßte es }	er } sie } wollte es }	er } sie } dürfte es }	er } sie } möchte es }	er } sie } sollte es }
wir könnten	wir müßten	wir wollten	wir dürften	wir möchten	wir sollten
ihr könntet	ihr müßtet	ihr wolltet	ihr dürftet	ihr möchtet	ihr solltet
Sie könnten	Sie müßten	Sie wollten	Sie dürften	Sie möchten	Sie sollten
sie könnten	sie müßten	sie wollten	sie dürften	sie möchten	sie sollten

Note that whilst the Imperfect Subjunctive forms of **wollen** and **sollen** are indistinguishable from those of the straightforward Imperfect Tense, those of the other modal verbs are distinguished by the addition of an ***Umlaut***.

1.2 Expression of Conditions

One way of expressing a condition is to use a **wenn** clause together with the present tense. The verb of the main clause may be in the present or the future tense:

> Wenn ich Zeit habe, werde ich mit dir ins Theater gehen.
> Wenn ich Zeit habe, gehe ich mit dir ins Theater. *If I have time, I'll go to the theatre with you.* (i.e. I'm not sure yet—I may or may not go.)

If, however, the condition is subject to a greater degree of improbability, uncertainty or potentiality than in the above example, then the use of the Imperfect Subjunctive is called for:

> Wenn ich Zeit **hätte, würde** ich mit dir ins Theater gehen.
> *If I had time, I would go to the theatre with you.* (i.e. I haven't got time, so I am **not** going with you.)
> Wenn ich reich **wäre, würde** ich eine Weltreise machen.
> *If I were rich, I would go on a world tour.* (i.e. I am not rich, so I almost certainly won't be going.)
> Wenn Sie in Amerika arbeiten **wollten, würden** Sie eine Arbeitsgenehmigung beantragen müssen.
> *If you wanted to work in America, you would have to apply for a work permit.* (i.e. It's not been made clear whether you want to work in America or not.)
> Wenn ich vor dem Haus parken **dürfte, wäre** alles viel leichter.
> *If I were allowed to park outside the house, everything would be much easier.* (i.e. I'm not allowed to park there—which is a considerable nuisance. This could of course be an indirect request for permission to park outside the house.)
> Wenn du auswandern **könntest, hättest** du bestimmt bessere Aussichten.
> *If you could emigrate, you would no doubt have better prospects.* (i.e. There is a possibility that you might be able to emigrate).

In sentences like the last two examples, it is possible to use **würde . . . sein** and **würde . . . haben** respectively instead of **wäre** and **hätte**:

> Wenn ich vor dem Haus parken dürfte, **würde** alles viel leichter **sein**.
> Wenn du auswandern könntest, **würdest** du bestimmt bessere Aussichten **haben**.

The word **so** or **dann** is often inserted between the **wenn** clause and the main clause:

Wenn ich reich wäre, **so** würde ich eine Weltreise machen.
Wenn ich vor dem Haus parken dürfte, **dann** wäre alles viel leichter.

It is also possible to omit the **wenn** and move the verb to the initial position:

Wäre ich reich, so würde ich eine Weltreise machen.
Dürfte ich vor dem Haus parken, dann wäre alles viel leichter.

When a wish is expressed, the **wenn** clause can stand on it own:

Wenn ich nur reich wäre!	*If only I were rich!*
Wäre ich nur reich!	
Wenn ich nur die Zeit hätte!	*If only I had the time!*
Hätte ich nur die Zeit!	

In all of the above examples, the **wenn** clause comes before the main clause. It is of course possible for the main clause to come first, followed by the **wenn** clause:

Ich würde mit dir ins Theater gehen, wenn ich Zeit hätte.
Ich würde eine Weltreise machen, wenn ich reich wäre.

2 Collocations

The term ***collocation*** simply means 'placing together'. In the context of language, it refers to a pair or group of words that frequently occur together (or **co-occur**). Examples of collocations in English are:

a *confirmed* bachelor	(adjective + noun)
an *inveterate* liar	(adjective + noun)
to rain *heavily*	(verb + adverb)
to *encounter* difficulties	(verb + noun)
to *put on* an exhibition	(verb + noun)

It may be possible to substitute an alternative word or words for the italicised word in some of the above collocations, but the number of substitutions that can be made is very small. For instance, it may be possible to substitute *confirmed* for *inveterate*, but it is not possible to say *an inveterate bachelor*. Whilst *to meet* and *to encounter* are very similar in meaning, one does not normally talk of *meeting difficulties*, although one might *run into difficulties*. It is certainly possible to *mount an exhibition* or even *to organise* one, but it is doubtful whether further verbs can be substituted here without a change of meaning. As native speakers of English, we intuitively know whether a collocation sounds correct or not. We have no such intuition about a foreign language. Each collocation must be learned as it is encountered.

Examples of German collocations that appeared in the **Dialog** of this **Lektion** are:

auf Schwierigkeiten stoßen	(verb + preposition + noun)
Kenntnisse vorweisen können	(verb + verb + noun)
ein Gelegenheit wahrnehmen	(verb + noun)
Erfahrungen sammeln	(verb + noun)

Further examples that have occurred elsewhere include:

stark regnen	(verb + adverb) **Lektion 10**
eine Ausstellung veranstalten	(verb + noun) **Lektion 13 VS**

3 Prepositions with the Genitive Case

For the sake of completeness the **Genitive Case** was mentioned in the **Grammatik** section of **Lektion 11** when adjectival endings were being dealt with. The examples given contained the preposition **statt** (*instead of*) which is followed by the genitive case. In this unit two further prepositions requiring the use of the genitive, **trotz** (*in spite of, despite*) and **wegen** (*on account of*) were introduced. Of the prepositions which require the use of the genitive, the most commonly used are:

angesichts (*in view of*), **(an)statt** (*instead of*), **ausschließlich/exklusive** (*exclusive of*), **außerhalb** (*outside of*), **beiderseits** (*on both sides of*), **bezüglich** (*concerning, with regard to*), **diesseits** (*on this side of*), **einschließlich/inklusive** (*inclusive of*), **innerhalb** (*inside of*), **jenseits** (*on the other side of*), **laut** (*according to*), **trotz** (*in spite of*), **während** (*during*), **wegen** (*on account of*).

The distinctive feature of the genitive case in the masculine and neuter singular is an **-s** on both the article (or possessive adjective etc.) ***and*** on the noun:

Während seines Lebens	*During his life*
Jenseits des Rheins	*On the other side of the Rhine*
Trotz des schlechten Wetters	*Despite the bad weather*
Wegen des starken Verkehrs	*On account of the heavy traffic*

Nouns of one syllable often add **-es** instead of **-s** in the genitive:

Während des Krieges	*During the war*
Diesseits des Hauses	*On this side of the house*

In the feminine singular and masculine, neuter and feminine plural, the distinctive feature is an **-r** on the article (or possessive adjective etc.):

Wegen der Arbeitslosigkeit	*On account of (the) unemployment*
Trotz der frischen Luft	*Despite the fresh air*
Angesichts ihrer Freundlichkeit	*In view of her (their) friendliness*
Trotz der vielen Schwierigkeiten	*Despite the many difficulties*
Trotz vieler Schwierigkeiten	*Despite many difficulties*
Angesichts Ihrer guten Englischkenntnisse	*In view of your good knowledge* (lit. *knowledges*) *of English*

Informally and colloquially the dative is often used instead of the genitive after many of the above listed prepositions. Since the dative and genitive are indistinguishable in the feminine singular, the use of the dative is noticeable only in the masculine and neuter singular and in the plural (all genders):

> Trotz dem Wetter; Wegen dem Regen; Während dem Krieg; Wegen den vielen Leuten; Während den folgenden Monaten.

4 Double infinitives

In **Lektion 5** a number of examples were given of double infinitives, which appear at the end of a sentence or clause, following a finite verb:

> Ich kann heute abend leider nicht **essen gehen**.
> Möchtest du den Mann auch **kennenlernen**?
> Möchtest du auch **spazierengehen**?

Sometimes, as in the last two examples, the two verbs are considered to be a unit and are therefore written as one word.

Conditional sentences often contain a double infinitive. One such sentence occurred in the **Dialog:**

> Sie müßten natürlich sehr gute Englischkenntnisse **vorweisen können**.

Sentences such as:

> Müßte ich aber nicht eine Arbeitsgenehmigung beantragen?

can also be expressed using a **würde** construction, which then produces a double infinitive at the end:

> Würde ich aber nicht eine Arbeitsgenehmigung **beantragen müssen**?

Übungen

ÜBUNG 14.1 Was kann man auch sagen?

1 An Ihrer Stelle würde ich nach Amerika auswandern.

(*a*) Ich rate Ihnen, nach Amerika auszuwandern.
(*b*) Ich rate Ihnen, nicht nach Amerika auszuwandern.
(*c*) In Amerika gibt es viele freie Stellen.

2 Sie hätten dann bessere Aussichten.
(*a*) Sie hätten dann eine schöne Aussicht auf den Park.
(*b*) Sie würden dann bessere Aussichten haben.
(*c*) Sie würden dann besser aussehen.

3 Sie müßten natürlich gute Englischkenntnisse vorweisen können.
(*a*) Sie müßten natürlich den ganzen Tag Englisch sprechen.
(*b*) Sie würden natürlich Ihre Deutschkenntnisse vergessen müssen.
(*c*) Sie müßten natürlich sehr gut Englisch sprechen, lesen und schreiben können.

4 Müßte ich ein Visum beantragen?
(*a*) Würde ich ein Visum beantragen müssen?
(*b*) Könnte ich ein Visum beantragen?
(*c*) Würde ich ein Visum beantragen können?

5 Könnte ich mit dem Visum auch nach Kanada fahren?
(*a*) Würde ich mit dem Visum auch nach Kanada fahren können?
(*b*) Würde ich mit dem Visum auch nach Kanada fahren müssen?
(*c*) Sollte ich mit dem Visum auch nach Kanada fahren?

6 Wegen der Arbeitslosigkeit im eigenen Lande wandern viele Menschen aus.
(*a*) Viele Menschen wandern aus, auch wenn sie im eigenen Lande eine gute Stellung haben.
(*b*) Viele Leute wandern aus, weil sie im eigenen Lande keine Arbeit finden.
(*c*) Wenn es keine Arbeitslosigkeit gibt, dann wollen die meisten Leute im eigenen Lande arbeiten.

ÜBUNG 14.2 **Welche Antwort paßt?**

Eine Reise in die USA

1 Wo könnte ich in London Informationen über Reisen in die USA bekommen?
(*a*) In jedem Reisebüro.
(*b*) In Ihrem Reisepaß.
(*c*) Beim Verkehrsamt.

2 Müßte ich für eine Reise in die USA ein Visum beantragen?
(*a*) Nein, Visen kosten natürlich Geld.
(*b*) Ja, Sie würden ein Visum brauchen.
(*c*) Ja, für die Bundesrepublik braucht man ein Visum.

3 Dürfte ich Sterling-Reiseschecks in die USA mitnehmen?
(*a*) Nein, Sie dürften nur Reiseschecks mitnehmen.
(*b*) Reiseschecks könnten Sie auf Ihrer Bank kaufen.
(*c*) Ja, sicher.

4 Müßte ich in Hotels übernachten?
(*a*) Nein, natürlich nicht.
(*b*) Natürlich dürften Sie in Hotels übernachten.
(*c*) Ja, Sie dürften auch bei Freunden übernachten.

5 Dürfte ich britische Würste für einen Bekannten in Boston mitnehmen?
(*a*) Ja, in Boston gibt es viele britische Würste.
(*b*) Nein, es ist verboten (*forbidden*), Fleisch mitzunehmen.
(*c*) Ja, Sie dürften Ihren Bekannten in Boston besuchen.

6 Dürfte ich mit meinem Wagen in die USA fahren?
(*a*) Ja, klar. In den USA sieht man viele Autos aus Europa.
(*b*) Nein, sie dürften nur mit Ihrem Wagen fahren.
(*c*) Ja, aber Sie müßten mit Ihrem Wagen fahren.

ÜBUNG 14.3 Sagen Sie es anders.
Replace the phrases in italics as indicated in the examples:

Ein Spaziergang im Wald

Weil das Wetter sehr schön war, sind wir gestern nachmittag aufs Land gefahren.
Wegen des schönen Wetters . . .
Obwohl der Verkehr auf den Straßen ziemlich stark war, waren wir innerhalb einer Stunde schon mitten im Wald.
Trotz des starken Verkehrs . . .

1 *Weil die Luft im Wald frisch war*, konnten wir einen angenehmen Spaziergang machen.

2 *Obwohl das Wetter herrlich war*, haben wir im Wald nur wenige andere Menschen gesehen.
3 *Weil der Spaziergang sehr lang war*, sind wir nach 2 Stunden alle müde geworden.
4 *Obwohl es im Wald sonst nur wenige Wanderer gab*, hatten wir Glück – das Wald-Café war auf!
5 *Obwohl die Preise im Wald-Café sehr hoch waren*, haben wir Kaffee und Kuchen bestellt.
6 *Weil der Weg zum Auto zurück sehr lang war*, haben wir nur eine halbe Stunde im Café gesessen.
7 *Weil wir auf dem Rückweg* (way back) *viel Pausen* (pauses) *gemacht haben*, haben wir erst um 7 Uhr wieder den Parkplatz erreicht.
8 *Weil um diese Zeit der Verkehr ziemlich schwach war*, sind wir schnell nach Hause gekommen.

ÜBUNG 14.4 Ergänzen Sie.

Insert **würde, hätte, wäre, müßte, könnte** as appropriate.

Wenn ich nur ein Auto hätte!

Wenn ich ein Auto hätte, . . . (1) . . . ich nicht mehr um 6 Uhr aufstehen. Ich . . . (2) . . . dann bis 7 Uhr schlafen und . . . (3) . . . auch mehr Zeit zum Frühstücken. Ich . . . (4) . . . erst um 7.30 Uhr losfahren und . . . (5) . . . trotzdem noch pünktlich im Betrieb ankommen.

Nach der Arbeit . . . (6) . . . ich im Sommer manchmal aufs Land fahren und das schöne Wetter ausnutzen. Die Heimreise (*journey home*) . . . (7) . . . auch viel kürzer als die mit dem Bus und mit der Bahn. Einmal im Monat . . . (8) . . . ich am Wochende meine Eltern besuchen—die lange Reise . . . (9) . . . dann viel leichter als sonst. Ich . . . (10) . . . natürlich auch mit dem Wagen im Urlaub wegfahren.

ÜBUNG 14.5 Wie kann man es anders sagen?

Rephrase the sentences as indicated in the examples:

Nur weil ich keine Zeit habe, gehe ich nicht mit dir ins Kino.
Wenn ich die Zeit hätte, würde ich mit dir ins Kino gehen.
Nur weil Heinz so müde ist, kann er dir nicht in der Küche helfen.
either: ***Wenn er nicht so müde wäre, würde er dir in der Küche helfen können.***

or ***Wenn er nicht so müde wäre, könnte er dir in der Küche helfen.***

1 Nur weil ich so viel zu tun habe, fahre ich nicht fürs Wochenende weg.
2 Nur weil Klaus arbeitslos ist, kann er sich die Reise nach Amerika nicht leisten.
3 Nur weil für Sabine die Fahrt ins Büro so kurz ist, kann sie länger als ihre Kolleginnen (*colleagues*) schlafen.
4 Nur weil wir in München keine Freunde oder Verwandten haben, müssen wir im Hotel übernachten.
5 Nur weil Dieter keine Probleme hat, ist er so freundlich (*friendly*).
6 Nur weil Jan und Paula starke Raucher sind, lade ich sie nicht zum Abendbrot ein.
7 Nur weil Manfred kein Auto hat, fährt er mit dem Zug zur Arbeit.
8 Nur weil Thea krank ist, muß ich die Kinder von der Schule abholen.

Verstehen Sie?

1 Konversation

Herr Kaiser hat einen Autounfall

Herr Göller from the Traffic Police calls in at Herr Kaiser's office to have a few words with Herr Kaiser about his car accident. When his secretary, Frau Jahn, discovers who Herr Göller is, she tries to keep him until Herr Kaiser returns. Note how politely they address each other.

Herr Göller Entschuldigen Sie, bitte. Wäre es möglich, mit Herrn Kaiser zu sprechen?

Frau Jahn Herr Kaiser ist leider im Moment nicht da. Könnten Sie in einer Stunde wieder vorbeikommen?

Herr Göller Dazu hätte ich heute keine Zeit mehr.

Frau Jahn Könnte ich ihm also etwas ausrichten?

Herr Göller Würden Sie ihm bitte sagen, daß Herr Göller von der Verkehrspolizei da war wegen seines Autounfalls.

Frau Jahn Ich werde ihm Bescheid sagen, Herr Göller. Oder kann ich Ihnen vielleicht etwas zu trinken anbieten?

Herr Kaiser müßte bald wieder da sein.

Herr Göller Ich müßte eigentlich in einer halben Stunde wieder im Büro sein, aber vielleicht könnte ich doch noch ein paar Minuten auf Herrn Kaiser warten. Also, ein Glas Mineralwasser würde ich sehr gerne trinken. Bei diesem warmen Wetter bekommt man schnell Durst.

der Unfall (¨e) *accident*	**jemandem etwas ausrichten** *to give someone a message*
möglich *possible*	**der Durst** *thirst*
dazu *for that*	

Richtig (R) oder Falsch (F)?

1 Herr Kaiser möchte mit Herrn Göller sprechen.
2 Herr Kaiser ist im Moment nicht im Büro.
3 Herr Göller hat keine Zeit, wieder vorbeizukommen.
4 Frau Jahn soll Herrn Kaiser ausrichten, daß Herr Göller da war.
5 Herr Göller ist von der Kriminalpolizei.
6 Er kann nicht auf Herrn Kaiser warten.
7 Er würde gerne ein Glas Mineralwasser trinken.
8 Wenn das Wetter warm ist, hat man schnell Durst.

2 Lesetexte

Text A

Lesen Sie den Text, und versuchen Sie, die Fragen zu beantworten. Nur wenn Sie auf Schwierigkeiten stoßen, sollten Sie sich die 'wichtigen Vokabeln' ansehen.

der Herzinfarkt (–e) (*heart attack*)	**der Hausarzt (¨e)** *GP, family doctor*
der Notfall (¨e) (*case of*) *emergency*	**gemütlich** *snug*(*ly*)
die Sprechstunde (-n) *consultation*	**drehen** *to turn*
das Krankenhaus (¨er) *hospital*	**die Gesundheit** *health*
schließen *to close*	**unterwegs** *on the way, on the road*
die Klingel (-n) *bell*	**die Stechuhr (-en)** *time-clock*
abstellen (*sep.*) *to turn off*	**verschreiben** *to prescribe*
schonen *to spare, save*	**die Berufung** *vocation*

3.15 Uhr. Ein Herzinfarkt

Wenn sich Notfälle an Sprechstunden halten müßten, könnten die Krankenhäuser bis 8 Uhr morgens schließen, die Nachtdienst-Apotheken die Klingel abstellen, die Notarzt-Taxifahrer ihre Autos schonen, und der Hausarzt würde sich noch einmal gemütlich auf die andere Seite drehen.
Woran wir dann am meisten sparen würden, wäre aber unser aller Gesundheit. Und so sind Nacht für Nacht mehr als Tausend Ärzte in der Bundesrepublik unterwegs, um ihren Patienten zu helfen. Ohne die Gesundheit nach der Stechuhr zu verschreiben.

Mensch und Medizin sind die Berufung des Arztes

1 What change would it be possible to make if emergencies had to keep to consultation hours?
2 Who would, under the same circumstances, be able to turn off their door-bells?
3 Who would be able to spare their cars?
4 What would the GP be able to do?
5 What would we, however, be economising on most of all?
6 How many doctors are there out on the road every night in (the Federal Republic of) Germany?
7 What is their aim?
8 What process is not carried out according to the time-clock?

Text B Lesen Sie den Text.

Much of the vocabulary that occurs in this text has already been introduced, other words are recognisable because of their similarity to English. It should be possible to work out the meaning of the few remaining vocabulary items from the context and for this reason, no vocabulary list is supplied at this point. All words are, however, listed in the back of the book.

„... kommt jetzt der Intercity, der durch ganz Europa fährt, und der heißt EuroCity.“

„Meine sehr verehrten Damen und Herren, liebe Freunde!
Der Intercity hat einen europäischen ‚Verwandten‘ bekommen: den EuroCity. 64 EC-Züge täglich verbinden seit Beginn des Sommerfahrplans über 200 Städte in 13 Ländern Europas miteinander. Damit sind wir den Vereinigten Staaten von Europa ein gutes Stück nähergekommen.
Die schnellen EuroCitys starten von über 60 Bahnhöfen der Deutschen Bundesbahn, machen unterwegs nur wenig Zwischenhalte und bringen Sie direkt ins Zentrum wichtiger europäischer Metropolen. Und das mit all dem Komfort, der Ihnen auf Ihren Intercity-Reisen selbstverständlich geworden ist:
Freundliche EC-Betreuer begrüßen Sie am Bahnsteig, helfen Ihnen beim Einsteigen mit dem Gepäck, begleiten Sie zu Ihrem Platz und sorgen dafür, daß Sie es auch richtig bequem haben. Die EC-Betreuer sprechen meistens mehrere Sprachen, so daß in ganz Europa für gute Verständigung gesorgt ist.
Wie übrigens auch für Ihr leibliches Wohl. Denn im EuroCity-Zugrestaurant tragen viele internationale Köche auf ihre Art dazu bei, Ihnen die Reise so angenehm wie möglich zu machen.
EuroCity heißt also für Sie: Überall in Europa, wo Sie das EC-Zeichen sehen, haben Sie die Garantie, unbeschwert, komfortabel und sicher reisen zu können. Wie im Intercity.
Ich danke Ihnen für den herzlichen Empfang des neuen EuroCity und wünsche Ihnen im Namen der Bahnen Europas immer eine schöne Reise.“

Deutsche Bundesbahn DB

Beantworten Sie die Fragen:

1 How is the EuroCity service described here?
2 What has this service brought those involved closer to being?
3 What three advantages of the EuroCity trains are listed here?
4 What four duties are performed by EuroCity stewards before departure of a EuroCity train?
5 How are EuroCity stewards able to make themselves understood throughout Europe?
6 What kind of personnel have been appointed to cater for the physical well-being of passengers and where are they to be found?
7 What guarantee does the EC sign offer?
8 What does the ‘announcer’ wish us, and in whose name?

15 Es kommt darauf an

In this unit you will learn further ways of asking for information and of offering advice.

Dialog

Anita Juarez has gone into a travel agency to enquire about passport requirements for a visit to Britain. She also finds out about ways of paying for goods other than by cash. She is not interested in booking a flight, as she plans to travel by car with three others.

Anita Juarez Guten Tag. Könnten Sie mir bitte sagen, ob ich einen Reisepaß brauche, um nach Großbritannien zu fahren?

Hanna Martin Es kommt darauf an, ob Sie die deutsche Staatsangehörigkeit haben oder nicht.

Anita Juarez Mein Vater ist Spanier, aber meine Mutter ist Deutsche. Ich bin in Deutschland geboren und bin auch hier groß geworden.

Hanna Martin Dann genügt Ihr Personalausweis. Mit Ihrem deutschen Personalausweis können Sie in alle Länder der Europäischen Gemeinschaft reisen, und Großbritannien gehört ja zu den Mitgliedsstaaten der EG.

Anita Juarez Gut, danke. Dann hätte ich auch gerne noch gewußt, wieviel Geld ich mitnehmen darf.

Hanna Martin Soviel wie Sie wollen! Bloß würde ich Ihnen davon abraten, Bargeld in großen Mengen mitzunehmen.

Anita Juarez Ach ja. Da kaufe ich lieber Reiseschecks. Dann kann ich mich darauf verlassen, daß mein Urlaubsgeld gesichert ist.

Hanna Martin Das stimmt. Außerdem darf ich Sie vielleicht darauf aufmerksam machen, daß Sie auch noch Euroschecks in Pfund Sterling ausstellen können. Und in vielen Geschäften kann man natürlich mit der Kreditkarte bezahlen.

Anita Juarez Ich finde es günstig, wo möglich mit Kreditkarte einzukaufen, da ich dann erst am Ende des Monats abrechnen muß! Als Studentin bin ich sowieso davon abhängig, daß mir meine Eltern finanzielle Hilfe leisten.

Hanna Martin Da werden Sie sicher so billig wie möglich nach England kommen wollen. Kann ich Sie zu einem unserer Charterflüge überreden?

Anita Juarez Nein, danke. Wir fahren zu viert im Auto meines Freundes. Für Unterkunft ist auch gesorgt. Eine meiner spanischen Tanten ist mit einem Engländer verheiratet. Sie hat mich und meinen Freund dazu eingeladen, bei ihr mitten in London zu wohnen.

Hanna Martin Da haben Sie aber Glück gehabt!

der Reisepaß (¨e) *passport*
brauchen *to need*
um . . . zu . . . *in order to . . .*
Es kommt darauf an [, ob] *It depends [(on) whether]*
groß werden *to grow up*
genügen *to suffice*
der Personalausweis (-e) *personal identity card*
die Europäische Gemeinschaft *European Community*
reisen *to travel*
Großbritannien *Great Britain*
gehören *to belong*
der Mitgliedsstaat (-en) *member state*
Ich hätte gerne gewußt *I should like to have known*
mitnehmen (*sep.*) *to take along, take with one*
soviel wie *as much as*
bloß *only*
abraten (*sep.*) **von** (+*dat.*) *to advise against*
das Pfund Sterling (-) *pound sterling*
Euroschecks ausstellen *to make out Eurocheques*
die Kreditkarte (-n) *credit card*
günstig *favourable, convenient*
möglich *possible*
am Ende des Monats *at the end of the month*
abrechnen (*sep.*) *to settle up*
sowieso *in any case*
abhängig von *dependent on*
finanziell *financial(ly)*
Hilfe leisten *to give, render assistance*
überreden (*sep.*) **zu** (+*dat.*) *to persuade into, talk into*
der Charterflug (¨e) *charter flight*
Wir fahren zu viert *There are four of us going*
im Auto meines Freundes *in my friend's car*

das Bargeld *cash*
die Menge (-n) *quantity*
sich verlassen auf (+*acc.*) *to rely on*
sichern *to safeguard*
aufmerksam machen auf (+*acc.*) *to draw attention to*
Für Unterkunft ist auch gesorgt *Accommodation is taken care of, too*
eine meiner spanischen Tanten *one of my Spanish aunts*
einladen (*sep.*) **zu** (+*dat.*) *to invite (to)*

Fragen zum Dialog

1 Richtig (R) oder Falsch (F)?

1 Anita Juarez ist in Spanien geboren.
2 Sie hat aber deutsche Eltern.
3 Anita will nach Großbritannien fahren.
4 Mit einem deutschen Personalausweis kann man in alle Länder der EG reisen.
5 Großbritannien ist Mitgleid der EG.
6 Man sollte nicht Bargeld in großen Mengen in den Urlaub mitnehmen.
7 Anita wird Reiseschecks für ihren Urlaub kaufen.
8 In Großbritannien ist es oft möglich, mit Kreditkarte zu bezahlen.
9 Anita fliegt mit einer Chartergesellschaft nach England.
10 In London wird sie in einem billigen Hotel wohnen.

2 Welche Antwort paßt?

1 Brauche ich einen Reisepaß, wenn ich nach Großbritannien fahre?
(*a*) Nehmen Sie lieber Reiseschecks mit!
(*b*) Ja. Sie müssen auch ein Visum beantragen.
(*c*) Es kommt darauf an.

2 Sind Sie in Deutschland geboren?
(*a*) Es kommt darauf an.
(*b*) Ja, und ich bin auch hier groß geworden.
(*c*) Meine Mutter ist Deutsche, aber mein Vater ist Spanier.

3 Wieviel Geld darf ich nach Großbritannien mitnehmen?
(*a*) Sie dürfen nur Reiseschecks mitnehmen.

(*b*) Soviel wie Sie wollen!
(*c*) Bargeld darf man nur in kleinen Mengen mitnehmen.

4 Warum finden Sie es so günstig, mit der Kreditkarte zu bezahlen?
(*a*) Weil ich dann erst am Ende des Monats abrechnen muß!
(*b*) Weil ich dann Euroschecks in Pfund Sterling ausstellen kann.
(*c*) Weil mir meine Eltern finanzielle Hilfe leisten.

5 Kann ich Sie zu einem unserer Charterflüge überreden?
(*a*) Nein, danke. Da kaufe ich lieber Reiseschecks.
(*b*) Ja, gerne. Wir wollen zu viert im Auto meines Freundes fahren.
(*c*) Nein, danke. Ich fahre mit dem Wagen nach England.

Was Sie wissen sollten

Identity Cards and Registration

It often comes as a surprise to visitors from the English-speaking world that Germans are required to carry personal identity cards. Particularly in Britain, where even the driving licence does not carry the bearer's photograph, the idea of introducing identity cards is considered by many an infringement of personal liberty.

Despite protests from some quarters, the machine-readable identity card (**maschinenlesbarer Ausweis**) was gradually introduced from 1987 onwards. Machine-readable passports were introduced in 1988.

In Germany there is also a requirement to register with the Police (**die Anmeldepflicht**) and to notify the Police of any change of address (**sich ummelden**). Persons with a second home are required to declare which is legally their first and which their second residence (**erster und zweiter Wohnsitz**).

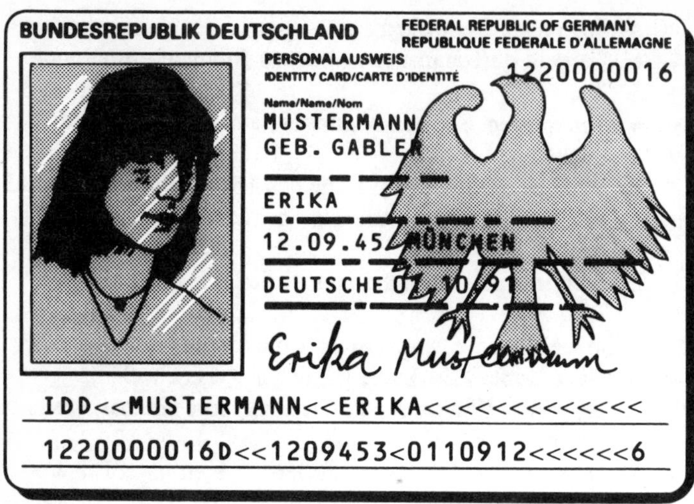

Wichtige Redewendungen

How to

1 *Ask for information*

(*a*) *in a direct way.*
Brauche ich einen Reisepaß?
Kann ich mit Kreditkarte bezahlen?
Wieviel Geld darf ich mitnehmen?
Wann kommt dieser Zug in München an?

(*b*) *in an indirect way.*

Könnten Sie mir bitte sagen,	ob ich einen Reisepaß brauche.
	ob ich mit der Kreditkarte bezahlen kann.
Ich hätte gerne gewußt,	wieviel Geld ich mitnehmen darf.
	wann dieser Zug in München ankommt.

2 *Advise someone against a course of action*

(*a*) *in a fairly informal way.*
Nehmen Sie lieber nicht Bargeld in großen Mengen mit.

Fahren Sie lieber nicht mit dem Wagen in die Stadtmitte.
Gehen Sie lieber nicht direkt nach dem Essen schwimmen.

(*b*) *in a rather formal way.*

Ich würde Ihnen davon abraten,	Bargeld in großen Mengen mitzunehmen. mit dem Wagen in die Stadtmitte zu fahren. direkt nach dem Essen schwimmen zu gehen.

Die Bankwelt (*The world of banking*)

das Sparkonto (-konten) *savings account*
das laufende Konto *current account*
der Geldschein (-e) (*bank*) *note, bill*
die Banknote (-n) *bank note*
der Geldautomat (-en) *cash dispenser*
die Kasse *cash desk, till, check-out*
die Devisen (*f. pl.*) *foreign currency*
das Scheckbuch (¨er) *cheque book*
die Münze (-n) *coin*
das Markstück (¨e) (*one*) *mark piece*
der Pfennig (-/e) *pfennig**
der Groschen (-) 10 *pfennig piece*
der Zinssatz (¨e) *interest rate*
der Wechselkurs (-e) *exchange rate*

*100 *Pfennige* = 1 *Mark*

Grammatik

1 Infinitive clauses

Certain expressions in both English and German often require what is termed an ***infinitive clause*** to complete the sense of the sentence:

e.g.,	Haben Sie Zeit, Ich habe versucht, Er hat mir geraten,	etwas zu tun.
	Have you (got) time *I tried* *He advised me*	*to do something.*

Note that in German the infinitive (in the case above **zu tun**) comes at the end of the clause. In fact, a few examples of such clauses have occurred in earlier units:

Lektion 6:	Hast du Zeit, **mit mir essen zu gehen?**
Lektion 8:	Dann rate ich Ihnen, **mal in den Englischen Garten zu gehen.**
Lektion 9:	Ich habe versucht, **bei dir anzurufen.**
Lektion 14:	Ich habe jede Gelegenheit wahrgenommen, **Englisch zu sprechen.**

and in this unit:

Ich wurde Ihnen davon abraten, **Bargeld in großen Mengen mitzunehmen.**
Ich finde es günstig, **wo möglich mit Kreditkarte einzukaufen.**
Sie hat mich und meinen Freund dazu eingeladen, **bei ihr im Zentrum Londons zu wohnen.**

Note that a comma separates the infinitive clause from the rest of the sentence (as in the above examples) except where the clause consists only of **zu** and the infinitive:

Ich habe keine Zeit **zu essen.**

Other expressions that frequently produce an infinitive construction include:

Ich habe Lust, Ich habe Angst, Ich habe vergessen, Ich hoffe, Ich habe vor, Es ist wichtig, Es lohnt sich,	etwas zu tun.
I have the inclination *I am afraid* *I have forgotten* *I hope* *I intend* *It is important*	*to do something.*
It is worth(while)	*doing something.*

2 *Um . . . zu . . .*

A further variation on the infinitive clause is the **um . . . zu . . .** (*in order* *to . . .*) clause. The **um** marks the beginning of the clause and the infinitive, as always, appears at the end:

> Brauche ich einen Reisepaß, **um nach Großbritannien zu fahren**? *Do I need a passport (in order) to go to Britain?*
> Dora ging ins Geschäft, **um ein Kleid zu kaufen.** *Dora went into the shop (in order) to buy a dress.*
> Du arbeitest zu schnell, **um genau sein zu können.** *You work too quickly to be able to be accurate.*

As in the above examples, the use of **um . . . zu . . .** normally indicates purpose, intention or marks the consequence of an action.

3 *(an)statt . . . zu . . . , ohne . . . zu . . .*

The prepositions **(an)statt** (*instead of*) and **ohne** (*without*) may also be used as conjunctions to introduce infinitive clauses:

> Gestern spielte Dieter Fußball, **(an)statt** in die Schule zu gehen.
> *Dieter played football yesterday instead of going to school.*
> **Statt** um 11 Uhr ins Bett zu gehen, arbeitete Klaus die ganze Nacht.
> *Instead of going to bed at 11 o'clock Klaus worked the whole night.*
> Jutta verließ das Restaurant, **ohne** zu bezahlen.
> *Jutta left the restaurant without paying.*
> Birgit setzte sich, **ohne** ihren Freunden ein Wort zu sagen.
> *Birgit sat down without saying a word to her friends.*

Note that, in these examples, the infinitive clause in German is rendered by an *-ing* clause in English.

4 Indirect questions introduced by *ob*

Direct questions such as:

> Brauche ich einen Reisepaß?
> *and* Haben Sie die deutsche Staatsangehörigkeit?

can be made into indirect questions as follows:

> Könnten Sie mir sagen, **ob** ich einen Reisepaß brauche.
> Ich hätte gern gewußt, **ob** Sie die deutsche Staatsangehörigkeit haben.

Note that the dependent clause is introduced by the word **ob** (*whether*) and that, as in the indirect questions dealt with in **Lektion 8**, the verb goes to the end of the clause.

5 *darauf, davon, usw.*

The form **da-** + preposition is often used in German to express what is rendered in English by a preposition + *it*. For example **davon** (*of it, from it*), **damit** (*with it*), **dafür** (*for it*). If the preposition begins with a vowel, then an additional **-r-** is inserted: **darauf** (*on it*), **darüber** (*above it*), **daraus** (*out of it*).

Examples that have occurred so far include:

> Ich habe mit ihnen Französisch geredet und **dadurch** meine Französischkenntnisse verbessert.
> *I spoke French with them and thus* (lit. *through it*) *improved my knowledge of French*. **Lektion 9**.
> Ich möchte Ihnen ein paar Fragen stellen, wenn Sie nichts **dagegen** haben.
> *I should like to ask you a few questions if you don't mind* (lit. *if you have nothing against it*). **Lektion 12 VS**.
> Sonneschein und Temperaturen bis zu 25 Grad und **darüber** . . .
> *Sunshine and temperatures up to 25 degrees and above* (lit. *above it*). **Lektion 13**.
> Sie würden nichts **dabei** verlieren.
> *You wouldn't lose anything thereby* (lit. *by it*). **Lektion 14**.

6 Prepositions associated with nouns, adjectives and verbs

Prepositions often occur in association with

(*a*) nouns	Er bekämpfte seine **Angst vor** dem Tod. *He fought his **fear of** death.*
(*b*) adjectives	Sie ist **von** ihren Eltern **abhängig**. *She is **dependent on** her parents.*
(*c*) verbs	Ich **verlasse mich auf** deine Hilfe. ***I am relying on** your assistance.*

The link between the noun/adjective/verb and the preposition is sometimes very close and sometimes somewhat looser. For instance, if in the sentence

> Ich verlasse mich auf deine Hilfe.

the prepositional phrase **auf deine Hilfe** is omitted, the remaining phrase **ich verlasse mich** makes no sense on its own. This shows that there is a very close link between the verb **sich verlassen** and the preposition **auf**. However, in the sentence

> Frank und Anna haben uns zu einem Drink eingeladen. *Frank and Anna have invited us for a drink.*

the prepositional phrase **zu einem Drink** may be omitted and we are still left with a complete sentence. The link between the verb **einladen** and the preposition **zu** is in this case less close than that between **sich verlassen** and **auf**.

Often prepositions of this kind introduce not merely a noun (as in the above examples) but a clause:

> Ich verlasse mich darauf, daß du mir morgen hilfst. *I am relying on your helping me tomorrow.*
> Frank und Anna haben uns (dazu) eingeladen, heute abend bei ihnen zu essen. *Frank and Anna have invited us to eat at theirs this evening.*

Note that the **da(r)** + preposition construction is often used to provide the link between the main clause and the dependent clause, although it may be omitted in those instances where the link between the noun/adjective/verb and the preposition is a loose one.

Examples from the **Dialog** are:

> Es kommt darauf an, ob Sie die deutsche Staatsangehörigkeit haben oder nicht.
> Bloß würde ich Ihnen (davon) abraten, Bargeld in großen Mengen mitzunehmen.
> Dann kann ich mich darauf verlassen, daß mein Urlaubsgeld gesichert ist.
> Außerdem darf ich sie vielleicht darauf aufmerksam machen, daß Sie auch noch Euroschecks in Pfund Sterling ausstellen können.
> Als Studentin bin ich sowieso davon abhängig, daß mir meine Eltern finanzielle Hilfe leisten.
> Sie hat mich und meinen Freund (dazu) eingeladen, bei ihr im Zentrum Londons zu wohnen.

Two more verbs which occurred in the **Dialog, sorgen für** and **überreden (zu)** may be used to produce sentences of this kind:

> Wir haben dafür gesorgt, daß Unterkunft in einem Hotel reserviert ist.
> *We have seen to it that accommodation in an hotel has been reserved.*
> Sie hat uns (dazu) überredet, nach Berlin zu fliegen.
> *She persuaded us to fly to Berlin.*

7 Genitive Case

The genitive case is used not only after certain prepositions (see **Lektion 14**), but also in many instances where, in English, either the preposition *of* or the 'possessive' *s* would be used:

> at the end **of** the day/at the day's end
> the mother **of** John/John's mother
> at the beginning **of** next week (although ***not*** in this instance: at next week's beginning)

Examples of the genitive which occurred in the **Dialog** are:

> Sie können in alle Länder **der Europäischen Gemeinschaft** (*fem. sing.*) reisen.
> *You can travel to all countries of the European Community.*
> . . . da ich erst am Ende **des Monats** (*masc. sing.*) abrechnen muß.
> *. . . as I don't have to pay until the end of the month*
> Kann ich Sie zu einem **unserer Charterflüge** (*masc. pl.*) überreden?
> *Can I persuade you to (take) one of our charter flights?*

As already pointed out in **Lektion 14**, the distinctive feature of the masculine and neuter singular forms in the genitive is an **s** on both the article (or possessive adjective etc.) and the noun. When the noun is of one syllable only, the ending is often **es**:

Wer ist der Vater diese**s** Mädchen**s**?	*Who is the father of this girl?*
am Ende des Krieg**es**	*at the end of the war*
in der Nähe meines Haus**es**	*near my house*

The distinctive feature of the feminine singular and of the plural (all genders) is an **r**. No ending is added to the noun:

das Auto meine**r** Mutter	*my mother's car*
am Ende de**r** Geschichte	*at the end of the story*
die Wohnung meine**r** Freunde	*my friends' flat*

Proper names normally take an **-s** in the genitive:

die Königin Englands/Englands Königin	*The Queen of England*
die Museen Kölns/Kölns Museen	*Cologne's museums*

Proper names ending in a sibilant (**s, ß, tz, z, x**) take an apostrophe in the genitive (which is of course only noticeable in the written language):

Klaus' Schwester   Fritz' Wagen   Agnes' Buch

The genitive is often avoided, particularly in informal German, by introducing the preposition **von** (+*dat.*):

> in der Nähe von meinem Haus
> das Auto von meiner Mutter
> die Wohnung von meinen Freunden
> die Königin von England
> die Schwester von Klaus

It is also fairly common in German to join two nouns together, using the genitive **(e)s** to effect the combination:

der Monatsanfang	*the beginning of the month*
das Jahresende	*the end of the year*
die Landeshauptstadt	*regional capital*

Remember that in expressions of quantity neither the genitive nor **von** (+*dat.*) is required (see **Lektion 7**):

ein Glas Weißwein; zwei Tassen Tee; ein Kilo Tomaten

Übungen

ÜBUNG 15.1 Was kann man auch sagen?

1 Wann fährt der nächste Zug nach Paris?
(*a*) Fährt dieser Zug nach Paris?
(*b*) Bitte sagen Sie mir, wann der nächste Zug nach Paris fährt.
(*c*) Fährt der nächste Zug nach Paris?

2 Ich rate Ihnen davon ab, mit dem Zug nach Paris zu fahren.
(*a*) Fahren Sie lieber nicht mit dem Zug nach Paris.
(*b*) Es ist eine gute Idee, mit dem Zug nach Paris zu fahren.
(*c*) Möchten Sie nicht mit dem Zug nach Paris fahren?

3 Ich habe aber keine Lust, mit dem Bus zu fahren.
(*a*) Ich finde die Busfahrt aber zu teuer.
(*b*) Mit dem Bus möchte ich aber lieber nicht fahren.
(*c*) Ich fahre aber sehr gerne mit dem Bus.

4 Dann rate ich Ihnen zu fliegen.
(*a*) Dann könnte ich vielleicht fliegen.
(*b*) Haben Sie dann Zeit zu fliegen?
(*c*) Dann wäre es eine gute Idee zu fliegen.

5 Ich fliege nicht gern.
(*a*) Fliegen gefällt mir nicht.
(*b*) Ich habe nicht vor zu fliegen.
(*c*) Ich nehme jede Gelegenheit wahr zu fliegen.

6 Ich möchte unbedingt mit der Bahn fahren.
(*a*) Ich hoffe, mit der Bahn zu fahren.
(*b*) Ich möchte unbedingt nicht mit dem Bus fahren.
(*c*) Ich will unbedingt mit dem Zug fahren.

ÜBUNG 15.2 Was paßt zusammen?

Whilst at first glance a number of combinations seem possible, in fact only one combination in each instance will provide a series of sentences that together form a meaningful unit.

Pläne für den Sommerurlaub

1 Ich habe vor, . . .
2 Ich habe also gestern angefangen, . . .
3 Ich finde es wichtig, . . .
4 Ich bin der Meinung, daß es sich nicht lohnt, . . .
5 Ich habe deshalb die Gelegenheit wahrgenommen, . . .
6 Ich habe leider keine Zeit, . . .
7 Ich werde aber versuchen, . . .
8 Ich hoffe natürlich auch, . . .

(*a*) in einem Hotel zu wohnen.
(*b*) während meines Aufenthaltes nur Spanisch zu sprechen.
(*c*) ein ganzes Jahr in Spanien zu arbeiten.
(*d*) die Sehenswürdigkeiten Madrids besichtigen zu können.
(*e*) Spanisch zu lernen.
(*f*) im kommenden Sommer nach Spanien zu fahren.
(*g*) für den Monat Juli die Wohnung eines deutschen Freundes in Madrid zu mieten.
(*h*) wenigstens ein paar Worte (*words*) Spanisch sprechen zu können.

ÜBUNG 15.3 Herr Droste möchte nach Amerika fahren

Herr Droste bombards his travel agent with questions about his trip to the United States. Re-phrase the pairs of sentences as indicated in the examples.

> Muß ich ein Visum beantragen? Das möchte ich gerne wissen.
> ***Ich möchte gerne wissen, ob ich ein Visum beantragen muß.***
> Wieviel Geld brauche ich für 3 Wochen? Könnten Sie mir das sagen?
> ***Könnten Sie mir sagen, wieviel Geld ich für 3 Wochen brauche?***

1 Kann ich in den Vereinigten Staaten Euroschecks ausstellen? Ich möchte mich danach erkundigen.
2 Haben die Banken auch sonnabends auf? Das muß ich unbedingt wissen.
3 Kann ich mit meiner Kreditkarte zahlen? Könnten Sie mir das sagen?

4 Wie steht der Wechselkurs des Dollars? Das sollten Sie ja wissen.
5 Was kostet der Flug München—New York? Das können Sie mir wohl sagen?
6 Wie lange dauert der Flug? Das hätte ich auch noch gerne gewußt.
7 Brauche ich ein Visum? Das verstehe ich immer noch nicht!
8 Wer bin ich? Wissen Sie denn nicht?!

ÜBUNG 15.4 Sagen Sie es anders.

Beispiele: Die Schwester von meinem neuen Freund ist sehr arrogant.
Die Schwester ***meines neuen Freundes*** ist sehr arrogant.
Das Auto von dieser Schwester ist natürlich ganz neu.
Das Auto ***dieser Schwester*** ist natürlich ganz neu.

1 Das Auto von meinem Freund ist dagegen schon 12 Jahre alt.
2 Mir gefällt es aber besser als das neue Auto von seiner arroganten Schwester.
3 Ich finde die Form von alten Autos viel schöner.
4 Meinem Freund gefällt das Haus von meinen Eltern.
5 Schon die Lage von diesem Haus ist sehr attraktiv.
6 Es steht in der Nähe von einem schönen Wald.
7 Das Haus war ein Geschenk von meinem Großvater an meinen Vater.
8 So ein Haus kostet heute viel mehr als das neue Auto von der Schwester von meinem neuen Freund!

ÜBUNG 15.5 Ergänzen Sie.

Insert **dafür, davon, dazu, darauf** as appropriate:

Werner Du! Ich verlasse mich . . . (1) . . . , daß du morgen nachmittag mit mir nach Wien fährst.

Nikola Du weißt ja, daß es . . . (2) . . . abhängig ist, daß der Chef morgen nicht im Büro ist.

Werner Ich werde . . . (3) . . . sorgen, daß er morgen den ganzen Tag zu Hause bleibt!

Nikola Könnte ich dich nicht . . . (4) . . . überreden, erst nach 5.00 Uhr loszufahren?

Werner Nein. Dann hätten wir keine Zeit . . . (5) . . . , in Wien ins Theater zu gehen.

Nikola Na, gut. Aber ich rate dir . . . (6) . . . ab, mich vom Büro abzuholen.

ÜBUNG 15.6 Sagen Sie es anders.

Ein guter Rat

Beispiele: Du solltest zu Hause bleiben können und nicht die ganze Zeit fernsehen.
Du solltest zu Hause bleiben können, ***ohne die ganze Zeit fernzusehen***.

Du solltest früh ins Bett gehen. Dann könntest du früher aufstehen.
Du solltest früh ins Bett gehen, ***um früher aufstehen zu können***.

Du solltest früher aufstehen und nicht so lange schlafen.
Du solltest früher aufstehen, ***anstatt so lange zu schlafen***.

1 Du solltest einkaufen gehen können und nicht jedesmal neue Kleidung kaufen.

2 Du solltest heute abend deine Oma besuchen und nicht ins Kino gehen.

3 Du solltest zu Mittag im Büro essen. Dann könntest du länger arbeiten.

4 Du solltest zu Hause Mineralwasser trinken und nicht jeden Abend in die Kneipe gehen.

5 Du solltest weniger essen. Dann könntest du schlank werden.

6 Du solltest deinen Urlaub hier verbringen. Dann könntest du viel Geld sparen.

7 Du solltest im Restaurant essen können und nicht jedesmal das teuerste Gericht bestellen.

8 Und du? Du solltest den Mund halten und nicht so viel Unsinn (*nonsense*) reden!

Verstehen Sie?

1 Konversation

Eine Reise nach China

Herr Schulz makes enquiries in his local travel agency about a visit he hopes to make to China.

Herr Schulz	Guten Tag. Ich hätte gern gewußt, ob es möglich ist, als Tourist nach China zu reisen.
Frau Falke	Möglich ist es schon. Wir können zum Beispiel preiswerte Gruppenreisen mit festgelegten Programmen anbieten.
Herr Schulz	Was für Reisedokumente muß man haben?
Frau Falke	Es kommt darauf an, ob Sie Bundesbürger sind, oder nicht.
Herr Schulz	Ich bin Bundesbürger, aber meine Freundin, die auch mitfahren will, ist Japanerin.
Frau Falke	Also, zur Einreise nach China benötigen Bürger der Bundesrepublik einen gültigen Reisepaß, eine Einreisegenehmigung und ein Visum. Nach der erforderlichen Dokumentation für Japaner müßte ich mich erkundigen.
Herr Schulz	Und wie beantragt man die Einreisegenehmigung beziehungsweise das Visum?
Frau Falke	Wir besorgen alle erforderlichen Genehmigungen.
Herr Schulz	Kann man auch Individualreisen unternehmen?
Frau Falke	Ja, selbstverständlich. Wenn Sie Ihre Reiseroute selbst bestimmen wollen, können wir Ihnen auch Hotelzimmer buchen.
Herr Schulz	Vielen Dank für die Auskunft.

anbieten (*sep.*) *to offer*
die Gruppenreise (-n) *package tour* (lit. *group travel*)
festgelegt *fixed*
der Bundesbürger (-) *citizen of the Federal Republic*
benötigen *to require*
die Einreise (-n) *entry*
gültig *valid*
erforderlich *required, necessary*
beziehungsweise *alternatively, or*
besorgen *to take care of, see to*
bestimmen *to determine, decide on*
buchen *to book*
die Auskunft (¨e) *information*

Richtig (R) oder Falsch (F)?

1 Es ist möglich, als Tourist nach China zu reisen.
2 Man kann zum Beispiel mit einer Gruppe dorthin reisen.
3 Herr Schulz möchte wissen, was für Reisedokumente man benötigt, um nach China zu reisen.
4 Er fährt allein nach China.
5 Bürger der Bundesrepublik Deutschland brauchen zur Einreise nach China nur einen gültigen Reisepaß.
6 Frau Falke weiß nichts über die erforderliche Dokumentation für Japaner.
7 Man darf nur mit einer Reisegruppe nach China reisen.
8 Man kann die Reiseroute selbst bestimmen.

2 Lesetexte

Text A

Lesen Sie den Text, und versuchen Sie, die Fragen zu beantworten. Nur wenn Sie auf Schwierigkeiten stoßen, sollten Sie sich die 'wichtigen Vokabeln' ansehen.

Ihre Eintrittskarte für die Welt

In Deutschland und in mehr als 160 Ländern weltweit sind Sie bei über 5,4 Millionen EUROCARD-Akzeptanzstellen immer willkommen. Bei Fluggesellschaften, Reisebüros, Autovermietungen. In Hotels, Restaurants, Geschäften. Und Sie können den Bargeldservice im In- und Ausland bei mehr als 120 000 Geschäftsstellen von Kreditinstituten nutzen. Für 100 Mark Jahresbeitrag bietet Ihnen die EUROCARD in Verbindung mit der international verbreiteten MasterCard und Access in Großbritannien eines der dichtesten Akzeptanznetze rund um die Welt.

Fragen Sie nach den weiteren Vorteilen und Zusatzleistungen der EUROCARD. Und zwar dort, wo Sie auch Ihre eurocheque-Karte bekommen. Ihr kontoführendes Kreditinstitut hält EUROCARD-Anträge für Sie bereit.

EUROCARD: Eine Empfehlung der deutschen Banken und Sparkassen.

1 In which countries is EUROCARD accepted?
2 Give six examples of places where you might wish to use your EUROCARD.
3 What further EUROCARD service is offered both at home and abroad?
4 What does the figure of 100 Marks represent?
5 How is it that EUROCARD is so widely accepted?
6 Where can one enquire about the further advantages and additional facilities offered by EUROCARD?
7 Where can you pick up the application form?
8 By whom is EUROCARD recommended?

die Eintrittskarte (-n) *entrance ticket*
willkommen *welcome*
die Geschäftsstelle (-n) *business outlet*
die Fluggesellschaft (-en) *airline company*
die Autovermietung (-en) *car rental*
der Jahresbeitrag (¨e) *annual subscription*
die Verbindung (-en) *association*
verbreitet *wide-spread*
dicht *dense*
der Vorteil (-e) *advantage*
die Zusatzleistung (en) *additional service*
kontoführend *account holding*
der Antrag (¨e) *application*
bereithalten *to keep (ready)*
die Empfehlung *recommendation*

Text B

Lesen Sie den Text.

Try to work out the meaning of the relatively few words that have as yet not been introduced. All words are however listed in the back if you do have difficulties.

5 Millionen VISA-Partner laden Sie ein, bargeldlos . . .

. . . **im Restaurant** zu speisen oder einen kleinen **Imbiß** einzunehmen, die **Friseur-** und **Blumenladenrechnung** zu begleichen, das **Taxi** oder die **KFZ-Reparatur** zu bezahlen, im **Kaufhaus** das eine oder andere zu besorgen, den **Urlaub** im **Reisebüro** zu buchen, **Flugtickets** und **Schiffspassagen** abzurechnen, **Hotelrechnungen** auszugleichen, mal außer der Reihe Freunde **einzuladen** und zu **bewirten**, in der **Boutique** oder im **Laden** nebenan die günstige Gelegenheit zu nutzen, wann immer Sie möchten.
Und vieles mehr.

Nehmen Sie *diese Einladung* an.

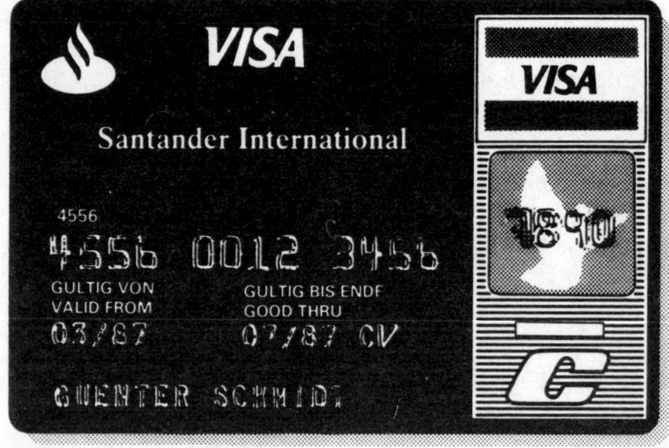

16 Ich habe starke Kopfschmerzen

In this unit you will learn ways of talking about illnesses and ailments.

Dialog

Herr Berg has been suffering from bad headaches, so he makes an appointment to see Dr Klein. She quickly diagnoses his problem, refers him to a specialist and prescribes him tablets.

Dr. Klein Guten Tug, Herr Berg. Wie kann ich Ihnen behilflich sein?

Herr Berg Guten Tag, Frau Doktor. Ich bekomme jetzt seit zwei oder drei Jahren ziemlich oft starke Kopfschmerzen. Gestern habe ich wieder den ganzen Tag Kopfschmerzen gehabt, und ich habe mich deshalb entschlossen, zu Ihnen zu kommen.

Dr. Klein Das tut mir aber leid. Wie fühlen Sie sich sonst, und wie lange dauern jedesmal die Kopfschmerzen?

Herr Berg Ungefähr zwölf Stunden. Beim Aufwachen sind die Kopfschmerzen schon ziemlich stark. Wenn ich dann aufstehe, wird mir übel. Manchmal muß ich mich auch übergeben.

Dr. Klein Und die Kopfschmerzen erscheinen gerade dann, wenn Sie besonders viel zu erledigen haben, nicht wahr?

Herr Berg Genau! Das ist eben ein Problem, das immer wieder auftaucht. Aber wie haben Sie das denn wissen können?

Dr. Klein Weil Ihre Symptome typisch sind für Menschen, die an Migräne leiden. In solchen Fällen spielt der Streß fast immer eine Rolle. Wir müssen auch feststellen, ob Sie gegen gewisse Nahrungsmittel oder Getränke—wie zum Beispiel Käse oder Rotwein—allergisch sind.

Herr Berg Ach was! Soll ich denn etwa auf den guten Rotwein, den ich so gerne trinke, verzichten?

Dr. Klein Nicht unbedingt. Ich empfehle Ihnen einen Facharzt, der Ihnen bestimmt helfen kann. Vorläufig verschreibe ich Ihnen Tabletten, die Sie einnehmen müssen, sobald Sie Kopfschmerzen bekommen.

Herr Berg Ich bedanke mich, Frau Doktor. Diesen Besuch hatte ich seit langem verschoben. Jetzt bin ich aber erleichtert.

Wie kann ich Ihnen behilflich sein? *How can I help you?*
oft *often*
starke Kopfschmerzen (*m. pl.*) *bad headache(s)*
sich entschließen *to decide, resolve*
jedesmal *every time, each time*
beim Aufwachen *upon awakening*
mir wird übel *I feel sick*
sich übergeben *to vomit*
besonders *especially*
erledigen *to deal with, do*
genau *precisely*
ein Problem, das immer wieder auftaucht *a problem that keeps on cropping up*
immer wieder *again and again*
auftauchen (*sep.*) *to crop up, turn up*
das Symptom (-e) *symptom*
der Mensch (-en) (*wk. noun*) *human being*
die Migräne *migraine*
leiden an/unter (+*dat.*) *to suffer from*
für Menschen, die an Migräne leiden *for people who suffer from migraine*
solch- *such*
der Fall (¨e) *case*
der Streß *stress*
eine Rolle spielen *to play a role*
feststellen (*sep.*) *to find out, ascertain*
gewiß *certain*
das Nahrungsmittel (-) *food(stuff)*
der Käse (-) *cheese*
allergisch gegen (+*acc.*) *allergic to*
etwa *an intensifier indicating surprise or indignation*
verzichten (auf+*acc.*) *to do without, abstain from*
nicht unbedingt *not necessarily*
der Facharzt (¨e) *specialist (doctor)*
vorläufig *for the time being*
einnehmen (*sep.*) *to take (of tablets, meals, etc.)*
sobald *as soon as*
sich bedanken *to say thank you*
verschieben *to postpone*
erleichtert *relieved*

Fragen zum Dialog

1 Richtig (R) oder Falsch (F)?

1 Herr Berg bekommt seit zwei oder drei Monaten ziemlich oft starke Kopfschmerzen.
2 Weil er auch gestern Kopfschmerzen gehabt hat, hat er sich entschlossen, zum Arzt zu gehen.
3 Die Kopfschmerzen dauern meistens nur zwei Stunden.
4 Wenn Herr Berg Kopfschmerzen hat, wird ihm beim Aufstehen übel.
5 Er bekommt die Kopfschmerzen, wenn er unter Streß leidet.
6 Seine Symptome sind nicht besonders typisch für Menschen, die an Migräne leiden.
7 Dr Klein empfiehlt Herrn Berg einen Facharzt.
8 Herr Berg trinkt sehr gerne Rotwein.
9 Herr Berg muß die Tabletten, die ihm Dr Klein verschreibt, jeden Tag einnehmen.
10 Herr Berg wollte schon seit langem zum Arzt, ist aber erst heute dazu gekommen.

2 Welche Antwort paßt?

1 Ich bekomme seit zwei Jahren ziemlich oft starke Kopfschmerzen.
(*a*) Das tut mir aber leid.
(*b*) Das finde ich aber günstig!
(*c*) Da haben Sie recht!

2 Und wie fühlen Sie sich sonst, wenn Sie Kopfschmerzen bekommen?
(*a*) Das ist ein Problem, das immer wieder auftaucht.
(*b*) Gestern habe ich wieder den ganzen Tag Kopfschmerzen gehabt.
(*c*) Mir wird übel, wenn ich aufstehe.

3 Wie haben Sie wissen können, wann meine Kopfschmerzen erscheinen?
(*a*) Weil ich mich manchmal übergeben muß.
(*b*) Weil Ihre Symptome typisch sind für Menschen, die an Migräne leiden.
(*c*) Weil ich heute besonders viel zu erledigen habe.

4 Darf ich dann keinen Rotwein mehr trinken?
   (*a*) Nicht unbedingt.
   (*b*) Soviel wie Sie wollen.
   (*c*) Ach, wie schade!

5 Ich empfehle Ihnen einen Facharzt, der Ihnen bestimmt helfen kann.
   (*a*) Das glaube ich Ihnen.
   (*b*) Ich bedanke mich, Frau Doktor.
   (*c*) Das wäre kein Problem.

Was Sie wissen sollten

Health Insurance in Germany

Almost all Germans enjoy the protection of health insurance or 'sickness insurance' (**Krankenversicherung**). Most are compulsorily insured with one of the health insurance companies (**Krankenkassen**) within the welfare state system. The best-known of these is the **AOK** (**Allgemeine Ortskrankenkasse**—*general local health insurance company*).

Because **Krankenkassen** are relatively rich, they are able to provide a very high standard of health care. For instance, waiting lists for operations are virtually unknown and very generous provision is made for convalescence. The German tradition of taking a **Kur** (*rest cure*) at a **Kurort** (*spa*) is also supported by the **Krankenkassen**. Despite all this, some people take out an additional insurance with a private health insurance company for non-essential extras, such as a private room during a stay in hospital.

When a patient requires medical attention, he or she presents a health insurance form (**Krankenschein**) which the doctor completes and submits for the payment of medical fees.

British visitors to Germany may obtain free urgent medical treatment by presenting Form E111 (issued by the DSS) to the nearest **AOK** office. This office will issue a **Krankenschein** which grants free treatment by any doctor or dentist belonging to the scheme.

Immer in
Ihrer Nähe

Wir haben für Sie geöffnet:

Mo–Fr	8.00–12.00 Uhr
	und 14.00–15.30 Uhr

Tel. erreichen Sie uns:

Mo–Fr	7.15–16.00 Uhr

Ein automatischer Anrufbeantworter
nimmt Ihre Gespräche außerhalb der
angegebenen Zeiten entgegen.

der Spezialist
für Sozialversicherung

Wichtige Redewendungen

Three ways of talking about aches and pains

1	Ich habe	Kopfschmerzen.	*I have*	*a headache*
		Zahnschmerzen.		*toothache.*
		Ohrenschmerzen.		*earache.*
		Halsschmerzen.		*a sore throat.*
		Rückenschmerzen.		*backache.*
		Bauchschmerzen/ Magenschmerzen.		*stomach-ache.*

2 Ich habe Schmerzen	im Bauch/Magen.	*I have a pain in my*	*stomach.*
	in der Hand.		*hand.*
	im Rücken.		*back.*
	im Auge.		*eye.*
	in der Nase.		*nose.*
	im Fuß.		*foot.*

3 Mein	Bein	tut weh.	*My*	*leg*	*hurts.*
Meine	Hand			*hand*	
Mein	Knie			*knee*	
Meine	Schulter			*shoulder*	
Meine	Augen	tun weh.	*My*	*eyes*	*hurt.*
	Füße			*feet*	
	Hände			*hands*	
	Ohren			*ears*	

For certain parts of the body all three of the patterns listed above may be used:

Ich habe Rückenschmerzen.
Ich habe Schmerzen im Rücken.
Mein Rücken tut weh.

For others, only two of the three patterns will normally be appropriate:

Ich habe Schmerzen im Bein.
Mein Bein tut weh.
(*but rarely*, *if ever*, Ich habe Beinschmerzen.)

Krankheiten (*Illnesses*)

die Masern (*pl*) *measles*	**die Erkältung** *cold*
Mumps (*masc or fem*) *mumps*	**die Grippe** *influenza*
die Windpocken *chicken pox*	**das Fieber** *fever*
die Halsentzündung *throat infection*	**der Krebs** *cancer*
der Schnupfen (-) *cold, snuffles*	**der Husten (-)** *cough*

Ich bin (stark) erkältet. *I have a (heavy) cold.*
Ich habe einen (leichten) Schnupfen. *I have a (slight) cold/the snuffles.*
Sie hat (hohes) Fieber. *She has a (high) temperature.*

Grammatik

1 Relative Clauses

The following sentences from the **Dialog** contain examples of ***relative clauses*** (indicated in bold typeface). Each relative clause is introduced by a ***relative pronoun*** (in italic) which in English is translated by *which, that who(m)* etc.:

> Das ist eben ein Problem, ***das*** **immer wieder auftaucht.**
> Ihre Symptome sind typisch für Menschen, ***die*** **an Migräne leiden**.
> Soll ich denn etwa auf den guten Rotwein, ***den*** **ich so gerne trinke**, verzichten?
> Ich empfehle Ihnen einen Facharzt, ***der*** **Ihnen bestimmt helfen kann**.
> Ich verschreibe Ihnen Tabletten, ***die*** **Sie einnehmen müssen**, sobald Sie Kopfschmerzen bekommen.

Note that the relative pronoun agrees in number and gender with the noun to which it refers in the main clause. The case of the relative pronoun depends on its function within the relative clause. For instance, in the second example above:

> . . . , den ich so gerne trinke, . . .

the relative pronoun **den** is masculine and singular because it refers to **Rotwein** in the main clause. It is in the accusative case because it is the object of the relative clause.

Relative pronouns may not be omitted in German, whereas in English they often are:

> Der Mann, dem du gestern geholfen hast, hat vor einer Stunde angerufen.
> *The man* (*whom*) *you helped yesterday phoned an hour ago.*

As in English, relative pronouns are often used together with prepositions:

> Wie heißt der Student, mit dem Dagmar ins Kino gegangen ist?
> *What's the name of the student* ***with whom*** *Dagmar has gone to the cinema?*

In German, however, the preposition may not be separated from the relative pronoun as it often is in English:

> *What's the name of the student* ***who*** *Dagmar has gone to the cinema* ***with****?*

Here is a summary of relative pronouns:

	Masculine	*Feminine*	*Neuter*	*Plural* (*Masc., Fem & Neut.*)
	Der Mann,	Die Frau,	Das Kind,	Die Männer, Frauen, Kinder,
Nominative	**der** ...	**die** ...	**das** ...	**die** ...
Accusative	**den** ...	**die** ...	**das** ...	**die** ...
Genitive	**dessen** ...	**deren** ...	**dessen** ...	**deren** ...
Dative	**dem** ...	**der** ...	**dem** ...	**denen** ...

Here are some examples of relative pronouns in use:

Nominative

Wie heißt der Ingenieur, **der** für Frau Schmidt arbeitet?
Kennen Sie die Frau, **die** mir gestern geholfen hat?
Ich möchte ein Auto kaufen, **das** nicht zu teuer ist.
Wie heißen die Leute, **die** im alten Haus in der Kantstraße wohnen?

Accusative

Das ist der Student, **den** ich jeden Tag sehe.
Wo wohnt die alte Dame, für **die** du arbeitest?
Wie heißt das Dorf, durch **das** wir gerade gefahren sind?
Da findest du die Gärten, durch **die** ich so gerne spaziere.

Genitive

Hast du den Mann eingeladen, **dessen** Frau in unserem Büro arbeitet?
Kennt ihr die Lehrerin, **deren** Sohn einen Unfall gehabt hat?
Ist das nicht das Kind, **dessen** Mutter Betriebswirtschaft studiert?
Monika und Klaus, **deren** Eltern im 3. Stock wohnen, möchten zu Jochens Party kommen.

Dative

Wie heißt der Kunde, mit **dem** Ilona essen gegangen ist?
Die Engländerin, mit **der** Werner verheiratet ist, kommt aus Bristol.
Das Haus, in **dem** Norbert und Henny jetzt wohnen, ist sehr schön.
Die Freunde, mit **denen** wir in Urlaub gehen wollen, haben zwei Kinder.

You will see that, in common with other subordinate clauses, the verb in the relative clause is sent to the end of that clause. The relative clause begins with a comma and ends with either a comma, or full stop or a question mark.

The relative pronoun should be as close as possible to the noun to which it refers, but it is sometimes preferable to finish the main clause before starting the relative clause, e.g.:

Konntest du dem Mann helfen, dessen Frau im Krankenhaus liegt?

rather than:

Konntest du dem Mann, dessen Frau im Krankenhaus liegt, helfen?

Sometimes **welch-** plus the appropriate ending is used as a relative pronoun instead of **der, die, das.** Whilst it is generally considered stylistically unaesthetic, it can be used to avoid a clash between the relative pronoun and the definite article and/or the demonstrative pronoun:

Welche Mutter hat ihr Kind verloren?
Die, ***welche*** (*rather than* ***die***) die Party organisiert hat.

2 Verbs as nouns

In German the infinitive form of a verb may be made into a noun (or ***nominalised***) simply by assigning to it the neuter definite article **das** and by capitalising the initial letter. Such nominalisation is often achieved in English by using the **-ing** form:

spielen	*to play*	das Spielen	*the playing*
tanzen	*to dance*	das Tanzen	*the dancing*

Nominalisation is often used when a more formal effect is desired:

Das Sprechen mit dem Fahrer ist während der Fahrt verboten.

rather than:

Es ist verboten, während der Fahrt mit dem Fahrer zu sprechen.

Sometimes the definite article is omitted in both German and English:

Rauchen verboten No smoking

The **Dialog** contains an example of a nominalised verb used together with the preposition **bei** which here has the meaning of *upon:*

Beim Aufwachen sind die Kopfschmerzen schon ziemlich stark.

It would also have been possible, in this instance, to say:

Wenn ich aufwache, sind die Kopfschmerzen schon ziemlich stark.

Beim, im and **am** are all used with the verb **sein** to mean *in the process of*, although the use of **am** is considered colloquial:

Franz ist beim Schreiben.	*Franz is (in the process of) writing.*
Maria ist beim Arbeiten.	*Maria is (in the process of) working.*
Unsere Gäste sind im Weggehen.	*Our guests are (in the process of) leaving.*
Ich bin am Verhungern.	*I am (in the process of) starving.*

A further preposition commonly used with nominalised verbs is **zu**.

Hast du was zum Schreiben?	*Have you got something to write with?*
Ich habe nichts mehr zum Lesen.	*I have nothing left to read.*
Sie kam nicht zum Trinken.	*She didn't get as far as drinking (anything).*
Das ist zum Kotzen! (*vulgar*)	*That's enough to make you puke!*

3 Weak nouns

There is a group of masculine nouns which take **-(e)n** in all cases except the nominative singular. Such nouns are sometimes referred to as **weak nouns** and are designated in the glossary with the abbreviated note: (*wk. noun*). A number of such nouns have already been introduced:

Assistent **(L13)**	Kunde **(L12)**
Automat **(L15)**	Mensch **(L5)**
Bauer **(L5)**	Musikant **(L13)**
Franzose **(L2)**	Prinz **(L13)**
Herr **(L2)**	Russe **(L5)**
Journalist **(L2)**	Schwede **(L2)**
Junge **(L3)**	Soldat **(L10)**
Kandidat **(L11)**	Student **(L2)**
Kollege **(L14)**	Tourist **(L1)**

Here are a few examples of weak nouns in use:

Hast du einen neuen Assistenten?
Von diesem Automaten bekommt man nur Kaffee.
Das Leben eines Bauern kann sehr hart sein.
Sie ist mit einem amerikanischen Soldaten verheiratet.

Note that **der Herr** is slightly irregular in that **-n** is taken in the singular, but **-en** is taken in the plural:

Kennst du Herrn Klingenfelder?
Die Herren aus Frankreich sind sehr freundlich.

4 Perfect Tense of Modal Verbs

As has already been pointed out in **Lekton 12**, the modal verbs (**wollen, müssen, können,** etc.) tend to be used more often in the Imperfect Tense than in the Perfect Tense. Since, however, modal verbs are sometimes used in the Perfect Tense, it is as well to be able to recognise these forms when they occur.

The past participles of the commonly found modal verbs are as follows:

wollen	müssen	können	sollen	dürfen
gewollt	gemußt	gekonnt	gesollt	gedurft

These past participles are used only when there is no infinitive dependent on the modal verb:

Warum hast dieses Buch nicht genommen? Ich habe es nicht **gewollt**.
Warum hat Klaus nicht vor dem Haus geparkt? Das hat er nicht **gedurft**.

When—as is more often the case—there is an infinitive dependent on the modal verb, the infinitive form of the modal is used instead of the past participle. The resulting double infinitive then appears as the end of the sentence or clause:

Ich habe gestern nachmittag ins Kino **gehen wollen**.
Ich habe aber um 2 Uhr zum Arzt **gehen müssen**.
Deshalb habe ich den Film nicht **sehen können**.

If the double infinitive construction appears in a subordinate clause, the auxiliary verb (**haben**) is not sent to the end as might be expected, but is placed instead ***before*** the double infinitive:

Warum hast du gestern nachmittag nicht ins Kino gehen können?
Weil ich um 2 Uhr zum Arzt **habe gehen müssen**.
Ach schade. Ich bin auch nicht hingegangen, weil ich nicht alleine **habe sitzen wollen**.

Übungen

ÜBUNG 16.1 Was kann man auch sagen?

1 Guten Tag. Wie kann ich Ihnen behilflich sein?

(*a*) Guten Tag. Wie kann ich ihnen helfen?
(*b*) Guten Tag. Können Sie mir helfen?
(*c*) Guten Tag. Wie kann ich Ihnen helfen.

2 Ich habe Schmerzen im Rücken.
(*a*) Ich bin auf dem Rückweg.
(*b*) Ich habe Rückenschmerzen.
(*c*) Meine Beine tun weh.

3 Das ist ein Problem, das bei vielen Patienten auftaucht.
(*a*) Probleme findet man bei vielen Patienten.
(*b*) Ich habe viele Patienten, die Probleme haben.
(*c*) Viele Patienten haben dieses Problem.

4 Ich habe große Schwierigkeiten beim Aufstehen.
(*a*) Ich habe große Schwierigkeiten, wenn ich aufstehen will.
(*b*) Ich finde es ganz unmöglich, aufzustehen.
(*c*) Ich kann gar nicht aufstehen.

5 Sie haben am Wochenende bestimmt in Ihrem Garten gearbeitet!
(*a*) Sie haben am Wochenende bestimmt in ihrem Garten gearbeitet!
(*b*) Sie haben am Wochenende sicher in Ihrem Garten gearbeitet!
(*c*) Sie haben am Wochenende sicher in seinem Garten gearbeitet!

6 Wie haben Sie das wissen können?
(*a*) Das haben Sie wissen können!
(*b*) Wie konnten Sie das wissen?
(*c*) Haben Sie das nicht wissen können?

7 Um diese Jahreszeit gibt es ja im Garten viel zu erledigen.
(*a*) Im Garten gibt es ja um diese Jahreszeit viel zu tun.
(*b*) Um diese Jahreszeit gibt es ja im Garten wenig zu tun.
(*c*) Im Garten gibt es ja immer viel zu erledigen.

8 Sind Rückenschmerzen dann typisch für Gärtner?
(*a*) Leiden dann alle Gärtner an Rückenschmerzen?
(*b*) Leiden dann viele Gärtner an Rückenschmerzen?
(*c*) Bin ich dann ein typischer Gärtner?

ÜBUNG 16.2 **Sagen Sie es anders.**
Beispiele: Hans hat Schmerzen im Bauch.

Sein Bauch tut weh.
Greta hat Schmerzen in den Augen.
Ihre Augen tun weh.

1 Oma hat Schmerzen in den Knien.
2 Dieter hat Schmerzen in der rechten Schulter.
3 Frau Braun hat Schmerzen im linken Fuß.
4 Herr Leinert hat Schmerzen in den Händen.
5 Christel hat Ohrenschmerzen.
6 Manfred hat Schmerzen in der Nase.
7 Gerd hat Rückenschmerzen.
8 Ich habe Magenschmerzen.

ÜBUNG 16.3 **Was paßt zusammen?**

Urlaub in Spanien

1 Meinen Sommerurlaub verbringe ich dieses Jahr mit zwei Kolleginnen, . . .
2 Wir wollen nach Spanien zur Insel (*Island*) Ibiza fliegen, . . .
3 Wir haben eine Wohnung in einem Haus gemietet, . . .
4 In der Nähe von der Wohnung gibt es mehrere Restaurants, . . .
5 Eine Freundin von mir, . . . , hat mir ein paar Tips gegeben.
6 Mein Bruder, . . . , hat mir auch gesagt, wo man am besten schwimmen kann.
7 Mit einem Wagen, . . . , wollen wir die ganze Insel besichtigen.
8 Hoffentlich werden wir ein paar Leute kennenlernen, . . .

(*a*) in dem nur Deutsche wohnen
(*b*) deren Mann 2 Jahre lang auf Ibiza gearbeitet hat, und die deshalb die Insel sehr gut kennt
(*c*) die ungefähr 160 Kilometer südwestlich von Valencia liegt
(*d*) die ich im Büro bei der Firma Schneider kennengelernt habe
(*e*) den wir schon hier in Deutschland gemietet haben
(*f*) mit denen wir Deutsch sprechen können!
(*g*) der letztes Jahr seinen Urlaub dort verbracht hat
(*h*) in denen man deutsches Essen bekommen kann

ÜBUNG 16.4 **Ergänzen Sie.**

Insert the following as appropriate.

deren, durch den, dessen, den, das, der, die, in denen, in dem, in der

Wo möchten sie wohnen?

Theo Naumann möchte in einem Land wohnen,
. . . (1) . . . irgendwo im Süden liegt.
. . . (2) . . . man Deutsch oder Englisch spricht.
. . . (3) . . . Bevölkerungszahl relativ klein ist.

Elke Anders möchte in einer Großstadt wohnen,
. . . (4) . . . es viele Parks und viele Bäume gibt.
. . . (5) . . . nur wenig Industrie hat.
. . . (6) . . . Kulturleben reichhaltig ist.

Manfred Meyer möchte in der Nähe von einem Wald wohnen,
. . . (7) . . . nur wenige Leute kennen.
. . . (8) . . . man am Wochenende spazieren kann.
. . . (9) . . . noch nicht unter saurem Regen leidet.

Sie möchten alle in Ländern wohnen,
. . . (10) . . . es keine Kriege gibt.

ÜBUNG 16.5 Join the following pairs of sentences together as shown in the examples:

Ich komme aus einer kleinen Stadt. Sie heißt Lauenburg.
Ich komme aus einer kleinen Stadt, ***die Lauenburg heißt.***

Diese Stadt liegt an der Elbe im Norden Deutschlands. Die Stadt existiert seit dem 13. Jahrhundert.

Diese Stadt, ***die seit dem 13. Jahrhundert existiert***, liegt an der Elbe im Norden Deutschlands.

1 Die Stadt Lauenburg hat ungefähr 11 000 Einwohner. Sie liegt im Bundesland Schleswig-Holstein.
2 Ich wohne in der Elbstraße. Diese Straße ist der älteste Teil (*part*) Lauenburgs.
3 In der Elbstraße liegt auch das alte Rathaus. Im alten Rathaus findet man heute das Elbschiffahrtsmuseum.
4 In Lauenburg sieht man auch die alte Brücke. Über diese Brücke hat man früher Salz von Lüneburg nach Lübeck transportiert.
5 Ich arbeite in einem Fotogeschäft. Es liegt am Marktplatz.
6 Dorthin kommen viele Touristen. Diese Touristen wollen die Altstadt besichtigen.
7 Wir verkaufen auch Postkarten. Die Besucher schicken (*send*) die Postkarten in alle Welt.

8 Jeden Tag kommen neue Menschen ins Geschäft. Ich kann oft diesen Menschen beim Kaufen eines Fotoapparates helfen.

ÜBUNG 16.6 Sagen Sie es anders.

Use the more commonly found Imperfect Tense form instead of the Perfect Tense form as in the following examples.

Gestern habe ich in der Stadtmitte einkaufen müssen.

Gestern mußte ich in der Stadtmitte einkaufen.

Ich habe meiner Tochter ein Geschenk zum Geburtstag kaufen wollen.

Ich wollte meiner Tochter ein Geschenk zum Geburtstag kaufen.

1 Ich habe aber lange nach einem Parkplatz suchen müssen.
2 Im Parkhaus habe ich nicht parken können, weil alles besetzt war.
3 Auf der Straße habe ich nicht parken dürfen, weil es zwischen 7.00 Uhr und 18.00 Uhr verboten ist.
4 Ich habe 2 Kilometer außerhalb der Stadtmitte fahren müssen.
5 Da habe ich endlich einen Parkplatz finden können.
6 Dann habe ich zu Fuß wieder in die Stadtmitte zurückgehen müssen.
7 Nach langem Suchen habe ich das ideale Geschenk finden können.
8 Bloß habe ich dann wieder 2 Kilometer zum Auto zurückgehen müssen!
9 Das habe ich eigentlich nicht gewollt.
10 Das habe ich einfach gemußt.

Verstehen Sie?

1 Konversation

Eine Erkältung

Ralf Steuber consults his doctor about a heavy cold that he is having difficulties in throwing off.

Ralf Steuber Guten Morgen, Dr. Glöckner.

Dr. Glöckner Guten Morgen, Herr Steuber. Was für Beschwerden haben Sie?

Ralf Steuber Ich bin jetzt seit 3 Wochen stark erkältet und fühle mich gar nicht wohl.

Dr. Glöckner	Das muß dann mehr als eine Erkältung sein. Wissen Sie, ob Sie Fieber haben? Haben Sie die Temperatur gemessen?
Ralf Steuber	Ja, heute morgen: 37,6 (siebenunddreißig sechs). Ich habe auch Schwierigkeiten beim Atmen und muß ziemlich oft husten.
Dr. Glöckner	Ich möchte Ihnen die Lungen abhören. Machen Sie bitte den Oberkörper frei (. . .) Und jetzt holen Sie tief Luft!
Ralf Steuber	Au, das tut aber weh, Herr Doktor!
Dr. Glöckner	Ja, Sie haben eine Lungenentzündung. Sind Sie Raucher?
Ralf Steuber	Ja, ist das schlimm?
Dr. Glöckner	Natürlich ist das schlimm. Rauchen ist gesundheitsschädlich, und kann sogar Krebs und Herzkrankheiten verursachen.
Ralf Steuber	Ja, ich weiß. Ich sollte mir endlich das Rauchen abgewöhnen.
Dr. Glöckner	Das sollten Sie unbedingt.

Der Bundesgesundheitsminister: Rauchen gefährdet Ihre Gesundheit.

die Beschwerde (-n) *complaint, trouble*
messen *to measure*
atmen *to breathe*
husten *to cough*
die Lunge (-n) *lung*
abhören *to sound, listen to*
der Oberkörper *upper part of the body*
Holen Sie tief Luft! *take a deep breath*
der Raucher (-) *smoker*
schlimm *bad*
schädlich *harmful*
verursachen *to cause*
sich das Rauchen abgewöhnen *to give up smoking*

Richtig (R) oder Falsch (F)?

1 Ralf Steuber fühlt sich seit einem Monat krank.
2 Dr Glöckner sagt, daß es nur eine Erkältung ist.
3 Ralf findet es manchmal schwer, Luft zu holen.
4 Ralf muß seine Jacke und sein Hemd ausziehen.
5 Dr Glöckner hört ihm die Lungen ab.
6 Er findet es nicht schlimm, daß Ralf Raucher ist.

7 Rauchen kann nicht nur Krebs, sondern auch Herzkrankheiten verursachen.
8 Ralf sollte deshalb nicht weiterrauchen.

2 Lesetext

Lesen Sie den Text, und versuchen Sie, die Fragen zu beantworten.

Neues aus der Medizin

Schnupfen. Wenn die Nase verschlossen ist, hilft ein Heizkissen im Genick, rät die Kieler Ärztin Dr. Ursula Langhagel. Das Kissen soll so heiß wie möglich sein. Vor allem beim Einschlafen ist diese befreiende Wärmewirkung sehr angenehm.

Grippe. Mit einer starken Erkältung sollte man sich nicht ans Autosteuer setzen. Denn die Schnupfen- und Grippe-Viren beeinträchtigen die Reaktionsfähigkeit stärker als etwa 0,8 Promille Alkohol im Blut, entdeckte der englische Forscher Dr. Andrew Smith von der Universität Sussex.

(*Bunte*, Heft 52)

Atemluft. Machen Sie auch bei Kälte öfter mal das Fenster auf, empfehlen Wissenschaftler des Bundesgesundheitsamtes. Die Innenraumluft kann durch Formaldehyd, Tabakrauch, Abgase aus defekten Gasherden und Haushaltssprays gesundheitsschädlich sein.

verschlossen *blocked up*
das Kissen (-) *cushion, pad*
das Genick (-e) (*nape of the*) *neck*
einschlafen (*sep.*) *to fall asleep*
die Wärme *warmth, heat*
die Wirkung (-en) *effect*
das Fenster (-) *window*

der Rauch *smoke*
das Abgas (-e) *(exhaust) fumes*
der Herd (-e) *stove*
das Steuer (-) *steering-wheel*
die Fähigkeit (-en) *ability, capability*
das Promille (-) *thousandth (part)*
0,8 Promille 80 *millilitres*

1 When can a heated pad in the nape of the neck be of benefit?
2 How hot should the pad be?
3 When can this heat treatment be particularly pleasant?
4 What do scientists of the Federal Office of Health recommend us to do?
5 What harmful substances are often found in the air indoors?
6 When should we not drive a car, according to information in this text?
7 By what are our reactions impaired?
8 To what extent are they impaired?

17 Die Täter werden noch gesucht

In this unit you will encounter the 'passive voice'.

Dialog

Karin Rebel is eager to tell her flat-mate, Antje Augst, about the robbery at the bank where she works. They listen to the news to find out more details.

Karin Rebel Was denkst du, was heute passiert ist?! Auf unsere Bank hat man einen Raubüberfall verübt!

Antje Augst Was? Wurdest du etwa verletzt?

Karin Rebel Ach, nein! Aber fast 20 000 Mark sind gestohlen worden.

Antje Augst Und die Täter sind mit dem Geld entkommen?

Karin Rebel Das weiß ich nicht. Ich glaube, sie werden noch gesucht. Mach mal das Radio an. Es ist gleich 6 Uhr. Bayern 3 bringt Nachrichten. Vielleicht wird über den Raubüberfall berichtet. (*Antje macht das Radio an.*)

Nachrichtensprecher . . . Nach offiziellen Aussagen sollen die Staatsausgaben für Sozialleistungen, Bildung und Gesundheit um mehr als 10 Millionen Mark gekürzt werden.

München. Bei einem bewaffneten Raubüberfall auf die Dresdner Bank in der Leopoldstraße sind heute nachmittag gegen 14 Uhr 30 fast 20 000 Mark erbeutet worden. Nach Augenzeugenberichten handelte es sich um drei maskierte Männer, die mit vorgehaltener Pistole die Herausgabe des Geldes erzwangen. Einer der Täter wurde von einem Bankkunden überwältigt und konnte anschließend von der Polizei verhaftet werden. Den anderen beiden Tätern gelang die Flucht in einem bereitste-

henden Pkw. Das Auto wurde wenig später verlassen aufgefunden.
Bamberg. Wegen Brandstiftung sind in der vergangenen Nacht zwei Mitglieder der Nationaldemokratischen Partei Deutschlands festgenommen worden . . . (*Karin macht das Radio aus.*)

Antje Augst Hoffentlich werden deine Bankräuber noch gefaßt. Bis du von der Polizei verhört worden?

Karin Rebel Ja, aber ich konnte keine Auskunft geben, da ich während des ganzen Überfalls in unserem Restaurant Kaffee getrunken habe!

Was denkst du, was heute passiert ist? *What do you think happened today?*
der Raubüberfall (¨e) (auf+*acc.*) *robbery, raid (on)*
verüben *to carry out, commit*
verletzt *injured, hurt*
stehlen *to steal*
der Täter (-) *perpetrator, (here) culprit, criminal*
entkommen *to get away*
anmachen (*sep.*) *to put on, turn on*
die Nachrichten (*f. pl.*) *news*
Vielleicht wird über den Raubüberfall berichtet *Perhaps there'll be a report on the raid;* (lit. *Perhaps will be reported on the raid*)
die Aussage (-n) *statement, report*
die Staatsausgaben (*f. pl.*) *state spending, expenditure*
die Sozialleistung (-en) *social benefit*
um (+*acc.*) *by*
kürzen *to cut, reduce*
Die Staatsausgaben sollen gekürzt werden *State expenditure is to be cut*
bewaffnet *armed*
erbeuten *to carry off, take*
nach Augenzeugenberichten (*m. dat. pl.*) *according to eye-witness reports*
sich handeln um *to be a question of, to concern*
maskiert *masked*
mit vorgehaltener Pistole *at pistol point*
die Herausgabe *handing over, surrender*
erzwingen *to force*
überwältigen *to overpower, overwhelm*
verhaften *to arrest*
gelingen *to succeed*
die Flucht (-en) *flight, escape*
Den anderen beiden gelang die Flucht *The other two managed to get away;* (lit. *To the other two succeeded the escape*)
bereitstehen (*sep.*) *to stand by*
in einem bereitstehenden Pkw *in a waiting car*
verlassen *to leave, abandon, desert*
auffinden (*sep.*) *to find, discover*
die Brandstiftung *arson, fire-raising*
vergangen *past*

die Nationaldemokratische Partei Deutschlands (NPD) *National Democratic Party of Germany*
festnehmen (*sep.*) *to apprehend, arrest*
ausmachen (*sep.*) *to put off, turn off*
der Räuber (-) *robber*
fassen *to catch, apprehend*
verhören *to question, interrogate*

Fragen zum Dialog

1 Richtig (R) oder Falsch (F)?

1 Man hat auf die Bank, wo Karin arbeitet, einen Raubüberfall verübt.
2 Karin wurde während des Überfalls schwer verletzt.
3 Die Täter haben fast 20 000 Mark gestohlen.
4 Radio Bayern berichtet über den Raubüberfall.
5 Der Raubüberfall wurde gegen 14 Uhr 30 auf die Dresdner Bank in der Münchner Leopoldstraße verübt.
6 Drei maskierte Männer haben mit vorgehaltener Pistole die Herausgabe des Geldes erzwungen.
7 Drei Bankkunden haben einen der Täter überwältigt.
8 Dieser Täter wurde dann von der Polizei verhaftet.
9 Die anderen beiden Täter sind in einem Auto entkommen.
10 Karin hat nichts vom Überfall gesehen, weil sie die ganze Zeit im Restaurant war.

2 Welche Antwort paßt?

1 Auf unsere Bank hat man einen Raubüberfall verübt.
(*a*) Was! Sind die Täter mit dem Geld entkommen?
(*b*) Genau! Das ist eben ein Problem, das immer wieder auftaucht.
(*c*) Da hast du aber Glück gehabt!

2 Wurdest du etwa verletzt?
(*a*) Das weiß ich nicht.
(*b*) Nicht unbedingt.
(*c*) Ach, nein. Ich war die ganze Zeit in unserem Restaurant.

3 Sind die Täter mit dem Geld entkommen?
(*a*) Ach, nein! Aber fast 20 000 Mark sind gestohlen worden.
(*b*) Das weiß ich nicht. Ich glaube, sie werden noch gesucht.
(*c*) Nein, es handelte sich um drei maskierte Männer.

4 Wurde nicht einer der Täter von einem Bankkunden überwältigt?
(*a*) Doch. Er wurde dann anschließend verhaftet.
(*b*) Nein. Ihnen gelang die Flucht in einem bereitstehenden Auto.
(*c*) Ja, aber ich konnte keine Auskunft geben.

5 Wird das Auto, in dem zwei der Täter entkommen sind, noch gesucht?
(*a*) Das weiß ich nicht. Ich glaube, sie werden noch gesucht.
(*b*) Nein. Es wurde wenig später verlassen aufgefunden.
(*c*) Es kommt darauf an, ob man die Bankräuber gefaßt hat oder nicht.

Was Sie wissen sollten

Broadcasting in Germany

Public broadcasting institutions exist in Germany both at the regional level (**Landesrundfunkanstalten**) and at the federal level (**Deutschlandfunk, Deutsche Welle** and **ZDF**). All of these apart from ZDF run radio stations.

The ten **Landesrundfunkanstalten** jointly form the **ARD (Arbeitsgemeinschaft der öffentlich-rechtlichen Rundfunkanstalten Deutschlands)** which is responsible for Germany's first terrestrial television channel »**Deutsches Fernsehen**«, or »**Erstes Programm**«, as it is commonly known. Individually the regional institutions transmit their own »**Drittes Programm**« or Channel 3. Channel 2 or »**Zweites Programm**« is the responsibility of **Zweites Deutsches Fernsehen (ZDF)**.

Öffentlich-rechtliche Rundfunkanstalten
(Broadcasting institutions under public law)

BR	Bayerischer Rundfunk (München)
HR	Hessischer Rundfunk (Frankfurt am Main)
LK	Länderkette (Berlin)
NDR	Norddeutscher Rundfunk (Hamburg)
RB	Radio Bremen (Bremen)
SR	Saarländischer Rundfunk (Saarbrücken)
SFB	Sender Freies Berlin (West Berlin)
SDR	Süddeutscher Rundfunk (Stuttgart)
SWF	Südwestfunk (Baden-Baden)
WDR	Westdeutscher Rundfunk (Köln)

	Deutsche Welle (Köln)
DLF	Deutschlandfunk (Köln)
ZDF	Zweites Deutsches Fernsehen (Mainz)

This picture is further complicated by local radio stations (of which there are many in all the main conurbations) and by satellite and cable TV. Satellite broadcasting offers reception throughout Western Europe of many of the terrestrial German channels (such as **WEST 3** and **Bayern 3**), additional public broadcasting channels (such as **3sat** and **EINS plus**) and private channels (such as **SAT 1** and **RTL plus**). Certain radio stations are also available via satellite. Satellite reception outside Europe is in certain cases possible by means of special satellite links. For instance, the University of Queensland in Brisbane, Australia, receives many of the European transmissions.

When you are driving in Germany, it is advisable to tune in on the FM band, **UKW—Ultrakurzwelle** (lit. *ultra short wave*), for information on local driving conditions. The frequency of the relevant station will be given at intervals along the **Autobahn**.

For German-learners with no access to satellite reception, it may be helpful to know that **Deutsche Welle** broadcasts on short wave (6075 kHz). Clear reception of BBC World Service broadcasts in German (**Morgenmagazin/Heute aktuell**) is available in the UK on Medium Wave (648 kHz) and many German-speaking stations can be picked up in the UK on Medium Wave after dark (see p. xii).

Wichtige Redewendungen

How to

1 Say that something is being done

(*a*) Man sucht die Täter noch.
(*b*) Die Täter werden noch gesucht.

(*a*) Im Bayerischen Rundfunk bringt man jetzt Nachrichten.
(*b*) Im Bayerischen Rundfunk werden jetzt Nachrichten gebracht.

(*a*) Man berichtet gerade über den Raubüberfall.
(*b*) Es wird gerade über den Raubüberfall berichtet.

(*a*) Man macht das Radio an.
(*b*) Das Radio wird angemacht.

2 *Say that something has been done, was done*

(*a*) Heute nachmittag hat man einen Raubüberfall verübt.
(*b*) Heute nachmittag wurde ein Raubüberfall verübt.
(*c*) Heute nachmittag ist ein Raubüberfall verübt worden.

(*a*) Man hat fast 20 000 Mark gestohlen.
(*b*) Fast 20 000 Mark wurden gestohlen.
(*c*) Fast 20 000 Mark sind gestohlen worden.

(*a*) Man hat einen Täter überwältigt.
(*b*) Ein Täter wurde überwältigt.
(*c*) Ein Täter ist überwältigt worden.

(*a*) Man hat das Auto verlassen aufgefunden.
(*b*) Das Auto wurde verlassen aufgefunden.
(*c*) Das Auto ist verlassen aufgefunden worden.

(*a*) Man hat zwei Mitglieder der NPD festgenommen.
(*b*) Zwei Mitglieder der NPD wurden festgenommen.
(*c*) Zwei Mitglieder der NPD sind festgenommen worden.

Radio, Fernsehen und audio-visuelle Technologie (*Radio, television & audio-visual technology*)

das Radio (-s) *radio (set)*
der Fernseher (-) *television set*
der Fernsehapparat (-e) *television set*
die Kassette (-n) *cassette*
die Schallplatte (-n) *record*
der Sender (-) *station*
der Kassettenrecorder (-) *cassette recorder*
der Videorecorder (-) *video recorder*
die Hi-Fi-Anlage (-n) *hi-fi system*
die Box (-en) *speaker*
die Aufnahme (-n) *recording*
die Sendung (-en) *broadcast*

Grammatik

1 Participles—present and past

The formation of the ***past participle*** and its role in forming the perfect tense have been dealt with in earlier **Lektionen**. So far no mention has been made of the ***present participle***, since its use is much rarer in German than in English. For instance, the English present continuous tense is formed by using the verb *to be* together with the present participle (the *-ing* form of the verb):

What is Martina ***doing***? She's ***playing*** Tennis.

Whereas in German this question and answer would of course simply be rendered as:

Was macht Martina? Sie spielt Tennis.

Nevertheless, the present participle ***does*** exist in German. It is therefore as well to know that the present participle is formed by adding **-d** to the infinitive:

spielen-**d**	*playing*	lächeln-**d**	*smiling*
lachen-**d**	*laughing*	tanzen-**d**	*dancing*

1.1 Use of participles as adjectives

Both present and past participles may be used as adjectives. The **Dialog** of **Lektion 17** contains examples of one present participle and four past participles used as attributive adjectives:

in einem **bereitstehenden** Pkw
bei einem **bewaffneten** Raubüberfall
mit **vorgehaltener** Pistole
in der **vergangenen** Nacht
drei **maskierte** Männer

and one past participle used as a predicative adjective:

Das Auto wurde (. . .) **verlassen** aufgefunden.

Some participles have come to be perceived as adjectives rather than participles. Many of these are listed as adjectives in dictionaries. Examples that have already been encountered in earlier **Lektionen** include:

anstrengend **(L10)** *tiring*
fließend **(L2)** *fluent* (*lit. flowing*)
laufend **(L15)** *current* (*lit. running*)
besetzt **(L8)** *occupied, taken*
erkältet **(L16)** *with a cold*
geboren **(L9)** *born*
gelegen **(L4)** *situated*
geschieden **(L2)** *divorced*
verboten **(14)** *forbidden*
verwitwet **(L2)** *widowed*

Other frequently found examples include:

auffallend *striking, conspicuous*
aufregend *exciting*
erschütternd *shattering*
reizend *charming*
rührend *touching*
überraschend *surprising*
aufgeregt *excited, nervous, worked up*
empört *incensed, indignant*
enttäuscht *disappointed*
erschöpft *exhausted*
gelassen *calm, cool, composed*
überrascht *surprised*
verrückt *mad, crazy, insane*

Use of participles as adverbs

Many participles may also be used as adverbs:

Sie ist auffallend intelligent.	*She is strikingly (remarkably) intelligent.*
Er lächelte reizend.	*He smiled charmingly.*
Sie spielte überraschend gut.	*She played surprisingly well.*
Er sah sie empört an.	*He looked at her indignantly.*
Sie hörte ihm gelassen zu.	*She listened to him calmly.*

2 Passive Voice

When the initiator of an action, often referred to as the 'agent', is expressed as the subject of the sentence, the verb is said to be in the **active voice**:

The police	are seeking	three masked men.
Die Polizei	sucht (*NB: singular!*)	drei maskierte Männer.
subject/ initiator(s)	*verb (active)*	*direct object/ sufferer(s)*

If, however, the 'sufferer' of the action (i.e. normally the direct object in an active sentence) is expressed as the subject of the sentence, the verb is said to be in the **passive voice**:

Three masked men	are being sought	(by the police).	
Drei maskierte Männer	werden	(von der Polizei)	gesucht.
subject/ sufferer	*verb . . . (passive)*	*prepositional phrase/ initiator(s)*	*. . . verb*

Note that in the passive sentence the expression of the initiator(s) of the action is optional, whereas in the active sentence it is usually obligatory.

The use of the passive in German tends to be a mark of rather formal language, such as that found in news reporting, in textbooks, in formal speeches etc. This does ***not***, however, mean that the passive is never used in informal speech and writing.

2.1 Formation of the passive

The passive is formed by using the verb **werden** (in the relevant tense) together with the past participle of the verb in question:

Present Passive
Unser neues Haus **wird** von der Firma Bernhardt **gebaut**.
Our new house is being built by the firm of Bernhardt.
Imperfect Passive
Unser altes Haus **wurde** vor dem ersten Weltkrieg **gebaut**.
Our old house was built before the First World War.
Perfect Passive
Die neue Schule **ist** noch nicht **gebaut worden**.
The new school has not yet been built.

Note that in perfect passive sentences the past participle of **werden** loses the prefix **ge-** and becomes **worden**.

Future Passive
Morgen abend **wird** diese Rolle von Max Ammer **gespielt werden**.
Tomorrow evening this role will be played by Max Ammer.

The present passive is also often used with future meaning:

Hoffentlich **werden** deine Bankräuber noch **gefaßt**.
I hope your bank robbers will still be caught.

2.2 Modal verbs and the passive infinitive

The general rule that modal verbs are followed by a second verb in the infinitive form also applies in the passive. The passive infinitive consists of the past participle of the verb in question together with the infinitive **werden**:

Die Staatsausgaben für Sozialleistungen sollen gekürzt werden. *State expenditure for social benefits is to be cut.*
Mein Auto muß bis morgen repariert werden. *My car must be repaired by tomorrow.*
Das kann leider nicht gemacht werden. *That cannot be done, I'm afraid.*
Hier darf nicht geraucht werden. *Smoking is not allowed here.* (lit. *Here may not be smoked.*)

2.3 Subjectless passives

The passive is sometimes used in German where in English a passive would not be possible. For instance:

Vielleicht wird über den Raubüberfall berichtet. *Perhaps there'll be a report on the raid.* (lit. *Perhaps will be reported on the raid.*)
In meiner Wohnung wird nicht geraucht. *There is no smoking in my flat.* (*i.e. it's not allowed.*)
Jetzt wird gegessen! *Now there will be some eating done!/Now eating will take place!*
Dort wurde früher getanzt. *Dancing used to take place there (formerly).*

Note that in all the above examples the passive verb has no subject. In fact, the 'dummy subject' **es** is used when there is no adverbial, prepositional phrase, etc. to take up the first slot in the sentence:

> Es wurde gegessen und getrunken. *There was eating and drinking.*

2.4 Dative verbs in the passive

Verbs which in German are followed by the dative, such as **begegnen** *to encounter*, **dienen** *to serve*, **helfen** *to help*, **raten** *to advise*, **schaden** *to harm, hurt* and **nützen** *to be of use*, cannot be made passive in the usual way. It is, however, possible to produce a kind of passive, if the dative object is retained:

> **Deiner Gesundheit** wird durch das Rauchen nicht gedient. *Your health is not served by smoking.*
> **Diesen Flüchtlingen** muß geholfen werden. *These refugees must be helped.*
> **Ihm** wurde geraten, zu Hause zu bleiben. *He was advised to stay at home.*

These are, in fact, subjectless passives like those in ***2.3*** above. What would in English be the subject of the passive sentence, is a dative object in German. Note that the verb **muß** in the second example above is in the ***singular*** and not the plural as one might at first glance expect.

2.5 Passive agent

As already stated above in the introductory notes on the passive, passive sentences do not have to include mention of the initiator of the action, the 'agent'. When, however, mention of the agent *is* required, the agent is normally introduced in association with the preposition **von**:

> Dieses Haus wurde von Flüchtlingen gebaut. *This house was built by refugees.*
> Dieser Baum ist vom Blitz getroffen worden. *This tree has been/was hit by lightning.*

A prepositional phrase introduced by **durch** is sometimes found in passive sentences. Such phrases do not normally denote the 'true' agent:

> Wir wurden durch die protestierenden Demonstranten aufgehalten. *We were delayed by (because of) the protesting demonstrators.*

In this example, there was no intention on the part of the demonstrators to cause a delay, but a delay occurred because of their demonstrating. In fact, if **von** were used here instead of **durch** the sentence would take on a different and more sinister meaning:

> Wir wurden von den protestierenden Demonstranten aufgehalten. *We were stopped by the protesting demonstrators (who didn't want to let us through).*

2.6 Active infinitive with passive meaning

In such sentences as

> Das ist kaum zu glauben. *That is scarcely to be believed.*

we find a contrast between English which uses the passive infinitive and German which uses the ordinary active infinitive. Other examples are:

> Diese Tür ist nicht zu öffnen. *This door cannot* (*must not*) *be opened.*
> Dem Kranken ist nicht mehr zu helfen. *The patient* (lit. *sick person*) *cannot be helped any more* (*i.e. is beyond help*).

2.7 'False' passives

When the verb **sein** rather than the verb **werden** is used with a past participle, the resultant sentence cannot be described as a true passive:

> Die Tür ist geschlossen. *The door is closed.*

Here the past participle **geschlossen** is closer in function to an adjective than to an element in the passive construction. This kind of 'false' passive is termed **Zustandspassiv** (*passive of state*) in German, because the focus is on the state (in this instance, that of being closed) rather than on the action or occurrence, as in the 'true' passive or **Vorgangspassiv** (*passive of occurrence*).

2.8 Use of man *as an alternative to the passive*

Amongst the examples of the use of **man** (*one*) that have occurred throughout the course, one in **Dialog 9** is a good illustration of the use of this impersonal pronoun as an alternative to a passive construction. This possibility is almost always available when the passive version does not specify the agent:

> Hélène hat man dort in der Personalabteilung angestellt. *Hélène was given an appointment in the personnel office there.*

Note that whilst English has to use a passive construction here, German offers the choice between the **man** construction and the passive:

> Hélène wurde dort in der Personalabteilung angestellt.

Dialog 17 contains a further example of the use of **man** as an alternative to the passive:

> Auf unsere Bank hat man einen Raubüberfall verübt.

instead of

> Auf unsere Bank ist ein Raubüberfall verübt worden.

More examples of this use of **man** are given in the **Wichtige Redewendungen** section of this **Lektion**. Note that as soon as the agent is specified, it is no longer possible to use the **man** construction:

	Die Täter werden noch gesucht. *or* Man sucht die Täter noch.
BUT	Die Täter werden noch von der Polizei gesucht. (No **man** construction possible)

The use of **man** is usually felt to be slightly less formal than the use of the passive.

Übungen

ÜBUNG 17.1 Was kann man auch sagen?

1 Auf unser Geschäft hat man heute einen Raubüberfall verübt!
- (*a*) Auf unser Geschäft wird heute ein Raubüberfall verübt!
- (*b*) Auf unser Geschäft ist heute ein Raubüberfall verübt worden.
- (*c*) Auf unser Geschäft wird man heute einen Raubüberfall verüben!

2 Was? Haben euch die Täter verletzt?
- (*a*) Was? Seid ihr von den Tätern verletzt worden?
- (*b*) Was? Habt ihr die Täter verletzt?
- (*c*) Was? Bist du verletzt worden?

3 Nein. Aber man hat mehr als 5 000 DM gestohlen.
- (*a*) Nein. Aber man wollte mehr als 5 000 DM stehlen.
- (*b*) Nein. Aber mehr als 5 000 DM sollen gestohlen worden sein.
- (*c*) Nein. Aber mehr als 5 000 DM sind erbeutet worden.

4 Konnte die Polizei die Täter fassen?
  (*a*) Sind die Täter von der Polizei gefaßt worden?
  (*b*) Konnten die Täter von der Polizei gefaßt werden?
  (*c*) Hat die Polizei die Täter gefaßt?

5 Einen der beiden Täter hat unser Chef überwältigt.
  (*a*) Einer der beiden Täter ist von unserem Chef überwältigt worden.
  (*b*) Einer der beiden Täter hat unseren Chef überwältigt.
  (*c*) Beide Täter haben unseren Chef überwältigt.

6 Der andere konnte aber in einem bereitstehenden Auto flüchten.
  (*a*) Dem anderen ist aber die Flucht in einem bereitstehenden Auto gelungen.
  (*b*) Die anderen sind aber in einem bereitstehenden Auto geflüchtet.
  (*c*) Der andere hat aber den Chef in einem bereitstehenden Auto mitgenommen.

7 Er ist wenig später verhaftet worden.
  (*a*) Man hat sie wenig später verhaftet.
  (*b*) Man hat ihn wenig später verhört.
  (*c*) Man hat ihn wenig später festgenommen.

8 Die beiden Räuber werden jetzt verhört.
  (*a*) Du hast wohl die beiden Räuber gehört?
  (*b*) Man verhört jetzt die beiden Räuber.
  (*c*) Mann hat die beiden Räuber schon verhört.

ÜBUNG 17.2 Was paßt zusammen?

Put the following phrases into the most appropriate order:

(*a*) handelte es sich um einen 21jährigen Mann,
(*b*) Das Auto wurde wenig später verlassen aufgefunden.
(*c*) Bei einem bewaffneten Raubüberfall
(*d*) Dem Täter gelang die Flucht
(*e*) Nach Augenzeugenberichten
(*f*) in einem bereitstehenden Pkw.
(*g*) die Herausgabe des Geldes erzwang.
(*h*) sind heute gegen 10 Uhr 15 fast 15 000 Mark erbeutet worden.
(*i*) der mit vorgehaltener Pistole
(*j*) auf die deutsche Bank in der Weinheimer Hauptstraße

ÜBUNG 17.3 Ergänzen Sie.

Use the following words in the most appropriate places in the text:

(*a*) verrückt	(*b*) rührend	(*c*) anstrengend	(*d*) gelassen
(*e*) überrascht	(*f*) erschöpft	(*g*) enttäuscht	(*h*) empört

Gestern fand ich die Arbeit besonders . . . (1) . . . Als ich zwei Stunden später als üblich total . . . (2) . . . wieder nach Hause kam, war ich etwas . . . (3) . . .— da wartete mein Freund Peter auf mich und wollte noch ins Kino gehen. »Bist du . . . (4) . . . ? Ich gehe sofort ins Bett!«, sagte ich . . . (5) . . .. Er sah zuerst ein wenig . . . (6) . . . aus. Dann antwortete er . . . (7) . . . , »Du hast sicher Hunger. Ich koche dir 'was«. Ich fand es . . . (8) . . . , daß er bereit war, für mich zu kochen, anstatt ins Kino zu gehen.

ÜBUNG 17.4 Hans und Trudi Hansen wollen mit dem Auto nach Großbritannien. Was muß alles gemacht werden?

Beispiele: Das Auto zur Inspektion bringen.
Das Auto muß zur Inspektion gebracht werden.

Den Führerschein (*driver's licence*) nicht vergessen!
Der Führerschein darf nicht vergessen werden.

1 Geld wechseln.
2 Die Katze ins Tierheim (lit. *animal home*) bringen.
3 Die Urlaubsversicherung nicht vergessen!
4 Die Zeitungen abbestellen (*cancel*).
5 Die Überfahrt Calais-Dover buchen.
6 Die Personalausweise mitnehmen.
7 Das englische Wörterbuch (*dictionary*) nicht vergessen!
8 Die Hotelzimmer reservieren.

ÜBUNG 17.5 Lesen Sie.

Imagine that you are writing the script for a radio broadcast of this recipe. Make as much use of the passive as possible and include the words **zuerst, dann, danach** (*after that*) **zum Schluß** (*finally*):

1 Zuerst werden die Champignons gewaschen und fein geschnitten.
2 Dann wird die Zwiebel . . .

der Champignon (-s) *button mushroom*	**zudecken** *to cover*
das Mehl *flour*	**sieben** *to sieve*
der Eßlöffel *dessert spoon*	**pürieren** *to purée*
der Rahm *cream*	**die Pfanne** *pan*
die Petersilie *parsley*	**zerlassen** *melted*
waschen *to wash*	**einrühren** *to stir in*
die Brühe *stock*	**würzen** *to season*
	bestreuen *to sprinkle*

Champignonrahmsuppe
(für 4 Personen)

Zutaten:

250 g Champignons	¼ Liter Brühe	3 Eßlöffel Rahm
1 kleine Zwiebel	½ Liter Milch	Petersilie
30 g Butter	Salz	
30 g Mehl	Pfeffer	

Zubereitung:

1. Die Champignons waschen und fein schneiden.
2. Die Zwiebel schülen und schneiden.
3. Die Champignons und die Zwiebel in der Brühe zum Kochen bringen.
4. Zudecken und 20–30 Minuten kochen.
5. Sieben oder im Mixer pürieren.
6. Das Mehl in einer zweiten Pfanne zur zerlassenen Butter geben und 1 Minute kochen.
7. Zuerst die Milch und dann das Champignonpüree einrühren.
8. Die Suppe mit Salz und Pfeffer würzen.
9. Die Suppe zum Kochen bringen, rühren, zudecken und 10–15 Minuten kochen.
10. Den Rahm einrühren und mit Petersilie bestreuen.

ÜBUNG 17.6 Sagen Sie es anders.

Beispiele: ***Die Architektur von Berlin***

Der Funkturm (*Radio tower*): Den 150m hohen Funkturm erbaute (*built*) man 1926 zur deutschen Funkausstellung.

Der 150m hohe Funkturm wurde 1926 zur deutschen Funkausstellung erbaut.

Die Kongreßhalle: Hugh A. Stubbins hat die Kongreßhalle 1957 als US-Beitrag zur Internationalen Bauausstellung entworfen (*designed*).

Die Kongreßhalle ist 1957 von Hugh A. Stubbins als US-Beitrag zur Internationalen Bauausstellung entworfen worden.

1 **Das Brandenburger Tor:** Carl Gotthard Langhans errichtete (*erected*) das Brandenburger Tor zwischen 1788 und 1791.

2 **Das Schloß Charlottenburg:** J. A. Nering hat das Schloß Charlottenburg 1695 als Sommersitz für die Kurfürstin (*electoral princess*) Sophie Charlotte begonnen.
3 **Das Reichstagsgebäude:** Paul Wallot erbaute in den Jahren von 1884 bis 1894 das Reichstagsgebäude im Stil der Neorenaissance. Nach der Kriegszerstörung hat man das Reichstagsgebäude im Originalstil wiedererrichtet.
4 **Das Hansaviertel:** Das Hansaviertel haben 48 international bekannte Architekten nach dem zweiten Weltkrieg errichtet.
5 **Die Freiheitsglocke** (*Liberty Bell*): Die Freiheitsglocke im Schöneberger Rathaus schenkte das amerikanische Volk den Berlinern im Jahre 1950.
6 **Das alte Museum:** Zwischen 1824 und 1830 hat K. F. Schinkel das alte Museum erbaut.
7 **Der Dom:** Den Dom hat J. Raschdorff in den Jahren 1894–1905 erbaut. Den Dom hat man in den 80er Jahren des 20. Jahrhunderts restauriert.
8 **Das Palais unter den Linden:** Das Palais unter den Linden errichtete Ph. Gerlach im Jahre 1732. Man hat es in den Jahren 1968–9 wiederaufgebaut und erweitert.

Verstehen Sie?

1 Radiosendung

Instead of the usual conversation, a radio broadcast of traffic news is included at this point. Since traffic reports contain rather specialised vocabulary, the vocabulary list is longer than usual. Such vocabulary is, however, very important to anyone planning to drive in German-speaking countries.

Verkehrsmeldungen

SWF 3 Radiodienst mit Meldungen zur Verkehrslage. Auf der Autobahn Frankfurt-Kassel in beiden Richtungen zwischen dem Hattenbacher-Dreieck und Homberg (Bezirk Kassel) durch hohes Verkehrsaufkommen zähflüssiger Verkehr mit zeitweiligem Stillstand.

Die Unfallstellen auf der Autobahn Basel-Karlsruhe zwischen Offenburg und Bühl sind geräumt. Jedoch besteht in diesem Streckenabschnitt noch zähflüssiger Verkehr mit zeitweiligem Stillstand. Den Verkehrsteilnehmern wird empfohlen, die Autobahn bereits bei der Anschlußstelle Lahr zu verlassen und über die Bundesstraßen 3 oder 36 in Richtung Karlsruhe auszuweichen.

Bundesautobahn Basel Richtung Freiburg zwischen Müllheim und Bad Krozingen wegen Bergungsarbeiten ist der rechte Fahrstreifen gesperrt. Auch dort muß mit Stauungen und Behinderungen gerechnet werden.

Auf der Bundesstraße 10 zwischen Ulm und der Autobahnanschlußstelle Ulm West 5 Kilometer Stau wegen Baustelle und starken Verkehrsaufkommens. Der Verkehr wird auf der B 10 in Richtung Geislinger Steige umgeleitet.

Am Grenzübergang Wasserbillig bei der Einreise nach Luxemburg durch hohes Verkehrsaufkommen zähflüssiger Verkehr. Auch hier ist mit Stauungen zu rechnen.

So weit die Verkehrsmeldungen.

die Meldung (-en) *report, announcement*
das Dreieck (-e) *triangle (intersection)*
das Aufkommen *appearance, amount*
zähflüssig *slow-moving*
zeitweilig *occasional, at times*
räumen *to clear*
jedoch *however*
bestehen *to exist*
der Streckenabschnitt *section*
der Verkehrsteilnehmer *driver* (lit. *traffic participant*)
bereits *already*
die Anschlußstelle (-n) *junction*
verlassen *to leave*
ausweichen *to get out of the way*
die Bergung *rescue, recovery*
der Fahrstreifen (-) *lane*
sperren *to close off*
die Stauung (-en) *tailback, jam*
die Behinderung (-en) *obstruction*
rechnen mit *to reckon on, expect*
der Stau (-e *or* **-s)** *tailback*
die Baustelle (-n) *roadworks* (lit. *construction site*)
umleiten (*sep.*) *to divert*
der Grenzübergang (¨e) *border crossing point*

Richtig (R) oder Falsch (F)?

1 Auf der Autobahn Frankfurt Kassel besteht in Richtung Kassel zähflüssiger Verkehr mit zeitweiligem Stillstand.
2 Zwischen Offenburg und Bühl auf der Autobahn Basel-Karlsruhe besteht auch zähflüssiger Verkehr mit zeitweiligem Stillstand.
3 Die Unfallstellen auf dieser Autobahn sind aber geräumt.

4 Den Verkehrsteilnehmern auf dieser Strecke wird geraten, über die Bundesstraßen 3 oder 36 auszuweichen.
5 Wegen einer Baustelle ist zwischen Heitersheim und Bad Krozingen der rechte Fahrstreifen der Autobahn Basel-Karlsruhe in Richtung Freiburg gesperrt.
6 Auf der Bundesstraße 10 besteht ein Stau von 5 Kilometer Länge.
7 Dort wird der Verkehr umgeleitet.
8 Bei der Einreise nach Luxemburg ist am Grenzübergang Wasserbillig mit Stauungen zu rechnen.

2 Lesetext

Lesen Sie den Text, und versuchen Sie, die Fragen zu beantworten.

Polizei überwältigt den Täter

Ohne schwere Folgen endete am Mittwochabend ein Raubüfall auf die Hauptkasse des Kaufhauses Hertie in der Freiburger Stadtmitte. Der Täter, der fünf Angestellte als Geiseln genommen hatte, konnte 17 Minuten nach der ersten Alarmmeldung überwältigt werden.

Wie von der Polizei am Gründonnerstag zu erfahren war, hatte der 23 jährige Mann tags zuvor gegen 18 Uhr das Kaufhaus betreten und darum gebeten, zum Personalbüro gebracht zu werden, da er einen Job suche. Plötzlich aber bedrohte er den ihn begleitenden Angestellten mit einer Pistole und verlangte, in den Raum gebracht zu werden, in dem sich die Hauptkasse befindet.

An der Hauptkasse wartete er, bis Vertreter der einzelnen Abteilungen kamen, um die Tageseinnahmen abzuliefern. Dem Vernehmen nach hatte er schließlich fünf Geiseln genommen und 40 000 Mark erbeutet. Das Geschehen an der Hauptkasse war zunächst weder von anderen Angestellten noch von Kunden im Kaufhaus bemerkt worden. Um 18.29 Uhr aber gelang es einer Sekretärin im Kassenraum, einen Hilferuf nach draußen zu schicken, ohne daß dies der Täter mitbekam. Der unbemerkt alarmierte Kaufhaus-Mitarbeiter telefonierte sofort mit der Polizei.

Um 18.46 Uhr drangen Kriminalpolizisten in den Hauptkassenraum ein, um den überraschten Täter zu überwältigen und festzunehmen. Der 23 jährige wurde am Donnerstag ausführlich vernommen. Das Motiv für den Überfall dürfte in finanziellen Problemen des jungen Mannes zu suchen sein. Er ist arbeitslos und hat nach den bisherigen Erkenntnissen der Polizei hohe Schulden.

(*Badische Zeitung*)

die Hauptkasse *cashier's office*
die Geisel (-n) *hostage*
betreten *to enter*
bitten *to ask, request*
bedrohen *to threaten*
sich befinden *to be situated*
der Vertreter (-) *representative*
abliefern *to hand over*
die Tageseinnahmen *the day's takings*
das Geschehen *events, happenings*
bemerken *to notice*

eindringen in (+*acc.*) *to force an entry into* **der Polizist (-en)** *policeman* **die Schuld (-en)** *debt*

1 What was the precise location of the robbery?
2 Who was taken hostage?
3 What happened only 17 minutes after the alarm had been raised?
4 On what pretext had the attacker asked to be taken to the personnel office?
5 What had he then demanded, whilst threatening an employee with a firearm?
6 What did he wait for and what did he manage to do?
7 Why were these events not immediately reported?
8 Who eventually called the police and what had alerted this person's attention?
9 What happened at 6.46 pm?
10 What seems to be the motive for the crime and what is the personal situation of the attacker?

18 Da stimme ich mit dir überein

In this unit you will learn further ways of expressing agreement and disagreement, as well as how to say what would have happened if certain circumstances had prevailed.

Dialog

Holger Breit questions Heike Bogner about her recent trip to Sri Lanka. She is full of enthusiasm, but Holger is rather sceptical.

Holger Breit Heike! Ich dachte, du wärest noch mit deinem Mann in Sri Lanka. Wie hat's dir dort eigentlich gefallen? Sei mal ehrlich!

Heike Bogner Einfach prima! Obwohl wir eigentlich geschäftlich in Sri Lanka waren, war das für mich eine der interessantesten Reisen, die ich je gemacht habe.

Holger Breit Tatsächlich? Meine Schwester hat mir auch versichert, nachdem sie ihre Hochzeitsreise dorthin gemacht hatte, daß ein Besuch nach Sri Lanka unbedingt zu empfehlen sei. Ich lasse mich aber nur schwer überzeugen.

Heike Bogner Ich bin letzte Woche selbst zum erstenmal dorthin geflogen. Bis dahin war ich immer der Ansicht gewesen, Länder der Dritten Welt haben mir nichts zu bieten. Jetzt bin ich aber ganz anderer Meinung.

Holger Breit Wie läßt sich so was erklären? Der Lebensstandard soll in Sri Lanka viel niedriger sein als in der Bundesrepublik. Die Nachteile des Lebens dort sind ja bekannt.

Heike Bogner Das stimmt. Aber die Landschaft ist wunderschön und das Klima ist auch während unseres europäischen Winters warm und sonnig. Zwar hat das Land große Probleme, wie zum Beispiel, Rassenkonflikte, Armut, Arbeitslosigkeit und Obdachlosigkeit. Man darf aber nicht vergessen, daß solche Probleme auch in vielen der reichsten Länder der Welt existieren.

Holger Breit Das mag wohl sein, und das sehe ich schon ein. Was ich aber so entsetzlich daran finde, ist, daß die reichen Länder der Welt so wenig Hilfe leisten für die Länder der Dritten Welt.

Heike Bogner Da stimme ich mit dir vollkommen überein. Um so wichtiger ist es also, daß Deutsche in solche Länder fahren, um Kontakt zu den Leuten der Dritten Welt herzustellen. Gerade der persönliche Kontakt zu ganz gewöhnlichen Menschen war für mich am allerinteressantesten.

Holger Breit Wärest du aber trotzdem nicht lieber nach Gran Canaria oder Teneriffa geflogen, wenn du die Wahl gehabt hättest? Es wäre zu dieser Jahreszeit dort bestimmt genauso warm gewesen wie in Sri Lanka.

Heike Bogner Sicher. Aber ich glaube kaum, daß ich mehr Spaß gehabt hätte. Ich freue mich schon auf meine nächste Reise!

Sei mal ehrlich! *Be honest now!*
geschäftlich *on business*
je *ever*
tatsächlich *really, actually, in fact*
versichern (+*dat.*) *to assure*
die Hochzeitsreise *honeymoon (trip)*
lassen *to let*
Ich lasse mich nur schwer überzeugen *I'm difficult to convince* (lit. *I let myself be convinced . . .*)
bis dahin *up to that point*
Ich war der Ansicht gewesen, *I had been of the view,*
bieten *to offer*
Jetzt bin ich ganz anderer Meinung *Now I'm of quite a different opinion*
so (et)was *something like that*
Wie läßt sich so was erklären? *How can something like that be explained?*
der Lebensstandard *standard of living*
niedrig *low*
der Nachteil (-e) *disadvantage*
die Landschaft (-en) *landscape*
das Klima *climate*
sonnig *sunny*
der Rassenkonflikt (-e) *racial conflict*
die Armut *poverty*
die Obdachlosigkeit *homelessness*
Man darf nicht vergessen . . . *One mustn't forget . . .*
Das mag wohl sein *That may well be*
Das sehe ich schon ein *I do see that*

entsetzlich *dreadful, awful, appalling*
übereinstimmen (sep.) **mit** (+dat.) *to agree with*
vollkommen *completely, entirely*
um so wichtiger *all the more important*
Kontakt herstellen (zu +*dat.*) *to establish contact (with)*
gewöhnlich *ordinary, usual(ly)*
Das war am allerinteressantesten *That was the most interesting (thing) of all*
Wärest du nicht lieber nach Gran Canaria geflogen? *Wouldn't you rather have flown to Gran Canaria?*
... wenn du die Wahl gehabt hättest *... if you had had the choice*
Es wäre dort genauso warm gewesen *It would have been just as warm there*
sich freuen auf *to look forward to*

Fragen zum Dialog

1 Richtig (R) oder Falsch (F)?

1. Heike hat es in Sri Lanka sehr gut gefallen.
2. Die Schwester von Holger war mal auf ihrer Hochzeitsreise in Sri Lanka.
3. Heike ist letzte Woche schon zum dritten Mal nach Sri Lanka geflogen.
4. Sie ist jetzt der Meinung, daß die Länder der Dritten Welt ihr doch etwas zu bieten haben.
5. Die Landschaft in Sri Lanka ist leider nicht besonders schön.
6. Sri Lanka hat große Probleme, wie zum Beispiel Rassenkonflikte, Armut, Arbeitslosigkeit und Obdachlosigkeit.
7. In den reichsten Ländern existieren solche Probleme natürlich nicht.
8. Heike findet es wichtig, daß Deutsche Kontakt zu Bürgern der Dritten Welt herstellen.
9. Zu dieser Jahreszeit wäre es in Gran Canaria nicht so warm gewesen wie in Sri Lanka.
10. Heike hätte bestimmt viel mehr Spaß gehabt, wenn sie nach Gran Canaria geflogen wäre.

2 Welche Antwort paßt?

1. Ich dachte, du wärest noch in Sri Lanka.
   (*a*) Ich bin schon in Colombo.
   (*b*) Ich bin gestern schon zurückgekommen.
   (*c*) Ich bin erst heute hingeflogen.

2 Wie hat's dir dort eigentlich gefallen?
   (*a*) Sicher.
   (*b*) Einfach prima!
   (*c*) Das mag wohl sein.

3 Das war für mich eine der interessantesten Reisen, die ich je gemacht habe.
   (*a*) Tatsächlich?
   (*b*) Einfach prima!
   (*c*) Das stimmt.

4 Ein Besuch nach Sri Lanka ist unbedingt zu empfehlen.
   (*a*) Das mag wohl sein. Ich lasse mich aber nur schwer überzeugen.
   (*b*) Sei mal ehrlich!
   (*c*) Mir hat's dort einfach prima gefallen.

5 Wärest du aber trotzdem nicht lieber nach Gran Canaria geflogen?
   (*a*) Das stimmt.
   (*b*) Bestimmt nicht.
   (*c*) Da stimme ich mit dir vollkommen überein.

Was Sie wissen sollten

Immigration to Germany

During the 1950s and early 1960s, the years of the **Wirtschaftswunder** (economic miracle), hundreds of thousands of refugees from the Eastern territories were successfully absorbed into Western Germany. As the economy continued to grow labour was recruited from southern European countries, such as Spain, Italy, Yugoslavia, Greece and above all from Turkey. Workers from these countries were offered short-term contracts and were referred to as **Gastarbeiter** (guest workers), since the intention was that they should return to their homeland on completion of their contract. Despite the declared policy that **»Die Bundesrepublik ist kein Einwanderungsland«** (*The Federal Republic is not an immigration country*) many guest workers did manage to obtain longstay residence permits and to bring over their families and dependants. Furthermore, citizens of European Community states nowadays have the right to reside anywhere in the Community.

Because the German constitution or Basic Law (**Grundgesetz**) guarantees the right to political asylum, the numbers of asylum-seekers (**Asylanten**) from such countries as Sri Lanka, Lebanon and Iran have increased in recent years. Difficulties in distinguishing genuine political refugees from economic refugees have led to problems and to attempts at tightening the vetting procedures for granting asylum. The official policy concerning economic refugees is to attempt to stem the flow by supplying generous aid to the home countries of would-be emigrants in order to raise the standard of living and preclude the need for emigration.

A further source of immigration to Germany has been the influx of 'ethnic Germans' (**Volksdeutsche**) from Poland and the Soviet Union. Although of German ancestry, many of these immigrants have little or no command of German and have had only limited success in finding employment and integrating into German society.

Wichtige Redewendungen

How to

1 *Express agreement*

(*a*) Da stimme ich mit dir (völlig) überein.
(*b*) Da bin ich ganz deiner Meinung.
(*c*) Darüber sind wir uns einig.
(*d*) Da hast du (völlig) recht.
(*e*) Das stimmt.
(*f*) Richtig!

2 *Express disagreement*

politely
(*a*) Da stimme ich nicht (ganz) mit dir überein.
(*b*) Ich bin da (ganz) anderer Meinung.
(*c*) Darüber sind wir uns leider nicht einig.
more directly
(*d*) Da hast du (völlig) unrecht.
(*e*) Das stimmt nicht.
bluntly
(*f*) Unsinn!

3 *Concede a point and go on to add a further argument*

(*a*) Das mag wohl sein, aber . . .

(*b*) Da hast du vielleicht recht, aber . . .
(*c*) Das sehe ich schon ein, aber . . .
(*d*) Sicher, aber . . .

Die Wirtschaft (*the economy*)

der Preis (-e) *price*
die Kosten (*pl.*) *costs*
das Angebot *supply*
die Nachfrage *demand*
der Lohn (¨e) *wage*
das Gehalt (¨er) *salary*
die Vollbeschäftigung *full employment*
der europäische Binnenmarkt *European single* (lit. *internal*) *market*
der Unternehmer (-) *entrepreneur*
der Arbeitgeber (-) *employer*
der Arbeitnehmer (-) *employee*
die Gewerkschaft (-en) *trade union*
der Gewinn (-e) *profit*
der Umsatz *turnover*
der Arbeitsplatz (¨e) *job, place of work*
die Marktwirtschaft *market economy*
die Planwirtschaft *planned economy*

Grammatik

1 Superlative

We use what is known as the ***superlative*** form to express extremes (e.g. *fastest*, *slowest*). In English we produce the superlative form of the adjective either by adding ***-est*** (*oldest*, *youngest*) or by adding ***most*** in front of the adjective (*most interesting*, *most practical*). In German only the **-(e)st** form exists:

Der schnell**ste** Flug	*The fastest flight*
Die billig**ste** Wohnung	*The cheapest apartment*
Das interessant**este** Beispiel	*The most interesting example*

Those adjectives which add an ***Umlaut*** in the comparative form (see **Lektion 6**) do so in the superlative as well:

Der **älteste** Einwohner	*The oldest inhabitant*
Die **stärkste** Frau	*The strongest woman*
Das **dümmste** Kind	*The most stupid child*

Note that **groß** and **gut** have irregular superlative forms:

Das **größte** Haus	*The biggest house*
Die **beste** Lösung	*The best solution*

You will see from the above examples that the **-st** suffix is more common that **-est**. The extra **-e-** is sometimes needed to 'oil the works' and to make the superlative form easier to pronounce.

Note that the superlative form of the adverb is **am -(e)sten**:

Dieser Wagen fährt **am schnellsten**	*This car goes fastest*
Dieses Ehepaar tanzt **am besten**.	*This (married) couple dances best.*

The adverbial form is often used with the verb **sein** to be:

Dieser Student ist **am klügsten** *This student is cleverest*

as opposed to

Dieser Student ist **der klügste** *This student is the cleverest (student).*

2 Pluperfect tense

The ***pluperfect tense*** is used to describe an action or state further in the past than the main (perfect or imperfect tense) reference point of the sentence:

Main reference point	
imperfect tense	*Pluperfect tense*
Als ich aufstand,	**hatten** meine Freunde schon **gefrühstückt**.
When I got up	*my friends* ***had*** *already* ***breakfasted.***

The pluperfect tense is formed in German by using the imperfect tense of the appropriate auxiliary verb **haben** (i.e. **hatte/hattest/hatten**) or **sein** (i.e. **war/warst/waren**) together with the past participle:

Nachdem ich die Zeitung **gelesen hatte**, spielte ich Karten. *After I* ***had read*** *the paper, I played cards.*
Ich wollte Karin besuchen, aber sie **war** schon in Urlaub **gefahren**. *I wanted to visit Karin, but she* ***had*** *already* ***gone*** *on holiday.*

3 Pluperfect subjunctive

The ***pluperfect subjunctive*** is used for expressing 'unreal' conditions in the past. That is to say, conjectures are made as to what might have happened, if circumstances had been different. There are a number of examples of the pluperfect subjunctive in the last two exchanges of **Dialog 18**:

Wärest du nicht lieber nach Teneriffa **geflogen**, wenn du die Wahl **gehabt hättest**? *Wouldn't you rather have flown to Teneriffe, if you had had the choice?*

Es **wäre** zu dieser Jahreszeit genauso warm **gewesen** wie in Sri Lanka. *It would have been just as warm at this time of the year as in Sri Lanka.*
Aber ich glaube kaum, daß ich mehr Spaß **gehabt hätte**. *But I hardly think that I would have had more fun.*

As you can see from the above examples, the pluperfect subjunctive is formed by using the imperfect subjunctive of the appropriate auxiliary verb **haben** (i.e. **hätte/hättest/hätten**) or **sein** (i.e. **wäre/wärest/wären**) together with the past participle.

When modal verbs are used in conditional sentences of this kind, the infinitive form of the modal verb rather than the past participle is used:

Ich **hätte** nach Berlin **fliegen können**, wenn ich 2 Tage freibekommen hätte. *I could have flown to Berlin, if I had got 2 days off.*
Das **hättest** du nicht **machen sollen**! *You ought not to have done that!*

4 Constructions with *lassen*

The verb **lassen** is used in a number of different ways and with a number of different meanings.

4.1 When used as a main verb, **lassen** can cover the meaning of (*a*) *to leave* and (*b*) *to stop* in English:

(*a*)	Du kannst deine Sachen hier lassen.	*You can leave your things here.*
	Laß mich nicht allein!	*Don't leave me alone!*
(*b*)	Laß das!	*Stop that!*
	Er kann das Rauchen nicht lassen.	*He can't stop smoking.*

4.2 **Lassen** can also be used with the meaning of *to allow*, *let*. In this case a second verb infinitive is normally required:

Laß mich bitte vorne sitzen!	*Let me sit in front, please!*
Mein Vater läßt mich sein Auto waschen.	*My father lets me wash his car.*

4.3 **Dialog 18** contains two examples of a further use of **lassen**. Here **lassen** is used together with a reflexive pronoun and a second verb infinitive:

Ich lasse mich nur schwer überzeugen. *I am difficult to convince* (lit. *I let myself be convinced only with difficulty*)
Wie läßt sich so was erklären? *How can something like that be explained?* (lit. *How does something like that explain itself?*)

This construction may often be used in preference to the passive:

> Das läßt sich nicht machen./Das kann nicht gemacht werden. *That cannot be done.*
> Seine Frage ließ sich leicht beantworten./Seine Frage konnte leicht beantwortet werden. *His question was easily answered.*

4.4 Finally, **lassen** is used (as a modal auxiliary verb) together with a second verb infinitive to mean *to have something done/ get something done:*

> Christel läßt sich ein neues Haus bauen. *Christel is having herself a new house built.*
> Ich muß mir heute die Haare schneiden lassen. *I must get my hair cut today.*
> Wir haben ihr zum Geburtstag Blumen schicken lassen. *We had flowers sent to her for her birthday.*

5 Sequencing of sentence elements

Attention has already been drawn to certain word-order possibilities in German—for instance the placing in initial position (or ***fronting***) of the pronominal object in **Lektion 13**. It will already have become clear that the sequencing of sentence elements is considerably more flexible in German than in English. In fact it is usually possible for any sentence element (other than the verb in declarative sentences) to appear in initial position:

Anna	hat gestern für ihre Mutter ein Geschenk gekauft.
Gestern	hat Anna für ihre Mutter ein Geschenk gekauft.
Für ihre Mutter	hat Anna gestern ein Geschenk gekauft.
Ein Geschenk	hat Anna gestern für ihre Mutter gekauft.

Generally speaking, the initial position is often occupied by information taken for granted by both the speaker and the listener(s):

> **Anna** hat ein Geschenk gekauft. **Das Geschenk** ist für ihre Mutter. **Ihre Mutter** ist leider krank.

The most important, and usually, new information is found towards the end of the sentence, where the main stress tends to fall.

However, the initial position ***can*** be used to highlight and give emphasis to certain information:

> **Herr Baumann** habe ich nicht gesehen. **Mit seiner Frau** habe ich gesprochen.

Almost any sentence element may be highlighted in this way, including the past participle:

Gesprochen hat er nicht. **Nur gelächelt** hat er.

6 Indirect or Reported Speech

The difference between **direct** and **indirect** (or **reported**) **speech** is best illustrated by an example:

Helga says:	»Klaus, ich bin krank«.	(Direct Speech)
Klaus reports:	»Helga sagte mir, **sie sei krank**«.	(Indirect Speech)

There is not scope within the framework of this course to list all the various details concerning indirect speech. For recognition purposes, it will suffice to know that the subjunctive is frequently found in sentences containing indirect speech:

Dagmar sagte, ihr Freund **wäre** gestern abend bei ihr gewesen. Er **hätte** stundenlang mit ihr geredet.

The use of the subjunctive sometimes casts an element of doubt on the claim being made:

Er behauptete, er hätte das Geld nie erhalten. *He claimed he had never received the money* (*but I'm not at all sure*).

The imperfect subjunctive forms of certain commonly found verbs are listed in **Lektion 14**. The present subjunctive forms of the frequently used verbs **sein** and **haben** are listed in section 7 below.

7 Present subjunctive of *sein* and *haben*

sein		**haben**	
ich sei	wir seien	ich habe	wir haben
du seiest	ihr seiet	du habest	ihr habet
Sie seien	Sie seien	Sie haben	Sie haben
er / sie / es } sei	sie seien	er / sie / es } habe	sie haben

8 Extended participial phrases

One structure that has not yet been introduced in the course, but which you will need to recognise if you are to understand ***formal***

German, is what is known as the ***extended participial phrase***. This phrase occupies the slot in the sentence normally occupied by an attributive adjective and contains either a present participal or a past participal:

> Die Zahl der /**in der Bundesrepublik arbeitenden**/ Ausländer ist im vergangenen Jahr gesunken.
> *The number of foreigners/**working in the Federal Republic**/fell last year.*

> Die /**im Herbst veröffentlichte**/ Zahl der Arbeitslosen ist weiter angestiegen.
> *The unemployment figure(s)/**published in the autumn**/ showed a further rise.* (lit. *has risen further.*)

The participial phrase can sometimes be quite long:

> Wir begrüssen die /**am 8. Dezember 1987 beim sowjetisch-amerikanischen Gipfel in Washington getroffene**/ Übereinkunft.
> *We welcome the agreement /**reached in Washington at the Soviet-American summit on 8th December 1987**/.*

This phenomenon hardly exists in English, except in such fixed expressions as *a never-to-be-forgotten evening*. In the three examples above it is possible to produce an acceptable English version by placing the participial phrase ***after*** the noun. A full relative clause is, however, sometimes the best solution in English:

> Das /**aus dem hohen Baum gefallene**/ Tier lief unversehrt davon.
> *The animal, /**which had fallen from the tall tree**/, ran off unscathed.*

Übungen

ÜBUNG 18.1 Welches Hotel sollen wir nehmen?

Hotel	*Das Insel-Hotel*	*Das Dom-Hotel*	*Das Crest-Hotel*
Anzahl der Betten	22	200	560
Preis pro Bett DM	60	240	350
Lage	zentral	1 km von d. Stadtmitte	5 km von d. Stadmitte
gebaut	1935	1887	1988
Comfort	*	**	****

State which hotel is cheapest, dearest, etc. according to the following pattern:

teuer **Am teuersten ist das Crest-Hotel.**
günstig **Am günstigsten liegt das Insel-Hotel.**

1 alt. 2 klein. 3 modern. 4 groß. 5 billig. 6 bequem. 7 zentral. 8 weit von der Stadtmitte entfernt.

ÜBUNG 18.2 Was paßt zusammen?

Put the following sentences into the most appropriate order:

1 Der läßt sich leider nicht mehr reparieren.
2 Was? Bist du etwa verletzt worden?
3 Dann bekommst du einen neuen von der Versicherung, oder?
4 Nein, aber mein schöner, alter Wagen ist völlig kaputt.
5 Kannst du ihn nicht reparieren lassen?
6 Klaus! Ich dachte, du wolltest heute nach Köln.
7 Ja, aber ich habe gestern abend meinen Wagen kaputtgefahren (*smashed up*).
8 Wahrscheinlich. Aber mein alter Borg-Ward war ja etwas Besonderes.

ÜBUNG 18.3 Lesen Sie die Beispiele, und machen Sie weiter.

Der vielbeschäftigte Vater

Heute bin ich um 6 Uhr aufgestanden.
Dann habe ich meine beiden Söhne geweckt.
Nachdem ich heute um 6 Uhr aufgestanden war, habe ich meine beiden Söhne geweckt.

Dann habe ich Kaffee gekocht.
Nachdem ich meine beiden Söhne geweckt hatte, habe ich Kaffee gekocht.

1 Dann habe ich meine Söhne zur Schule gebracht.
2 Dann habe ich im Supermarkt eingekauft.
3 Dann habe ich die Wohnung saubergemacht (*cleaned*).
4 Dann habe ich das Mittagessen zubereitet (*prepared*).
5 Dann habe ich meine Söhne von der Schule abgeholt.
6 Dann haben wir zusammen zu Mittag gegessen.
7 Dann haben wir eine Stunde lang Karten gespielt.
8 Dann sind wir schwimmen gegangen.

ÜBUNG 18.4 Lesen Sie die Beispiele, und machen Sie weiter.

Hat Ingrid alles falsch gemacht?

Ich habe nicht im Mai, sondern im November Urlaub gehabt.
Hättest du nicht lieber im Mai Urlaub gehabt?
Ich bin nicht mit Freunden, sondern alleine in Urlaub gefahren.
Wärest du nicht lieber mit Freunden in Urlaub gefahren?

1 Ich bin nicht nach Berlin, sondern nach München gefahren.
2 Ich habe dort nicht bei Freunden, sondern bei Verwandten gewohnt.
3 Ich bin dort nicht ins Theater, sondern in die Oper gegangen.
4 Ich habe nicht die Frauenkirche, sondern die Theatinerkirche besichtigt.
5 Ich habe nicht die Alte, sondern die Neue Pinakothek besucht.
6 Ich habe im Hofbräuhaus nicht Bier, sondern Mineralwasser getrunken.
7 Ich bin nicht im Englischen Garten, sondern im Hauptbahnhof spazierengegangen.
8 Ich habe nicht zwei Wochen, sondern nur eine Woche Urlaub gehabt.

ÜBUNG 18.5 Sagen Sie es anders.

Es ist schwer, Peter zu überzeugen.
Peter läßt sich (nur) schwer überzeugen.
Wie kann man so was erklären?
Wie läßt sich so was erklären?

1 Das kann man leider nicht machen.
2 Es ist nicht leicht, seine Fragen zu beantworten.
3 Kann ich dich nicht überreden?
4 Dieses Fenster kann man nicht öffnen.
5 Dieses Wort kann man nicht übersetzen (*translate*).
6 Wie kann man feststellen, wer kommt?
7 Das Problem kann man einfach nicht lösen (*solve*).
8 Wie kann man so etwas behaupten?

ÜBUNG 18.6 Was Karin behauptete.

Karin explained to her friend Lena what happened when she was supposed to meet Franz yesterday. Lena passed this information on to Franz, although she is not too sure about Karin's story.

Karin zu Lena: »Ich habe gestern vor dem Café Krause 20 Minuten auf Franz gewartet.«
Lena zu Franz: ***»Karin behauptete, sie hätte gestern vor dem Café Krause 20 Minuten auf dich gewartet.«***
Ich bin dann ins Café reingegangen.
Sie wäre dann ins Café reingegangen.

1 Ich habe mich ans Fenster gesetzt.
2 Ich habe eine Tasse Kaffee bestellt.
3 Ich habe die ganze Zeit zum Fenster hinausgeschaut.
4 Der Franz ist aber einfach nicht gekommen.
5 Ich habe mir noch einen Kaffee bringen lassen.
6 Dann ist der Peter reingekommen und hat sich zu mir gesetzt.
7 Der hat mich eingeladen, mit ihm ins Kino zu gehen.
8 Nur aus diesem Grunde bin ich mit Peter ins Kino gegangen.

Verstehen Sie?

1 Konversation

Silke Hahn and Wolf Kampe are discussing the question of immigration to Germany. Silke is in favour of a liberal policy, whilst Wolf is for stricter controls.

Wolf Kampe Also, ich bin der Meinung, wir sollten unsere Grenzen jetzt schließen für die Ausländer.

Silke Hahn Aber Wolf! Wie kannst du so 'was sagen? Das ist ja reine Ausländerfeindlichkeit.

Wolf Kampe Ach was! Gegen Ausländer habe ich ja nichts. Die sollen bloß im eigenen Lande bleiben.

Silke Hahn Dann hätten wir keine Touristen mehr in Deutschland.

Wolf Kampe An Touristen denke ich ja nicht. Die dürfen schon kommen, weil sie dann wieder nach Hause gehen, nachdem sir ihr Geld hier ausgegeben haben. Nein, ich rede von denen, die hier bleiben wollen und Sozialleistungen von unserem Staat erwarten.

Silke Hahn Wenn du damit die Asylanten meinst, darfst du zwei Punkte nicht vergessen. Erstens müssen die meisten das eigene Land verlassen, weil sie dort verfolgt werden. Und zweitens müssen sie irgendwie leben, wenn sie hier sind. Man kann ja nicht erwarten, daß jeder Asylant sofort fließend Deutsch spricht und einen Arbeitsplatz findet.

Wolf Kampe Das mag schon sein, aber ich finde, daß viel zu viele jetzt kommen wollen, und daß die große Mehrheit eher aus wirtschaftlichen als aus politischen Gründen kommt.

Silke Hahn Da muß man schon unterscheiden zwischen den beiden Gruppen, das gebe ich gerne zu. Aber das im Grundgesetz verbürgte Recht auf Asyl für politisch Verfolgte muß erhalten bleiben.

Wolf Kampe Das klingt ja alles schön und gut. Wie man aber eindeutige Beweise erbringt, daß ein Asylant im eigenen Land tatsächlich verfolgt wurde, möchte ich gerne wissen.

Silke Hahn Man muß es trotzdem versuchen. Für manche Leute kann ein zu Unrecht abgelehnter Antrag auf Asyl leider das Todesurteil bedeuten.

rein *pure*
die Ausländerfeindlichkeit *hostility towards foreigners*
der Punkt (-e) *point*
verfolgen *to persecute*
irgendwie *somehow*
die Mehrheit *majority*
eher *sooner, rather*
wirtschaftlich *economic*
unterscheiden *to distinguish, differentiate*
zugeben (*sep.*) *to admit*
verbürgen *to guarantee*
das Recht (auf +*acc.*) *right (of, to)*
das Asyl *asylum*
erhalten *to preserve*
klingen *to sound*
Das ist alles schön und gut *That's all well and good*
eindeutig *clear, unambiguous*
Beweise erbringen *to provide proof*
tatsächlich *actually, really*
zu Unrecht *wrongfully, wrongly*
ablehnen *to reject*
das Todesurteil *death sentence*

Richtig (R) oder Falsch (F)?

1 Wolf ist gegen die weitere Einwanderung von Ausländern in die Bundesrepublik.
2 Silke ist da ganz anderer Meinung.

3 Wolf hat nichts gegen Ausländer, wenn sie bloß nicht nach Deutschland kommen wollen.
4 Damit hat er natürlich nicht Touristen gemeint.
5 Touristen dürfen nicht kommen, weil sie nie wieder nach Hause gehen.
6 Wolf hat es nicht gern, wenn Asylanten Geld vom Staat erhalten.
7 Die meisten Asylanten verlassen das eigene Land, weil sie dort arbeitslos sind.
8 Wolf findet, die meisten kommen, weil sie ein wirtschaftlich besseres Leben suchen.
9 Silke ist für die Erhaltung des Asylrechts in der Bundesrepublik.
10 Wenn ein Antrag auf Asyl zu Unrecht abgelehnt wird, kann es für den Asylbewerber den Tod bedeuten.

2 Lesetext

Lesen Sie den Text, und versuchen Sie, die Fragen zu beantworten.

Das Recht auf Asyl

Nach Artikel 19 des Grundgesetzes wird politisch Verfolgten ein Asylrecht verbürgt. Wegen des wachsenden Zustroms von Asylbewerbern in die Bundesrepublik wird jedoch dieses Grundrecht auf Asyl immer restriktiver interpretiert.

Wegen der geringen Zahl der Asylbewerber in den Anfangsjahren der Bundesrepublik gab es kaum Probleme mit dem Asylrecht. Erst gegen Ende der 70er Jahre nahmen die Zahlen explosionsartig zu, und im Jahre 1980 wurden Maßnahmen ergriffen, um die Einreise Asylsuchender einzudämmen. Weitere Bestimmungen zur Bekämpfung des Asylmißbrauchs wurden 1987 eingeführt. Anfang der 90er Jahre haben viele Politiker für ein neues Ausländergesetz argumentiert.

In früheren Jahren entstammten Asylbewerber hauptsächlich den »sozialistischen« Ländern Osteuropas. Heute kommen sie nicht nur aus Osteuropa, sondern auch aus afrikanischen und asiatischen Ländern.

Die Hauptschwierigkeit bei der Gewährung vom Asylrecht ist die Unterscheidung zwischen rein wirtschaftlichen und echt politischen Gründen für die Antragstellung. Kein Asylrecht wird bei wirtschaftlichen und allgemeinen Notlagen gewährt.

wachsen *to grow*
der Zustrom *influx*
das Grundrecht (-e) *basic right*
gering *low, small (of numbers)*
zunehmen (*sep.*) *to increase*
Maßnahmen ergreifen *to adopt measures*
eindämmen (*sep.*) *to check, stem*
die Bestimmung (-en) *regulation*
die Bekämpfung *combatting*
der Mißbrauch *abuse*
einführen *to introduce*
der Politiker (-) *politician*
das Gesetz (-e) *law*
entstammen (+*dat.*) *to come from*
hauptsächlich *mainly, predominantly*
die Hauptschwierigkeit (-en) *main difficulty*
die Gewährung *granting*
echt *genuine(ly)*
die Antragstellung *submission of an application*
die Notlage (-n) *serious difficulty*

1 To which people is the right of asylum guaranteed by Article 19 of the Basic Law?
2 How is this basic right being interpreted as a result of the growing influx of applicants for asylum?
3 During what period were there hardly any problems with the right to asylum and why was this so?
4 When did the numbers of applicants rise dramatically?
5 What did the 1987 measures attempt to combat?
6 Where did asylum-seekers mainly come from in the earlier years?
7 Where do they additionally come from nowadays?
8 What main difficulty is encountered when granting the right of asylum?
9 What happens in cases of economic and general hardship?

Zusatzmaterialien

The following materials are intended to offer you additional practice in listening to and reading German. They are authentic extracts taken from the West German media. You will find that all the structures and most of the vocabulary have already been encountered in the course book.

Verstehen Sie?

Nachrichtensendung A

Hören Sie zu, und versuchen Sie folgende Fragen zu beantworten:

1 With what robbery is a comparison here being drawn?
2 Who raided what in the present robbery and where did the raid take place?
3 What was stolen?
4 Who have the Frankfurt Police not yet given details of?
5 How did the robbers stop the vehicle which they planned to raid?
6 What was the driver forced to do at pistol point?
7 What happened then?

ÜBERFALL AUF GOLD- UND DIAMANTENTRANSPORT

Im Stil der britischen Postzugräuber von 1963 haben zwei Maskierte in der Nähe des Frankfurter Flughafens einen Kleintransporter überfallen. Die Beute—Gold, Platin und Rohdiamanten im Wert von 3,3 Millionen Mark. Die bewaffneten Täter entkamen unerkannt. Über die Besitzer der geraubten Wertsachen machte die Frankfurter Polizei bislang keine Angaben. Die Tat ereignete sich nach ihrer Darstellung so: Die Räuber postierten gestern abend bei Kelsterbach einen Personenwagen quer auf der Fahrbahn. Als der Kleinlaster ausweichen wollte, sprang einer der Täter auf. Mit vorgehaltener Pistole zwang er den Fahrer, in ein Waldstück zu fahren. Dort wurde die Millionenbeute in einen Pkw umgeladen.

(*ZDF »Heute«*)

der Diamant (-en) *diamond*
der Postzugräuber (-) *mail-train robber*
die Beute *loot*
das Platin *platinum*
Roh- *rough (uncut)*
der Wert (-e) *value*
der Besitzer (-) *owner*
die Wertsachen (*f. pl.*) *valuables*
die Tat *deed*
sich ereignen *to happen, occur*
die Darstellung (*here*) *account*
quer *diagonal(ly)*
die Fahrbahn *carriageway*
aufspringen (*sep.*) *to jump onto*
zwingen *to force, compel*
das Waldstück (-e) *wood*
umladen *to transfer, reload*

Nachrichtensendung B

Hören Sie zu, und versuchen Sie folgende Fragen zu beantworten:

1 What effect did the Whitsun holiday rush have at the Bad Reichenhall border crossing point?
2 What does the figure of 20,000 represent?
3 Why was it not only the patience of hitch-hikers that was stretched?
4 Where did the motorway pile-up occur?
5 What were the weather conditions at the time?
6 What were the results of the pile-up?
7 What were the main causes of the pile-up?
8 What does the figure of 1 million marks represent?

Auf bundesdeutschen Autobahnen

Die Reisewelle zu Pfingsten ist am Nachmittag ins Rollen gekommen. Staus und zähflüssiger Verkehr auf der A8 München-Salzburg am Grenzübergang Bad Reichenhall. Weit über 20 000 Bundesbürger haben sich vor den Feiertagen in Richtung Österreich aufgemacht. Nicht nur die Geduld von Trampern wurde strapaziert. Auch Urlauber mit eigenen Fahrzeugen mußten Wartezeiten bis zu einer Stunde in Kauf nehmen.

Massenkarambolage auf der

Autobahn Stuttgart–München. Bei starkem Regen und schlechten Sichtverhältnissen sind zwischen Mühlhausen und Merklingen 118 Fahrzeuge in 36 Unfälle verwickelt worden. Dabei wurden 19 Menschen zum Teil schwer verletzt. Überhöhte Geschwindigkeit, sowie ungenügender Abstand waren Hauptursachen des Unglücks. Der Schaden wird über auf 1 Million Mark geschätzt.

(*ZDF »Heute«*)

das Pfingsten (-) *Whitsun*
der Feiertag (-e) *public holiday*
die Geduld *patience*
der Tramper (-) *hitch-hiker*
der Urlauber (-) *holiday-maker*
das Fahrzeug (-e) *vehicle*
die Wartezeit (-en) *wait*
in Kauf nehmen *to accept*
die Massenkarambolage (-n) *pile-up*
die Sichtverhältnisse (*pl.*) *visibility*
überhöht *excessive*
die Geschwindigkeit (-en) *speed*
der Abstand (¨e) *distance*
der Schaden (¨) *damage*

Lesetext A

Lesen Sie den Text.

Sommer läßt auf sich warten

Bonn (ddp)—Der von Wetterpropheten angekündigte »Jahrhundertsommer« läßt vorerst zu wünschen übrig. Am Wochenende legte sich ein grauer Wolkenschleier über das Bundesgebiet. Gute Nachrichten kamen nur vom Allgemeinen Deutschen Automobil Club (ADAC) aus München: Die Urlauber konnten ohne größere Staus in Richtung Süden reisen.

Zu Hause mußten die Bundesbürger auf Sommerfreuden verzichten. So herrschte dem Münchner Wetteramt zufolge in den Alpen »nicht gerade Bergwanderwetter«. Immer wieder gingen Schauer nieder, die Fernsicht war »nahezu auf Null reduziert«. Auch an den Küsten präsentierte sich das Wetter bei Temperaturen um zwanzig Grad nicht gerade freundlich. In Sylt wurden nach einer Sturmwarnung vorsorglich sogar die Strandkörbe abgebaut.

Die Autofahrer mußten dagegen kaum mit Verkehrsbehinderungen rechnen. Wie der ADAC mitteilte, kam es trotz Ferienbeginns in Berlin auf den Autobahnen aus der Großstadt nicht zu hohem Verkehrsaufkommen. Auch in den Ausflugsgebieten blieb alles ruhig.

(*Süddeutsche Zeitung*)

ankündigen *to announce*	**der Strandkorb (¨e)** *wicker beach chair*
der Schleier (-) *veil, haze*	**abbauen** *to take down*
der Berg (-e) *mountain*	**mitteilen** *to report*
die Fernsicht *(long distance) visibility*	**der Ausflug (¨e)** *excursion*

Fragen

1 What is, for the time being at least, leaving quite a lot to be desired?
2 What was the weather like at the weekend in Germany?
3 What was the good news from the ADAC in Munich?
4 What was the weather like in the Alps according to the Munich weather office?
5 What precautions were taken on the island of Sylt and why?
6 What advantages did the weather bring for car-drivers?
7 Why might one have expected heavy traffic on the motorways out of Berlin?
8 What were conditions like in the holiday resorts?

Lesetext B

Lesen Sie den Text

US-Studie: Frauen nirgends völlig gleichberechtigt

Washington (dpa)—In keinem Land der Welt sind die Frauen völlig gleichberechtigt. Zu diesem Schluß kommt eine Studie des »Population Crisis Committee« (PCC) in Washington, das sich für die freiwillige Familienplanung einsetzt. Untersucht wurden die Verhältnisse in 99 Ländern.

Nach den Bewertungskriterien (Gesundheit, Familienverhältnisse, Bildung, Beschäftigung und soziale Gleichstellung) geht es den Schwedinnen am besten,. gefolgt von den Frauen in Finnland, den USA, Norwegen, Kanada und Dänemark. Am schlimmsten diskriminiert würden die Frauen in Bangladesh. Die Bürgerinnen der Bundesrepublik stehen in der Statistik an 17. Stelle —hinter der UdSSR, Bulgarien und Ungarn.

Die Studie weist auf eine tiefe Kluft zwischen Industrie- und Entwicklungsländern hin. Eine Schwedin mit ein bis zwei Kindern habe eine Lebenserwartung von 81 Jahren, drei von fünf schwedischen Frauen seien erwerbstätig und nahezu alle könnten lesen und schreiben. Das Durchschnittsalter der Frau in Bangladesh sei dagegen nur 49 Jahre.

(*Süddeutsche Zeitung*)

nirgends *nowhere*	**die Beschäftigung** *employment*
gleichberechtigt *enjoying equal rights*	**hinweisen auf** (+*acc*) *to indicate*
der Schluß *conclusion*	**die Kluft (¨e)** *gulf, gap*
untersuchen *to investigate*	**die Entwicklung (-en)** *development*
das Verhältnis *condition, situation*	**die Erwartung (-en)** *expectancy*
die Bewertung *evaluation*	**erwerbstätig** *employed*
	der Durchschnitt (-e) *average*

Fragen

1 What conclusion has the PCC study come to?
2 What does the figure of 99 represent?
3 What were the study's evaluation criteria?
4 In which 6 countries do women fare best?
5 Why is Bangladesh mentioned?
6 Why has the Federal Republic no reason to be proud of its achievements in this area?
7 What does the study reveal?
8 What information is provided here about Swedish women?

You should now be in a position to tackle on your own—aided only by the careful use of a good dictionary—spoken or written German material of your own choosing.

Viel Spaß!

Key to the Exercises

RICHTIG ODER FALSCH?
For these sections, an 'R' indicates that the statement is true. Otherwise the correct version is given.

Lektion 1

RICHTIG ODER FALSCH?
1 R. 2 Michael Stein kommt aus Hamburg. 3 R. 4 Rainer König ist aus Salzburg. 5 R.

WELCHE ANTWORT PAßT?
1 (*b*). 2 (*a*). 3 (*b*). 4 (*c*).

ÜBUNGEN
1.1A 1 Ich heiße Schubert, Anita Schubert. 2 Ich komme aus Deutschland, aus Düsseldorf.
1.1B 1 Ich heiße Ziegler, Kurt Ziegler. Ich komme aus Deutschland, aus Köln. 2 Ich heiße Lowe, Tracy Lowe. Ich komme aus Australien, aus Sydney. 3 Ich heiße Sanchez, Juan Sanchez. Ich komme aus Spanien, aus Madrid. 4 Ich heiße Rebel, Heide Rebel. Ich komme aus Österreich, aus Wien.
1.2 1 Mein Name ist . . . 2 Ist Ihr Name . . . ? 3 Ist sein Name . . . ? 4 Ihr name ist . . . 5 Ist ihr Name . . . ?
1.3 1 bin, bin 2 Ist 3 ist 4 Sind 5 sind.
1.4 1 (*d*). 2 (*c*). 3 (*b*). 4 (*a*).
1.5 1 (*d*). 2 (*b*). 3 (*a*). 4 (*c*).

KONVERSATION (RICHTIG ODER FALSCH?)
1 R. 2 Sie ist aus Manchester. 3 R. 4 Südtirol ist in Italien, nicht in Österreich.

LESETEXT
1 A centre for tourism and conferences (congresses). 2 Not only from Germany but also from other European countries, from North America, from Japan, indeed from the whole world.

Lektion 2

RICHTIG ODER FALSCH?
1 Frau Dr. Koch ist aus Chicago. 2 R. 3 Sie ist Deutsche. 4 R. 5 Sie ist Ärztin. 6 R. 7 R. 8 Er spricht es nicht sehr fließend.

FRAGEN
1 Sie wohnt in Chicago. 2 Sie ist Ärztin. 3 Nein, er ist Englischlehrer. 4 Ja, er spricht sehr gut Spanisch. 5 Er spricht auch sehr gut Französisch.

ÜBUNGEN
2.1 1 Ich heiße Rainer Nauman. Ich bin Deutscher und wohne in Frankfurt. Ich bin ledig und bin Graphiker von Beruf. 2 Ich heiße Helga Aue. Ich bin Schweizerin und wohne in Zürich. Ich bin verheiratet und bin Verkäuferin von Beruf. 3 Ich heiße Karl Miller. Ich bin Kanadier und wohne in Toronto. Ich bin geschieden und bin Arzt von Beruf. 4 Ich heibe Barbara Martin. Ich bin Australierin und wohne in Sydney. Ich bin verwitwet und bin Lehrerin von Beruf. 5 Ich heiße Christel Kuhn. Ich bin Österreicherin und wohne in Salzburg. Ich bin verheira-

tet und bin Ärztin von Beruf.
2.2 1 Was sind Sie von Beruf? 2 Sind Sie verheiratet? 3 Sind Sie Deutscher? 4 Wo wohnen Sie? 5 Sprechen Sie Französisch (Spanisch)?
2.3 1 (*c*). 2 (*a*). 3 (*c*). 4 (*a*). 5 (*c*). 6 (*b*).
2.4 5-3-6-1-4-2.
2.5 1 (*d*). 2 (*g*). 3 (*b*). 4 (*a*/*c*). 5 (*c*/*a*). 6 (*h*). 7(*f*). 8 (*e*).

KONVERSATION (RICHTIG ODER FALSCH?)
1 Olaf kommt aus Köln. 2 R. 3 Olaf ist verheiratet. 4 R. 5 Werner wohnt jetzt in London. 6 R. 7 R. 8 R.

LESETEXT
A 1 Austrian; 28; salesman. 2 To come to London on vacation. 3 Someone who understands German.
B 1 widowed; secretary. 2 She's learning English as a hobby. 3 They should write to her. 4 They must live in the city centre.

Lektion 3

RICHTIG ODER FALSCH?
1 Das Haus liegt in der Nähe von Füssen. 2 R. 3 R. 4 Der Garten ist etwas klein aber sehr schön. 5 Renate hat zwei Jungen und ein Mädchen. 6 R. 7 Die Kinder kennen das Schloß noch nicht. 8 Das Haus kostet (nur) eintausend Mark im Monat.

FRAGEN
1 Es ist ein Einfamilienhaus, modern und groß. 2 Ja, es ist ziemlich groß. 3 Ja. 4 Ja, sie kennt das Schloß schon. 5 Nein, er findet das Haus sehr preiswert.

ÜBUNGEN
3.1 1 Sie hat (nur) ein Gästezimmer. 2 Nein, sie hat zwei Schlafzimmer. 3 Sie hat ein Bad und eine Dusche. 4 Sie hat zwei Balkons. 5 Es ist 25 (fünfundzwanzig) Quadratmeter groß. 6 Es ist 20 (zwanzig) Quadratmeter groß. 7 Nein, er ist (nur) 18 (achtzehen) Quadratmeter groß. 8 Nein, sie ist (nur) cirka 125 (hundertfünfundzwanzig) Quadratmeter groß. 9 Sie liegt in Freiburg im Breisgau.
3.2 1 (*b*). 2 (*c*). 3 (*a*). 4 (*c*). 5 (*a*). 6 (*b*).
3.3 1 liegt. 2 in der Nähe von. 3 (ziemlich) neu. 4 Was kostet. 5 (ziemlich) billig. 6 ist 25m² groß.
3.4 1 (*c*). 2 (*d*). 3 (*e*). 4 (*b*). 5 (*f*). 6 (*a*).
3.5 1 Ich wohne in Berlin. Ich habe eine Wohnung in Charlottenburg. Die Wohnung ist 120 Quadratmeter groß und kostet 450,–Mark im Monat. 2 Ich wohne in Köln. Ich habe ein Haus in der Severinstraße. Das Haus ist 350 Quadratmeter groß und kostet 1200,–Mark im Monat. 3 Ich wohne in Bremen. Ich habe ein Zimmer in der Violenstraße. Das Zimmer ist 28 Quadratmeter groß und kostet 180,–Mark im Monat. 4 Ich wohne in München. Ich habe ein Haus im Englischen Garten. Das Haus ist 420 Quadratmeter groß und kostet 1550,–Mark im Monat. 5 Ich wohne in Rothenburg. Ich habe ein Zimmer am Marktplatz. Das Zimmer ist 18 Quadratmeter groß und kostet 120,–Mark im Monat.

KONVERSATION (RICHTIG ODER FALSCH?)
1 R. 2 Die Wohnung ist nur klein. 3 R. 4 Das ist ja preiswert (billig). 5 R. 6 Sie ist in der Kaiserstraße. 7 Die Wohnung hat eine Dusche. 8 R.

LESETEXT
1 Sie haben eine Wohnung. 2 Travemünde liegt nicht weit von Lübeck

(in der Nähe von Lübeck). 3 Er findet die Wohnung phantastisch. 4 Sie hat drei (3) Zimmer. 5 Ja, sie gehen oft schwimmen. 6 Sie finden die Ostsee sehr kalt. 7 Er wohnt in München.

Lektion 4

RICHTIG ODER FALSCH?
1 J. 2 N. 3 N. 4 J. 5 J. 6 J.

WELCHE ANTWORT PAẞT?
1 (*b*). 2 (*c*). 3 (*a*). 4 (*b*). 5 (*b*).

ÜBUNGEN
4.1 1 Das Schloßhotel in Karlsruhe hat 180 (hundertachtzig) Betten. Einzelzimmer kosten von 143,– (hundertdreiundvierzig) bis 160,– (hundertsechzig) Mark. Doppelzimmer kosten von 215,– (zweihundertfünfzehn) bis 253,– (zweihundertdreiundfünfzig) Mark. 2 Das Hotel Körner in Hannover hat 140 (hundertvierzig) Betten. Einzelzimmer kosten von 109,– (hundertneun) bis 129,– (hundertneunundzwanzig) Mark. Doppelzimmer kosten von 139,– (hundertneununddreißig) bis 163,– (hundertdreiundsechzig) Mark. 3 Das Hotel Bristol in Köln hat 60 (sechzig) Betten. Einzelzimmer kosten von 113,– (hundertdreizehn) bis 165,– (hundertfünfundsechzig) Mark. Doppelzimmer kosten von 175,– (hundertfünfundsiebzig) bis 240,– (zweihundertvierzig) Mark. 4 das Hotel Domus in Kassel hat 66 (sechsundsechzig) Betten. Einzelzimmer kosten von 99,– (neunundneunzig) bis 119,– (hundertneunzehn) Mark. Doppelzimmer kosten von 155,– (hundertfünfundfünfzig) bis 177,– (hundertsiebenundsiebzig) Mark.
4.2 1 Peter Trost möchte ein Einzelzimmer mit Dusche. Er möchte aber keinen Parkplatz in der Tiefgarage. 2 Bernd und Claudia Hummel möchten ein Doppelzimmer mit Bad und Dusche. Sie möchten auch einen Parkplatz in der Tiefgarage. 3 Anna Lohr möchte ein Einzelzimmer mit Bad. Sie möchte auch einen Parkplatz in der Tiefgarage. 4 Paul Krause und Sylvia Bachmann möchten zwei Einzelzimmer mit Bad oder Dusche. Sie möchten auch einen Parkplatz in der Tiefgarage.
4.3 1 Wir haben leider keine Einzelzimmer mehr mit Dusche. 2 Wir haben leider keine Doppelzimmer mehr mit Bad. 3 Wir haben leider keine Doppelzimmer mehr mit Dusche. 4 (Nein.) Wir haben leider keine Zimmer mehr frei.
4.4 1 Ja, in Österreich kann man Deutsch sprechen. 2 Nein, in Norwegen versteht man meistens kein Spanisch. 3 Nein, in Dänemark versteht man meistens kein Französisch. 4 Ja, in Australien kann man Englisch sprechen. 5 Ja, in Belgien kann man Französisch sprechen. 6 Nein, in Neuseeland kann man meistens kein Deutsch sprechen.
4.5 1 eine Küche. 2 ein Eßzimmer. 3 zwei Schlafzimmer. 4 einen Fernsehraum 5 zwei Abstellräume. 6 ein WC (eine Toilette). 7 ein Badezimmer. 8 eine Dusche.

KONVERSATION (RICHTIG ODER FALSCH?)
1 Heike Klein möchte ein Einzelzimmer mit Dusche. 2 Sie möchte das Einzelzimmer für drei Nächte haben. 3 R. 4 R. 5 Das Zimmer kostet mit Frühstück hundertfünfundzwanzig (125) Mark. 6 R. 7 R.

LESETEXT
1 Holidays and conferences. 2 In an excellent (lit. best) situation in

Berchtesgaden. Five minutes from the town centre. 3 The Watzmann. 4 The atmosphere. 5 Ten minutes outside the town centre. Close to the motorways to Cologne and Belgium. 6 A mini-golf course and a coffee terrace. 7 It has been completely renovated, is in an idyllic position. The style is classical baroque. 8 Comfort and atmosphere. 9 40 km south of Munich. 10 Bellaria and Schloß: One conference room for up to 20 people. Kronprinz: Conference rooms for 20 to 120 people.

Lektion 5

RICHTIG ODER FALSCH?

1 Udo möchte heute nachmittag ins Kino gehen. 2 R. 3 R. 4 Ruth muß morgen schon um sechs Uhr aufstehen. 5 Der Film dauert ungefähr zwei Stunden. 6 R. 7 R. 8 Er kann Ruth erst um Viertel nach acht treffen. 9 R. 10 R.

WELCHE ANTWORT PAẞT?

1 (*b*). 2 (*a*). 3 (*b*). 4 (*c*). 5 (*b*).

ÜBUNGEN

5.1 1 Es ist fünf Uhr morgens. 2 Es ist fünf Uhr nachmittags. 3 Es ist ein Uhr mittags. 4 Es ist acht Uhr abends. 5 Es ist ein Uhr nachts. 6 Es ist elf Uhr abends. 7 Es ist zwölf Uhr mittags. 8 Es ist neun Uhr abends.

5.2 1 In Mexiko City ist es erst 6 Uhr abends. 2 In San Franzisko ist es erst 4 Uhr nachmittags. 3 In Hamburg ist es schon 1 Uhr nachts. 4 In Sydney ist es schon 10 Uhr morgens. 5 In Wellington ist es schon 12 Uhr mittags. 6 In Karatschi ist es schon 5 Uhr morgens. 7 In Hong Kong ist es schon 8 Uhr morgens. 8 In Moskau ist es schon 3 Uhr morgens.

5.3A 1 Um Viertel vor 10 muß ich für Frau Körner einkaufen. 2 Um halb 11 möchte ich mit Dieter schwimmen gehen. 3 Um 12 Uhr mittags möchte ich in der »Forelle« essen gehen. 4 Um Viertel nach 1 (eins) muß ich für Frau Körner arbeiten. 5 Um Viertel nach 4 muß ich Beate abholen. 6 Um Viertel vor 5 möchte ich mit Beate Tennis spielen. 7 Um halb 7 möchte ich ins Kino gehen. 8 Um 10 Uhr möchte ich mit Dieter und Beate tanzen gehen.

5.3B 1 Um Viertel vor 10 kauft er für Frau Körner ein. 2 Um halb 11 geht er mit Dieter schwimmen. 3 Um 12 Uhr mittags geht er in der »Forelle« essen. 4 Um Viertel nach 1 (eins) arbeitet er für Frau Körner. 5 Um Viertel nach 4 holt er Beate ab. 6 Um Viertel vor 5 spielt er mit Beate Tennis. 7 Um halb 7 geht er ins Kino. 8 Um 10 Uhr geht er mit Dieter und Beate tanzen.

5.4 1 muß. 2 kann. 3 muß. 4 können. 5 müssen. 6 muß. 7 mußt. 8 können.

5.5 1 (*d*). 2 (*e*). 3 (*f*). 4 (*a*). 5 (*c*). 6 (*b*).

KONVERSATION (RICHTIG ODER FALSCH?)

1 Die Zeit ist jetzt zwei Minuten vor Zwei Uhr nachmittags. 2 R. 3 R. 4 R. 5 Die Oper »Carmen« dauert zweieinhalb Stunden. 6 R. 7 Das Pop-Musik-Karussel endet um drei Uhr nachmittags. 8 R.

LESETEXT

1 They divide the German Reich (to the west of the Oder-Neiße-Line) into 4 zones. 2 With a blockade of the 3 western sectors of Berlin. 3 By the Berlin Air Lift. 4 It introduces its own new currency. 5 (*a*) The 3 western zones become the Federal Republic. (*b*) The Soviet Zone becomes the German Democratic

Republic. 6 Because the GDR is a socialist country. 7 One that is organised according to the principles of social market economy. 8 Travel to West Berlin and to the Federal Republic. 9 Thousands of GDR citizens visit West Berlin and the Federal Republic. 10 This is the day on which the GDR ceases to exist and becomes part of the Federal Republic. (The day of German unity.)

Lektion 6

RICHTIG ODER FALSCH?

1 R. 2 R. 3 Robert muß erst gegen 10 wieder zu Hause sein. 4 R. 5 Robert geht übermorgen in die Oper. 6 R. 7 R. 8 Im Bohlweg sind die Geschäfte viel interessanter als in der Hauptstraße. 9 R. 10 Die meisten Touristen besichtigen das Schloß und den Dom und gehen dann einkaufen.

WELCHE ANTWORT PAßT?

1 (*c*). 2 (*b*). 3 (*a*). 4 (*c*). 5 (*b*).

ÜBUNGEN

6.1 1 (*i*). 2 (*h*). 3 (*f*). 4 (*b*). 5 (*j*). 6 (*c*). 7 (*d*). 8 (*e*). 9 (*a*). 10 (*g*).

6.2 1 Mittwoch um 8 Uhr geht sie ins Theater. 2 Donnerstag um Viertel nach 7 geht sie mit Klaus in den Ratskeller. 3 Freitag um halb 11 geht sie mit Doris und Claudia in die Discothek. 4 Samstag um Viertel nach 9 geht sie ins Kabarett. 5 Sonntag um 2 Uhr geht sie mit Käthe ins Konzert.

6.3A 1 Ja, aber dieses hier ist noch teurer als das da drüben. 2 Ja, aber dieser hier ist noch schöner als der um die Ecke. 3 Ja, aber das hier ist noch interessanter als das da drüben. 4 Ja, aber das hier ist noch kleiner als das im zweiten Stock. 5 Ja, aber die hier ist noch größer als die in Düsseldorf. 6 Ja, aber die hier ist noch moderner als die in der Hauptstraße.

6.3B 1 Welches Hotel ist teurer? Dieses hier? 2 Welcher Garten ist schöner? Dieser hier? 3 Welches Geschäft ist interessanter? Dieses hier? 4 Welches Zimmer ist kleiner? Dieses hier? 5 Welche Fußgängerzone ist größer? Diese hier? 6 Welche Wohnung ist moderner? Diese hier?

6.4 1 Mir gefällt sie. 2 Mir gefallen sie nicht. 3 Mir gefällt er. 4 Mir gefällt es. 5 Mir gefällt sie nicht. 6 Mir gefallen sie nicht. 7 Mir gefällt es. 8 Mir gefällt er nicht.

6.5 1 (*c*). 2 (*b*). 3 (*a*) 4 (*f*). 5 (*e*). 6 (*d*).

KONVERSATION (RICHTIG ODER FALSCH?)

1 R. 2 Die Taxifahrerin kennt das Hotel. 3 R. 4 R. 5 Am Kurfürstendamm findet man die ganzen Geschäfte, Kinos, Cafés, Restaurants und Nachtklubs. 6 Otto Lamm kennt Berlin noch gar nicht. 7 R. 8 Otto Lamm kommt aus Buxtehude (i.e. from the back of the beyond!).

LESETEXT

1 16. 2 It is the state parliament. 3 Because they are city states. 4 It is the largest state in the Federal Republic. 5 That of the Netherlands and Belgium together. 6 The population of Bavaria and the population of Munich. 7 It has the largest population of all the states. 8 In the Ruhr. 9 Bonn.

Lektion 7

RICHTIG ODER FALSCH?

1 Der Kellner empfiehlt ihnen die Forelle und den Rehbraten. 2 R. 3 R. 4 Robert ißt auch eine Vorspeise. (Er bekommt eine kalte Schinkenplatte.) 5 Als Hauptgericht nimmt Robert die bayerische Schweinshaxe mit

Kartoffelknödel und Salat. 6 R. 7 R. 8 R. 9 R. 10 R.

WELCHE ANTWORT PAẞT?

1 (*b*). 2 (*a*). 3 (*c*). 4 (*a*). 5 (*b*).

ÜBUNGEN

7.1 1 (*a*). 2 (*c*). 3 (*a*). 4 (*c*). 5 (*c*). 6 (*b*).

7.2 1 (*c*). 2 (*e*). 3 (*d*). 4 (*a*). 5 (*b*).

7.3 1 Mir geht's nicht so gut. 2 Ihr geht's gut. 3 Ihr geht's nicht so gut. 4 Ihm geht's gut. 5 Ihnen geht's gut. 6 Uns geht's nicht so gut.

7.4 1 Bringen Sie uns eine Flasche Moselwein. 2 Geh mit mir ins Kino. 3 Fahr doch schneller. 4 Nimm hier Platz. 5 Fangen Sie sofort an. 6 Stehen Sie um halb sieben auf.

7.5 1 In Düsseldorf habe ich sehr viel zu tun. 2 Deshalb muß ich um 6 Uhr aufstehen. 3 Um halb 7 kommt mein Freund Holger und holt mich ab. 4 Von Frankfurt nach Düsseldorf fährt man ungefähr 2 Stunden. 5 Hoffentlich sind wir dann gegen halb 9 schon in Düsseldorf. 6 Am Abend wollen wir noch ins Theater gehen. 7 Nachher müssen wir natürlich wieder 2 Stunden auf der Autobahn fahren. 8 Wahrscheinlich sind wir erst gegen 1 Uhr morgens wieder zu Hause.

KONVERSATION (RICHTIG ODER FALSCH?)

1 Als Vorspeise bestellt Sonja eine Gemüsesuppe. 2 R. 3 Sie möchte statt dessen einen gemischten Salat. 4 Zum Trinken bestellt sie einen Apfelsaft. 5 R. 6 Zum Nachtisch bestellt Sonja einen gemischten Eisbecher ohne Sahne. 7 R. 8 Den Kaffee möchte sie erst nachher (erst nach dem Eisbecher) haben.

LESETEXT

1 Potatoes: diced; apples: in quarters. 2 $\frac{1}{2}$ litre; salt and sugar. 3 Till they are soft; on a low heat. 4 They are diced and fried.

Lektion 8

RICHTIG ODER FALSCH?

1 R. 2 Andrea gibt ihnen den Stadtplan und die Informationsblätter. 3 Jörg und sein Freund haben acht Tage (eine Woche) Urlaub. 4 R. 5 R. 6 R. 7 Sie kennen sich in München nicht aus. 8 R. 9 R. 10 Andrea wünscht ihnen viel Vergnügen.

WELCHE ANTWORT PAẞT?

1 (*b*). 2 (*c*). 3 (*a*). 4 (*c*). 5 (*b*).

ÜBUNGEN

8.1 1 Hätten Sie vielleicht ein Zimmer frei? 2 Möchtest du vielleicht heute nachmittag mit mir Tennis spielen? 3 Möchten Sie vielleicht morgen mit uns zum Olympischen Dorf hinausfahren? 4 Hättest du vielleicht Zeit, mit uns spazierenzugehen? 5 Möchtest du vielleicht mit uns eine Flasche Wein trinken? 6 Hätten Sie vielleicht einen Tisch für vier Personen?

8.2A 1 (*h*). 2 (*f*). 3 (*a*). 4 (*e*). 5 (*b*). 6 (*g*). 7 (*d*). 8 (*c*).

8.2B 1 In der Fußgängerzone. 2 Auf der Bank. 3 Im Restaurant. 4 In der Discothek. 5 Auf der Liegewiese. 6 Im Park.

8.3 1 Ich empfehle allen Touristen, den Dom zu besichtigen. 2 Der Arzt rät meiner Frau, in Urlaub zu fahren. 3 Klaus schlägt vor, heute abend italienisch zu essen. 4 Mein Freund Peter rät mir, mal nach Berlin zu fahren. 5 Der Empfangsherr empfiehlt der Dame, Zimmer 21 zu nehmen. 6 Hans rät den Engländern, in diesem See nicht schwimmen zu gehen.

8.4 1 Ich weiß nicht, wann sie ins Kino gehen. 2 ..., wie lange der Film dauert. 3 ..., was sie nach dem Film machen. 4 ..., wohin sie nachher gehen. 5 ..., wann sie nach Hause fahren. 6 ..., wo sie zur Zeit wohnen.
8.5 1 (*d*). 2 (*g*). 3 (*e*). 4 (*j*). 5 (*b*). 6 (*c*). 7 (*i*). 8 (*a*). 9 (*f*). 10 (*h*).
8.6 1 Hinter dem Markt und links von der Paulskirche. 2 Vor der Stadtbibliothek und links von dem Karlsbrunnen. 3 Hinter dem Parkplatz und rechts von der Paulskirche. 4 Zwischen dem Markt und dem Parkplatz und vor der Paulskirche. 5 Zwischen den Toiletten und dem Polizeiwagen und vor dem Karlsbrunnen. 6 Links von der Wurstbude und vor dem Markt. 7 Rechts von der Wurstbude und vor dem Parkplatz. 8 Vor der Wurstbude.

KONVERSATION (RICHTIG ODER FALSCH?)
1 R. 2 Sie wollen zu Fuß dorthin gehen. 3 R. 4 Links vom Odeonsplatz ist die Brienner Straße. 5 Vom Odeonsplatz bis zum Karolinenplatz sind es vielleicht 500 Meter. 6 R. 7 Die Alte Pinakothek steht auf der linken Seite. 8 R. 9 Wenn das Museum zuhat, gehen Jörg und Bodo einfach durch die Gegend weiterspazieren. 10 R.

LESETEXT
1 Between two bridges over the Rhine and flanked by the 'Hofgarten' (Court garden). 2 Pubs, discos, old breweries and boutiques. 3 To the south, behind the Karlsplatz (Karl's Square). 4 A mixture of old dwelling houses, new institutes of arts, antique shops and galleries. There are also a few restaurants and bars here. 5 A square kilometre. 6 The approximate number of eating places (of all kinds) in the old city. 7 Because they are full and the seats nearly always all taken. 8 Sit outside. 9 Eat one's fill; Eat very well. 10 Narrow (lanes). 11 Everyone (lit. everything) is tolerant here. 12 As an example of the quiet oases that are to be found here and there.

Lektion 9

RICHTIG ODER FALSCH?
1 R. 2 Es hat sich aber niemand gemeldet. 3 R. 4 Die Fahrt von Freiburg nach Straßburg hat ungefähr eine Stunde gedauert. 5 R. 6 Dann hat er den Dom besichtigt. 7 R. 8 Er hat am Nachmittag stundenlang mit ihnen Karten gespielt. 9 Er hat mit ihnen Französisch geredet. 10 R. 11 R. 12 Hélène hat dort bei einer Reisegesellschaft gearbeitet.

WELCHE ANTWORT PAßT?
1 (*b*). 2 (*c*). 3 (*b*). 4 (*a*). 5 (*b*).

ÜBUNGEN
9.1 1 (*i*). 2 (*j*). 3 (*a*). 4 (*c*). 5 (*g*). 6 (*b*). 7 (*d*). 8 (*e*). 9 (*k*). 10 (*h*). 11 (*l*). 12 (*f*).
9.2 1 (*b*). 2 (*c*). 3 (*a*). 4 (*b*). 5 (*a*). 6 (*c*).
9.3 4-1-9-10-7-2-6-3-8-5
9.4 1 Haben Sie denn letztes Jahr Ihrem Vater eine Flasche Cognac zum Geburtstag geschenkt? 2 Haben Sie denn letztes Jahr in den Sommerferien in Frankreich gearbeitet? 3 Sind Sie denn letzte Woche am Sonntag den ganzen Tag im Bett geblieben? 4 Haben Sie sich denn letzte Woche am Freitag Abend in der »Eisdiele« einen Eisbecher bestellt? 5 Haben Sie denn letztes Jahr im Urlaub in Italien versucht, Italienisch zu lernen? 6 Haben Sie denn

letztes Jahr an Ihrem Geburtstag mit Heike Fischer getanzt?

9.5 1 Um 2 Uhr habe ich meine Tochter in Neuß besucht. 2 Ich habe vor ihrer Wohnung geparkt. 3 Ich habe mich sehr gefreut, meine Tochter zu sehen. 4 Ich habe mich in die Küche gesetzt, und habe es mir bequem gemacht. 5 Meine Tochter hat noch eine Stunde in der Küche gearbeitet. 6 Wir haben über dies und das geredet. 7 Um 3 Uhr hat sie sich gesetzt, und hat sich eine halbe Stunde ausgeruht. 8 Um halb 4 hat sie meine Enkelin vom Kindergarten abgeholt. 9 Ich habe dann mit meiner Enkelin gespielt. 10 Um 4 Uhr hat meine Tochter Kaffee gekocht.

KONVERSATION

1 4 years. 2 She studied in Stuttgart and looked for work in the Stuttgart area after her studies. 3 In the sales department at Pfauters'. 4 Pfauters have a branch in Chicago. 5 Improve her knowledge of English. 6 Because she wants to improve her Spanish and Pfauters do not have a branch in Spain. 7 Because they have their HQ in Madrid. 8 Dagmar would have to work at least a year in Ludwigsburg with the firm first.

LESETEXT (RICHTIG ODER FALSCH?)

1 Paul Rosenbaum hat am 30. Oktober Geburtstag. 2 Er ist verheiratet und hat einen Sohn und eine Tochter. 3 R. 4 Von 1969 bis 1975 hat er ein Wirtschaftsgymnasium in Düsseldorf besucht. 5 R. 6 R. 7 Er hat Betriebswirtschaftslehre an der Ruhr-Universität Bochum studiert. 8 R. 9 R. 10 Seit 1985 ist er Personalleiter der Firma *Rosenbaum Werkzeugmaschinen.*

Lektion 10

RICHTIG ODER FALSCH?

1 R. 2 Thomas und Christel haben drei Wochen Urlaub genommen. 3 Sie sind mit dem Wagen nach England gefahren. 4 R. 5 Es war (schon) ziemlich spät, als Christel und Thomas in Dover angekommen sind. 6 R. 7 R. 8 Sie haben in Canterbury am ersten Tag schlechtes Wetter gehabt. 9 R. 10 Sie sind dort dreimal ins Theater gegangen.

WELCHE ANTWORT PAßT?

1 (*c*). 2 (*b*). 3 (*a*). 4 (*b*). 5 (*a*).

ÜBUNGEN

10.1 1 Wann steht ihr morgen auf? 2 Wann fahrt ihr los? 3 Wer bringt euch zum Bahnhof? 4 Wann habt ihr eu(e)re Fahrkarten gelöst? 5 Wie lange dauert die Fahrt Düsseldorf Wien? 6 Wann kommt ihr in Wien an? Wer holt euch vom Bahnhof ab? 8 Wie lange wollt ihr in Wien bleiben?

10.2 1 (*c*). 2 (*a*). 3 (*b*). 4 (*a*). 5 (*c*). 6 (*b*).

10.3 3-1-10-4-8-6-5-2-9-7 or 3-1-10-4-8-6-2-5-9-7.

10.4 1 Frau Stein habe ich schon angerufen. 2 Die Flugscheine habe ich noch nicht vom Reisebüro abgeholt. 3 Das Hotelzimmer (Die Hotelzimmer) habe ich schon reserviert. 4 Ein Taxi habe ich noch nicht bestellt. 5 Sonnenöl habe ich schon gekauft. 6 Mietze habe ich noch nicht zu Frau Böhm gebracht.

10.5 1 Von 1928 bis 1937 hat er das Kaiser-Wilhelm-Gymnasium in Köln besucht. 2 1937 hat er das Abitur gemacht. 3 (Auch im Jahre) 1937 hat er in Bonn die Buchhandelslehre begonnen. 4 1939 hat er an der Universität Köln Germanistik studiert. 5 Von 1939 bis 1945 ist er

Soldat im Zweiten Weltkrieg gewesen/... war er Soldat im Zweiten Weltkrieg. 6 1942 hat er Annemarie Zech geheiratet. 7 Von 1946 bis 1949 hat er Kurzgeschichten in Zeitungen und Zeitschriften veröffentlicht. 8 1949 ist sein erstes Buch (*Der Zug war pünktlich*) erschienen. 9 Von 1949 bis 1985 hat er viele literarische Werke geschrieben. 10 1972 hat er den Nobelpreis für Literatur erhalten. 11 1985 is er am 16. Juli in Hürtgenwald/Eifel gestorben.

KONVERSATION (RICHTIG ODER FALSCH?)
1 R. 2 Horst war 1945 erst 4 Jahre alt. 3 R. 4 R. 5 Horst hat nach dem Krieg zusammen mit seiner Schwester in den Ruinen gespielt. 6 In der Zwei-Zimmer-Wohnung haben Horst und Gerda im Schlafzimmer geschlafen. 7 R. 8 R.

LESETEXT
1 They arrived punctually yesterday evening. Trudi and Hans picked them up by car from the airport. 2 At 11 o'clock they went for a walk on the Kurfürstendamm. Night life in Berlin doesn't start until about 11. 3 The Reichstag building and the Brandenburg Gate. 4 They are making a coach tour round Berlin. 5 A few old postcards of Berlin. 6 No. He looked for some, but didn't find any. 7 20s' and 30s' china. The prices were too high for them. 8 In a little Turkish restaurant in Charlottenburg. They were probably the only Germans there. 9 They wanted to have a rest.

Lektion 11

RICHTIG ODER FALSCH?
1 Stefans Eltern haben angerufen, daß sie morgen um 14 Uhr 23 am Hauptbahnhof eintreffen. 2 R. 3 R. 4 R. 5 Er geht mit Peter im neuen Sportzentrum schwimmen. 6 R. 7 R. 8 Reinhard kennt Stefans Eltern noch gar nicht. 9 Stefans Mutter ist klein und ziemlich dick. 10 Stefans Vater hat ein schmales Gesicht und braune Augen. 11 Er trägt meistens einen Hut, weil er fast keine Haare mehr hat. 12 R.

WELCHE ANTWORT PAẞT?
1 (*b*). 2 (*c*). 3 (*c*). 4 (*a*). 5 (*b*).

ÜBUNGEN
11.1A 1 Sein Gesicht ist rot. 2 Seine Augen sind braun. 3 Seine Haare sind sehr kurz. 4 Seine Ohren sind groß. 5 Sein Mund ist klein.
11.1B 1 Ihr Gesicht ist schmal. 2 Ihre Augen sind grün. 3 Ihre Haare sind lang und braun. 4 Ihre Nase ist klein. 5 Ihr Mund ist ziemlich groß.
11.2 A Beate: 1 Am Arbeitsplatz trägt Beate eine dunkelgrüne Jacke, einen braunen Rock, eine hellgrüne Bluse und braune Lederschuhe. 2 Zu Hause trägt sie eine grüne Hose, eine gelbe Bluse, einen gelben Pullover und grüne Sportschuhe.
11.2 B Frank: 1 Am Arbeitsplatz trägt Frank eine graue Jacke, eine schwarze Hose, eine dunkelblaue Krawatte und graue Lederschuhe. 2 Zu Hause trägt er eine schwarze Hose, ein graues Hemd, einen grauen Pullover und schwarze Lederschuhe.
11.2 C Peter: 1 Am Arbeitsplatz trägt Peter einen blauen Anzug, ein hellblaues Hemd, eine schwarze Krawatte und schwarze Lederschuhe. 2 Zu Hause trägt er eine braune Hose, ein gelbes Hemd, einen grünen Pullover und keine Schuhe.
11.3 1 (*d*). 2 (*f*). 3 (*a*). 4 (*c*). 5 (*h*). 6 (*b*). 7 (*e*). 8 (*g*).

11.4 1 (*b*). 2 (*e*). 3 (*f*). 4 (*j*). 5 (*i*). 6 (*h*). 7 (*c*). 8 (*d*). 9 (*g*). 10 (*a*).
11.5 1 Nein, morgen wird er den ganzen Tag arbeiten. 2 Wirst du mit der Bahn kommen? 3 Nein, morgen werde ich doch meinen neuen Wagen bekommen! 4 Ach ja! Du wirst also mit dem Wagen fahren. 5 Natürlich! Hoffentlich wird es nicht zu viel Verkehr auf den Straßen geben. 6 Glaubst du, du wirst meine Wohnung finden? 7 Oh ja! Wenn nicht, dann werde ich dich anrufen. 8 Gut. Ich werde dich dann gegen 10 erwarten.

KONVERSATION (RICHTIG ODER FALSCH?)
1 R. 2 R. 3 Herr Herzog möchte Fräulein Bauer morgen besuchen. 4 R. 5 Es kann mit dem Flughafenbus oft sehr lange dauern, bis man in die Stadtmitte kommt. 6 R. 7 R. 8 Er liest »Die Frankfurter Rundschau«. 9 R. 10 Fräulein Brauer wird morgen ein graues Kostüm und eine graue Brille tragen.

LESETEXT
1 Car of the year. 2 56 journalists from 17 European countries. 3 The 'Car Oscar'. 4 They looked very carefully (lit. closely, precisely) at all the candidates. 5 Modern technology. Modern, aerodynamic styling. 6 People (lit. the person, human being). 7 Your personal car of the year. 8 You and everyone that travels with you.

Lektion 12

RICHTIG ODER FALSCH?
1 Dr Walz ist Gymnasiallehrer von Beruf. 2 R. 3 R. 4 Seine Frau und er haben mehrere Jahre lang gespart, bis . . . 5 Als Junge hatte Herr Jahn nur einen ganz primitiven Fotoapparat. 6 R. 7 R. 8 R. 9 R. 10 Heutzutage gibt es so viele arbeitslose Lehrer.

WELCHE ANTWORT PAßT?
1 (*c*). 2 (*b*). 3 (*a*). 4 (*b*). 5 (*a*).

ÜBUNGEN
12.1 1 Und wo warst du denn? 2 Ich war mit meiner Freundin in Österreich. 3 Hattet ihr schönes Wetter? 4 Ja, wir hatten Glück. 5 Wart ihr in Wien? 6 Nein, wir waren in Salzburg und Innsbruck. 7 Wart ihr in Salzburg im Mozarthaus? 8 Nein, wir hatten leider keine Zeit dazu.
12.2 1 mußte. 2 konnte. 3 wollte. 4 durfte. 5 sollte. 6 sollten. 7 wollte. 8 konnte. 9 durfte. 10 mußte.
12.3A 1 Weil wir uns ein eigenes Geschäft kaufen wollten, mußten wir mehrere Jahre lang sparen. 2 Weil ich mich immer fürs Fotografieren interessiert habe, habe ich mir ein Fotogeschäft gekauft. 3 Weil ich mit meinem neuen Beruf zufrieden bin, bin ich jetzt nur selten krank. 4 Weil meine Frau und zwei Söhne im Geschäft mitarbeiten, kann ich ein paar Stunden für mich allein haben. 5 Weil wir abends noch Kundenbesuche machen müssen, können wir nur selten zusammen ausgehen. 6 Weil mein dritter Sohn sich nicht für unser Geschäft interessiert, hat er sich einen anderen Beruf ausgesucht. 7 Weil wir fünf Personen in der Familie sind, brauchen wir einen ziemlich großen Wagen. 8 Weil wir hier sehr viele Freunde und Bekannte haben, wohnen wir so gerne in Weissach.
12.3B 1 Wir mußten mehrere Jahre lang sparen, denn wir wollten uns ein eigenes Geschäft kaufen. 2 Ich habe mir ein Fotogeschäft gekauft, denn ich habe mich immer fürs Fotografieren interessiert. 3 Ich bin jetzt nur

selten krank, denn ich bin mit meinem neuen Beruf zufrieden. 4 Ich kann ein paar Stunden für mich allein haben, denn meine Frau und zwei Söhne arbeiten im Geschäft mit. 5 Wir können nur selten zusammen ausgehen, denn wir müssen abends noch Kundenbesuche machen. 6 Mein dritter Sohn hat sich einen anderen Beruf ausgesucht, denn er interessiert sich nicht für unser Geschäft. 7 Wir brauchen einen ziemlich großen Wagen, denn wir sind fünf Personen in der Familie. 8 Wir wohnen so gerne in Weissach, denn wir haben so viele Freunde und Bekannte hier.

12.4 1 Obwohl ich nur wenig Geld verdiene, habe ich viel Geld für Bier ausgegeben. 2 Obwohl es sehr spät war, bin ich noch auf eine Party gegangen. 3 Obwohl ich am nächsten Tag arbeiten mußte, bin ich erst um 4 Uhr nach Hause gegangen. 4 Obwohl ich gar kein Geld mehr hatte, bin ich mit einem Taxi nach Hause gefahren. 5 Obwohl meine Eltern natürlich schon geschlafen haben, mußte ich sie leider wecken. 6 Obwohl sie sehr böse auf mich waren, haben sie das Taxi bezahlt. 7 Obwohl ich normalerweise um 7 Uhr aufstehe, hat mich mein Vater heute schon um halb 7 geweckt. 8 Obwohl ich nur zwei Stunden geschlafen hatte, mußte ich aufstehen und zur Arbeit gehen.

12.5 1 oder. 2 daß. 3 Wenn. 4 damit. 5 aber. 6 Obwohl. 7 Bis. 8 Als.

KONVERSATION (RICHTIG ODER FALSCH?)

1 R. 2 Lothar arbeitet bei der Deutschen Bank. 3 R. 4 Lothar wollte nach dem Abitur Anglistik studieren. 5 R. 6 Für Akademiker ist es (heutzutage) sehr schwer, eine Stellung zu finden. 7 R. 8 R.

LESETEXT

1 The first years at work. 2 Studying or training is now beginning to pay off. Plans can now be made and the future can be planned. 3 The financial adviser (from the **Sparkasse** savings bank). 4 Firstly, the amounts saved grow into a considerable sum which can be included in one's plans for later. Secondly, risk insurance sees to it that the whole family is safeguarded. 5 An entirely firm (solid) basis for one's future.

Lektion 13

RICHTIG ODER FALSCH?

1 R. 2 R. 3 Viele Wohnungen waren in Berlin zerstört. 4 R. 5 R. 6 Zuerst mußte Maria zu Fuß in die Schule gehen. Erst später konnte sie mit der S-Bahn fahren. 7 Marias Vater war 5 Jahre lang in russischer Gefangenschaft. 8 Als er aus der Gefangenschaft zurückkehrte, hat Maria ihren Vater nicht mehr erkannt. (. . . , erkannte Maria ihren Vater nicht mehr.) 9 R. 10 R.

WELCHE ANTWORT PAẞT?

1 (*b*). 2 (*a*). 3 (*c*). 4 (*b*). 5 (*b*).

ÜBUNGEN

13.1 1 (*c*). 2 (*a*). 3 (*b*). 4 (*b*). 5 (*a*). 6 (*c*). 7 (*b*). 8 (*a*).

13.2 Er hat noch geschlafen. Ich habe meinen Bademantel angezogen, bin in die Küche gegangen und habe Kaffee gekocht. Ich habe zum Fenster hinausgeschaut. Im Park haben schon Kinder gespielt. Ich habe mich ins Wohnzimmer gesetzt, habe das Radio angemacht und eine Tasse Kaffe getrunken. »Wird er mir glauben?«, habe ich gedacht und bin ins Schlafzimmer gelaufen, wo ich Peter aus einem tiefen Schlaf geweckt habe.

13.3 1 (*g*). 2 (*c*). 3 (*e*). 4 (*h*). 5 (*a*). 6 (*i*). 7 (*f*). 8 (*b*). 9 (*d*). 10 (*j*).

13.4 6-4-1-3-8-7-2-5.

13.5 1 Von 1928 bis 1937 besuchte er das Kaiser-Wilhelm-Gymnasium in Köln. 2 1937 machte er das Abitur. 3 1937 begann er in Bonn die Buchhandelslehre. 4 1939 studierte er an der Universität Köln Germanistik. 5 Von 1939 bis 1945 war er Soldat im Zweiten Weltkrieg. 6 1942 heiratete er Annemarie Zech. 7 Von 1946 bis 1949 veröffentlichte er Kurzgeschichten in Zeitungen und Zeitschriften. 8 1949 erschien sein erstes Buch (*Der Zug war pünktlich*). 9 Von 1949 bis 1985 schrieb er viele literarische Werke. 10 1972 erhielt er den Nobelpreis für Literatur. 11 1985 starb er am 16. Juli in Hürtgenwald/Eifel.

KONVERSATION (RICHTIG ODER FALSCH?)

1 Lutz Bönzli ist Forschungsassistent an der Freien Universität Berlin. 2 R. 3 R. 4 R. 5 Sie waren damals 6 Leute in einem Zimmer. 6 R. 7 Ihr Mann ist bei Stalingrad gefallen. 8 Ihre Kinder haben ihren Vater eigentlich nie gekannt.

LESETEXT

1 One of the best known German artists. 2 Because he turned away from the traditional concepts of sculpture (plastic art). 3 Because they were made of fat, hide, felt, honey and wax. 4 They still want to know, 'Is that supposed to be art?' 5 He felt that every person is an artist in a certain sense. 6 They put on a big exhibition of his works.

Lektion 14

RICHTIG ODER FALSCH?

1 Marta Friedl fährt nur bis Heilbronn. 2 R. 3 R. 4 Sie hat noch Verwandte in Deutschland. 5 R. 6 Stefan hat Mathematik studiert./Stefan ist fertig mit dem Studium. 7 R. 8 R. 9 Stefan hat immer jede Gelegenheit wahrgenommen, Englisch zu sprechen. 10 R.

WELCHE ANTWORT PAßT?

1 (*a*). 2 (*c*). 3 (*b*). 4 (*b*). 5 (*c*).

ÜBUNGEN

14.1 1 (*a*). 2 (*b*). 3 (*c*). 4 (*a*). 5 (*a*). 6 (*b*).

14.2 1 (*a*). 2 (*b*). 3 (*c*). 4 (*a*). 5 (*b*). 6 (*a*).

14.3 1 Wegen der frischen Luft im Wald ... 2 Trotz des herrlichen Wetters ... 3 Wegen des langen Spaziergangs ... 4 Trotz der wenigen Wanderer im Wald ... 5 Trotz der hohen Preise im Wald-Café ... 6 Wegen des langen Wegs zum Auto zurück ... 7 Wegen der vielen Pausen auf dem Rückweg ... 8 Wegen des ziemlich schwachen Verkehrs ...

14.4 1 müßte. 2 könnte. 3 hätte. 4 könnte. 5 würde. 6 würde/könnte. 7 wäre. 8 würde/könnte. 9 wäre. 10 würde/(könnte).

14.5 1 Wenn ich nicht so viel zu tun hätte, würde ich fürs Wochenende wegfahren. 2 Wenn Klaus nicht arbeitslos wäre, könnte er sich die Reise nach Amerika leisten/würde er sich die Reise nach Amerika leisten können. 3 Wenn für Sabine die Fahrt ins Büro nicht so kurz wäre, könnte sie nicht länger als ihre Kolleginnen schlafen/würde sie nicht länger als ihre Kolleginnen schlafen können. 4 Wenn wir in München Freunde oder Verwandte hätten, müßten wir nicht im Hotel übernachten/würden wir nicht im Hotel übernachten müssen. 5 Wenn Dieter Probleme hätte, wäre er nicht so freundlich. 6 Wenn Jan und Paula nicht starke Raucher wären, würde ich sie zum Abendbrot einladen. 7 Wenn Manfred ein Auto hätte, würde er nicht mit dem Zug zur Arbeit fahren. 8 Wenn Thea nicht krank wäre, müßte ich nicht die Kinder von der Schule abholen/würde ich nicht die Kinder von der Schule abholen müssen.

KONVERSATION (RICHTIG ODER FALSCH?)

1 Herr Göller möchte mit Herrn Kaiser sprechen. 2 R. 3 R. 4 R. 5 Herr Göller ist von der Verkehrspolizei. 6 Er kann (doch) ein paar Minuten auf Herrn Kaiser warten. 7 R. 8 R.

LESETEXTE

A 1 Hospitals could be closed until 8.00 a.m. 2 Night service chemists. 3 Emergency doctor-taxi drivers. 4 Turn over snugly onto his/her other side. 5 The health of all of us. 6 More than a thousand. 7 To help people. 8 Prescribing health.

B 1 As the European relative of the Intercity. 2 United States of Europe. 3 They run from more than 60 stations, they make only few stops en route. They take passengers directly into the centre of the main European metropolises. 4 They greet you on the platform, help you aboard with your luggage, accompany you to your seat and see to it that you are really comfortable. 5 They mostly speak several languages. 6 International cooks; in the EuroCity restaurant car. 7 Carefree, comfortable and safe travel. 8 A good journey; in the name of the railways of Europe.

Lektion 15

RICHTIG ODER FALSCH?

1 Anita Juarez ist in Deutschland geboren. 2 Sie hat einen spanischen Vater und eine deutsche Mutter. 3 R. 4 R. 5 R. 6 R. 7 R. 8 R. 9 Anita fährt mit dem Auto nach England. 10 In London wird sie bei einer Tante (bei ihrer Tante) wohnen.

WELCHE ANTWORT PAẞT?

1 (*c*). 2 (*b*). 3 (*b*). 4 (*a*). 5 (*c*).

ÜBUNGEN

15.1 1 (*b*). 2 (*a*). 3 (*b*). 4 (*c*). 5 (*a*). 6 (*c*).

15.2 1 (*f*). 2 (*e*). 3 (*h*). 4 (*a*). 5 (*g*). 6 (*c*). 7 (*b*). 8 (*d*).

15.3 1 Ich möchte mich danach erkundigen, ob ich in den Vereinigten Staaten Euroschecks ausstellen kann. 2 Ich muß unbedingt wissen, ob die Banken auch sonnabends aufhaben. 3 Könnten Sie mir sagen, ob ich mit meiner Kreditkarte zahlen kann? 4 Sie sollten ja wissen, wie der Wechselkurs des Dollars steht. 5 Sie können mir wohl sagen, was der Flug München-New York kostet. 6 Ich hätte auch noch gerne gewußt, wie lange der Flug dauert. 7 Ich verstehe immer noch nicht, ob ich ein Visum brauche. 8 Wissen Sie denn nicht, wer ich bin?!

15.4 1 Das Auto meines Freundes ... 2 ... das neue Auto seiner arroganten Schwester. 3 ... die Form alter Autos ... 4 ... das Haus meiner Eltern. 5 ... die Lage dieses Hauses ... 6 ... in der Nähe eines schönen Waldes. 7 ... ein Geschenk meines Großvaters ... 8 ... das neue Auto der Schwester meines neuen Freundes!

15.5 1 darauf. 2 davon. 3 dafür. 4 dazu. 5 dazu. 6 davon.

15.6 1 ..., ohne jedesmal neue

Kleidung zu kaufen. 2 . . . , anstatt ins Kino zu gehen. 3 . . . , um länger arbeiten zu können. 4 . . . , anstatt jeden Abend in die Kneipe zu gehen. 5 . . . , um schlank werden zu können. 6 . . . , um viel Geld sparen zu können. 7 . . . , ohne jedesmal das teuerste Gericht zu bestellen. 8 . . . , anstatt so viel Unsinn zu reden!

KONVERSATION (RICHTIG ODER FALSCH?)
1 R. 2 R. 3 R. 4 Er fährt mit seiner Freundin nach China. 5 . . . eine Einreisegenehmigung und ein Visum. 6 R. 7 Man kann auch Individualreisen nach China unternehmen. 8 R.

LESETEXT
A In Germany and in more than 160 countries world-wide. 2 Airlines, travel agencies, car rental firms, hotels, restaurants, shops. 3 Cash dispenser facility. 4 The annual subscription. 5 It is associated with MasterCard and Access. 6 Where you get your eurocheque card. 7 At the credit institution where you have your account. 8 German banks and savings banks.

Lektion 16

RICHTIG ODER FALSCH?
1 Herr Berg bekommt seit zwei oder drei Jahren ziemlich oft starke Kopfschmerzen. 2 R. 3 Die Kopfschmerzen dauern meistens ungefähr zwölf Stunden. 4 R. 5 R. 6 Seine Symptome sind (ganz) typisch für Menschen, die an Migräne leiden. 7 R. 8 R. 9 Herr Berg muß die Tabletten, die ihm Dr Klein verschreibt, dann einnehmen, sobald er Kopfschmerzen bekommt. 10 R.

WELCHE ANTWORT PAßT?
1 (*a*). 2 (*c*). 3 (*b*). 4 (*a*). 5 (*b*).

ÜBUNGEN
16.1 1 (*a*).2 (*b*). 3 (*c*). 4 (*a*). 5 (*b*). 6 (*b*). 7 (*a*). 8 (*b*).
16.2 1 Ihre Knie tun weh. 2 Seine rechte Schulter tut weh. 3 Ihr linker Fuß tut weh. 4 Seine Hände tun weh. 5 Ihre Ohren tun weh. 6 Seine Nase tut weh. 7 Sein Rücken tut weh. 8 Mein Magen tut weh.
16.3 1 (*d*). 2 (*c*). 3 (*a*). 4 (*h*). 5 (*b*). 6 (*g*). 7 (*e*). 8 (*f*).
16.4 1 das. 2 in dem. 3 dessen. 4 in der. 5 die. 6 deren. 7 den. 8 in dem. 9 der. 10 in denen.
16.5 1 Die Stadt Lauenburg, die im Bundesland Schleswig-Holstein liegt, hat ungefähr 11 000 Einwohner. 2 Ich wohne in der Elbstraße, die der älteste Teil Lauenburgs ist. 3 In der Elbstraße liegt auch das alte Rathaus, in dem man heute das Elbschiffahrtsmuseum findet. 4 In Lauenburg sieht man auch die alte Brücke, über die man früher Salz von Lüneburg nach Lübeck transportiert hat. 5 Ich arbeite in einem Fotogeschäft, das am Marktplatz liegt. 6 Dorthin kommen viele Touristen, die die Altstadt besichtigen wollen. 7 Wir verkaufen auch Postkarten, die die Besucher in alle Welt schicken. 8 Jeden Tag kommen neue Menschen ins Geschäft, denen ich oft beim Einkaufen eines Fotoapparates helfen kann.
16.6 1 Ich mußte aber lange nach einem Parkplatz suchen. 2 Im Parkhaus konnte ich aber nicht parken, . . . 3 Auf der Straße durfte ich nicht parken, . . . 4 Ich mußte 2 Kilometer außerhalb der Stadtmitte fahren. 5 Da konnte ich endlich einen Parkplatz finden. 6 Dann mußte ich zu Fuß wieder in die Stadtmitte zurückgehen. 7 Nach langem Suchen konnte ich dann das ideale Geschenk finden. 8 Bloß mußte ich dann

wieder 2 Kilometer zum Auto zurückgehen! 9 Das wollte ich eigentlich nicht. 10 Das mußte ich einfach.

KONVERSATION (RICHTIG ODER FALSCH?)
1 Ralf Steuber fühlt sich seit 3 Wochen krank. 2 Dr Glöckner sagt, daß das mehr als eine Erkältung sein muß. 3 R. 4 R. 5 R. 6 Er findet es natürlich schlimm, daß Ralf Raucher ist. 7 R. 8 R.

LESETEXT
1 When the nose is blocked up. 2 As hot as possible. 3 Whilst going to sleep. 4 Open the window, even when it's cold. 5 Formaldehyde, tobacco smoke, fumes from defective gas stoves and household sprays. 6 With a heavy cold. 7 The cold and 'flu viruses. 8 To a greater extent than by having 80 millilitres of alcohol per litre of blood in the bloodstream.

Lektion 17

RICHTIG ODER FALSCH?
1 R. 2 Karin wurde während des Überfalls nicht verletzt. 3 R. 4 R. 5 R. 6 R. 7 Ein Bankkunde hat einen der Täter überwältigt. 8 R. 9 R. 10 R.

WELCHE ANTWORT PAẞT?
1 (*a*). 2 (*c*). 3 (*a*). 4 (*a*). 5 (*b*).

ÜBUNGEN
17.1 1 (*b*). 2 (*a*). 3 (*c*). 4 (*b*). 5 (*a*). 6 (*a*). 7 (*c*). 8 (*b*).
17.2 *c-j-h-e-a-i-g-d-f-b*.
17.3 1 (*c*). 2 (*f*). 3 (*e*). 4 (*a*). 5 (*h*). 6 (*g*). 7 (*d*). 8 (*b*).
17.4 1 Geld muß gewechselt werden. 2 Die Katze muß ins Tierheim gebracht werden. 3 Die Urlaubsversicherung darf nicht vergessen werden. 4 Die Zeitungen müssen abbestellt werden. 5 Die Überfahrt Calais-Dover muß gebucht werden. 6 Die Personalausweise müssen mitgenommen werden. 7 Das englische Wörterbuch darf nicht vergessen werden. 8 Die Hotelzimmer müssen reserviert werden.
17.5 Zuerst werden die Champignons gewaschen und fein geschnitten. Die Zwiebel wird geschält und geschnitten. Die Champignons und die Zwiebel werden dann in der Brühe zum Kochen gebracht. Sie werden zugedeckt und 20 bis 30 Minuten gekocht. Danach werden sie gesiebt oder im Mixer püriert. Das Mehl wird dann in einer zweiten Pfanne zur zerlassenen Butter gegeben und 1 Minute gekocht. Zuerst wird die Milch und dann das Champignonpüree eingerührt. Die Suppe wird dann mit Salz und Pfeffer gewürzt. Sie wird zum Kochen gebracht, gerührt, zugedeckt und 10 bis 15 Minuten gekocht. Zum Schluß wird der Rahm eingerührt und die Suppe wird mit Petersilie bestreut.
17.6 1 Das Brandenburger Tor wurde zwischen 1788 und 1791 von Carl Gotthard Langhans errichtet. 2 Das Schloß Charlottenburg ist 1695 als Sommersitz für die Kurfürstin Sophie Charlotte von J. A. Nering begonnen worden. 3 Das Reichstagsgebäude wurde in den Jahren von 1884 bis 1894 im Stil der Neorenaissance von Paul Wallot erbaut. Nach der Kriegszerstörung ist das Reichstagsgebäude im Originalstil wiedererrichtet worden. 4 Das Hansaviertel ist von 48 international bekannten Architekten nach dem Zweiten Weltkreig errichtet worden. 5 Die Freiheitsglocke im Schöneberger Rathaus wurde vom amerikanischen Volk im Jahre 1950 den Berlinern geschenkt. 6 Zwischen 1824 und 1830 ist das alte Museum von K. F.

Schinkel erbaut worden. 7 Der Dom ist von J. Raschdorff in den Jahren 1894 bis 1905 erbaut worden. Der Dom ist in den 80er Jahren des 20. Jahrhunderts restauriert worden. 8 Das Palais unter den Linden wurde von Ph. Gerlach im Jahre 1732 errichtet. Es ist in den Jahren 1968–9 wiederaufgebaut und erweitert worden.

RADIOSENDUNG (RICHTIG ODER FALSCH?)
1 R. 2 R. 3 R. 4 R. 5 Wegen Bergungsarbeiten ist zwischen Müllheim und Bad Krozingen der rechte Fahrstreifen . . . gesperrt. 6 R. 7 R. 8 R.

LESETEXT
1 The cashier's office of the ***Hertie*** department store in the centre of Freiburg. 2 Five employees. 3 The attacker was overpowered. 4 Looking for work. 5 To be taken to the room in which the cashier's office is located. 6 For the representatives of the individual departments to hand in their day's takings. He took five hostages and stole 40 000 marks. 7 Because the happenings in the cashier's office were at first not noticed either by the other employees or by customers in the store. 8 A colleague in the store. The appeal for help (unnoticed by the attacker) from a secretary in the cashier's office. 9 The criminal police forced an entry into the main cashier's office, overpowered and apprehended the surprised attacker. 10 Financial problems; unemployed and deep in debt.

Lektion 18

RICHTIG ODER FALSCH?
1 R. 2 R. 3 Heike ist letzte Woche zum erstenmal dorthin geflogen. 4 R. 5 Die Landschaft in Sri Lanka ist wunderschön. 6 R. 7 Auch in vielen der reichsten Länder der Welt existieren solche Probleme. 8 R. 9 Zu dieser Jahreszeit wäre es in Gran Canaria genauso warm gewesen wie in Sri Lanka. 10 Heike glaubt kaum, daß sie mehr Spaß gehabt hätte, wenn sie nach Gran Canaria geflogen wäre.

WELCHE ANTWORT PAẞT?
1 (*b*). 2 (*b*). 3 (*a*). 4 (*a*). 5 (*b*).

ÜBUNGEN
18.1 1 Am ältesten ist das Dom-Hotel. 2 Am kleinsten ist das Insel-Hotel. 3 Am modernsten ist das Crest-Hotel. 4 Am größten ist das Crest Hotel. 5 Am billigsten ist das Insel-Hotel. 6 Am bequemsten ist das Crest-Hotel. 7 Am zentralsten liegt das Insel-Hotel. 8 Am weitesten von der Stadtmitte entfernt liegt das Crest-Hotel.
18.2 6-7-2-4-5-1-3-8.
18.3 1 Nachdem ich Kaffee gekocht hatte, habe ich . . . 2 Nachdem ich meine beiden Söhne zur Schule gebracht hatte, habe ich . . . 3 Nachdem ich im Supermarkt eingekauft hatte, habe ich . . . 4 Nachdem ich die Wohnung saubergemacht hatte, habe ich . . . 5 Nachdem ich das Mittagessen zubereitet hatte, habe ich . . . 6 Nachdem ich meine Söhne von der Schule abgeholt hatte, haben wir . . . 7 Nachdem wir zusammen zu Mittag gegessen hatten, haben wir . . . 8 Nachdem wir eine Stunde lang Karten gespielt hatten, sind wir . . .
18.4 1 Wärest du nicht lieber nach Berlin gefahren? 2 Hättest du nicht lieber bei Freunden gewohnt? 3 Wärest du dort nicht lieber ins Theater gegangen? 4 Hättest du nicht lieber die Frauenkirche besichtigt? 5 Hättest du nicht lieber die Alte

Pinakothek besucht? 6 Hättest du im Hofbräuhaus nicht lieber Bier getrunken? 7 Wärest du nicht lieber im Englischen Garten spazierengegangen? 8 Hättest du nicht lieber zwei Wochen Urlaub gehabt?

18.5 1 Das läßt sich leider nicht machen. 2 Seine Fragen lassen sich nur schwer beantworten. 3 Läßt du dich nicht überreden? 4 Dieses Fenster läßt sich nicht öffnen. 5 Dieses Wort läßt sich nicht übersetzen. 6 Wie läßt sich feststellen, wer kommt? 7 Das Problem läßt sich einfach nicht lösen. 8 Wie läßt sich so was behaupten?

18.6 1 Sie hätte sich ans Fenster gesetzt. 2 Sie hätte eine Tasse Kaffee bestellt. 3 Sie hätte die ganze Zeit zum Fenster hinausgeschaut. 4 Du wärest aber einfach nicht gekommen. 5 Sie hätte sich noch einen Kaffee bringen lassen. 6 Dann wäre der Peter reingekommen und hätte sich zu ihr gesetzt. 7 Der hätte sie eingeladen, mit ihm ins Kino zu gehen. 8 Nur aus diesem Grunde wäre sie mit Peter ins Kino gegangen.

KONVERSATION (RICHTIG ODER FALSCH?)

1 R. 2 R. 3 R. 4 R. 5 Touristen dürfen kommen, weil sie dann wieder nach Hause gehen, nachdem sie ihr Geld in Deutschland ausgegeben haben. 6 R. 7 Die meisten Asylanten verlassen das eigene Land, weil sie dort verfolgt werden. 8 R. 9R. 10 R.

LESETEXT

1 To those who are politically persecuted. 2 More and more restrictively. 3 In the initial years of the Federal Republic; on account of the small number of applicants for asylum. 4 Towards the end of the Seventies. 5 The abuse of asylum. 6 From the 'socialist' countries of eastern Europe. 7 African and Asian countries. 8 Distinguishing between purely economic and genuinely political reasons for submitting an application. 9 No right to asylum is granted.

Zusatzmaterialien

NACHRICHTENSENDUNG A

1 The British mail train robbery of 1963. 2 Two masked people raided a van near Frankfurt airport (near Kelsterbach). 3 Gold, platinum and uncut diamonds valued at 3.3 million marks. 4 The owners of the stolen valuables. 5 They stationed a car diagonally across the carriageway. 6 Drive to a wood. 7 The loot was transferred to a car.

NACHRICHTENSENDUNG B

1 Tailbacks and slow-moving traffic. 2 The number of Germans who have set off towards Austria before the start of the holiday. 3 Holidaymakers with their own vehicles had to put up with waits of up to an hour as well. 4 On the Stuttgart-Munich motoway, between Mühlhausen and Merklingen. 5 Heavy rain and poor visibility. 6 118 vehicles in 36 accidents; 19 injured, some seriously. 7 Excessive speed and driving too close (lit. insufficient distance). 8 The estimated damage.

LESETEXT A

1 The 'Summer of the Century' heralded by the weather prophets. 2 A grey cloud haze lay over the whole area. 3 Holiday-makers were able to travel South without any really long tailbacks. 4 Not exactly the weather for hiking in the mountains. Constant showers; long-range visibility reduced practically to zero. 5 The

wicker beach chairs were stowed away because of a gale warning. 6 There were hardly any delays. 7 It was the beginning of the holidays in Berlin. 8 Quiet.

LESETEXT B

1 That women do not enjoy equality in any country in the world. 2 The number of countries in which the circumstances of women were investigated. 3 Health, family circumstances, employment and equality of social status. 4 Sweden, Finland, USA, Norway, Canada and Denmark. 5 It is the country in which women suffer the greatest discrimination. 6 It occupies the 17th place. 7 A great gap between the industrialised countries and the developing countries. 8 A Swedish woman with one or two children has a life expectancy of 81 years. Three out of five Swedish women are gainfully employed and nearly all can read and write.

German—English Vocabulary

Abbreviations: L—Lektion; VS—Verstehen Sie?; ZM—Zusatzmaterialien. *masc.—masculine; fem.—feminine; neut.—neuter; pl.—plural; sep.—separable; wk. noun—weak noun; acc.—accusative; gen.—genitive; dat.—dative; sub. conj.—subordinating conjunction;* **indicates verb uses* sein *to form perfect tense.*

abbauen (*sep.*) *to take down, dismantle* ZM
abbestellen (*sep.*) *to cancel (newspapers etc.)* L17
der Abend (-e) *evening* L2
das Abendbrot (-e) *supper, evening meal* L5
abends *in the evening* L5
aber *but, however* L2, L13
die Abfahrt (-en) *departure* L14
das Abgas (-e) *(exhaust) fumes* L16 VS
sich etwas abgewöhnen (*sep.*) *to give something up* L16 VS
abhängig (von +m *dat.*) *dependent (on)* L15
abholen (*sep.*) *to pick up* L5
abhören (*sep.*) *to sound, listen to* L16 VS
das Abitur *school leaving exam (needed for university entrance)* L9 VS, L12
ablehnen (*sep.*) *to reject* L18 VS
abliefern (*sep.*) *to hand over* L17 VS
abraten (*sep.*) von (+*dat.*) (rät ab, riet ab, abgeraten) *to advise against* L15
abrechnen (*sep.*) *to settle (a bill)* L15
der Abschluß (die Abschlüsse) *conclusion, final examination* L12
abschmecken (*sep.*) *to season, flavour* L7 VS
der Abschnitt (-e) *section* L17 VS
absichern (*sep.*) *to safeguard, protect* L12 VS
der Abstand *distance, space* ZM
abstellen (*sep.*) *to turn off* L14 VS
der Abstellraum (¨e) *store room* L3
die Abteilung (-en) *department* L9
sich abwenden von (*sep.*) (wendet ab, wendete ab, abgewendet *or* wendet ab, wandte ab, abgewandt) *to turn away from* L13 VS
ach so *oh, I see* L1
die Ader (-n) *vein* L13
aerodynamisch *aerodynamic* L11 VS
afrikanisch *African* L18 VS
ägyptisch *Egyptian* L8 VS
die Akademie (-n) *academy, college* L13 VS
der Akademiker (-) *graduate* L12 VS
die Aktionskünstler (-) *action painter* L13 VS
aktiv *active(ly)* L13 VS
aktuell *topical(ly)* L17
das Akzeptanznetz (-e) *network of outlets (lit. network of acceptance)* L15 VS
die Akzeptanzstelle (-n) *outlet (lit. place of acceptance)* L15 VS
alarmieren *to alert, alarm* L17 VS
die Alarmmeldung (-en) *giving the alert* L17 VS
der Alkohol (-e) *alcohol* L16 VS
all- *all* L8 VS
vor allem *above all* L16 VS
die Allee (-n) *avenue* L6
allein(e) *alone* L12
aller- *of all, by far* L18
am allerinteressantesten *most interesting by far* L18
allerdings *certainly* L9 VS
allergisch (gegen +*acc.*) *allergic (to)* L16
alles *everything* L2 VS, L8
allgemein *general* L16

die Alliierten (*masc. plur.*) *the Allies* L5 VS
als (1) *than* L6
als (2) *as* L7
als (3) *when* (*one event in the past; cf* wenn *whenever, if*) L9
also *well, then* L5
alt *old* L2 VS, L3
die Altbauwohnung (-en) *older dwelling, flat* L12
das Altbier *strong dark beer* L8 VS
das Alter (-) *age* L12
die Altstadt *old city* L8 VS
Amerika *America* L1
der Amerikaner (-) *American (male)* L2
die Amerikanerin (-nen) *American (female)* L2
amerikanisch *American* L5
das Amt (¨er) *office* ZM
an (1) (+*acc/dat.*) *on* (*in dates*), *at* L1 VS, L7
an (2) *to* L2 VS
anbieten (*sep.*) (bietet an, bot an, angeboten) *to offer* L14 VS
ander- *other, different* L1 VS, L12
anders (als) *different(ly) (from)* L1
anderthalb *one and a half* L10
der Anfang (¨e) *beginning* L12
anfangen (*sep.*) (fängt an, fing an, angefangen) *to begin, start* L5
die Anfangsjahre (*n. pl.*) *initial years* L18 VS
die Angabe (-n) *detail* ZM
das Angebot *offer, supply* L11 VS, L18
angenehm *pleasant* L14 VS
angesichts (+*gen.*) *in view of* L14
der/die Angestellte (*adj. noun*) *employee, white-collar worker* L12 VS
die Anglistik *English Language & Literature* L12 VS
der Angriff (-e) *attack* L13 VS
die Angst (¨e) *fear* L15
Angst haben (vor +*dat.*) *to be afraid (of)* L15
ankommen* (*sep.*) (kommt an, kam an, angekommen) *to arrive;* L10
es kommt darauf an *it depends (on)* L15
die Ankunft (¨e) *arrival* L11 VS, L14
die Ankunftshalle (-n) *arrivals (hall)* L11 VS
anmachen (*sep.*) *to put on, turn on* L17
die Anmeldepflicht *compulsory registration* L15
annehmen (1) (*sep.*) (nimmt an, nahm an, angenommen) *to assume* L13 VS
annehmen (2) (*sep.*) *to accept* L15 VS
anrufen (*sep.*) (ruft an, rief an, angerufen) *to call up, telephone* L9
sich anschauen (*sep.*) *to have a look at;* Schauen Sie es sich an *Have a look at it* L3
anschließend *following that, next* L9
die Anschlußstelle (-n) *junction* L17 VS
ansehen (*sep.*) (sieht an, sah an, angesehen) *to look at;* L10
Wir möchten es uns ansehen *We'd like to have a look at it*
das Ansehen(-) *esteem, regard* L13 VS
ansehnlich *considerable, impressive* L12 VS
die Ansicht (-en) *view, opinion* L18
Ich bin der Ansicht, daß . . . *I am of the view that . . .* L18
die Anstalt (-en) *institution* L17
anstatt (+*gen.*) *instead of* L14
(an)statt . . . zu . . . *instead of* L15
ansteigen* (*sep.*) (steigt an, stieg an, angestiegen) *to increase, go up* L18
anstellen (*sep.*) *to appoint* L9
anstrengend *strenuous, tiring* L10
die Antiquität (-en) *antique* L8 VS
das Antiquitätengeschäft (-e) *antique shop* L8 VS
der Antrag (¨e) *application* L15 VS
die Antragstellung *submission of an application* L18 VS
die Antwort (-en) *answer* L1
antworten *to answer* L3
die Anzahl (-en) *number* L18
sich anziehen (*sep.*) (zieht an, zog an, angezogen) *to get dressed* L8
der Anzug (¨e) *suit* L11

die AOK (Allgemeine Ortskrankenkasse) *General Local Health Insurance Company* L16
der Apfel(¨) *apple* L7
der Apfelsaft *apple juice* L7
die Apotheke (-n) *chemist's (shop)* L12
der April *April* L1 VS, L13
die Arbeit (-en) *work* L9
arbeiten *to work* L5
der Arbeiter (-) *worker* L18 VS
die Arbeiterklasse *working class* L18 VS
der Arbeitgeber (-) *employer* L18
die Arbeitsgemeinschaft (-en) *association* L17
die Arbeitsgenehmigung (-en) *work permit* L14
arbeitslos *unemployed, jobless* L12
die Arbeitslosigkeit *unemployment* L13
der Arbeitnehmer (-) *employee* L18
der Arbeitsplatz (¨e) (1) *place of work, workplace* L11
der Arbeitsplatz (¨e) (2) *job* L18
arbeitsunfähig *incapable of work, unfit for work* L12 VS
die Architektur *architecture* L11
argumentieren *to argue* L18 VS
der Arm (-e) *arm* L11
die Armut *poverty* L18
arrogant *arrogant* L15
die Art (-en) (1) *kind, sort* L8 VS
die Art (-en) (2) *way, method* L14 VS
der Artikel (-) *article* L14
der Arzt (¨e) *doctor (male)* L2
die Arztin (-nen) *doctor (female)* L2
asiatisch *Asian* L18 VS
der Assistent (*wk. noun*) *assistant* L13 VS
der Ast (¨e) *branch, bough* L13
das Asyl *asylum* L18 VS
der Asylant (en) *asylum-seeker* L18 VS
der Asylbeweber (-) *applicant for asylum* L18 VS
der Asylmißbrauch *abuse of asylum* L18 VS
das Asylrecht *right of asylum* L18 VS
der Asylsuchende (*adj. noun*) *asylum-seeker* L18 VS
atmen *to breathe* L16 VS
die Atmosphäre (-n) *atmosphere* L4 VS
attraktiv *attractive* L15
auch *also, too* L1
auf (+*acc/dat*) *on, at* L2
  Auf Wiedersehen! *Goodbye!* L8 VS
  Auf Wiederhören! *Goodbye! (on the telephone)* L11 VS
der Aufenthalt (-e) *stay, residence* L14
die Aufenthaltserlaubnis (-se) *residence permit* L14
auffallend *striking(ly), conspicuous(ly)* L17
auffinden (*sep.*) (findet auf, fand auf, aufgefunden) *to find, discover* L17
die Aufgabe (-n) *task* L11 VS
aufgeführt *listed* L8
aufgeregt *excited, nervous, worked up* L17
aufhaben (*sep.*) (hat auf, hatte auf, aufgehabt) *to be open (of shops etc.)* L8 VS
aufhalten (*sep.*) (hält auf, hielt auf, aufgehalten) *to delay, hold up, detain* L17
aufhören (*sep.*) *to cease, stop* L5 VS
sich aufmachen (*sep.*) *to set out, start out* ZM
aufmerksam *attentive* L15
aufmerksam machen auf (+*acc.*) *to draw attention to* L15
die Aufnahme (-n) *recording* L17
aufnehmen (*sep.*) (nimmt auf, nahm auf, aufgenommen) (1) *to take in;* L13
aufnehmen (*sep.*) (nimmt auf, nahm auf, aufgenommen) (2) *to record* L17
aufnehmen (*sep.*) (nimmt auf, nahm auf aufgenommen)
aufregend *exciting* L17
der Aufschnitt *slices of cold meat or cheese* L5
aufspringen* (*sep.*) (auf +*acc.*) (springt auf, sprang auf, aufgesprungen) *to jump onto* ZM
aufstehen* (*sep.*) (steht auf, stand auf, aufgestanden) *to get up, stand up* L5

auftauchen* (*sep.*) *to crop up, turn up* L16
aufteilen (*sep.*) *to divide (up)* L5 VS
aufwachen* (*sep.*) *to wake up* L16
der Aufzug (¨e) *lift* L4
das Auge (-n) *eye* L11
der Augenblick (-e) *moment* L13 VS
der Augenzeuge (-n) (*wk. noun*) *eyewitness* L17
der Augenzeugenbericht (-e) *eyewitness report* L17
der August *August* L5 VS, L13
aus (+*dat.*) *from, out of* L1
ausbilden (*sep.*) *to train, instruct, educate* L14
die Ausbildung *training* L12 VS
der Ausblick (-e) auf *view, outlook onto* L4 VS
der Ausflug (¨e) *excursion* ZM
das Ausflugsgebiet (-e) *area to which excursions are made* ZM
ausführlich *detailed, in detail* L17 VS
die Ausgaben (*fem. pl.*) *expenditure* L17
ausgeben (*sep.*) (gibt aus, gab aus, ausgegeben *to spend (of money)* L6
ausgezeichnet *excellent* L7
ausgleichen (*sep.*) (gleicht aus, glich aus, ausgeglichen) *to settle (a bill)* L15 VS
sich auskennen (*sep.*) (kennt aus, kannte aus, ausgekannt) *to know one's way around* L8
die Auskunft (¨e) *information* L15 VS, L17
das Ausland *foreign countries* L12 VS
im Ausland *abroad*
der Ausländer (-) *foreigner* L14
das Ausländergesetz *law pertaining to foreigners* L18 VS
ausmachen (*sep.*) *to put off, turn off* L17
ausrichten (*sep.*) *to tell, pass on (a message)* L14 VS
sich ausruhen (*sep.*) *to have a rest* L8
die Aussage (-n) *statement, report* L17
ausschließlich (+*gen.*) *exclusive of, excluding* L14
aussehen (*sep.*) (sieht aus, sah aus, ausgesehen) *to look, seem* L11
außer (+*dat.*) *out of* L15 VS
außerdem *besides, in addition* L14
außerhalb von *outside (of)* L4 VS
außerhalb (+*gen*) *outside of* L14
die Aussicht (-en) *view, prospect* L10 VS, L14
die Aussichtsplattform (-en) *viewing platform* L10 VS
die Ausstattung (-en) *fittings, equipment* L11 VS
ausstellen (*sep.*) *to make out (a cheque)* L15
die Ausstellung (-en) *exhibition* L13 VS, L17
sich etwas aussuchen (*sep.*) *to choose something (for oneself)* L12
der Ausstausch *exchange* L18
Australien *Australia* L1
der Australier (-) *Australian (male)* L2
die Australierin (-nen) *Australian (female)* L2
auswandern* (*sep.*) *to emigrate* L14
ausweichen* (*sep.*) (weicht aus, wich aus, ausgewichen) *to get out of the way, escape* L17 VS
der Ausweis (-e) *(identity) card* L15
das Auto (-s) *car* L8 VS, L10
die Autobahn (-en) *motorway* L4 VS, L13
der Autofahrer (-) *car driver* ZM
der Automat (-en) (*wk. noun*) *(vending/slot) machine* L15
das Autosteuer (-) *car steering-wheel* L16 VS
der Autounfall (¨e) *car accident* L14 VS
die Autovermietung (-en) *car rental (firm)* L15 VS
die Avantgardekunst *avant-garde art* L13 VS

die Bäckerei (-en) *baker's (shop)* L12
der Backstein (-e) *brick* L13 VS
das Bad (¨er) *bath* L3
der Bademantel (¨) *bath-robe* L13
das Badezimmer (-) *bathroom* L3
die Bahn (-en) *railway, railroad* L10
mit der Bahn *by rail* L10

der Bahnhof (¨e) *railway station* L8
der Bahnsteig (-e) *platform* L14
bald *soon* L3
der Balkon (-s) *balcony* L3
die Banane (-n) *banana* L7
die Bank (-en) *bank* L8
der/die Bankangestellte (*adj. noun*) *bank employee* L12 VS
die Banklehre (-n) *banking apprenticeship* L12 VS
die Banknote (-n) *bank note* L15
der Bankräuber (-) *bank robber* L17
die Bankwelt *world of banking* L15
die Bar (-s) *bar* L8 VS
das Bargeld *cash* L15
bargeldlos *cashless, without cash* L15 VS
der Bargeldservice *cash (dispenser) service* L15 VS
der/das Barock *baroque* L4 VS
die Basis (die Basen) *basis* L12 VS
der Bau (*no pl.*) *building, construction* L5 VS, L17
die Bauausstellung (-en) *building exhibition, architectural exhibition* L17
der Bauch (¨e) *belly, stomach* L16
die Bauchschmerzen (*masc. pl.*) *stomach-ache* L16
bauen *to build* L11
der Bauer (-n) (*wk. noun*) *peasant, farmer* L5
das Bauernbrot *coarse rye bread* (*lit. peasant's bread*) L5
der Baum (¨e) *tree* L13
die Baustelle (-n) *roadworks, construction site* L17 VS
bayerisch *Bavarian* L7
Bayern *Bavaria* L6 VS
beantragen *to apply for* L14
beantworten *to answer* L2
der Becher (-) *cup, glass, mug, beaker* L7
sich bedanken *to say thank you* L16
bedeuten *to mean* L5 VS
die Bedienung *service* L6
die Bedingung (-en) *condition* L13 VS
bedrohen *to threaten* L17 VS
beeinträchtigen *to impair, reduce* L16 VS
sich befinden (befindet, befand, befunden) *to be situated* L17 VS
befreien *to free, release* L16 VS
begegnen (+*dat.*) *to encounter, meet* L17
der Beginn (*no pl.*) *beginning* L14 VS
beginnen (beginnt, begann, begonnen) *to begin* L1 VS
begleichen (begleicht, beglich, beglichen) *to settle* (*a bill*) L15 VS
begleiten *to accompany* L14 VS
begrüßen *to greet, welcome* L14 VS, L18
behaupten *to maintain, claim* L18
behilflich *helpful, of assistance* L16
die Behinderung (-en) *obstruction* L17 VS
bei (+*dat.*) *at, with* L7
beide *both* L1
beiderseits (+*gen.*) *on both sides of* L14
das Bein (-e) *leg, bone* L11
das Beispiel (-e) *example* L8 VS
zum Beispiel *for example* L8 VS
der Beitrag (¨e) *contribution, subscription* L15 VS, L17
beitragen (*sep.*) zu (trägt bei, trug bei, beigetragen) *to contribute to* L14 VS
beitreten* (*sep.*) (tritt bei, trat bei, beigetreten) *to join* L5 VS
bekämpfen *to fight* (*against*) L15
die Bekämpfung *combating* L18 VS
bekannt *well-known, famous* L13 VS, L18
der Bekannte (*adj. noun*) (*male*) *acquaintance* L9
die Bekannte (*adj. noun*) (*female*) *acquaintance* L9
die Bekleidung *clothing* L11
bekommen (bekommt, bekam, bekommen) *to get* L4 VS, L13
Belgien *Belgium* L1
bemerken *to notice* L17 VS
benötigen *to require* L15 VS
bequem *comfortable* L3
die Bequemlichkeit *comfort* L4 VS
bereit *prepared, willing, ready* L2 VS
bereithalten (*sep.*) (hält bereit, hielt bereit, bereitgehalten) *to keep* (*ready*) L15 VS

bereits *already* L17 VS
bereitstehen (*sep.*) (steht bei, stand bei, bereitgestanden) *to be ready, stand by* L17
der Berg (-e) *mountain, hill* ZM
das Bergwanderwetter *weather for hiking in the mountains* ZM
die Bergungsarbeiten (*fem. pl.*) *rescue work, recovery work* L17 VS
der Bericht (-e) *report* L17
berichten (über +*acc.*) *to report (on)* L10
der Beruf (-e) *occupation, profession* L2
berufsbildend *vocational* L12
das Berufsleben *working life, professional life* L12 VS
die Berufsschule (-n) *vocational school* L11
berufstätig *working* L12 VS
die Berufung *vocation* L14 VS
berühmt *famous* L3
die Besatzung (en) *occupation* L13
die Besatzungszone (-n) *zone of occupation* L13
beschäftigt *busy* L18
die Beschäftigung *employment* ZM
jmdm. Bescheid sagen *to let someone know* L11
beschreiben (beschreibt, beschrieb, beschrieben) *to describe* L11
die Beschwerde (-n) *complaint, trouble* L16 VS
besetzt *occupied, taken* L8 VS
besichtigen *to view, to have a look at* L6
besiegen *to conquer* L5 VS
der Besitzer (-) *owner, proprietor* ZM
besonders *especially* L16
besorgen *to take care of, get (for someone)* L15 VS
besser- *better* L14
best- *best* L4 VS, L6
am besten (*adv.*) *best* L6
bestehen (besteht, bestand, bestanden) (1) *to pass (exams)* L12 VS
bestehen (besteht, bestand, bestanden) (2) *to exist* L17
bestellen *to order* L7
bestimmen *to determine, decide on* L15
bestimmt *certainly, definitely* L3
die Bestimmung (-en) *regulation* L18 VS
bestreuen *to sprinkle* L17
der Besuch (-e) *visit* L12
besuchen *to visit, to attend* L5, L9 VS, L10
der Betrag (¨e) *amount* L12 VS
betreten (betritt, betrat, betreten) (1) *to step on, walk on* L8
betreten (betritt, betrat, betreten) (2) *to enter* L17 VS
der Betreuer (-) *person in charge of looking after someone, minder* L14 VS
der Betrieb (-e) (1) *factory, works, concern* L9 VS, L11
der Betrieb (2) *bustle* L12
es gibt wenig Betrieb *there's little going on*
die Betriebswirtschaft *business management, business economics* L9 VS
die Betriebswirtschaftslehre *business management studies* L9 VS
das Bett (-en) *bed* L3
die Beute *haul, loot* ZM
die Bevölkerungszahl *population* L6 VS
bevor (*sub. conj.*) *before* L8 VS, L12
bewaffnet *armed* L17
der Beweis (e) *proof* L18 VS
der Bewerber (-) *applicant* L18 VS
die Bewerbung (-en) *application* L14
die Bewertung *evaluation, assessment* ZM
das Bewertungskriterium (-ien) *(evaluation) criterion* ZM
bewirten *to entertain (to a meal)* L15 VS
bezahlen *to pay (for)* L7
die Beziehungen (*fem. pl.*) *connections, contacts* L13
der Bezirk (-e) *administrative district, region* L17 VS
bezüglich (+*gen.*) *concerning, with regard to* L14
die Bibliothek (-en) *library* L8
das Bier (-e) *beer* L7
bieten (bietet, bot, geboten) *to offer* L15 VS, L18

die Bildung *education* L9 VS, L17
das Bildungssystem (-e) *educational system* L12
billig *cheap* L18
der Binnenmarkt *internal market* L18
die Birne (-n) *pear* L7
bis (+*acc.*) (1) *up to, until, by* L4
bis zu (+*dat.*) *up to, until* L4
bis (*sub. conj.*) (2) *until* L12
bisher *(up) until now* L12
bisherig *previous, up until now* L17 VS
bislang *until the present time, as yet* ZM
bißchen *bit L8*
bitte *please* L1
bitte schön *there you are; yes please?* L4
bitten (bittet, bat, gebeten) *to ask, request* L17 VS
das Blatt (¨er) *sheet, leaf* L8
blau *blue* L11
das Blech *metal* L13
die Blechlawine (-n) *vast column of cars* L13
bleiben* (bleibt, blieb, geblieben) *to stay, remain* L8
der Blick (-e) *glance, look* L5 VS
der Blitz (-e) *lightning* L17
die Blockade (-n) *blockade* L5 VS
bloß *only* L9 VS, L15
die Blume (-n) *flower* L15 VS, L18
der Blumenladen (¨) *flower shop* L15 VS
der Blumenkohl (-e) *cauliflower* L7
die Bluse (-n) *blouse* L11
das Blut *blood* L16 VS
die Bohne (-n) *bean* L7
die Bombe (-n) *bomb* L13 VS
der Bombenangriff (-e) *bomb attack* L13 VS
böse (auf +*acc.*) *angry (with)* L12
die Boutique (-n) *boutique* L8 VS
die Box (-en) *speaker* L17
die Brandstiftung *fire-raising, arson* L17
braten (brät, briet, gebraten) *to fry, roast* L7 VS
die Bratwurst (¨e) *fried sausage* L8 VS
brauchen *to need* L11 VS, L15
das Brauhaus (¨er) *brewery* L8 VS
braun *brown* L11
brennen (brennt, brannte, gebrannt) *to burn* L10
der Brief (-e) *letter* L11 VS
die Brille (-n) *pair of glasses* L11 VS
bringen (bringt, brachte, gebracht) *to bring* L5 VS
britisch *British* ZM
das Brot *bread* L5
die Brücke (-n) *bridge* L6
der Bruder (¨) *brother* L9
die Brühe (-n) *stock, clear soup* L17
der Brunnen (-) *fountain, well* L8
die Brust (¨e) *chest, breast* L11
das Buch (¨er) *book* L10
buchen *to book* L15 VS
der Buchhandel *book trade* L10
die Buchhandlung (-en) *bookshop* L12
die Bude (-n) *kiosk, stand* L8
das Büf(f)et(t) *buffet* L5
Bulgarien *Bulgaria* ZM
die Bundesautobahn (-en) *federal motorway* L17 VS
die Bundesbahn *Federal Railway* L14
der Bundesbürger (-) *citizen of the Federal Republic* L15 VS, L18
das Bundesgebiet *(area of) the Federal Republic* ZM
das Bundesgesundheitsamt *Federal Office of Health* L16 VS
der Bundesgesundheitsminister *Federal Minister of Health* L16 VS
das Bundesland (¨er) *federal state* L6 VS
die Bundesrepublik *Federal Republic* L5 VS
die Bundesstraße (n) *federal road (maintained by the Federal Government)* L17 VS
der Bürger (-) *citizen* L5 VS
die Bürgerin (-nen) *(female) citizen* ZM
das Büro (-s) *office* L9
der Bus (-se) *bus* L10
die Busfahrt (-en) *bus trip, bus journey* L12
die Busrundfahrt (-en) *bus tour* L10 VS

die Butter *butter* L11
das Butterbrot (-e) *sandwich* L11
aus Buxtehude kommen *to come from the back of beyond* L6 VS

das Café (-s) *café, coffee house* L6
der Champignon (-s) *(button) mushroom* L17
die Champignonrahmsuppe *cream of mushroom soup* L17
die Chance (-n) *chance* L9 VS
der Charterflug (¨e) *charter flight* L15
der Chef (-s) *chief, head, boss* L5 VS, L13
chemisch *chemical* L12
die chemische Reinigung *dry cleaning, dry cleaner's* L12
cirka *approximately* L3
der Club (-s) *club* ZM
die Cola (-s) *coke* L7

da (1) *there, at that time, so* L1 L5
da (*sub. conj.*) (2) *as, since* L12
da drüben *over there* L1
dabei *by it, with it* L14
dadurch *in this way, (lit. through this)* L9
dafür *but (to compensate)* L2
dagegen (1) *against it* L12 VS
wenn Sie nichts dagegen haben *if you don't mind* L12 VS
dagegen (2) *on the other hand, however* ZM
bis dahin *up to that point* L18
damals *at that time* L9
die Dame (-n) *lady* L14 VS
damit (*sub. conj.*) (1) *so that* L11
damit (2) *with that* L14 VS
danach *after that* L5 VS
Dänemark *Denmark* L1
der Dank (*no plur.*) *thanks* L8 VS
Vielen Dank *many thanks* L8 VS
danke *thank you* L2
danke schön *thank you very much* L4
danken (+*dat.*) *to thank* L14 VS
dann *then* L2 VS
darf (*inf.* dürfen) *may* L2
die Darstellung *account, description* ZM
darüber *above, beyond* L13
das *that* L1
daß (*sub. conj.*) *that* L11
das Datum (Daten) *date* L5 VS
datum (data) L9 VS
dauern *to last, to take (of time)* L5
dazu *to it* L14 VS
die DDR *GDR (German Democratic Republic)* L5 VS, L18
defekt *defective* L16 VS
die Definition (-en) *definition* L13 VS
dein *your (informal form)* L8
der Delegierte (*adj. noun*) *delegate* L1 VS
demokratisch *democratic* L5 VS
der Demonstrant (-en) (*wk. noun*) *demonstrator* L17
die Demonstration(-en) *demonstration* L5 VS
denn (1) *then* L3
denn (2) (*conj.*) *for* L12
denken (denkt, dachte, gedacht) *to think* L10
deshalb *for that reason, that is why* L2 VS, L12
die Destille (-n) *bar (dialect word)* L8 VS
deutsch *German* L2
Deutsch *German (language)* L2
die Deutsche (*adj. noun*) *German (female)* L2
der Deutsche (*adj. noun*) *German (male)* L2
die Deutsche Bundesbahn *German Federal Railway* L14
die Deutsche Demokratische Republik (DDR) *German Democratic Republic (GDR)* L5 VS
Deutschland *Germany* L1
die Devisen (*f. pl.*) *foreign currency* L15
der Dezember *December* L10 VS, L13
d.h. (=das heißt) *that means, i.e.*
der Dialog (-e) *dialogue* L1
der Diamant (-en) *diamond* ZM
dicht *dense* L15 VS
dick *fat, thick* L11
dienen (+*dat.*) *to serve* L17
der Dienst (-e) *service* L14 VS

der Dienstag (-e) *Tuesday* L6
dies- *this (one)* L6
diesmal *this time* L10 VS
diesseits (+*gen.*) *this side of* L14
dir (*dat. of* du) *you, to you* L6
direkt *direct(ly)* L3
die Discothek (-en) *discotheque* L6
diskriminieren *to discriminate (against)* ZM
doch (1) *yes (in response to a negative question)* L4
doch (2) *(emphatic particle, often used where 'do' + verb is found in English)* L9
Erzähl mir doch davon! *Do tell me about it!* L9
der Doktor (-en) *doctor* L2
die Doktorarbeit (-en) *doctoral thesis* L12
das Dokument (-e) *document* L15 VS
die Dokumentation *documentation* L15 VS
der Dom (-e) *cathedral* L6
der Donnerstag (-e) *Thursday* L6
das Doppelzimmer (-) *double room* L4
doppelt *double, doubly* L12 VS
das Dorf (¨er) *village* L8
dort *there* L3
dorthin *(to) there* L13
draußen *outside* L8 VS
drehen *to turn* L14 VS
das Dreieck (-e) *triangle (intersection)* L17 VS
dreimal *three times* L10
die Dreißiger Jahre *the Thirties* L10 VS
der Drink (-s) *(alkoholic) drink* L15
dritt- *third* L4
drittens *thirdly* L12 VS
die Drogerie (-n) *drug-store* L12
die Druckerei (-en) *printing works* L12
du *you (informal)* L5
dumm *stupid* L6
dunkel *dark* L11
durch (+*acc.*) *through, by* L6
durchfahren* (*sep.*) (bis) (fährt durch, fuhr durch, durchgefahren) *to travel, go through (to)* L14
der Durchschnitt *average* ZM
das Durchschnittsalter *average age* ZM
sich durchsetzen (*sep.*) *to win through, be successful* L11 VS
dürfen (*modal verb*) (darf, durfte, gedurft) *to be allowed to* L4
der Durst *thirst* L14 VS
die Dusche (-n) *shower* L3
der D-Zug (¨e) *fast train* L14

eben *just, simply* L16
ebenfalls *likewise, also* L4 VS
echt *genuine(ly)* L18 VS
die Ecke (-n) *corner* L4
die EG (Europäische Gemeinschaft) *European Community* L15
das Ehepaar (-e) *(married) couple* L18
eher *rather, sooner* L18 VS
ehrlich *honest(ly)* L11 VS, L18
ehrlich gesagt *quite honestly* L11 VS
das Ei (-er) *egg* L5
eigen *own* L6 VS
eigentlich *actually* L3
das Eigentum *property* L9
die Eigentumswohnung (-en) *owner-occupied dwelling* L9
der Eilzug (¨e) *fast stopping train* L14
einbringen (*sep.*) (bringt ein, brachte ein, eingebracht) *to bring in* L10
eindämmen (*sep.*) *to check, stem* L18 VS
eindeutig *clear, unambiguous* L18 VS
eindringen* (*sep.*) (in +*acc.*) (dringt ein, drang ein, eingedrungen) *to force one's way (into), penetrate* L17 VS
einfach *simple, simply* L9
das Einfamilienhaus (¨er) *one-family house, detached house* L3
einführen (*sep.*) *to introduce* L5 VS
einig- *some* L11
einkaufen (*sep.*) *to shop* L5
einladen (*sep.*) (zu +*dat.*) (lädt ein, lud ein, eingeladen) *to invite (to)* L15
die Einladung (-en) *invitation* L15 VS

einmal *once* L14 VS
noch einmal *once again* L14 VS
einnehmen (*sep.*) (nimmt ein, nahm ein, eingenommen) *to take* (*a meal, medicine*) L15 VS, L16
einplanen (*sep.*) *to include in one's plans* L12 VS
die Einreise (-n) (in +*acc.*/nach) *entry* (*into*) L15 VS
die Einreisegenehmigung (-en) *entry permit* L15 VS
einrühren (*sep.*) *to stir in* L17
eins *one* L3
einschlafen* (*sep.*) (schläft ein, schlief ein, eingeschlafen) *to fall asleep* L16 VS
einschließlich (+*gen.*) *including, inclusive of* L14
einsehen (*sep.*) (sieht ein, sah ein, eingesehen) *to see, realise*
sich einsetzen für (*sep.*) *to support* (*the idea of*), *campaign for* ZM
einsteigen* (*sep.*) (in) (steigt ein, stieg ein, eingestiegen) *to get on, board* (*a vehicle*) L14 VS
einstig *former* L8 VS
sich eintragen (*sep.*) (trägt ein, trug ein, eingetragen) *to register* (*oneself*) L4
eintreffen* (*sep.*) trifft ein, traf ein, eingetroffen) *to arrive* L11
der Eintritt *entrance, admission* L15 VS
die Eintrittskarte (-n) *entrance ticket* L15 VS
die Einwanderung *immigration* L18
der Einwohner (-) *inhabitant* L5 VS, L18
einzeln *individual, separate* L17 VS
das Einzelzimmer (-) *single room* L4
einig *in agreement* L18
Darüber sind wir uns einig *We're in agreement on that* L18
einig- *some* L11
einzig *single, sole, solitary* L4
das Eis *ice, ice-cream* L7
der Eisbecher (-) *ice-cream sundae* L7
elegant *elegant, smart* L11
die Eltern (*pl.*) *parents* L9
der Empfang (¨e) *reception* L4
die Empfangsdame (-n) *receptionist* (*female*) L4
der Empfangsherr (-en) (*wk. noun*) *receptionist* (*male*) L4 VS
empfehlen (empfiehlt, empfahl, empfohlen) *to recommend* L7
die Empfehlung (-en) *recommendation* L15 VS
empört *indignant, incensed* L17
das Ende (-n) *end* L13
enden *to end, finish* L17 VS
endlich *finally, at last* L13
eng *narrow* L8 VS
England *England* L1
der Engländer (-) *Englishman* L2
die Engländerin (-nen) *Englishwoman* L2
Englisch *English* (*language*) L2
englisch *English* L2 VS
englischsprachig *English language, English-speaking* L14
der Enkel (-) *grandchild, grandson* L9
die Enkelin (-nen) *granddaughter* L9
enorm *enormous*(*ly*) L10 VS
entdecken *to discover* L16 VS
entfernt *distant* L4 VS, L18
entkommen* (entkommt, entkam, entkommen) *to escape, get away* L17
entlang (+*acc. if* entlang *follows the noun*) *along* L6
sich entschließen (für +*acc.*) (entschließt, entschloß, entschlossen) *to decide* (*on*), *resolve* L12 VS
entschuldigen *to excuse* L1
entsetzlich *dreadful, awful, appalling* L18
entsprechen (entspricht, entsprach, entsprochen) *to correspond to, be in accordance with* L18 VS
entstammen* (+*dat.*) *to come from* L18 VS
enttäuscht *disappointed* L17
entweder . . . oder . . . *either . . . or . . .* L17
entwerfen (entwirft, entwarf, entworfen) *to design* L17
die Entwicklung (-en) *development* ZM

das Entwicklungsland (¨er) *developing country* ZM
die Entzündung (-en) *inflammation, infection* L16
er *he etc.* (*masc. pronoun*) L1
erbauen *to build, construct* L17
erbeuten *to take* (*as loot*) L17
erbringen (erbringt, erbrachte, erbracht) *to provide, produce* L18 VS
die Erbse (-n) *pea* L7
die Erdbeere (-n) *strawberry* L7
die Erde (-n) *earth* L7 VS
sich ereignen *to occur, happen* ZM
erfahren (erfährt, erfuhr, erfahren) *to learn* L17 VS
die Erfahrung (-en) *experience* L14
erforderlich *requisite, necessary* L15 VS
ergänzen *to complete* L1
ergehen* (*impersonal*) (ergeht, erging, ergangen) L14 VS
  es ist ihm schlecht ergangen *he fared badly*
ergreifen (ergreift, ergriff, ergriffen) *to take, adopt* (*of measures*) L18 VS
erhalten (erhält, erhielt, erhalten) (1) *to receive* L10 (2) *to preserve, keep* L18 VS
die Erhaltung *keeping, preservation* L18 VS
erkältet sein *to have a cold* L16
die Erkältung (-en) *cold* L16
erkennen (erkennt, erkannte, erkannt) *to recognise* L11
die Erkenntnisse (*f. pl.*) *findings* L17 VS
erklären *to explain* L18
sich erkundigen (nach + *dat.*) *to enquire, inform oneself* (*about*) L8
die Erlaubnis (-se) *permission, permit* L14
erledigen *to deal with, do* L16
erleichtert *relieved* L16
die Eroberung (-en) *taking, capture* L13 VS
erreichen *to reach* L13
errichten *to erect* L17
erscheinen* (erscheint, erschien, erschienen) *to appear* L10
erschöpft *exhausted* L17
erschütternd *shattering* L17
erst *not until, only* L5
erst- *first* L6 VS
  zum erstenmal *for the first time* L6 VS
erstens *firstly* L12 VS
erstklassig *first class* L4 VS
erwähnen *to mention* L13 VS
erwarten *to expect, await* L5
die Erwartung (-en) *expectation, expectancy* ZM
erweitern *to extend* L13 VS, L17
erwerbstätig (*gainfully*) *employed* ZM
erzählen *to tell, narrate* L9
erzwingen (erzwingt, erzwang, erzwungen) *to force* L17
es *it etc.* (*neut. pronoun*) L2
der Esel (-) *ass, donkey* L13
essen (ißt, aß, gegessen) *to eat* L5
essen gehen *to go for a meal* L5
der Essig *vinegar* L7 VS
der Eßlöffel (-) *dessert spoonful* L17
das Eßzimmer (-) *dining room* L3
etwa (1) *an intensifier expressing surprise or indignation* L16
etwa (2) *for instance, say* L16 VS
etwas (1) *something* L5
etwas (2) *rather, somewhat* L3
  etwas Besonderes *something special* L18
euch (*acc. & dat. of* Ihr) *you, to you* L10
euer (Ihr-*form*) *your* L10
das Europa *Europe* L11 VS
europäisch *European* L1 VS, L18
die Europäische Gemeinschaft (EG) *European Community* L15
der Euroscheck (-s) *Eurocheque* L15
existieren *to exist* L5 VS, L16
exklusive (+ *gen.*) *exclusive of, excluding* L14
explosionsartig *explosive*(*ly*), *astronomical*(*ly*) L18 VS
der Expreßzug (¨e) *express train* L14

das Fach (¨er) *subject, specialism* L12
der Facharzt (¨er) *specialist* (*doctor*) L16
das Fachgeschäft *specialist shop* L12
fähig *capable, able* L18 VS

die Fähigkeit (-en) *ability, capability* L16 VS
die Fahrbahn *carriageway* ZM
fahren* (fährt, fuhr, gefahren) *to go (in a vehicle), to drive* L6
der Fahrer (-) *driver* ZM
die Fahrkarte (-n) *ticket* L8
der Fahrkartenschalter (-) *ticket office* L14
der Fahrplan (¨e) *timetable, schedule* L14
der Fahrpreis *fare* L14
der Fahrstreifen (-) *lane, carriageway* L17 VS
die Fahrt (-en) *journey, drive* L9
das Fahrzeug (-e) *vehicle* ZM
der Fall (¨e) *case* L11 VS, L16
auf jeden Fall *definitely, at all events* L11 VS
fallen* (fällt, fiel, gefallen) *to fall, die (in battle)* L13 VS, L18
falsch *wrong(ly)* L1
familiär *informal* L4 VS
die Familie (-n) *family* L9
die Familienfirma (-firmen) *family firm* L9 VS
der Familien-Paß (-Pässe) *family pass* L14
die Familienplanung *family planning* ZM
die Familienverhältnisse (*n. pl.*) *family circumstances* ZM
der Familienstand *marital status* L2
fassen *to catch, apprehend, seize* L17
fast *almost* L2 VS
der Februar *February* L13
feiern *to celebrate* L9
der Feiertag (-e) *public holiday* L5 VS, ZM
fein *fine(ly)* L17
die Feindlichkeit *hostility* L18 VS
das Fell (-e) *fur, hide* L13
das Fenster (-) *window* L16 VS
die Ferien (*pl.*) *holiday(s), vacation* L3 VS
der Ferienbeginn *start of the holidays* ZM
die Ferienwohnung (-en) *holiday apartment* L3 VS
das Ferienhotel (-s) *holiday hotel* L4 VS
Fernseh- *television* L4
der Fernsehapparat (-e) *television set* L17
der Fernseher (-) *television (set)* L17
fernsehen (*sep.*) (sieht fern, sah fern, ferngesehen) *to watch television* L10
der Fernsehraum (¨e) *TV room* L4
die Fernsicht *long-range visibility* ZM
fertig *ready, finished* L14
fertigstudieren (*sep.*) *to finish studying* L14
festlegen (*sep.*) *to fix, lay down, establish* L15 VS
festnehmen (*sep.*) (nimmt fest, nahm fest, festgenommen) *to arrest, detain, apprehend* L17
feststellen (*sep.*) *to find out, ascertain* L16
das Fett (-e) *fat, grease* L13
das Fieber (-) *fever, temperature* L16
der Film (-e) *film* L5
der Filz (-e) *felt* L13
finanziell *financial(ly)* L15
finden (findet, fand, gefunden) *to find* L3
der Finger (-) *finger* L11
Finnland *Finland* ZM
die Firma (Firmen) *firm, company* L9
der Fisch (-e) *fish* L7
flankieren *to flank* L8 VS
die Flasche (-n) *bottle* L7
das Fleisch *meat* L5
die Fleischerei (-en) *butcher's (shop)* L12
der Fleischsalat *meat salad* L5
fleißig *industrious, hard-working* L12 VS
fliegen* (fliegt, flog, geflogen) *to fly* L10
fleißend *fluent(ly)* L2
der Floh (¨e) *flea* L10 VS
der Flohmarkt (¨e) *flea-market* L10 VS
die Flucht (-en) *escape, flight* L17
flüchten* (vor + *dat.*) *to flee (from)* L13 VS
der Flüchtling (-e) *refugee* L13 VS
der Flug (¨e) *flight* L11 VS, L15
die Fluggesellschaft (-en) *airline company* L15 VS

der Flughafen (¨) *airport* L10
der Flughafenbus (-se) *airport bus* L11 VS
das Flugticket (-s) *plane ticket* L14
das Flugzeug (-e) *aeroplane* L10
der Flur (-e) *hall, lobby* L3
föderativ *federal* L6 VS
die Folge (-n) *consequence* L17 VS
folgend *following* L1
folgen (+*dat.*) *to follow* ZM
die Forelle (-n) *trout* L7
die Form (-en) *form, shape* L12 VS, L15
der Formaldehyd *formaldehyde* L16 VS
der Forscher (-) *researcher* L16 VS
die Forschung (-en) *research* L13 VS
der Forschungsassistent (*wk. noun*) *research assistant* L13 VS
der Fotoapparat (-e) *camera* L12
das Fotogeschäft (-e) *photographic shop* L12
fotografieren *to photograph* L12
das Fotografieren *photography* L12
die Frage (-n) *question* L1
fragen (nach +*dat.*) *to ask* (*for*) L2
Frankreich *France* L1
der Franzose (-n) (*wk. noun*) *Frenchman* L2
die Französin (-nen) *Frenchwoman* L2
Französisch *French* (*language*) L2
die Frau (-en) *woman, wife, Mrs.* L2
die Frauenkirche *Church of Our Lady* L18
das Fräulein (-) *young woman, Miss* L2
frei *free, vacant* L4
das Freibad (¨er) *open-air swimming pool* L3
freibekommen (*sep.*) (bekommt frei, bekam frei, freibekommen) *to get* (*time*) *off* L10 VS, L18
das Freie *open air* L13
die Freiheit (-en) *freedom, liberty* L17
die Freiheitsglocke (-n) *Liberty Bell* L17
die Freikörperkultur *nudism, naturism* L8
der Freistaat (-en) *free state* L6 VS
der Freitag (-e) *Friday* L6
fremd *strange, foreign* L14
die Freude (-n) *joy* ZM
sich freuen (auf +*acc.*) *to look forward to* L18
sich freuen (über +*acc.*) *to be pleased* (*about*) L9
der Freund (-e) *friend* L8
die Freundin (-nen) (*female*) *friend, girlfriend* L9
freundlich *friendly* L14
die Freundlichkeit *friendliness* L4 VS, L14
frisch *fresh* L14
der Friseur (-e) *hairdresser* L15 VS
der Frost *frost* L8
früh *early* L10
früher *earlier, formerly* L12
das Frühjahr *spring* L13 VS
das Frühstück (-e) *breakfast* L4
frühstücken *to have breakfast* L10
das Frühstücksbüf(f)et(t) (*self-service*) *breakfast buffet* L5
sich fühlen *to feel* (*well or ill*) L8
der Führerschein (-e) *driver's licence* L17
die Funkausstellung *broadcasting exhibition* L17
der Funkturm *radio tower* L17
für *for* L1 VS, L8
furchtbar *frightful*(*ly*) L11 VS
der Fuß (¨e) *foot* L8 VS, L11
zu Fuß *on foot* L8 VS
der Fußball (¨e) *football* L11
der Fußgänger (-) *pedestrian* L6
die Fußgängerzone (-n) *pedestrian precinct* L6

die Galerie (-n) *gallery* L8 VS
ganz *whole*(*ly*), *quite* L1 VS, L10
gar kein *no . . . at all* L12
das ist gar kein Problem *that's no problem at all*
gar nicht *not at all* L3 VS
garni (*see* Hotel garni)
die Garage (-n) *garage* L4 VS
die Garantie (-n) *guarantee* L14 VS
der Garten (¨) *garden* L3
der Gärtner (-) *gardener* L16
das Gas (-e) *gas* L16 VS
der Gasherd (-e) *gas stove* L16 VS
die Gasse (-n) *lane, alley* L6
der Gastarbeiter *guest worker* L18
das Gästezimmer (-) *guestroom* L3

die Gaststätte (-n) *eating place* L8 VS
das Gebäude (-) *building* L10 VS
geben (gibt, gab, gegeben) *to give* L3
es gibt *there is, there are* L1 VS, L3
das Gebiet (-e) *area, region* L6 VS
geboren *born; née* L9 VS, L15
der Gebrauch (¨e) *use* L12 VS
der Geburtstag (-e) *birthday* L7
Birgit hat morgen Geburtstag *It's Birgit's birthday tomorrow* L7
die Geduld *patience* ZM
gefährden *to endanger* L16 VS
gefährlich *dangerous* L12 VS
gefallen (gefällt, gefiel, gefallen) *to be pleasing* L6
mir gefällt das *I like that* L6
die Gefangenschaft *captivity* L13
gegen (1) (+*acc.*) *around, about* L5
gegen (2) (+*acc.*) *against* L10 VS
die Gegend (-en) *area, region* L8 VS
gegenüber (1) (+*dat.*) *opposite (to)* L4 VS
gegenüber (2) (+*dat.*) *compared with* L18
das Gehalt (¨er) *salary* L18
gehen* (geht, ging, gegangen) *to go* L2
wie geht es Ihnen? *how are you?* L2
geht das? *is that all right?* L4
es geht um *it is a matter of, it concerns* L12 VS
gehören *to belong* L4 VS, L15
die Geisel (-n) *hostage* L17 VS
gekleidet *dressed* L11
gekocht *boiled* L5
ein gekochtes Ei *boiled egg* L5
gelassen *calm(ly)* L17
gelb *yellow* L11
das Geld *money* L6
der Geldautomat (-en) (*wk. noun*) *cash dispenser* L15
der Geldberater (-) *financial adviser* L12 VS
der Geldschein (-e) *note (of money)* L15
gelegen *situated* L4 VS
die Gelegenheit (-en) *opportunity* L14
gelingen* (gelingt, gelang, gelungen) *to succeed, be successful* L17
es ist mir gelungen, . . . zu tun *I succeeded in doing . . .*
gelten als (gilt, galt, gegolten) *to be regarded as* L13
die Gemeinschaft (-en) *community* L15
gemischt *mixed* L7
das Gemüse (*no pl.*) *vegetable(s)* L7
der Gemüseladen (¨) *greengrocer's (shop)* L12
die Gemüsesuppe (-n) *vegetable soup* L7 VS
gemütlich *snug(ly)* L14 VS
genau *precise(ly), close(ly)* L11 VS, L16
genauso . . . wie . . . *just as . . . as . . .* L6
die Genehmigung (-en) *permit, permission* L14
das Genick (-e) *(nape of the) neck* L16 VS
genießen (genießt, genoß, genossen) *to enjoy* L13 VS
genug *enough* L14
genügen *to suffice* L15
das Gepäck *luggage* L4
die Gepäckaufbewahrung (-en) *left luggage office* L14
geprägt von *characterised by* L8 VS
gerade *just, precisely* L11
nicht gerade (*ironic*) *not exactly* ZM
geradeaus *straight ahead* L6
das Gericht (-e) *dish, course* L7
gering *low, small (of numbers)* L18 VS
die Germanistik *German language & literature* L10
gern(e) *with pleasure* L2
die Gesamtschule (-n) *comprehensive school* L12
das Geschäft (-e) *shop, business* L6
geschäftlich *on business* L18
die Geschäftsstelle (-en) *branch, branch office* L15 VS
das Geschehen (-) *happenings, events* L17 VS
das Geschenk (-e) *present* L9
die Geschichte (-n) *story, history* L10
geschieden *divorced* L2
geschlossen *shut, closed* L17

die Geschwindigkeit (-en) *speed* ZM
die Gesellschaft (-en) *company, society* L9
das Gesetz (-e) *law* L18 VS
das Gesicht (-er) *face* L11
gestern *yesterday* L9
die Gesundheit *health* L14 VS
gesundheitsschädlich *harmful to health* L16 VS
das Getränk (-e) *drink* L7
gewähren *to grant* L18 VS
die Gewährung *granting* L18 VS
die Gewerkschaft (-en) *trade union* L18
gewiß *certain* L13 VS, L16
der Gewinn (-e) *profit* L18
gewöhlich *ordinary, usual* L18
der Gipfel (-) *summit, peak* L18
das Glas (¨er) *glass* L7
das Glatteis *black ice* L8
glauben (+*dat.*) *to think, to believe* L6
gleich *right, just, immediately* L4
gleichberechtigt *equal, enjoying equal rights* ZM
die Gleichstellung *(equal) status* ZM
das Gleis (-e) *track* L14
die Glocke (-n) *bell* L17
das Glück *luck, fortune* L9
Glück haben *to be lucky* L9
sein Glück versuchen *to try one's luck* L13
glücklich *happy, lucky* L11 VS
das Gold *gold* ZM
das Golf *golf* L4 VS
der Golfplatz (¨e) *golf course* L4 VS
der Grad (-/-e) *degree* L13
die Grammatik *grammar* L1
der Graphiker *graphic artist, graphic designer* L2
grau *grey* L11
die Grenze (-n) *border, frontier* L5 VS
der Grenzübergang (¨e) *border crossing-point* L17 VS
der Grill (-s) *grill* L7
die Grilltomate (-n) *grilled tomato* L7 VS
die Grippe (-n) *influenza* L16
der Groschen (-) 10 *pfennig piece* L15
groß *large, big, tall* L3, L11
groß werden* *to grow up* L15
Großbritannien *Great Britain* L5 VS, L15
die Größe (-n) *size* L11
die Großeltern (*pl.*) *grandparents* L9
die Großstadt (¨e) *(large) city* L6 VS, ZM
größtenteils *for the greater part* L13
großzügig *generous* L11 VS
grün *green* L11
der Grund (¨e) *reason* L11 VS, L18
das Grundgesetz *basic law (German constitution)* L18
die Grundidee (-n) *basic idea* L12 VS
der Gründonnerstag *Maundy Thursday* L13
das Grundrecht (-e) *basic right* L18 VS
die Grundschule (-n) *primary school, elementary school* L12
die Grünen *the Greens (ecology movement)* L13 VS
die Gruppe (-n) *group* L15 VS
die Gruppenreise (-n) *package tour* L15 VS
grüß Gott! *hello; greeting in S. Germany and Austria* L2
grüßen *to greet* L10 VS
gültig *valid* L15 VS
günstig *favourable, convenient* L15
die Gurke (-n) *gherkin, cucumber* L5
der Gurkensalat *gherkin salad* L5
der Gürtel (-) *belt* L11
gut *good* L2
gutbezahlt *well-paid* L13
der Gymnasiallehrer (-) *grammar school teacher* L12
das Gymnasium (-ien) *academic secondary school, grammar school* L9 VS

das Haar (-e) *hair* L11
haben (hat, hatte, gehabt) *to have* L2 VS, L3
der Hahn (¨e) *cock, rooster, cockerel* L13
das Hähnchen (-) *chicken* L7
halb *half* L5
die Halle (-n) *hall, room* L3
das Hallenbad (¨er) *indoor swimming pool* L3

der Hals (¨e) *neck, throat* L11
die Halsentzündung (-en) *throat infection, sore throat* L16
die Halsschmerzen (*masc. pl.*) *sore throat* L16
halten (1) (hält, hielt, gehalten) *to hold, keep* L13
halten* (2) (hält, hielt, gehalten) *to stop, hold* L13
das Hammelfleisch *mutton* L7
die Hand (¨e) *hand* L11
sich handeln um *to be a question of, concern* L17
hart *hard* L13
hätten Sie . . . ? would you have . . . ? L8
der Hauptbahnhof (¨e) *main (train) station* L18
das Hauptgericht (-e) *main course* L7
die Hauptkasse (-n) *cashier's office* L17 VS
das Hauptquartier *headquarters* L9 VS
hauptsächlich *mainly* L18 VS
die Hauptschule (-n) *lit. main school (in some respects comparable to the British Secondary Modern School)* L12
der Hauptschulabschluß *final exam at the Hauptschule* L12
die Hauptschwierigheit (en) *main difficulty* L18 VS
die Hauptstadt (¨e) *capital city* L5 VS, L13
die Hauptstraße (-n) *High Street, main street* L6
die Hauptverkehrsader (-n) *main (traffic) artery* L13
das Haus (¨er) *house* L3
der Hausarzt (¨e) *family doctor, GP; resident doctor* L14 VS
Hause
  zu Hause *(at) home [position]* L5
  nach Hause *home [motion towards]* L6
hausgebraut *locally brewed* L8 VS
der Haushalt (-e) *household* L16 VS
die Haxe (-n) *leg (joint), knuckle (of meat)* L7
das Heim (-e) *home* L14
die Heimreise (-n) *journey home* L14
heiraten *to marry, get married* L9
heiß *hot* L5
heißen (heißt, hieß, geheißen) *to be called, mean* L1
das Heizkissen (-) *heating pad, cushion* L16 VS
helfen (+*dat.*) (hilft, half, geholfen) *to help* L2 VS, L7
hell *light (of colours, ale); bright* L11
das Hemd (-en) *shirt* L11
herausfinden (*sep.*) (findet heraus, fand heraus, herausgefunden) *to find out* L11 VS
die Herausgabe (-n) *handing over, surrender* L17
der Herbst (-e) *autumn, fall* L18
der Herd (-e) *stove, cooker* L16 VS
der Herr (-en) (*wk. noun*) *gentleman, Mr.* L2
Herr Ober *form of address to a waiter* L7
herrlich *great, wonderful* L10
die Herrschaften (*fem. pl.*) *lady and gentleman, (ladies and) gentlemen* L7
herrschen *to prevail, dominate* ZM
herstellen (*sep.*) *to manufacture, produce, make* L9 VS, L18
das Herz (-en) *heart* L8 VS, L13
  Ihm schlug das Herz bis zum Hals *His heart came into his mouth* L13
der Herzinfarkte (-e) *heart attack*
die Herzkrankheit (-en) *heart disease* L16 VS
herzlich *hearty, heartily, warm(ly)* L10 VS
heute *today* L5
heute abend *this evening* L5
heute morgen *this morning* L16 VS
heute nachmittag *this afternoon* L5
heutzutage *nowadays* L1 VS, L12
hier *here* L2
  von hier aus *from here* L6
hierher *here (towards the speaker)* L11
die Hi-Fi-Anlage *hi-fi system* L17
die Hilfe *help, aid, assistance* L15
Hilfe leisten *to give, render assistance* L15
der Hilferuf (-e) *call for assistance* L17 VS
die Himbeere (-n) *raspberry* L7

das Himbeereis *raspberry ice-cream* L7
der Himmel (-) *sky, heaven* L7 VS
hin
wo . . . hin? *where (to)?* L6
hin und zurück *there and back* L13
hinausfahren* (*sep.*) (fährt hinaus, fuhr hinaus, hinausgefahren) *to drive, go out (to)* L8
hinausschauen (*sep.*) *to look out* L13
zum Fenster hinausschauen *to look out of the window* L13
hingehen* (*sep.*) (geht hin, ging hin, hingegangen) *to go there* L8 VS
hinter (+*dat/acc.*) *behind* L8
hinüber *over (there)* L10 VS
hinüberschauen (*sep.*) *to look over* L10 VS
hinweisen auf (+*acc.*) *to point to, indicate* ZM
historisch *historical* L5 VS
die Hitze *heat* L7 VS, L8
das Hobby (-s) *hobby* L2 VS
hoch (hoh-) *high(ly)* L10 VS
das Hochdeutsch *High German* L8
die Hochschule (-n) *institution of higher education (eg. university)* L12
die Hochschullehrer(-) *university teacher* L12
die Hochschulreife *academic standard required for entrance to university* (lit. *university maturity*) L12
die Hochzeitsreise *honeymoon trip* L18
das Hofbräuhaus *famous beer hall in Munich* L18
hoffen *to hope* L15
hoffentlich *hopefully* L3
der Hofgarten (¨) *Court garden* L8
hoh- (*see* hoch)
holen *to fetch* L16 VS
Luft holen *to take, draw breath* L16 VS
holländisch *Dutch* L13 VS
der Honig *honey* L13 VS
hören *to hear* L8 VS
die Hose (-n) *pair of trousers* L11
das Hotel (-s) *hotel* L4 VS
das Hotel garni *bed and breakfast hotel* L4
das Hotelzimmer (-) *hotel room* L15 VS
der Hund (-e) *dog* L13
husten *to cough* L16 VS
der Husten (-) *cough* L16
der Hut (¨e) *hat* L11

ich *I* L1
ideal *ideal* L16
die Idee (-n) *idea* L14
idyllisch *idyllic* L4 VS
ihm (*dat. pronoun*) *(to) him* L7
ihnen (*dat. pronoun*) *(to) them* L7
ihnen (*dat. pronoun*) *(to) you)* L2
Ihr *your* L1
ihr (1) *her, their* L1
ihr (2) (*dat. pronoun*) *(to) her* L7
ihr (3) (Ihr *in correspondence*) *you (informal plural)* L10
der Imbiß (Imbisse) *snack* L15 VS
immer *always* L6
immer wieder *again and again* L16
die Individualreise (-n) *individual trip* L15 VS
die Industrie (-n) *industry* ZM
das Industrieland (¨er) *industrialised country* ZM
die Information (-en) *information* L8
das Informationsblatt (¨er) *leaflet* L8
der Ingenieur (-e) *engineer* L2
inklusive (+*gen.*) *inclusive of* L4 VS, L14
das Inland *home (country)* L15 VS
die Innenraumluft *indoor air* L16 VS
innerdeutsch *internal (within Germany)* L5 VS
innerhalb (+*gen.*) *inside (of)* L14
die Innovation (-en) *innovation* L13 VS
die Insel (-n) *island* L16
insgesamt *a total of, all told* L11 VS
die Inspektion *inspection, (car) service* L17
integriert *integrated* L5 VS
Intercity-Zug (¨e) *Inter-City train* L14 VS
interessant *interesting* L3
das Interesse (-n) *interest* L11
sich interessieren für (+*acc.*) *to be interested in* L10 VS, L12

international *international(ly)* L13 VS
interpretieren *to interpret* L18 VS
irgendwie *somehow* L18 VS
Irland *Ireland* L1
Italien *Italy* L1
italienisch *Italian* L8 VS

ja (1) *yes* L1, L2
ja (2) *indeed* L1 VS
ja (3) *after all, as you know* L2
die Jacke (-n) *jacket* L11
das Jahr (-e) *year* L2 VS, L3
der Jahresbeitrag (¨e) *annual subscription* L15 VS
die Jahreszeit (-en) *time of the year, season* L16
das Jahrhundert (-e) *century* L13 VS
jahrelang *for many years* L12
der Januar *January* L13
die Japanerin (-nen) *Japanese woman* L18 VS
japanisch *Japanese* L8 VS
je (1) *each* L6 VS
je (2) *ever* L18
die Jeans (*pl.*) *jeans* L8 VS
jed- *every, each* L5
jeden Tag *every day* L5
jedesmal *every time* L16
jedoch *however* L17 VS
jen- *that* L11
jenseits (+*gen.*) *the other side of* L14
jetzt *now* L2
jeweils *each, each time* L6 VS
der Job (-s) *job* L17 VS
der Journalist (-en) (*wk. noun*) *journalist* L2
die Jugend *youth* L12
der Jugendstil *art nouveau* L12
der Juli *July* L2 VS, L13
jung *young* L11
der Junge (-n) (*wk. noun*) *boy* L3
der Juni *June* L1 VS, L13
die Jury (-s) *Jury* L11 VS

das Kabarett (-e *or* -s) *cabaret* L6
der Kaffee *coffee* L4 VS, L5
die Kaffeeterrasse *coffee terrace* L4 VS
das Kalbfleisch *veal* L7
das Kalifornien *California* L14
kalt *cold* L3 VS, L7
die Kälte *cold* L8
Kanada *Canada* L1
der Kanadier (-) *Canadian* (*male*) L2
die Kanadierin (-nen) *Canadian* (*female*) L2
der Kandidat (-en) (*wk. noun*) *candidate* L11 VS
kann (*see* können)
kapitalistisch *capitalist* L5 VS
kaputt *broken, smashed* L18
kaputtfahren (*sep.*) (fährt kaputt, fuhr kapput, kaputtgefahren) *to smash up* (*a car*) L18
die Karambolage (-n) *collision, crash* ZM
der Karfreitag *Good Friday* L13
die Karte (-n) *card* L9
die Kartoffel (-n) *potato* L5
der Kartoffelknödel (-) *potato dumpling* L7
der Kartoffelsalat *potato salad* L5
das Karussell *car(r)ousel* L5 VS
der Käse (-) *cheese* L16
die Kasse (-n) *till, cash desk, check-out* L15
die Kassette (-n) *cassette* L17
der Kassettenrecorder (-) *cassette recorder* L17
kassieren (bei) *to collect money* (*from*) L7
die Katze (-n) *cat* L10
in Kauf nehmen *to accept, put up with* ZM
kaufen *to buy* L9
das Kaufhaus (¨er) *department store* L15 VS
kaum *scarcely, hardly* L10 VS, L17
kein *no, not a, not one* L4
der Keller (-) *cellar* L6
der Kellner (-) *waiter* L7
die Kellnerin (-nen) *waitress* L7
kennen (kennt, kannte, gekannt) *to know, be acquainted with* L3
kennenlernen (*sep.*) *to get to know* L5
die Kenntnisse (*fem. pl.*) *knowledge* L9
das Kfz (Kraftfahrzeug) *vehicle* L15 VS
kg = das Kilogramm (-e/-) *kilogram(me)* L7
das Kilo (-/-s) *Kilo* L7

der Kilometer (-), km. *kilometer* L4 VS, L13
das Kind (-er) *child* L2
der Kinderärztin (-nen) *paediatrician (female)* L2
der Kindergarten (¨) *nursery school, kindergarten* L12
das Kino (-s) *cinema, movie theatre* L5
die Kirche (-n) *church* L8
die Kirsche (-n) *cherry* L7
das Kissen (-) *cushion, pad* L16 VS
klar *clear(ly), of course* L10
die Klasse (-n) *class* L18 VS
klassisch *classical* L4 VS
das Kleid (-er) *dress* L11
kleiden *to dress, clothe* L11
die Kleidung *clothing* L12
klein *small, little* L3
die Kleinigkeit (-en) *small thing* L9
der Kleinlaster (-) *small truck, van* ZM
der Kleintransporter (-) *small truck, van* ZM
das Klima *climate* L18
die Klingel (-n) *bell* L14 VS
klingen (klingt, klang, geklungen) *to sound* L18 VS
die Kluft (¨e) *gulf, gap* ZM
klug *clever* L6
das Knie (-) *knee* L16
der Knödel (-) *dumpling* L7
die Kneipe (-n) *pub* L8 VS
der Koch (¨e) *cook* L14 VS
kochen *to boil, cook* L5, L7
der Kohl (-e) *cabbage* L7
die Kohlensäure *carbonic acid; fizz* L7
der Kollege (-n) (*wk. noun*) (*male*) *colleague* L14
die Kollegin (-nen) (*female*) *colleague* L14
der Komfort *comfort, luxury* L14 VS, L18
komfortabel *comfortable* L11 VS
kommen* (kommt, kam, gekommen) *to come* L1
komplett *completely, fully* L4 VS
die Konditorei (-en) *cake shop* L12
die Konferenz (en) *conference, meeting* L4 VS
das Konferenzhotel (-s) *conference hotel* L4 VS
die Konferenzmöglichkeit (-en) *conference facility* L4 VS
der Konferenzraum (¨e) *conference room* L4 VS
der Kongreß (-esse) *congress, conference* L1 VS
die Königin (-nen) *queen* L15
können (*modal verb*) (kann, konnte, gekonnt) *to be able* L2 VS, L3
der Kontakt (-e) *contact* L2 VS, L18
das Konto (-s) *account* L15
kontoführend *account holding* L15 VS
der Kontrast (-e) *contrast* L8 VS
der Kontrollpunkt (-e) *control point, checkpoint* ZM
kontrovers *controversial* L13 VS
die Konversation (-en) *conversation* L1
das Konzert (-e) *concert* L6
der Kopf (¨e) *head* L11
die Kopfschmerzen (*masc. pl.*) *headache* L16
der Korb (¨e) *basket, wicker* ZM
der Körper (-) *body* L11
der Körperteil (-e) *part of the body* L11
kosten *to cost* L3
die Kosten (*pl.*) *costs, expenses* L18
das Kostüm (-e) *costume* L11
das Kraftfahrzeug (-e) *vehicle* L15 VS
krank *ill, sick* L12
der Kranke (*adj. noun*) *sick person, patient* L17
das Krankenhaus (¨er) *hospital* L14 VS
die Krankenkasse (-n) *health insurance company, fund* L16
der Krankenschein (-e) *health insurance claim form* L16
die Krankenversicherung *health insurance* L16
die Krankheit (-en) *illness, disease* L16
die Krawatte (-n) (*neck*)*tie* L11
der Krebs (-e) *cancer* L16
das Kreditinstitut (-e) *credit institution* L15 VS

die Kreditkarte (-n) *credit card* L15
der Krieg (-e) *war* L10
das Kriegsende *end of the war* L13
die Kriegsgefangenschaft lit. *war captivity* L13
Er war in russischer Kriegsgefangenschaft *He was a Russian P.O.W.* L13
die Kriegszerstörung *destruction (caused) by war* L17
das Kriterium (-ien) *criterion* ZM
kritisch *critical* L11 VS
krumm *crooked* *L6*
die Küche (-n) *kitchen* L3
der Kuchen (-) *cake* L5
das Kulturinstitut (-e) *institute of arts* L8 VS
das Kulturleben *cultural life* L16
der Kunde (-n) (*wk. noun*) *customer* L12
der Kundenbesuch (-e) *visit to customer(s)* L12
die Kunst (¨e) *art* L13 VS
die Kunstakademie (-n) *academy of art* L13 VS
der Künstler (-) *artist* L13 VS
die Kur (-en) *(health, rest) cure* L16
die Kurfürstin (-nen) *electoral princess* L17
das Kurhaus (¨er) *spa rooms* L4 VS
der Kurort (-e) *health resort, spa* L16
kurz *short, brief(ly)* L5 VS, L13 VS
kürzen *to cut, reduce* L17
die Kurzwelle (-n) *short wave* L17
die Kusine (-n) *(female) cousin* L2
die Küste (-n) *coast* L10

lachen *to laugh* L17
lächeln *to smile* L17
der Laden (¨) *shop* L12
die Lage (-n) *position, situation* L3
das Lammfleisch *lamb* L7
das Land (¨er) (1) *country, countryside* L1 VS, L10
aufs Land fahren *to drive into the countryside* L10 VS
auf dem Lande *in the country(side)* L13
das Land (¨er) (2) *federal state* L6 VS
die Landeshauptstadt (¨e) *state capital* L6 VS, L15
das Landesparlament (-e) *state parliament* L6 VS
die Landesregierung (-en) *state government* L6 VS
die Landschaft (-en) *landscape, scenery* L18
der Landtag (-e) *federal diet, federal parliament* L6 VS
lang *long* L6
lange *long (of time)* L5
wie lange? *how long?* L5
die Länge *length* L17 VS
langsam *slow* L12
lassen (1) *to leave, stop* L18
lassen (2) *to let, allow* L18
lassen (3) + sich + *infinitive* L18
Wie läßt sich das erklären? *How can that be explained?*
lassen (4) + *infinitive* (läßt, ließ, gelassen) *to have, get (something done)* L18
der Laster (-) *truck, lorry* ZM
der Lastkraftwagen (-) (Lkw-s) *heavy goods vehicle* L10
der Lastwagen (-) *lorry, truck* L10
laufen* (läuft, lief, gelaufen) *to run, be on* L5
laufendes Konto *current account* L15
laut (+*gen.*) *according to* L14
das Leben (-) *life* L10 VS
leben *to live* L18 VS
die Lebensbedingungen (*fem. pl.*) *living conditions* L13 VS
die Lebenserwartung *life expectancy* ZM
der Lebenslauf (¨e) *curriculum vitae* L9 VS
die Lebensmittel (*neut. pl.*) *food(stuffs), groceries* L13
der Lebensstandard *standard of living* L18
das Leder *leather* L11
der Lederschuh (-e) *leather shoe* L11
ledig *single* L2
legen *to lay, put* L8
sich in die Sonne legen *to lie in the sun* L8
die Lehre (-n) *apprenticeship, training* L10

der Lehrer (-) *teacher (male)* L2
die Lehrerin (-nen) *teacher (female)* L2
leiblich *physical, bodily* L14 VS
leicht *easy, easily* L11 VS, L14
sich etwas leichtmachen (*sep.*) *to make something easy for oneself* L11 VS
leid tun: (es) tut mir leid *I'm sorry* L5
leiden (an + *dat.*/unter + *dat.*) (leidet, litt, gelitten) *to suffer (from)* L16
leider *unfortunately* L2
leihen (leiht, lieh, geliehen) *to lend* L12
leisten *to render (assistance)* L15
sich etwas leisten *to afford something* L12
die Leistung (-en) (1) *achievement, service* L15 VS
die Leistung (-en) (2) *payment, benefit* L17
die Leistung (-en) (3) *performance, output* L18 VS
die Lektion (-en) *lesson, course-unit* L1
lernen *to learn* L2 VS, L9
lesen (liest, las, gelesen) *to read* L1
der Lesetext (-e) *reading text* L1
die Leute (*pl.*) *people* L10 VS
lieb- *dear, nice* L7, L10 VS
lieber *rather*
  ich esse lieber . . . *I prefer to eat . . .* L7
liegen (*sometimes**) (liegt, lag, gelegen) *to lie* L3
der Liegewagen (-) *couchette car* L14
der Liegewagenplatz (¨e) *couchette* L14
die Liegewiese (-n) *lawn (for sunbathing)* L8
links *on the left, to the left* L6
der *or* das Liter (-) *litre* L7
literarisch *literary* L10 VS
locken *to tempt, lure* L13
der Löffel (-) *spoon* L17
der Lohn (¨e) *wage* L18
sich lohnen *to be worthwhile, to be worth it* L15
los *off* L6
  los geht's *off we go!* (lit. *off it goes!*) L6
  da war viel los! *there was a lot going on there* L10 VS
losfahren* (*sep.*) (fährt los, fuhr los, losgefahren) *to set off, drive off* L10
lösen (1) *to buy (a ticket)* L8
lösen (2) *to solve* L18
die Lösung *solution* L18
die Luft (¨e) *air* L14
die Luftbrücke *airlift* L5 VS
die Lunge (-n) *lung* L16 VS
die Lust *inclination* L15
Lust haben *to feel like (doing something)* L15

machen *to make, do* L8
die Macht (¨e) *power* L5 VS
das Mädchen (-) *girl* L3
mag (*see* mögen)
das Magazin (-e) *magazine* L17
der Magen (¨/-) *stomach* L11
die Magenschmerzen (*masc. pl.*) *stomach-ache* L16
der Mai *May* L10 VS, L13
mal (1) (*emphatic particle*)
  Gehen Sie mal . . . *Do go . . . , be sure to go . . .* L8
mal (2) *once* L12
das Mal (-e) *time*
  zum erstenmal *for the first time* L6 VS
man *one* L3
manch- *some, many a* L5
der Mann (¨er) *husband, man* L2
der Mantel (¨) *coat* L10 VS, L11
die Mark (-) *mark* L3
das Markstück (-e) *(one) mark piece* L15
der Markt (¨e) *market* L5 VS
der Marktplatz (¨e) *market place, market square* L6
die Marktwirtschaft *market economy* L5 VS
die Marmelade *jam* L5
der März *March* L13
die Maschine (-n) *machine, plane* L9 VS, L10
maschinenlesbar *machine-readable* L15
die Masern (*pl.*) *measles* L16
maskiert *masked* L17
der/die Maskierte (*adj. noun*) *masked person* ZM

die Massenkarambolage (-n) (*multiple*) *pile-up* ZM
die Maßnahme (-n) *measure* L18 VS
Maßnahmen ergreifen *to adopt measures* L18 VS
das Material (-ien) *material* ZM
die Mathematik *mathematics* L14
die Mathematiklehrer (-) *maths teacher* L14
die Mauer (-n) (*free-standing*) *wall* L5 VS
der Mechaniker (-) *mechanic* L2
die Medizin (-en) *medicine* L14 VS
das Mehl *flour* L17
mehr (als) *more* (*than*), *any more* L5
mehrer- *several* L12
die Mehrheit *majority* L18 VS
mehrmals *several times* L9
die Mehrwertsteuer (MWS) *Value Added Tax* (*VAT*) L6
mein *my* L1
meinen *to mean, think* L18
die Meinung (-en) *opinion* L13 VS
der Meinung sein *to be of the opinion* L13 VS
meist- *most* L6
meistens *mostly* L2
sich melden *to answer* (lit. *to announce oneself*) L9
die Meldung (-en) *report, announcement* L17 VS
die Menge (-n) *amount, quantity* L15
der Mensch (-en) (*wk. noun*) *person, human being* , (*in the pl.*) *people* L16
das Menü (-s) *set meal* L6
messen (mißt, maß, gemessen) *to measure* L16 VS
der *or* das Meter (-) *metre* L8 VS
die Metropole (-n) *metropolis* L1 VS
die Metzgerei (-en) *butcher's* (*shop*) L12
mich (*acc. pronoun*) *me* L2
die Miete (-n) *rent* L3
mieten *to rent* L10
das Mikrophon (-e) *microphone* L5 VS
die Milch *milk* L7
die Million (-en) *million* L5 VS
mindestens *at least* L9 VS
das Mineralwasser *mineral water* L7
der Minigolfplatz (¨e) *mini-golf course* L4 VS
die Minute (-n) *minute* L4 VS
mir (*dat. pronoun*) *to me, me* L2 VS
mischen *to mix* L7
die Mischung (-en) *mixture* L8 VS
der Mißbrauch *abuse* L18 VS
mit (+*dat.*) *with* L2 VS, L4
der Mitarbeiter (-) *colleague* L9 VS
mitarbeiten (*sep.*) *to work with* (*someone*), *co-operate* L12
mitbekommen (*sep.*) (bekommt mit, bekam mit, mitbekommen) *to get, understand, realise* L17 VS
das Mitbringsel (-) *small present* L9
miteinander *together, with each other* L14 VS
mitfahren* (*sep.*) fährt mit, fuhr mit, mitgefahren *to go along* L11
das Mitglied (-er) *member* L15
der Mitgliedsstaat (-en) *member state* L15
mithelfen (*sep.*) (hilft mit, half mit, mitgeholfen) *to help* (*together with others*) L13 VS
mitkommen* (*sep.*) (kommt mit, kam mit, mitgekommen) *to come along* L5
mitnehmen (*sep.*) (nimmt mit, nahm mit, mitgenommen) *to take along, take with one* L15
das Mittagessen (-) *lunch* L5
mittags *at lunchtime, at noontime* L5
die Mitte (-n) *middle, centre* L9
mitteilen *to report, inform* ZM
die Mittelklasse (-n) *medium class* (*of hotels*) L4 VS
der Mittelpunkt (-) *centre* L11 VS
mitten in (+*dat.*) *in the middle of* L15
mittler- *medium, middle* L12
der Mittwoch (-e) *Wednesday* L6
der Mixer (-) *mixer, blender* L17
möchte (n) (*from* mögen) *should like, would like* L4
das Modalverb (-en) *modal verb* L12
modern *modern* L3
mögen (*modal verb*) (mag, mochte, gemocht) *to like* L4
möglich *possible* L14 VS, L15
so . . . wie möglich *as . . . as possible* L16
die Möglichkeit (-en) *possibility* L12 VS

die Möhre (-n) *carrot* L7
der Moment (-e) *moment* L4 VS
Moment mal! *just a moment!* L11
der Monat (-e) *month* L3
im Monat August *in the month of August* L13
der Montag (-e) *Monday* L6
der Morgen (-) *morning* L2
morgen *tomorrow* L5
morgen abend *tomorrow evening* L5
morgen nachmittag *tomorrow afternoon* L5
morgens *of a morning* L5
der Mosel(wein) *Moselle wine* L7
das Motiv (-e) *motive* L17 VS
müde *tired* L12
Mumps (*masc. or fem.—no article*) *mumps* L16
der Mund (¨er) *mouth* L11
die Münze (-n) *coin* L10 VS, L15
das Museum (Museen) *museum* L10
die Musik *music* L5 VS
der Musikant (-en) (*wk. noun*) *musician, minstrel* L13
müssen (*modal verb*) (muß, mußte, gemußt) *to have to, must* L5
müßte (*from* müssen) *would have to* L11 VS
die Mutter (¨) *mother* L5
die MWS (Mehrwertsteuer) *VAT* (*Value Added Tax*) L6

nach (1) *to* (*of place names*) L1 VS
nach Hause *home* (*motion towards*) L6
nach (2) (+*dat.*) *after* L5 VS
nach (3) (+*dat.*) *according to* L5 VS
nachdem (*sub. conj.*) *after* L12
die Nachfrage *demand* L18
nachher *afterwards* L5
der Nachmittag *afternoon* L5
nachmittags *in the afternoon* L5
die Nachrichten (*fem. pl.*) *news* L5 VS
nächst- *next, nearest* L10
die Nacht (¨e) *night* L2
der Nachtdienst (-e) *night service, night duty* L14 VS
der Nachteil (-e) *disadvantage* L18
der Nachtisch *dessert, sweet* L7
der Nachtklub (-s) *night club* L6 VS
das Nachtleben *night life* L10 VS
nachts *in the night* L5
die Nähe *vicinity*
in der Nähe (von) *near(by), in the vicinity (of)* L15
näher *nearer* L14 VS
näherkommen* (*sep.*) (kommt näher, kam näher, nähergekommen) *to approach, come nearer* L14 VS
nahezu *nearly, almost, virtually* ZM
das Nahrungsmittel (-) *food(stuff)* L16
der Name (-n) *name* L1
nämlich *namely, you see* L3
die Nase (-n) *nose* L11
national *national* L5 VS
die Nationaldemokratische Partei Deutschlands (NPD) *National Democratic Party* L17
natürlich *naturally, of course* L1
der Nebel (-) *fog* L8
neben (+*acc/dat.*) *next to, near* L1
nebenan *next to one, next door* L7
der Neffe (-n) *nephew* L9
nehmen (nimmt, nahm, genommen) *to take* L4
nein *no* L1
nennen (nennt, nannte, genannt) *to name, call* L10
die Neorenaissance *neo-renaissance* L17
nett *nice* L11 VS
das Netz (-e) *net, network* L15 VS
neu *new* L5 VS
die Neubauwohnung (-en) *newly built dwelling, flat* L12
Neuseeland *New Zealand* L1
der Neuseeländer (-) *New Zealander* (*male*) L2
die Neuseeländerin (-nen) *New Zealander* (*female*) L2
nicht *not* L1
nicht . . . , sondern . . . *not . . . but . . .* L12
nicht nur . . . , sondern auch . . . *not only . . . but also . . .* L1 VS
nicht wahr? *isn't that so?* (lit. *not true?*) L1
die Nichte (-n) *niece* L9
nichts *nothing* L8
niedergehen* (*sep.*) (geht nieder, ging nieder, niedergegangen) *to descend, fall* (*of rain*) ZM

die Niederlande *the Netherlands* L6 VS
niedrig *low* L18
niemand *no-one, nobody* L9
noch *still* L3
noch nicht *not yet* L3
Nordamerika *North America* L1
normalerweise *normally, usually* L9
Norwegen *Norway* L1
die Not (-ë) *emergency, difficulty*
 die Wohnungsnot *housing shortage* L13 VS
der Notarzt (¨e) *doctor on emergency call* L14 VS
der Notfall (¨e) *(case of) emergency* L14 VS
die Notlage (-n) *serious difficulty, plight* L18 VS
der November *November* L5 VS, L13
die Null (-en) *zero, nought*
 die Stunde Null *zero hour* L5 VS, L13
die Nummer (-n) *number* L12
nur *only* L1 VS
nutzen *to use, make use of* L15 VS

die Oase (-n) *oasis* L8 VS
ob *whether, if* L8 VS, L15
die Obdachlosigkeit *homelessness* L18
Ober (*see* Herr Ober)
der Oberkörper (-) *upper part of the body*
 Machen Sie den Oberkörper frei! *Strip to the waist* L16
das Obst (*no pl.*) *fruit* L7
obwohl (*sub. conj.*) *although* L12
oder *or* L1
die Oder-Neiße-Linie *Oder-Neisse-Line (border between Germany and Poland)* L5 VS
öffentlich *public* L17
öffnen *to open* L5 VS, L17
öfters *from time to time* L10 VS
ohne *without* L7 VS, L8
ohne . . . zu . . . *without (. . .ing)* L15
das Ohr (-en) *ear* L11
die Ohrenschmerzen (*masc. pl.*) *earache* L16
die Ökonomie (-n) *economy* L5 VS

der Oktober *October* L5 VS, L13
das Olympische Dorf *the Olympic Village* L8
die Oma (-s) *Grandma* L10 VS
der Onkel (-) *uncle* L9
der Opa (-s) *Grandpa* L10
die Oper (-n) *opera* L5 VS, L6
die Orange (-n) *orange* L7
die Ordnung *order*
 in Ordnung bringen *to sort out* L11 VS
organisieren *to organise* L9
organisiert *organised* L5 VS, L9
die Orientierungsstufe (-n) lit. *orientation stage; usually a two-year period at commencement of secondary education* L12
das Original (-e) *original* L17
der Ort (-e) *place* L16
Österreich *Austria* L1
Österreicher (-) *Austrian (male)* L2
Österreicherin (-nen) *Austrian (female)* L2
Osteuropa *eastern Europe* L18 VS
Ostpreußen *East Prussia* L13
die Ostee *Baltic* L3 VS
oval *oval* L11

ein paar *a few* L5 VS, L8
der Park (-s) *park* L8
parken *to park* L4
das Parkhaus (¨er) *multi-storey carpark* L9
der Parkplatz (¨e) *parking place, parking lot* L4, L8
das Parlament (-e) *parliament* L6 VS
die Partei (-en) *(political) party* L17
die Party (-s) *party* L16
der Paß (Pässe) *pass, passport* L14
passen *to suit, fit* L1
passen zu (+*dat.*) *to go with* L1
passieren* *to happen* L17
die Pause (-n) *pause, break* L14
der Pelz (-e) *fur* L10 VS
der Pelzmantel (¨) *fur coat* L10 VS
pensioniert *retired, pensioned off* L12 VS
perfekt *perfect(ly)* L2
die Person (-en) *person* L4
die Personalabteilung (-en) *personnel department* L9

der Personalausweis (-e) *personal identity card* L15
das Personalbüro (-s) *personnel office* L9 VS
der Personalleiter (-) *personnel manager* L9 VS
der Personenkraftwagen (Pkw) *(private) car* L10
der Personenwagen *(private) car* ZM
der Personenzug (¨e) *slow train; passenger train* L14
persönlich *personal(ly)* L11 VS, L18
die Petersilie *parsley* L17
die Pfanne (-n) *pan* L17
der Pfeffer *pepper* L7 VS
der Pfeffersteak (-s) *pepper steak* L7 VS
der Pfennig (-/-e) *pfennig* L15
das Pfingsten (-) *Whitsun* ZM
der Pfirsich (-e) *peach* L7
die Pflaume (-n) *plum* L7
das Pfund (-/-e) *pound* L7
phantastisch *fantastic* L3 VS, L7
die Pistole (-n) *pistol* L17
der Pkw (-s) Personenkraftwagen (-) *(private) car* L17
der Plan (¨e) *plan* L5 VS, L8
planen *to plan* L12 VS
die Planung *planning* ZM
die Planwirtschaft *planned economy* L5 VS
die Plastik (-en) *sculpture, plastic art* L13 VS
der Plastiker (-) *sculptor* L13 VS
das Platin *platinum* ZM
die Platte (-n) (1) *plate, dish* L7
die Platte (-n) (2) *record, disc* L17
die Plattform (-en) *platform* L10 VS
der Platz (¨e) (1) *square* L6
der Platz (¨e) (2) *seat* L7
der Platz (3) *room, space* L11 VS
das Platzangebot *(amount of) space (offered)* L11 VS
Platz nehmen (nimmt Platz, nahm Platz, Platz genommen) *to take a seat* L7
plötzlich *suddenly* L17 VS
der Politiker (-) *politician* L18 VS
politisch *political(ly)* L18 VS
die Polizei *police* L8
der Polizeiwagen (-) *police car* L8
Pommes frites *(pl.)* *chips, French fries* L7
der Porree (-s) *leek* L7
das Porzellan (-e) *porcelain, china* L10 VS
die Post *post, mail* ZM
postieren *to station, position* ZM
die Postkarte (-n) *postcard* L10 VS
der Postzugräuber (-) *mail train robber* ZM
praktisch *practical(ly)* L3 VS, L6
sich präsentieren *to present oneself* ZM
der Preis (-e) *price* L10 V S, L18
preiswert *reasonably priced* L3
prima! *super! great!* L11
primitive *primitive, basic* L12
der Prinz (-en) *(wk. noun)* *prince* L13
das Prinzip (-ien) *principle* L5 VS
pro *per* L4
das Problem (-e) *problem* L2 VS, L11
das Produkt (-e) *product* L11 VS
der Produktionsleiter (-) *production manager* L9 VS
der Professor (-en) *Professor* L2
das Programm (-e) *programme* L5 VS, L17
der Programmhinweis (-e) *programme information* L5 VS
das Promille *thousandth (part)* L16 VS
  0,8 Promille 80 *millilitres (of alcohol per litre of blood)* L16 VS
protestieren *to protest* L17
die Prüfung (-en) *examination* L12 VS
der Pudding (-s) *(sort of) blancmange* L7
der Pulli (-s) *jumper, sweater* L11
der Pullover (-) *jumper, sweater* L11
der Pumpernickel *pumpernickel* L5
der Punkt (-e) *point* L18 VS, ZM
pünktlich *punctual(ly), on time* L10
das Püree (-s) *purée* L17
pürieren *to purée* L17

der Quadratkilometer (-) *square kilometer* L8 VS

der *or* das Quadratmeter (-) *square metre* L3
sich quälen *to struggle one's way* L13
die Qualität *quality* L7
der Qualitätswein (-e) *quality wine* L7
quer *diagonally, crosswise* ZM

das Radio (-s) *radio* L13
die Radiosendung (-en) *radio broadcast* L17 VS
der Rahm *cream* L17
der Rasen (-) *lawn* L8
der Rassenkonflikt (-e) *racial conflict* L18
raten (+*dat.*) (rät, riet, geraten) *to advise* L8
das Rathaus (¨er) *town or city hall* L6
der Ratskeller (-) *town hall cellar (normally a restaurant)* L6
rauben *to steal* ZM
der Räuber (-) *robber* L17
der Raubüberfall (¨e) (auf +*acc.*) *robbery, raid (on)* L17
der Rauch *smoke* L16 VS
rauchen *to smoke* L16
der Raucher (-) *smoker* L16 VS
der Raum (¨e) *room* L3
räumen *to clear* L17 VS
reagieren *to react* L5 VS
die Reaktion (-en) *reaction* L16 VS
die Reaktionsfähigkeit (-en) *ability to react* L16 VS
die Realschule (-n) *secondary school (leading to a leaving examination at 16+)* L12
rechnen mit (+ *dat.*) *to reckon on, expect* L17 VS
die Rechnung (-en) *bill* L15 VS
das Recht (-e) (auf +*acc.*) *right (to)* L18 VS
recht haben (hat recht, hatte recht, recht gehabt) *to be right* L6
rechtlich *legal(ly)* L17
rechts *to the right, on the right* L6
rechtzeitig *punctual(ly), on time* L10 VS
reden *to talk, speak* L9
die Redewendung (-en) *phrase, idiomatic expression* L1
reduzieren *to reduce* ZM
der Regen *rain* L8
die Regierung (-en) *government* L6 VS
der Regierungssitz *seat of government* L6 VS
regnen *to rain* L10
der Rehbraten (-) *roast venison* L7
reich *rich* L13
reichhaltig *extensive, wide-ranging* L11 VS
die Reichsbahn *former East German railway* L14
der Reichstag *the Parliament of the German Reich* L10 VS
das Reichstagsgebäude *the Reichstag building* L10 VS, L17
die Reihe (-n) *turn*
außer der Reihe *out of the ordinary, out of the normal run of things* L15 VS
rein *pure(ly)* L18
rein (=herein, hinein) *in* L18
reingehen* (*sep.*) (geht rein, ging rein, reingegangen) *to go in* L18
reinkommen* (*sep.*) (kommt rein, kam rein, reingekommen) *to come in* L18
die Reinigung *cleaning, cleaner's* L12
die Reise (-n) *journey, trip* L9
das Reisebüro (-s) *travel agency* L14
das Reisedokument (-e) *travel document* L15 VS
die Reisegesellschaft (-en) *travel company, tour operator* L9
reisen *to travel* L5 VS, L15
der Reisepaß (-pässe) *passport* L15
die Reiseroute (-n) *route, itinerary* L15 VS
der Reisescheck (-s) *traveller's cheque* L8
die Reisewelle (-n) (lit. *travel wave*) *holiday traffic* ZM
reizend *charming* L17
relativ *relative(ly)* L12 VS
die Reparatur (-en) *repair* L15 VS
reparieren *to repair* L17
die Republik (-en) *republic* L5 VS

renoviert *renovated* L4 VS
der Reserveschlüssel (-) *spare key* L11
reservieren *to reserve* L17
das Restaurant (-s) *restaurant* L6
restaurieren *to restore* L17
restriktiv *restrictive(ly)* L5 VS
retten *to rescue (from)* L5 VS
das Rezept (-e) *recipe* L7 VS
der Rhein *the Rhine* L8 VS
richtig (1) *correct, right* L1
richtig (2) *thoroughly, really* L9
die Richtung (-en) *direction* L10
das Rindfleisch *beef* L7
das Risiko (Risiken) *risk* L12 VS
die Risikoversicherung *risk insurance* L12 VS
der Rock (¨e) *skirt* L11
der Rohdiamant (-en) *rough, uncut diamond* ZM
die Rolle (-n) *role, part* L16
ins Rollen kommen *to start rolling, get under way* ZM
rot *red* L7
der Rotwein (-e) *red wine* L7
die Rübe (-n) *turnip* L7
der Rücken (-) *back* L16
die Rückenschmerzen (*masc. pl.*) *back pain* L16
der Rückweg *way back* L14
der Ruf (-e) *call, shout* L17
ruhig *quiet(ly), calm(ly)*
Nehmen Sie ruhig Platz *Feel free to sit down* L14
rühren *to stir; to touch* L17
rührend *touching* L17
das Ruhrgebiet *the Ruhr (area)* L6 VS
die Ruine (-n) *ruin* L10 VS
rund (1) *about, approximately* L8 VS
rund (2) *round* L11
rund um (+*acc.*) *(all) around* L8 VS
die Rundfahrt (-en) *round trip, tour* L10 VS
der Rundfunk *broadcasting* L17
die Rundfunkanstalt (-en) *broadcasting corporation* L17
rundlich *plump* L11 VS
runter (=herunter, hinunter) *down* L10 VS
runterfahren* (*sep.*) (fährt runter, fuhr runter, runtergefahren) *to drive down* L10 VS
der Russe (-n) (*wk. noun*) *Russian* L13 VS
russisch *Russian* L13
Rußland *Russia* L10 VS

die Sache (-n) *thing, matter* L10 VS, L18
der Saft (¨e) *juice* L7
sagen *to say* L1
die Sahne *cream* L7
der Salat (-e) *salad* L5
das Salz (-e) *salt* L7 VS
sammeln *to collect* L14
Erfahrungen sammeln *to gain experience* L14
der Samstag (-e) *Saturday (in Southern Germany)* L6
satt *full (up), replete* L7
sauber *clean* L18
saubermachen (*sep.*) *to clean* L18
sauer *sour, tart* L6
der saure Regen *acid rain* L16
der Sauerbraten (-) *braised beef (marinaded in vinegar)* L8 VS
die S-Bahn (-en) (=Stadtbahn) *railway network within a city* L13
schade *a pity*
wie schade! *what a pity!* L10
der Schaden (¨) *damage* ZM
schaden (+*dat.*) *to harm, damage, hurt* L17
schädlich *harmful* L16 VS
schälen *to peel* L7 VS, L17
die Schallplatte (-n) *record, disc* L17
der Schalter (-) *(ticket) window* L14
der Schankwein (-e) *draught wine* L7
schätzen *to estimate* ZM
schauen *to look* L13
der Schauer (-) *shower* ZM
der Scheck (-s) *cheque* L8
das Scheckbuch (¨er) *cheque book* L15
der Schein (-e) *(bank)note* L15
schenken *to give (as a present)* L7
schicken *to send* L16
das Schiff (-e) *ship, boat* L10
die Schiffahrt (-en) *shipping* L16
die Schiffspassage (-n) *boat fare* L15 VS

der Schinken (-) *ham* L7
die Schinkensplatte (-n) *ham platter* L7
die Schlachterei (-en) *butcher's (shop)* (*esp. in North Germany*) L12
der Schlaf *sleep* L13
schlafen (schläft, schlief, geschlafen) *to sleep* L5
der Schlafwagen (-) *sleeping car* L14
der Schlafwagenplatz (¨e) *sleeper* L14
das Schlafzimmer (-) *bedroom* L3
schlagen (schlägt, schlug, geschlagen) *to beat* L8 VS
Ihm schlug das Herz bis zum Hals *His heart came into his mouth* L13
schlank *slim* L11
schlecht *bad* L10
der Schleier (-) *veil, haze* ZM
schließen (schließt, schloß, geschlossen) *to shut, close, conclude* L14
schließlich *finally, in the end* L17 VS
schlimm *bad* L16 VS
der Schlips (-e) (*neck*)*tie* L11
das Schloß (Schlösser) *castle* L3
der Schluß (Schlüsse) *conclusion* ZM
der Schlüssel (-) *key* L4
schmal *narrow, thin* (*of face*) L11
schmecken *to taste* (*good*) L7
der Schmerz (-en) *pain* L16
schmieden *to forge, concoct, make* L12 VS
der Schnee *snow* L8
schneiden (schneidet, schnitt, geschnitten) *to cut, slice* L7 VS, L17
schnell *quick*(*ly*), *fast* L2 VS, L6
der Schnellzug (¨e) *fast train* L14
der Schnupfen (-) (*slight*) *cold, the snuffles* L16
die Schokolade *chocolate* L7
der Schokoladenpudding (-s) *chocolate blancmange* L7
schon (1) *already* L3
schon (2) *alright* L8
schön *beautiful, lovely, nice* L3
schonen *to spare, save* L14 VS
der Schoppen (-) *glass* (*of beer, wine etc.*) L7
Schottland *Scotland* L1
schrecklich *terrible* L14
schreiben (schreibt, schrieb, geschrieben) *to write* L2
der Schriftsetzer (-) *type-setter, compositor* L12
der Schriftsteller (-) *writer, author* L10
der Schuh (-e) *shoe* L11
die Schulbildung *schooling* (lit. *school education*) L9 VS
die Schuld (-en) *debt; fault* L17 VS
die Schule (-n) *school* L9 VS
das Schuljahr (-e) *school year* L12
die Schulter (-n) *shoulder* L11
schwach *weak* L7 VS, L14
der Schwager (¨) *brother-in-law* L9
die Schwägerin (-nen) *sister-in-law* L9
das Schwarzbrot *brown* (lit. *black, rye bread*) L5
der Schwede (-n) (*wk. noun*) *Swede* (*male*) L2
die Schwedin (-nen) *Swede* (*female*) L2
das Schwein (-e) *pig* L7
das Schweinefleisch *pork* L7
die Schweinshaxe (-n) *knuckle of pork* L7
der Schweizer (-) *Swiss* (*male*) L2
die Schweizerin (-nen) *Swiss* (*female*) L2
schwer *difficulty, heavy* L10 VS
die Schwester (-n) *sister* L9
die Schwiegermutter (¨) *mother-in-law* L9
die Schwierigkeit (-en) *difficulty*
auf Schwierigkeiten stoßen *to encounter difficulties* L14
schwimmen* (*also* haben) (schwimmt, schwamm, geschwommen) *to swim* L3
der See (-n) *lake* L3
die See (-n) *sea* L3 VS
sehen (sieht, sah, gesehen) *to see* L5
sehenswert *worth seeing* L10
die Sehenswürdigkeit (-en) *sight* (*worth seeing*) L3
sehr *very* L2
die Seide *silk* L8 VS
sein (1) *his, its* L1
sein (2)* (ist, war, gewesen) *to be* L1

seit (+*dat.*) *since* L1 VS, L8
seitdem *since then* L5 VS
die Seite (-n) *side, page* L8
das Sekretariat (-e) *office* L14
die Sekretärin (-nen) *secretary (female)* L2 VS
der Sektor (-en) *sector* L5 VS, L13
selbst *itself, myself, yourself etc.* L3
selbstverständlich (1) *taken for granted* L14 VS
selbstverständlich (2) *of course, naturally* L7 VS, L8
selten *seldom, rare(ly)* L12
senden (sendet, sendete, gesendet *or* sendet, sandte, gesandt) *to send* L13
der Sender (-) *(radio, TV) station* L17
die Sendung (-en) *broadcast* L17
der September *September* L5 VS, L13
der Service *service* L15 VS, L17
sich setzen *to sit (oneself) down* L7
sich *oneself* L4
sicher (1) *certain(ly), sure(ly)* L3
sicher (2) *no doubt* L9 VS
sicher (3) *safe(ly)* L11 VS, L13
die Sicherheit *safety* L11 VS
sichern *to safeguard* L15
die Sicht *visibility* ZM
Sie *you* L1
sie (*fem. pronoun & pl. pronoun*) *she, they* L1
sieben *to sieve* L17
der Sieg (-e) *victory* L5 VS
die Siegesmacht (¨e) *victorious power* L5 VS
sinken* (sinkt, sank, gesunken) *to fall, drop, sink* L18
der Sinn (-e) *sense* L13 VS
der Sitz (-e) *seat, residence* L6 VS, L17
sitzen (*sometimes**) (sitzt, saß, gesessen) *to sit* L8
der Skeptiker (-) *sceptic* L13 VS
so (et)was *something like that* L18
so ... wie ... *as ... as ...* L6
sobald *as soon as* L16
die Socke (-n) *sock* L11
sofort *immediately, straight away* L7
sogar *even* L10
der Sohn (¨e) *son* L9
solch- *such* L16
der Soldat (-en) (*wk. noun*) *soldier* L10
solid(e) *solid, firm* L12 VS
sollen (*modal verb*) (soll, sollte, gesollt) *to be supposed, ought* L10
C. soll sehr schön sein *C. is supposed to be very nice*
sollte(n) (*from* sollen) *ought, should* L1
der Sommer (-) *summer* L8 VS
der Sommerfahrplan (¨e) *summer timetable, summer schedule* L14 VS
die Sommerferien (*pl.*) *summer holidays* L9
die Sommerfreuden (*fem. pl.*) *joys of summer* ZM
der Sommersitz *summer residence* L17
der Sommertag (-e) *summer's day, day of summer* L13
der Sommerurlaub *summer vacation* L15
sondern (*see* nicht nur ... sondern auch ...)
der Sonnabend (-e) *Saturday* L6
die Sonne (-n) *sun* L6
der Sonnenschein *sunshine* L8
sonnig *sunny* L18
der Sonntag (-e) *Sunday* L6
sonst *otherwise* L12
sorgen für *to see to, take care of* L15
sorgen dafür, daß *to see to it that* L12 VS
die Sorte (-n) *sort, kind* L7
sortieren *to sort* L13 VS
soviel *so much* L11 VS
soviel wie *as much as* L15
sowie *as well as* L4 VS
sowieso *in any case, anyway* L15
die Sowjetunion *the Soviet Union* L5 VS
die Sowjetzone *Soviet zone* L5 VS
sozial *social* L5 VS, ZM
sozialistisch *socialist* L5 VS
die Sozialleistung (-en) *social (welfare) benefit* L17
die Sozialwohnung (-en) *welfare housing (similar to British council flat/house)* L12

Spanien *Spain* L1
der Spanier (-) *Spaniard (male)* L2
die Spanierin (-nen) *Spaniard (female)* L2
Spanisch *Spanish (language)* L2
spanisch *Spanish* L15
sparen *to save* L12
der Sparbetrag (¨e) *amount saved* L12 VS
die Sparform (-en) *form/method of saving* L12 VS
der Spargel (-) *asparagus* L7
die Sparkasse (-n) *savings bank* L9
das Sparkonto (-konten) *savings account* L15
der Spaß (¨e) *fun*
Viel Spaß! *Have fun!* L8 VS
Es hat Spaß gemacht *It was fun* L13 VS
spät *late* L10
später *later* L7
spazierengehen* (*sep.*) (geht spazieren, ging spazieren, spazierengegangen) *to go for a walk* L5
der Spaziergang (¨e) *walk* L8
einen Spaziergang machen *to go for a walk* L8
der Speck (-e) *bacon* L7 VS
die Speisekarte (-n) *menu* L7
speisen *to dine, eat (a meal)* L8 VS
sperren *to block, close off* L17 VS
spielen *to play* L5
der Spieler (-) *player (male)* L2
die Spielerin (-nen) *player (female)* L2
die Spitze (-n) *top* L13
der Sport *sport* L8
der Sportschuh (-e) *training shoe, plimsoll, sneaker* L11
Sport treiben (treibt Sport, trieb Sport, Sport getrieben) *to do sport* L8
das Sportzentrum (-zentren) *sports centre* L11
die Sprache (-n) *language* L2 VS, L12
die Sprachkenntnisse (*pl.*) *knowledge of languages* L9 VS
sprechen (spricht, sprach, gesprochen) *to speak* L2
die Sprechstunde (-n) *consultation* L14 VS
die Sprechstundenzeiten (*pl.*) *consultation hours* L14 VS
springen* (springt, sprang, gesprungen) *to jump, leap* ZM
der Staat (-en) *state* L1
die Staatsangehörigkeit *nationality* L2
die Staatsausgaben (*fem. pl.*) *state expenditure* L17
die Stadt (¨e) *town, city* L1
das Stadtbild (-er) *townscape, cityscape* L8 VS
die Stadtmitte (-n) *town centre, city centre* L9
das Stadtmuseum (-museen) *city museum* L8 VS
der Stadtplan (¨e) *map of the town or city* L8
die Stadtsprache (-n) *language of the city* L8
der Stadtstaat (-en) *city state* L6 VS
der Stadtteil (-e) *part of the city* L13 VS
das Stadtzentrum (-zentren) *town centre, city centre* L2 VS
der Stalinismus *Stalinism* L5 VS
stark *strong(ly)*
es regnet stark *it's raining heavily* L10
starten *to start, commence (a journey)* L14 VS
die Statistik *statistics* ZM
statt (+*gen*) *instead of* L11
statt dessen *instead (of that)* L7 VS
der Stau (-e *or* -s) *tailback* L17 VS
die Stauung (-en) *jam, tailback* L17 VS
das Steak (-s) *steak* L7 VS
die Stechuhr (-en) *time-clock* L14 VS
stehen (*sometimes**) (steht, stand, gestanden) *to stand* L1
stehenbleiben* (*sep.*) (bleibt stehen, blieb stehen, stehengeblieben) *to stop, come to a halt* L10
stehlen (stiehlt, stahl, gestohlen) *to steal* L17
steigen* (steigt, stieg, gestiegen) *to rise, go up, climb* L18
die Stelle (-n) (1) *post, vacancy* L9 VS
die Stelle (-n) (2) *place* L14

stellen *to put, pose (questions)* L12 VS
die Stellung (-en) *position, situation* L12 VS, L13
sterben* (stirbt, starb, gestorben) *to die* L10
die Steuer (-n) *tax* L6
das Steuer (-) *steering-wheel* L16 VS
der Stiefel (-) *boot* L11
der Stil (-e) *style* L4 VS, L17
die Stileinrichtung *style of furniture and fittings* L4 VS
still *quiet* L8 VS
der Stillstand *standstill* L17 VS
stimmen *to be right, correct* L1
der Stock (-) *storey (Brit), story (US), floor*
im dritten Stock *on the third floor (Brit), on the fourth floor (US)* L4
stören *to disturb* L13 VS
stoßen auf (+*acc.*) (stößt, stieß, gestoßen) *to encounter, come up against* L14
der Strand (¨e) *beach* ZM
der Strandkorb (¨e) *wicker beach chair* ZM
strapazieren *to strain, tax (patience)* ZM
die Straße (-n) *street* L6
die Strecke (-n) *section, stretch* L17 VS
der Streckenabschnitt (-e) *section* L17 VS
streng *strict, rigorous* L11 VS
der Streß *stress* L16
die Struktur (-en) *structure* L6 VS
der Strumpf (¨e) *stocking* L11
das Stück (-e/-) *piece, bit* L14 VS
der Student (-en) (*wk. noun*) *(male) student* L2
die Studentin (-nen) *(female) student* L2
die Studie (-n) *study, survey* ZM
studieren *to study* L9 VS
das Studium *study, studies* L9 VS, L14
die Stufe (-n) *stage, level* L12
der Stuhl (¨e) *chair* L8 VS
die Stunde (-n) *hour* L5
die Stunde Null *zero hour* L13
stundenlang *for hours on end* L9
der Sturm (¨e) *storm, gale* ZM
die Sturmwarnung (-en) *gale warning* ZM
das Styling *styling* L11 VS
suchen *to look for, seek* L2 VS, L9
Südbayern *Southern Bavaria* L3
der Süden *south* L13
der Südosten *the south east* L6 VS
südlich von *to the south of* L4 VS
südwestlich von *to the south west of* L16
die Summe (-n) *sum* L12 VS
der Supermarkt (¨e) *supermarket* L18
die Suppe (-n) *soup* L7
das Symptom (-e) *symptom* L16
das System (-e) *system* L12

der Tabak (-e) *tobacco* L16 VS
die Tablette (-n) *tablet* L16
der Tafelwein (-e) *table wine* L7
der Tag (-e) *day* L2
jeden Tag *every day* L5
eines Tages *one day* L10 VS
die Tageseinnahmen (*fem. pl.*) *the day's takings* L17 VS
das Tagesmenü (-s) *set meal of the day* L6
täglich *daily* L14 VS
tags zuvor *the day before* L17 VS
die Tante (-n) *aunt* L9
tanzen *to dance* L5
die Tasse (-n) *cup* L7
die Tat (-en) *deed, act, crime* ZM
der Täter (-) *perpetrator, culprit, criminal* L17
die Tätigkeit (-en) *employment*, lit. *activity* L9 VS
tatsächlich *real(ly), actual(ly)* L18
tauschen (gegen +*acc.*) *to exchange, swap (for)* L10 VS
tausend *thousand* L4
das Tausend (-e) *thousand* L5 VS, L13
das Taxi (-s) *taxi, cab* L6 VS, L10
der Taxifahrer (-) *(male) taxi driver* L14 VS
die Taxifahrerin (-nen) *(female) taxi driver* L6 VS
die Technik *technology, engineering* L11 VS

der Tee (-s) *tea* L7
der Teil (-e) *part* L16
zum Teil *partly* ZM
teilen *to divide* L5 VS
der Teilnehmer (-) *participant* L17 VS
die Teilung *division* L5 VS
telefonieren *to telephone* L8 VS
die Temperatur (-en) *temperature* L13
das Tennis *tennis* L2
der Tennisspieler (-) *tennis player (male)* L2
die Tennisspielerin (-nen) *tennis player (female)* L2
der Teppich (-e) *carpet* L10
teuer *dear, expensive* L3
der Text (-e) *text* L1
thailändisch *Thai* L8 VS
das Theater (-) *theatre* L6
das Ticket (-s) *(plane) ticket* L14
tief *deep* L13
die Tiefgarage (-n) *underground car park* L4
das Tier (-e) *animal* L17
das Tierheim (-e) *animal home, nursery* L17
der Tisch (-e) *table* L7
der Toast *toast* L11
der Tod (-e) *death* L15
das Todesurteil (-e) *death sentence* L18 VS
die Toilette (-n) *toilet* L8
tolerant *tolerant* L8 VS
das Tor (-e) *gate* L10 VS
total *total(ly)* L8 VS
der Tourismus *tourism* L1 VS
der Tourist (-en) (*wk. noun*) *tourist (male)* L1 VS, L6
die Tradition (en) *tradition* L4 VS
traditionell *traditional(ly)* L13 VS
tragen (trägt, trug, getragen) *to wear* L8 VS, L11
der Tramper (-) *hitch-hiker* ZM
der Transport (-e) *consignment, transport* ZM
transportieren *to transport* L16
treffen (trifft, traf, getroffen) (1) *to meet* L5
treffen (trifft, traf, getroffen) (2) *to hit* L17
treffen (trifft, traf, getroffen) (3) *to make, take, reach (an agreement, decision)* L18
das Treffen (-) *meeting, gathering* L18
treiben (treibt, trieb, getrieben) lit. *to drive; to do (sport)*
Sport treiben *to do sport* L8
trinken (trinkt, trank, getrunken) *to drink* L7
trotz (+*gen.*) *despite, in spite of* L14
trotzdem *nevertheless* L12
die Trümmer (*pl.*) *rubble, ruins* L13 VS
die Trümmerfrau (-en) *woman sorting rubble in German cities after World War II* L13 VS
tschüs! *bye!* L5
tun (tut, tat, getan) *to do* L5
die Tür *door* L17
der Türke (-n) (*wk. noun*) *Turk (male)* L2
die Türkin (-nen) *Turk (female)* L2
türkisch *Turkish* L10 VS
der Turm (¨e) *tower* L17
typisch (für +*acc.*) *typical(ly) (of)* L6

die U-Bahn (Untergrundbahn) *underground railway* L10
übel *ill, sick*
mir wird übel *I feel sick* L16
über (+*acc/dat.*) *over, above; more than* L8
überall *everywhere* L14 VS
die Übereinkunft (¨e) *agreement* L18
übereinstimmen (*sep.*) mit (+*dat.*) *to agree with* L18
die Überfahrt (-en) *crossing* L17
der Überfall (¨e) (auf +*acc.*) *attack, raid (on)* L17
überfallen (überfällt, überfiel, überfallen) *to attack, raid* ZM
sich übergeben (übvergibt, übergab, übergeben) *to vomit, be sick* L16
überhaupt *at all* L8
überhaupt nichts *nothing at all* L8
überhöht *excessive, too high* ZM
die Überlegung (-en) *consideration* L11 VS

übermorgen *the day after tomorrow* L6
übernachten *to spend the night* L13
überraschend *surprising* L17
überrascht *surprised* L17
überreden (zu +*dat.*) *to persuade* (*to have/do*) L15
übersetzen *to translate* L18
überwältigen *to overpower, overwhelm* L17
überzeugen *to convince* L18
üblich *usual, customary* L13 VS
übriglassen (*sep.*) (läßt übrig, ließ übrig, übriggelassen) *to leave* (*over*) ZM
Das läßt viel zu wünschen übrig *That leaves much to be desired*
übrigens *by the way* L14 VS
die Übung (-en) *exercise, drill* L1
die UdSSR (Union der Sozialistischen Sowjetrepubliken) *USSR* ZM
Uhr *o'clock, hour*(*s*) (*when stating the time*) L5
die Uhrzeit *time* (*of day*) L5
UKW (Ultrakurzwelle) *VHF, FM* L17
um (1) (+*acc.*) *around* L4
um (2) *at* (*of time*) L5
um wieviel Uhr? *at what time?*
um (3) (+ *acc.*) *by* L17
um so . . . *all the more* . . . L18
um . . . zu . . . in order to L15
die Umfrage (-en) *survey* L12 VS
die Umgebung *surrounding area* L3
umladen (*sep.*) (lädt um, lud um, umgeladen) to transfer, reload ZM
umleiten (*sep.*) to divert L17 VS
sich ummelden (*sep.*) *to re-register, inform* (*the Police*) *of a change of address* L15
der Umsatz (¨e) *turnover* L18
unbedingt *absolutely, without fail* L6 VS, L8
unbemerkt *unnoticed* L17 VS
unbeschwert *carefree* L14 VS
und *and* L1
unerkannt *unrecognised* ZM
unfähig *incapable, unable* L12 VS
der Unfall (¨e) *accident* L14 VS
die Unfallstelle (-n) *scene of an accident* L17 VS
Ungarn *Hungary* ZM
ungefähr *about, approximately* L5
ungenügend *insufficient*(*ly*) ZM
ungeplant *unplanned* L10
das Unglück (-e) *accident, disaster* ZM
unmöglich *impossible* L16
die Universität (-en) *university* L3 VS
unrecht haben *to be wrong* L18
zu Unrecht *wrongfully, wrongly* L18 VS
uns (*acc. & dat. pronoun*) *us, to us* L7
unser- *our* L8
der Unsinn *nonsense* L15
unter (+*acc./dat.*) *under, beneath* L5
die Untergrundbahn (-en) (*abbr.*) die U-bahn *underground railway* L10
die Unterkunft (¨e) *accommodation* L13
unternehmen (*insep.*) (unternimmt, unternahm, unternommen) *to undertake, do* L8
der Unternehmer (-) *entrepreneur, employer* L18
unterrichten *to teach, instruct* L12
unterscheiden (*insep.*) (unterscheidet, unterschied, underschieden) *to distinguish* L18 VS
die Unterscheidung *distinguishing* L18 VS
untersuchen *to investigate, examine* ZM
unterwegs *on the way, on the road* L14 VS
unversehrt *unscathed, in tact* L18
unzufrieden *dissatisfied* L12
der Urlaub (-e) *holiday, vacation, leave* L2
der Urlauber (-) *holiday-maker* ZM
das Urlaubsgeld *holiday money* L15
das Urteil (-e) *sentence, judgement* L18 VS
usw (=und so weiter) *etc., and so on* L6 VS

die Vanille *vanilla* L7
das Vanilleneis *vanilla ice-cream* L7
der Vater (¨) *father* L9
verabredet sein *to have an appointment, date* L11

veranstalten *to organise, mount (an exhibition)* L13 VS
die Verantwortung (-en) *responsibility* L12
verbessern *to improve* L9
verbinden (verbindet, verband, verbunden) *to join, connect, link* L14 VS
die Verbindung (-en) *connection, conjunction* L15 VS
verbieten (verbietet, verbot, verboten) *to forbid* L14
verboten *forbidden* L14
verbreitet *widespread* L15 VS
verbringen (verbringt, verbrachte, verbracht) *to spend (time)* L10
verbürgen *to guarantee* L18 VS
verdienen *to earn, deserve* L11 VS
verehrt *honoured* L14 VS
vereinigen *to unite* L1
die Vereinigten Staaten von Amerika *United States of America* L1
die Vereinigung *unification* L5 VS
verfolgen *to persecute* L18 VS
der Verfolgte (*adj. noun*) *persecuted person* L18 VS
vergangen *past* L17
vergessen (vergißt, vergaß, vergessen) *to forget* L15
verhaften *to arrest* L17
das Verhältnis (-se) *circumstance, condition* ZM
verheiratet (mit) *married (to)* L2
verhören *to question, interrogate* L17
der Verkäufer (-) *salesman* L2
die Verkäuferin (-nen) *sales woman* L2
die Verkaufsabteilung *sales department* L9 VS
der Verkehr *traffic* L11
das Verkehrsamt (¨er) *tourist information office* L4
das Verkehrsaufkommen *volume of traffic* L17 VS
die Verkehrsbehinderung (-en) *(traffic) obstruction, traffic delay* ZM
die Verkehrslage (-n) *traffic situation* L17 VS
Die Verkehrsmeldung (-en) *traffic report* L17 VS
die Verkehrspolizei *Traffic Police* L14 VS
der Verkehrsteilnehmer (-) *road-user* L17 VS
verlangen *to demand* L17 VS
verlassen (verläßt, verließ, verlassen) *to leave, abandon, desert* L17
sich verlassen auf (+*acc.*) *to rely on* L15
verletzen *to injure, wound, hurt* L17
verlieren (verliert, verlor, verloren) *to lose* L10 VS, L13
die Vermietung (-en) *rental (firm)* L15 VS
vernehmen (vernimmt, vernahm, vernommen) *to examine, question* L17 VS
das Vernehmen *examining, questioning* L17 VS
veröffentlichen *to publish* L10
verpassen *to miss* L11
verrückt *mad, crazy, insane* L17
verschieben (verschiebt, verschob, verschoben) *to postpone* L16
verschieden *different, various* L5 VS
verschlossen *closed (off)* L16 VS
verschreiben (verschreibt, verschrieb, verschrieben) *to prescribe* L14 VS, L16
versetzen *to move, transfer* L9
versichern *to assure* L18
die Versicherung (-en) *insurance* L12 VS
die Verständigung *communication, understanding* L14 VS
verstehen (versteht, verstand, verstanden) *to understand* L1
versuchen *to try, attempt* L9
der Vertreter (-) *representative* L17 VS
verüben *to commit, carry out* L17
verursachen *to cause* L16 VS
der/die Verwandte (*adj. noun*) *relative* L9
verwickeln in (+*acc.*) *to involve in* ZM
verwitwet *widowed* L2
verzichten (auf +*acc.*) *to do without, abstain from* L16
der Vetter (-) *(male) cousin* L9

der Videorecorder (-) *video recorder* L17
viel *a lot (of), much* L4
Viel Spaß *Have fun* (lit. *much fun*) L8 VS
Viel Vergnügen *Enjoy yourself* (lit. *much pleasure*) L8
viel- *many* L1 VS, L6
vielbeschäftigt *very busy* L18
Vielen Dank! *many thanks!* L8
vielleicht *perhaps* L2
zu viert *four in number* L15
wir fahren zu viert *there are four of us going* L15
das Viertel (-) *quarter* L5
die Villa (Villen) *villa* L13
das *or* der Virus (Viren) *virus* L16 VS
das Visum (Visen) *visa* L14
die Vokabel (-n) *vocabulary item; (pl.) vocabulary* Introduction
der Volksdeutsche *ethnic German* L18
die Volksmusik *folk music* L5 VS
die Volksschule *primary school, elementary school* L9 VS
voll *full, fully* L8 VS, L14
die Vollbeschäftigung *full employment* L18
völlig *complete(ly)* L18
vollkommen *complete(ly), perfect(ly)* L18
von (+*dat.*) *of, from* L2
vor (1) (+*acc/dat.*) *before, in front of, to (of time)* L5
vor allem *above all* L16 VS
vor (2) (+*dat.*) *ago*
vor zwei Jahren *two years ago* L9
vorankommen* (*sep.*) kommt voran, kam voran, vorangekommen) *to get on, make progress* L12 VS
vorbeikommen* (*sep.*) (kommt vorbei, kam vorbei, vorbeigekommen) *to come by, call in* L11
vorerst *for the present* ZM
vorgehalten *held in front* L17
mit vorgehaltener Pistole *at pistol point* L17
vorhaben (*sep.*) (hat vor, hatte vor, vorgehabt) *to intend* L15
vorher *beforehand* L5
vorläufig *for the time being* L16
vorlegen (*sep.*) *to present, show, produce* L15 VS
der Vormittag *morning*
am Vormittag *in the morning* L11
vorne *at the front* L18
vorschlagen (*sep.*) (schlägt vor, schlug vor, vorgeschlagen) *to suggest* L6
vorsorgen (*sep.*) *to make provisions* L12 VS
vorsorglich *as a precaution* ZM
die Vorspeise (-n) *starter* L7
sich vorstellen (sep.) *to imagine* L10 VS, L12
die Vorstellung (-en) *idea, concept* L13 VS
der Vorteil (-e) *advantage* L15 VS
vorwärts *forwards* L6
vorweisen (*sep.*) (weist vor, wies vor vorgewiesen) *to show, produce* L14

das Wachs (-e) *wax* L13 VS
wachsen* (wächst, wuchs, gewachsen) *to grow* L18 VS
der Wagen (-) *car* L5
die Wahl (-en) *choice* L18
wählen *to choose, elect* L11 VS
wahr *true* L1
während (+*gen*) *during* L14
wahrnehmen (*sep.*) (nimmt wahr, nahm wahr, wahrgenommen) *to perceive, take (an opportunity)* L14
wahrscheinlich *probably* L7
die Währung (en) *currency* L5 VS
der Wald (¨er) *woods, forest* L10
das Waldsterben *dying of the forests* L10
das Waldstück (-e) *woodland area* ZM
Wales *Wales* L1
wandern *to hike, ramble* ZM
wann? *when* L5
warm *warm* L3 VS, L18
die Wärme *warmth* L16 VS
die Wärmewirkung (-en) *heat effect, heat treatment* L16 VS
die Warnung (-en) *warning* ZM
warten (auf +*acc.*) *to wait (for)* L12
die Wartezeit (-en) *wait* ZM
was *what* L1
was? *what?* L2
was für? *what sort of . . . ?* L3

'was = etwas *something* L17
waschen (wäscht, wusch, gewaschen) *to wash* L17
der Waschsalon (-s) *launderette* L12
das Wasser (-) *water* L7
das WC (-s) *WC* L3
wechseln *to change* (*of money*) L8
der Wechselkurs (-e) *exchange rate* L15
die Wechselstube (-n) *exchange office* L9
wecken *to waken* L12
weder . . . noch . . . *neither . . . nor . . .* L10
der Weg (-e) *way, path, road* L6
wegen (+*gen.*) *on account of* L14
weggehen* (*sep.*) (geht weg, ging weg, weggegangen) *to go away* L7
weh tun *to hurt* L16
weich *soft* L7 VS
weil (*sub. conj.*) *because* L11
der Wein (-e) *wine* L7
weiß (*see* wissen)
weiß *white* L7
der Weißwein (-e) *white wine* L7
weit *far* L3
weiter- *further* L8
weitermachen (*sep.*) *to carry on, continue* L18
weiterrauchen (*sep.*) *to carry on smoking* L16 VS
weiterspazieren (*sep.*) *to walk on, stroll on* L8
welch-? *which?* L1
die Welle (-n) *wave* L17
die Welt (-en) *world* L1 VS, L10
der Weltkreig (-e) *World War* L10
die Weltreise (-n) *world tour* L14
weltweit *world-wide* L15 VS
wem? (*dat. pronoun*) *to whom?* L7
wenden (wendet, wendete, gewendet *or* wendet, wandte, gewandt) to turn L13
wenig *little, not much* L10 VS
ein wenig *a little* L10 VS
wenig- *few* L11
wenn *if, when*(*ever*) L2
wenigstens *at least* L14
wer? *who?* L1
werden* (1) (wird, wurde, geworden) *to become* L3
werden (2) (wird, wurde, geworden) *shall, will* (*forming future tense*) L8
werden* (3) (wird, wurde, worden) (*used to form passive voice*) L17
das Werk (-e) *work* L10
das Werkzeug (-e) *tool* L9 VS
die Werkzeugmaschine (-n) *machine tool* L9 VS
wert *worth* L10 VS
der Wert (-e) *value* ZM
die Wertsachen (*pl.*) *valuables* ZM
wertvoll *valuable* L10 VS
die Westalliierten (*pl.*) *Western Allies* L5 VS
westlich (+*gen.*) *to the west of* L5 VS
das Wetter *weather* L8
das Wetteramt (¨er) *meteorological office* ZM
wichtig *important* L1
wie? *how?* L1
wie lange? *how long?* L5
wie *like, as* L11 VS
wieder *again* L5 VS, L6
wiederaufbauen (*sep.*) *to re-build* L17
wiedererrichten (*sep.*) *re-erect* L17
das Wiederhören (*lit. hearing again*)
Auf Wiederhören! *Goodbye!* (*on the phone*) L11
wiedersehen (*sep.*) (sieht wieder, sah wieder, wiedergesehen) *to see again* L13
das Wiedersehen *seeing again*
Auf Wiedersehen! *Goodbye!* L8 VS
wienerisch *Viennese* L8 VS
wieviel? *how much, how many?* L3
Der wievielte ist heute? *What's the date today?* L13
das Wild *game; red deer* L7
willkommen *welcome* L15 VS
die Windpocken (*fem. pl.*) *chicken pox* L16
der Winter *winter* L18
wirklich *really* L10
die Wirkung (-en) *effect* L16 VS
die Wirtschaft (-en) *economy* L5 VS, L18
wirtschaftlich *economic* L18 VS
das Wirtschaftsgymnasium *grammar school* (*with an economics bias*) L9 VS, L13

das Wirtschaftswunder *economic miracle* L18
wissen (weiß, wußte, gewußt) *to know (a fact)* L1
der Wissenschaftler (-) *scientist, scholar* L16 VS
wo? *where?* L1
wo . . . her? *where . . . from?* L1
wo . . . hin? *where . . . to?* L6
woanders *somewhere else* L12
die Woche (-n) *week* L3
das Wochenende (-n) *weekend* L11
der Wochentag (-e) *day of the week, weekday* L6
woher? *where . . . from?* L1
wohin? *where . . . to?* L6
wohl (1) *no doubt, probably* L2
wohl (2) *well* L16 VS
das Wohl *well-being, welfare* L14 VS
wohnen *to live* L2
wohnhaft *resident* L13 VS
das Wohnhaus (¨er) *dwelling house* L8 VS
der Wohnort (-e) *(place of) residence* L2
der Wohnsitz (-e) *residence* L15
die Wohnung (-en) *flat, apartment, dwelling* L3
die Wohnungsnot *housing shortage* L13 VS
der Wohnungsplan (¨e) *plan of an apartment* L3
das Wohnzimmer (-) *living room* L3
die Wolke (-n) *cloud* L8
wollen (*modal verb*) (will, wollte, gewollt) *to want, intend, plan* L2 VS, L6
woran *on what* L14 VS
das Wort (-e/¨er) *word* L15
das Wörterbuch (¨er) *dictionary* L17
das Wunder (-) *miracle* L18
wunderbar *wonderful* L3 VS
wunderschön *very beautiful* L18
wünschen *to wish (for), want, desire* L7 VS, L8
die Wunschsendung (-en) *request programme* (lit. *broadcast*) L5 VS
würde (n) (*from* werden) *would* L4
der Würfel (-) *cube* L7 VS
in Würfel schneiden *to dice* L17
die Wurst (¨e) *sausage* L8
die Wurstbude (-n) *sausage stand* L8
würzen *to season* L17

zähflüssig *slow-moving (of traffic)* L17 VS
die Zahl (-en) *number* L3
zahlen *to pay* L7
zählen *to count* L12 VS
der Zahn (¨e) *tooth* L16
die Zahnschmerzen (*masc. pl.*) *toothache* L16
z.B. (=zum Beispiel) *e.g., for example* L8 VS
der Zeh (-en) *toe* L11
die Zehe (-n) *toe* L11
das Zeichen (-) *sign* L14 VS
der Zeichner (-) *artist*, lit. *drawer* L13 VS
zeigen *to show* L8
die Zeit (-en) *time*
zur Zeit *at present* L5
der Zeitpunkt (-e) *(point in) time* L12 VS
die Zeitschrift (-en) *journal, magazine* L10
die Zeitung (-en) *newspaper* L10
die Zeitungsdruckerei (-en) *newspaper print shop* L12
das Zeitungsgeschäft (-e) *newsagent's (shop)* L12
zeitweilig *occasional, at times* L17 VS
zentral *centrally* L6 VS, L18
das Zentrum (Zentren) *centre* L1 VS, L15
zerlassen (zerläßt, zerließ, zerlassen) *to melt* L17
zerstören *to destroy* L10 VS, L13
die Zerstörung *destruction* L17
ziemlich *fairly* L2
das Zimmer (-) *room* L3
der Zins (-en) (*usually pl.*) *interest* L15
der Zinssatz (¨e) *interest rate* L15
die Zitadelle (-n) *citadel* L8 VS
die Zone (-n) *zone, precinct* L5 VS, L6
zu (1) (+*dat.*) *to* L6 VS
zu (2) (+*infinitive*) *to* L6
zu (3) *too* L3

zu (4) *closed, to* L10
zu Hause *at home* L5
zubereiten (*sep.*) *to prepare, cook*
die Zubereitung *preparation* L7 VS
der Zucker *sugar* L7 VS
zudecken (*sep.*) *to cover* L17
zuerst (*at*) *first* L7
zufällig *by chance* L8 VS, L11
zufolge (*follows noun*) (+*dat.*) *according to* ZM
zufrieden *satisfied, contented* L12
der Zug (¨e) *train* L10
zugeben (*sep.*) (gibt zu, gab zu, zugegeben) *to admit* L18 VS
das Zugrestaurant (-s) *restaurant car* L14 VS
das Zug-Sekretariat *office services on board a train* L14
zuhaben (*sep.*) (hat zu, hatte zu, zugehabt) *to be closed* L8 VS
die Zukunft *future* L12 VS, L14
die Zukunftsaussicht (-en) *prospect for the future* L14
zunächst *at first* L17 VS
zunehmen (*sep.*) (nimmt zu, nahm zu, zugenommen) *to increase* L18 VS
zurück *back* L10
zurückfliegen* (*sep.*) (fliegt zurück, flog zurück, zurückgeflogen) *to fly back* L10
zurückgehen* (*sep.*) (geht zurück, ging zurück, zurückgegangen) *to go back* L16
zurückkehren* (*sep.*) *to return* L13
zurückkommen* (*sep.*) (kommt zurück, kam zurück, zurückgekommen) *to come back* L10 VS
zusammen *together* L2 VS, L5
zusammenpassen (*sep.*) *to go together* L5
sich zusammensetzen (*sep.*) *to sit down together* L11 VS
der Zusatz (¨e) *addition, supplement* L15 VS
die Zusatzleistung (-en) *additional service* L15 VS
zusätzlich *additional, supplementary* L13
das Zusatzmaterial (-ien) *supplementary material* ZM
der Zuschlag (¨e) *additional charge* L14
zuschlagpflichtig *subject to an additional charge* L14
der Zustand (¨e) *state, condition* L17
der Zustrom (¨e) *influx* L18 VS
die Zutaten (*pl.*) *ingredients* L7 VS
zuverlässig *reliable* L11 VS
die Zwanziger Jahre *the Twenties* L10 VS
zwar *in fact, actually* L15 VS, L18
die Zweigstelle (-n) *branch* L9
zweit- *second* L4 VS
zweitens *secondly* L12 VS
die Zwetschge (-n) *plum* L7
die Zwiebel (-n) *onion* L7
die Zwiebelsuppe (-n) *onion soup* L7
zwingen (zwingt, zwang, gezwungen) *to force, compel* ZM
zwischen (+*acc/dat.*) *between* L8
der Zwischenhalt (-e) *stop* (*on the way*) L14 VS

Index to Grammar Notes

The first number in each entry refers to the Unit, the second to the section within the Grammar of the Unit

BUSINESS GERMAN

ANDREW CASTLEY and DEBBIE WAGENER

Now that the European market place is truly with us, thousands of business people are finding that they need to be able to say more than just 'Guten Morgen' if they are to survive.

If you've never learnt German before, or if your German needs brushing up, this is the course for you.

Andrew Castley and Debbie Wagener have created a practical course that is both fun and easy to work through. They explain the language clearly along the way and give you plenty of opportunities to practise what you've learnt. The course structure means that you can work at your own pace, arranging your learning to suit your needs.

The course contains:

- A range of units of dialogues, culture notes, grammar and exercises
- Further units of cultural briefings – in German to give you more practice
- A pronunciation guide
- Verb tables
- An English-German glossary of business terms
- An extensive German-English vocabulary

By the end of the course you'll be able to participate fully and confidently in meetings, on the shop floor, on the telephone, or in the bar after work.

TEACH YOURSELF BOOKS